ACCOUNTING
IN LIFE AND HEALTH INSURANCE COMPANIES

Paul J. Zucconi, CPA

Contributing Authors
Gregory K. Benner, CPA
Donald C. Blackburn
Thomas M. Brown, CPA
David N. Cheek, CPA
Rod P. Farrell, CPA
Daniel C. Johnson, CPA
Joseph M. Jordan, CPA
Randall W. LeGallais, CA
Jerry R. Licari, CPA
Jerry L. Miller, CPA
John E. Schramm, Jr., CPA
John M. Vana

Edited by
Robert D. Land, FLMI

FLMI Insurance Education Program
Life Management Institute LOMA
Atlanta, Georgia

Textbook Project Team:

Project Editor	Robert D. Land, FLMI
Manuscript Editor, Curriculum	Richard Bailey, FLMI
Manuscript Editor, Examinations	Sean S. Gilley, FLMI, ALHC
Project Manager	Dennis W. Goodwin, FLMI

The **Life Office Management Association** is an international association founded in 1924. Through education, training, research, and information sharing, LOMA is dedicated to promoting management excellence in leading life and health insurance companies and other financial institutions. LOMA conducts research on various company operations, including financial planning, human resources, and information management. Among its activities is the sponsorship of the FLMI Insurance Education Program, an educational program intended primarily for home office and branch office employees.

The **FLMI Insurance Education Program** consists of two levels—Level I, "Fundamentals of Life and Health Insurance," and Level II, "Functional Aspects of Life and Health Insurance." Level I is designed to help students achieve a working knowledge of the life and health insurance business. Level II is designed to further the student's career development by providing a more detailed understanding of life and health insurance and related business and management subjects. Upon the completion of Level I, the student is awarded a certificate. Upon the completion of both levels, the student is designated a Fellow of the Life Management Institute (FLMI) and is awarded a diploma.

Copyright © 1987 LOMA (Life Office Management Association, Inc.)

Reprinted: November 1990, March 1994

All rights reserved. This text, or any part thereof, may not be reproduced or transmitted in any form or by any means, electronic or mechanical, including photocopying, recording, storage in an information retrieval system, or otherwise, without the prior written permission of the publisher.

While a great deal of care has been taken to provide accurate, current, and authoritative information in regard to the subject matter covered in this book, the ideas, suggestions, general principles, conclusions, and any other information presented here are for general educational purposes only. This text is sold with the understanding that it is neither designed nor intended to provide the reader with legal, accounting, investment, marketing, or other types of professional business management advice. If legal advice or other expert assistance is required, the services of a competent professional person should be sought.

ISBN 0-915322-85-4

Library of Congress Catalog Card Number: 86-82715

Printed in the United States of America

Preface

Accounting in Life and Health Insurance Companies has been developed for use in LOMA's FLMI Insurance Education Program. The primary purpose of this book is to provide an introduction to the accounting practices followed by life and health insurance companies in the United States and Canada as required by regulatory authorities. Throughout the text, the authors assume that readers have no accounting background other than a general understanding of basic commercial accounting principles, terms, and concepts. Accordingly, an attempt has been made to use terminology that is as non-technical as possible without sacrificing essential accuracy. The book is not intended to serve as a guide or manual for persons or companies attempting to establish an insurance accounting department.

The first two chapters of the book are designed to provide the student with an introduction to and overview of both life and health insurance accounting and the financial statements used by life and health insurance companies. Chapter 3 deals with the accounting information systems typically found in these companies. Chapters 4 through 11 cover the major accounts and transaction cycles found in life and health insurance companies. Chapter 12 addresses taxation, while Chapter 13 covers internal auditing and control. Chapter 14 describes generally accepted accounting principles for life and health insurers. Planning and budgeting is the topic of Chapter 15, and the concluding chapter addresses cost accounting in life and health insurance companies.

This book replaces the text, *Accounting for Life Insurance Companies*, by Charles L. Van House, Sr., FLMI, and W. Rogers Hammond, DBA, CPA. Certain portions of the material presented in that textbook have been updated for this book.

Many people have helped in the creation of this book. The following members of the firm of Peat, Marwick, Mitchell & Co. contributed to the development of the materials:

    Gregory K. Benner, CPA
    Thomas M. Brown, CPA
    Rod P. Farrell, CPA
    Daniel C. Johnson, CPA
    Joseph M. Jordan, CPA
    Randall W. LeGallais, CA
    Jerry R. Licari, CPA
    Jerry L. Miller, CPA
    John E. Schramm, Jr., CPA

Donald C. Blackburn, David N. Cheek, CPA, and John M. Vana—all of Peat, Marwick, Mitchell & Co.—also developed materials for this text. August H. Lehmann, CPA, CLU, ChFC, FLMI, Senior Vice President and Treasurer of Union Bankers Insurance Company, deserves special recognition for his efforts during the preliminary stages of this project. Alexa Selph composed the text's glossary and index.

A dedicated panel of reviewers contributed their time and expertise to this text. The following individuals reviewed the book for clarity, technical accuracy, and adherence to current industry practices:

    Anthony V. Betro, FLMI, Second Vice President
    Teachers Insurance and Annuity Association of America

    Fred P. Hauser, FSA, Senior Vice President and Controller
    Metropolitan Life Insurance Company

    Gordon H. Johnson, FCA, FLMI, Vice President—Finance
    The Imperial Life Assurance Company of Canada

    Wanda M. LaPrath, FLMI, Manager, Corporate Accounting
    E.F. Hutton Life Insurance Company

    A. John Mason, FLMI, Senior Claim Consultant
    The Prudential Insurance Company of America

    Richard D. Sonday, CPA, FLMI, Controller
    Lincoln Mutual Life Insurance Company

    Barbara Timpano, CPA, FLMI, Assistant Controller
    Metropolitan Life Insurance Company

The following members of the Course 7 Examinations Review Panel also reviewed the text:

>Alan E. Close, Accounting Officer
>Northwestern Mutual Life Insurance Company
>
>Roisin McArthur, FLMI, Information Systems Consultant
>The Canada Life Assurance Company

John M. Patrick, Vice President and Assistant Comptroller, The Prudential Insurance Company of America, reviewed several chapters in the earlier stages of text development.

Members of the LOMA staff also devoted their considerable energies to the development of *Accounting in Life and Health Insurance Companies*. Richard Bailey, FLMI, and Sean S. Gilley, FLMI, ALHC, both of the Life Management Institute staff, reviewed the text at each stage of its development process. Dani L. Long, FLMI, read the final manuscript and made many helpful suggestions. Stephen W. Forbes, Ph.D., FLMI, Senior Vice President of LOMA's Financial Planning and Control Division, also reviewed portions of the final manuscript. Kurt Fanstill, FLMI, contributed to the chapter on Accounting Information Systems. Dennis W. Goodwin, FLMI, Assistant Manager, Curriculum Department, supervised the development and production of the text. Finally, our special thanks go to Robert D. Land, FLMI, Associate, Curriculum Department, who directed the work of the entire project and who—as the editor and project leader—made an outstanding contribution to the book.

Paul J. Zucconi, CPA, et al.
Peat, Marwick, Mitchell & Co.
October 1986

Contents

1. **Introduction to Life and Health Insurance Accounting 1**
   Learning Objectives 1
   Introduction 1
   Statutory Accounting in the United States and Canada 3
     Differences between Life Accounting and
       GAAP Accounting
   Other Types of Life Insurance Accounting 12
     GAAP (Generally Accepted Accounting Principles)
     Tax Accounting
     Managerial Accounting
   Organization and Functions of a Life Accounting Department . 15
   Key Terms 16
   Review Questions and Exercises 16

2. **An Overview of Financial Statements Used by Life and Health
   Insurance Companies 17**
   Learning Objectives 17
   Introduction 17
   The Annual Statement 18
     Balance Sheet
     Summary of Operations
     Analysis of Operations
     Capital and Surplus Account
     Cash Flow Statement
     Five-Year Historical Data
     Analysis of Increase in Reserves during the Year
     Other Exhibits and Schedules

Annual Reports 49
   Other Reports
   Tax Returns
Internal Financial Information 50
Key Terms 51
Review Questions and Exercises 51

3. Accounting Information Systems 53
Learning Objectives 53
Introduction 53
Evolution of Automated Accounting Systems 54
Data Processing Terms and Concepts 54
A Financial and Managerial Accounting System 57
   Transaction Processing
   The General Accounting System
   The Client/Policy Accounting System
   The Investment Accounting System
Information Produced by Accounting Information Systems 67
Key Terms 68
Review Questions and Exercises 68

4. Premium and Commission Accounting 71
Learning Objectives 71
Introduction 71
Premium Control Process 72
Objectives of Premium Accounting 72
   Premium Income
   Premium Suspense
   Premium Deposits
   Unearned Premiums
   Advance Premiums
   Uncollected Premiums
Accounting for Commissions 80
   Commission Accounting Basics
Annual Statement Aspects—United States 83
   Exhibit 1
   Schedule T
   Health Insurance Premiums and Commissions
   Balance Sheet Information

Annual Statement Aspects—Canada 88
   Exhibit 1
   Exhibit 3
   Exhibit 12
   Miscellaneous
Key Terms 93
Review Questions and Exercises 93

5. Accounting for Bond and Stock Investments 95
Learning Objectives 95
Introduction 95
Accounting for Investment Income 96
   Canada
Accounting for Bonds and Stocks 99
   Bonds
   Stocks
Annual Statement Aspects of Bond and Stock Investments—
   United States 113
   Annual Statement Valuation of Bonds and Stocks
Annual Statement Aspects of Bond and Stock Investments—
   Canada 116
   Bonds
   Stocks
Key Terms 119
Review Questions and Exercises 119

6. Accounting for Other Investments 121
Learning Objectives 121
Introduction 121
Mortgage Loans 122
   Accounting for Mortgage Loans
Real Estate 127
   Accounting for Real Estate
Policy Loans 131
   Accounting for Policy Loans
Annual Statement Aspects of Other Investments—United States .. 135
   Mortgage Loans
   Real Estate
   Policy Loans
Annual Statement Aspects of Other Investments—Canada 139
Key Terms 139
Review Questions and Exercises 140

7. Policy Benefit Settlements 141
Learning Objectives 141
Introduction 141
Objectives of Policy Benefit Accounting 142
Policy Dividends 142
    Dividend Records
    Dividend Liabilities
    Dividend Payment Options
    Dividend Entries
    Disbursements of Dividends Held under an Option
Nonforfeiture Options 150
    Cash Surrender
    Reduced Paid-Up and Extended Term Insurance
Annual Statement Aspects—United States 153
Annual Statement Aspects—Canada 156
Key Terms 158
Review Questions and Exercises 159

8. Claim and Contract Settlement 161
Learning Objectives 161
Introduction 161
Life Insurance Claims 164
    Matured Endowment Payments
    Effects of Life Insurance Claim Settlements on Surplus
Health Insurance Claims 168
    Disability Claims
    Medical Expense Claims
Annuity and Supplementary Contract Payments 171
    Recording of Supplementary Contracts and Annuities
    Settlement of Supplementary Contracts and Annuities
Reinsurance Benefit Entries 173
Claim Records and Controls 174
Claim Liabilities 176
Annual Statement Aspects—United States 179
Annual Statement Aspects—Canada 181
Key Terms 186
Review Questions and Exercises 186

9. Other Assets, Other Liabilities, and Separate Accounts 187
Learning Objectives 187
Introduction 187

Other Assets 188
   Electronic Data Processing Equipment
   Reinsurance Ceded
   Net Adjustment in Assets and Liabilities due to Foreign
     Exchange Rates
Other Liabilities 192
   General Expenses Due or Accrued
   Agent Commissions Due and Accrued
   Taxes, Licenses, and Fees Due or Accrued, Excluding
     Federal Income Taxes
   Amounts Retained by the Company as Agent or Trustee
   Remittances and Items not Allocated
   Borrowed Money
   Dividends to Stockholders Declared and Unpaid
   Reinsurance in Unauthorized Companies
   Mandatory Securities Valuation Reserve
Separate Accounts 196
Key Terms 202
Review Questions and Exercises 202

10. **Capital and Surplus** 205
   Learning Objectives 205
   Introduction 205
   Capital 206
     Stock Companies
     Mutual Companies
   Surplus 210
     Calculation of Total Surplus
     Accounting for Changes in Surplus—United States
     Accounting for Changes in Surplus—Canada
   Minimum Capital and Surplus Requirements 220
   Key Terms 222
   Review Questions and Exercises 222

11. **Summary of U.S. and Canadian Annual Statements** 223
   Learning Objectives 223
   Introduction 223
   Expense Reporting 224
     Types of Expense Liabilities
     Annual Statement Presentation of Expenses
   Reconciliation of Ledger Assets (Exhibit 12)—
     United States 230

Analysis of Nonadmitted Assets and Related Items
  (Exhibit 14—United States) 231
    Prepaid Expenses
    Loans and Amounts Receivable
Fund Accounting—Canada 233
    Summary of Funds and Amounts Owing by the Company
    Analysis of Income by Fund
    Reconciliation of Funds
Other Annual Statement Reports 237
Use of Annual Statement Information 239
Key Terms 240
Review Questions and Exercises 241

12. Taxation of Life and Health Insurance Companies 249
Learning Objectives 249
Introduction 249
Premium Taxes 250
    Retaliatory Tax Laws
Taxes Based on Property Values 252
    Real Estate Taxes
    The Tangible Personal Property Tax
    The Intangible Personal Property Tax
    The Business Tax in Canada
Non-federal Income Taxes in the United States and Canada ...255
    United States
    Canada
Other State, Provincial, and Local Taxes 256
Federal Income Taxation—United States 257
    Definition of a Life Insurance Company
    LICTI under the 1984 Act
Federal Income Taxation—Canada 261
    The Federal Business Income Tax
Annual Statement Aspects of Taxation 266
Key Terms 268
Review Questions and Exercises 268

13. Internal Control and Auditing 269
Learning Objectives 269
Introduction 269

Internal Control 270
  Basic Concepts of Internal Accounting Control
  Methods Used in Maintaining an Effective Internal
    Accounting Control System
  Examples of Specific Types of Internal Controls
Auditing 277
  External Auditing and Internal Auditing
  Fiscal Auditing
  Performance or Operational Auditing
Key Terms 284
Review Questions and Exercises 285

14. **Generally Accepted Accounting Principles for Life and Health Insurance Companies** **287**
    Learning Objectives 287
    Introduction 287
    SAP and GAAP Philosophies 288
    Development of GAAP for the Life Insurance Industry 289
      The Audit Guide
    SAP-GAAP Comparisons 292
      Income Determination
      Asset Valuation
      Policy Reserve Valuation
      Dividends to Policyowners
      Dividends to Stockholders
      Changes in Surplus
      Federal Income Taxes
    Canadian Accounting Compared with U.S. SAP and GAAP ... 303
      Policy Acquisition Costs
      Nonadmitted Assets
      Marketable Securities
      Mortgage Loans
      Real Estate
      Policy Reserves
      Solvency Reserves
      Deferred Federal Income Taxes
    Key Terms 308
    Review Questions and Exercises 308

15. **Planning and Budgeting** **311**
    Learning Objectives 311
    Introduction 311

Planning 311
    Operations Planning and Strategic Planning
Budgeting 317
    Types of Budgets
    Budget Preparation
    Budget Analysis and Evaluation
Key Terms 326
Review Questions and Exercises 327

16. Cost Accounting 329
Learning Objectives 329
Introduction 329
The Uses and Purposes of Cost Accounting 330
    Basics of an Effective Cost Accounting System
Marginal Costs 332
Functional Costs 334
    Development of a Functional Cost Accounting System
    Cost Accumulation and Allocation
    Effective Utilization of Functional Cost Information
Key Terms 342
Review Questions and Exercises 342

Glossary 343

Index 359

1
Introduction to Life and Health Insurance Accounting

Learning Objectives

After reading this chapter, you should be able to:
- Understand the objectives of statutory accounting
- Describe the differences between life insurance accounting and accounting in non-insurance companies
- Distinguish between the going-concern concept and the liquidation concept
- Explain why many U.S. life companies maintain their ledgers on a cash basis
- Understand the concepts of nonledger accounts and the balance account
- Explain the difference between financial accounting and managerial accounting

Introduction

Accounting is an essential function for virtually all businesses. The processes of keeping books and of compiling, analyzing, and presenting financial information so the company can plan and budget for future operations are often crucial to a company's success or failure. The accounting function must be accurate, timely, and consistent in order to satisfy internal management, stockholders, regulatory authorities, and other parties interested in the company's operations.

For a number of reasons, a reliable accounting function is especially necessary for life and health insurers. The sheer volume of insurers' business—1985 premium income in the United States and Canada of $170 billion—requires an effective accounting process. Insurers are also responsible for a large amount of assets—$906 billion in 1985. Maintaining accounts for these assets is an enormous task. In addition, insurers have potential liabilities to millions of policyowners, and the accounting function must help assure that adequate reserves are maintained for those liabilities. Finally, the types of financial information that regulatory authorities require from insurers make an insurer's accounting function different from the accounting function in non-insurance, or commercial, companies.

The purpose of this text is to provide you with an understanding of the specific principles and practices applicable to the life and health insurance accounting function and with an understanding of the differences between the accounting practices of life and health insurers and of non-insurance companies. The terms *life insurance accounting* and *life accounting* are used in this text to represent accounting as practiced in the life and health insurance industry. *GAAP accounting* is the term used to represent the field of accounting as practiced outside the insurance industry. This type of accounting is based on generally accepted accounting principles (GAAP). While publicly held life and health insurance companies are, in certain cases, required to use GAAP (as you will learn later in this chapter and in more detail in Chapter 14), this text concentrates on accounting practices specific to life and health insurers. The special characteristics of life insurance accounting can be traced to two principal sources: the nature of the life insurance business and government regulation of the insurance industry. To a considerable degree, these two factors are interrelated.

The nature of the life and health insurance business can be described as the acceptance of mortality and morbidity risks, often on a long-term basis. The typical life and health insurance company also accepts annuity risks and other long-term risks that have, from an accounting standpoint, many of the same characteristics as mortality and morbidity risks. In order to assure the ability to pay the future claims and benefits resulting from the acceptance of such risks, insurers set aside portions of the premiums received on long-term business. These amounts, plus the interest that accumulates on them, must be sufficient to pay future claims and benefits. Policy reserve accounts are used to measure the company's ability to pay claims and benefits in later years when the amount of claim costs may exceed the amount of premiums received. One aspect of the insurance accounting function, then, is to help make sure that the insurer remains solvent so that it can pay these claims and benefits in later years. **Solvency** can be defined as a company's ability to meet its current and future obligations.

One way in which an insurer demonstrates its solvency is through the Annual Statement that regulatory authorities require each insurer to file. This report is frequently referred to as the *statutory Annual Statement*. Regulatory authorities generally consider the solvency of insurance companies to be both in the public interest and necessary for the protection of policyowners. Thus, Annual Statement forms have been designed to provide a large volume of information on the long-term stability of an insurer's financial position. Since the Annual Statement forms are standardized, they can also be used to compare insurers' solvency and financial position. The information requirements of the statutory Annual Statement have resulted in the development of life accounting practices that differ from the accounting practices of commercial companies. An understanding of the nature and objectives of the statutory Annual Statement form should help you in comprehending the life accounting methods described throughout this text.

Statutory Accounting in the United States and Canada

The phrase **statutory accounting** refers specifically to the accounting methods and principles that apply to the completion of the statutory Annual Statement. Most of the information in this chapter and in this entire text applies to the statutory accounting practices (SAP) that are directly related to preparation of the Annual Statement. Many other fields of accounting—such as managerial accounting and tax accounting—are relevant to an insurer's accounting function and are also discussed in this text.

The Annual Statement form used by insurers is designed to present information about the insurer's operations and financial performance. However, the Annual Statement emphasizes the solvency of the insurer rather than its annual performance for the reporting year. A life and health insurance company's Annual Statement contains a mass of data extracted from the company's accounting and statistical records. The information found in a company's Annual Statement includes

- a Balance Sheet
- a Summary of Operations
- a surplus account
- a cash flow statement
- many supporting exhibits, schedules, and supplemental questionnaires and reports

Governmental authorities prescribe the exact Annual Statement form that insurers must use. In the United States, each state mandates the use of the Annual Statement form recommended by the National Association of Insurance Commissioners (NAIC), a body composed of the insurance commissioners from each state and the District of Columbia. The terms *U.S. Annual Statement, Statement,* and *Blank* all are used to refer to the official NAIC form. Whenever the *Canadian Annual Statement* or *Canadian Blank* is mentioned, the reference is to the life and accident and sickness form prescribed by the federal Department of Insurance for use by Canadian companies registered under the Canadian and British Insurance Companies Act. The Canadian Annual Statement is identified as Form INS-54. The Annual Statement forms required in the United States and Canada are quite similar in structure. In this text, the term *Annual Statement* refers to either the U.S. or Canadian form. Note that the Annual Statement exhibits shown throughout this text are from the 1985 versions of the U.S. and Canadian forms. Changes are usually made in these forms from year to year.

Each company in the United States and Canada must file the appropriate Annual Statement shortly after the end of each calendar year in each state or province in which the company is licensed to do business. Companies licensed in both the United States and Canada must file separate forms in each country. A British, U.S., or other foreign company operating in Canada must file an Annual Statement form similar to Form INS-54 that covers only the company's Canadian business.

Although a company operating in the United States files the same basic NAIC form in each state, a number of different Annual Statement forms are required of life and health insurance companies operating in Canada. In addition to filing Form INS-54 with the federal government, most Canadian companies file a simpler form with the insurance department of each province in which they are licensed. A company licensed in only one province files a form similar to the federal form with the Insurance Department of its home province. Canadian companies licensed to do business in one or more states of the United States are required to file the official NAIC form with each of the states in which the company is licensed.

The next section of this chapter describes the differences between life accounting and GAAP accounting that result primarily from the governmental requirements of the Annual Statement form.

Differences between Life Accounting and GAAP Accounting

Life insurance accounting is distinguished from most non-insurance accounting in a number of ways. First, in life accounting, insurers value many assets on a more conservative basis than do other companies. Because of this more conservative valuation, certain assets are not admitted, i.e., not shown, on a life and health insurer's Balance Sheet. Another feature of life accounting is that, in many companies, journal entries generally are not made until cash transactions take place. This practice is referred to as **cash-basis accounting.** Many insurers that keep their journals on a cash basis compensate for accounting discrepancies that result from cash-basis accounting by maintaining a balance account. Use of a balance account keeps the basic accounting equation in balance at all times. Each of these unique aspects of life insurance accounting is discussed below.

Asset valuation

Accounting in a commercial company is concerned primarily with the needs of management and stockholders and, secondarily, with the needs of creditors. Commercial companies value their assets according to generally accepted accounting principles (GAAP), using the going-concern concept. The **going-concern concept** assumes, for financial reporting purposes, that the reporting company will continue to do business in the future. Thus, the value of a company's assets under the going-concern concept is the worth or value that the assets will have in the future operations of the business, rather than the assets' salvage or resale value.

In a life and health insurance company, however, the interests of management, stockholders (if any), and creditors are secondary in the minds of regulators to the interests of policyowners, who need assurance of the stability and solvency of the company. Life accounting, therefore, is solvency-oriented and uses more conservative asset valuation methods. By valuing assets more conservatively, insurers can demonstrate that, even if their assets were liquidated for relatively low amounts, present and future claims could still be met. To accomplish this conservative asset valuation, life insurance company assets are generally valued on a liquidation-value basis. The **liquidation concept** assumes—for the purposes of determining a company's financial position—that the company will have to terminate its operations immediately and liquidate all of its assets in order to satisfy the claims of creditors. Thus, under the liquidation concept, many assets are valued at the amount they could be sold for in the event of the company's liquidation as of the Balance Sheet date. The liquidation value of an asset is its market value, if one is readily available. If the market value for an asset is uncertain, usually no value is allowed for that asset.

The difference between these two valuation methods can be demonstrated by considering the treatment of certain assets under each method. A magazine publisher's subscription list, for example, could be valued as an asset under either method. The asset's value might be greater under the going-concern concept, however, if the publisher expected the list to generate future revenue, perhaps in the form of subscription renewals. Under the liquidation concept, the list's value might be limited to the price for which the list could be sold immediately, perhaps to another publisher or to a direct-mail advertiser. Possibly, the list could not be sold and would have no liquidation value whatsoever. As another example, furniture and equipment might be usable for years. Therefore, furniture and equipment are shown in a commercial company's financial statements at their depreciated asset values, which may be much higher than the market value that could be realized if those assets were sold to a used-equipment dealer.

Admitted assets and nonadmitted assets

The amount of assets that appears on a life insurance company's Annual Statement Balance Sheet is the total of the company's **admitted assets.** Admitted asset values can be defined as those values that are allowed by law or by insurance department ruling to be shown on the Annual Statement Balance Sheet. Assets not shown on the Annual Statement Balance Sheet are **nonadmitted assets.** Nonadmitted assets fall into two categories: (1) assets that are partially admitted and (2) assets that are entirely nonadmitted. Most assets in the first category are investments that have a lower market value than their current book value. Most assets in the second category are assets acquired in carrying out the normal process of doing business. Examples of this second category of nonadmitted assets are furniture, most equipment, and amounts advanced to agents against future commissions. The value of the second type of nonadmitted asset would be uncertain if a company became insolvent, so no part of these assets is admitted. Ownership of nonadmitted assets is not necessarily a sign of financial weakness in a company. Many items that might be accepted at their full value in GAAP accounting are nonadmitted in a life insurance statement. Some of the assets, such as amounts advanced to agents, may be fully collectible, but they are nonadmitted because of the conservatism of the liquidation concept.

The determination of how much of an insurer's assets can be admitted is most important when an insurer is valuing its investment holdings. Legislation or insurance department rulings specify the different methods of valuing different types of investments. For example, as prescribed by U.S. governmental authorities, the admitted value of certain bonds is their market value as of the Annual Statement date. Market values fluctuate from time to time and may vary considerably from book values. If an investment's book value is greater than its market value, the difference between these values is considered to be a *nonadmitted* asset. Thus, if a bond's book value is $350 but its market value is $300, and the bond's admitted value is its market value, the nonadmitted asset value relative to that investment is $50 ($350–$300). Nonadmitted asset values, as defined earlier, do not appear on an insurer's Balance Sheet. Exhibit 13 of the U.S. Annual Statement (shown in Figure 1-1) reflects the transition from assets' book values to the net admitted asset values to be used on the Balance Sheet.

In the Canadian Annual Statement, assets are shown at their book values. The book values of these assets are, therefore, the same as the admitted values. If the aggregate book value of stocks and certain bonds is higher than the aggregate market value of these items as determined by Canadian authorities, an insurer's accountant must either (1) reduce the book value of some items by crediting an appropriate asset account or (2) credit an Investment Reserve

FIGURE 1-1
Exhibit 13—U.S. Annual Statement.

Form 1 ANNUAL STATEMENT FOR THE YEAR 1985 OF THE _____ 14
                                                        Name

EXHIBIT 13—ASSETS

	(1) LEDGER ASSETS	(2) NON LEDGER ASSETS	(3) ASSETS NOT ADMITTED	(4) NET ADMITTED ASSETS (Cols. 1 + 2 − 3)
1. Bonds (Schedule D, Part 1)				
2. Stocks:				
2.1 Preferred stocks (Schedule D, Part 2, Section 1)				
2.2 Common stocks (Schedule D, Part 2, Section 2)				
3. Mortgage loans on real estate (Schedule B, Part 1, Sec. 1):				
3.1 First liens				
3.2 Other than first liens				
4. Real estate (Schedule A, Part 1):				
4.1 Properties occupied by the company (less $_____ encumbrances)				
4.2 Properties acquired in satisfaction of debt (less $_____ encumbrances)				
4.3 Investment real estate (less $_____ encumbrances)				
5. Policy loans				
6. Premium notes, including $_____ for first year premiums				
7. Collateral loans (Schedule C, Part 1)				
8.1 Cash on hand and on deposit:				
a. Cash in company's office				
b. Cash on deposit (Schedule E)				
8.2 Short-term investments (Schedule DA, Part 1)				
9.				
10. Other invested assets (Schedule BA, Part 1)				
11. Reinsurance ceded:				
11.1 Amounts recoverable from reinsurers (Schedule S, Part 1)				
11.2 Commissions and expense allowances due				
11.3 Experience rating and other refunds due				
11.4				
12. Other assets (give items and amounts):				
12.1 Agents' balances (gross debit $_____ less $_____ for doubtful accounts less $_____ credit balances)				
12.2 Bills receivable				0
12.3 Furniture and equipment				0
12.4 Cash advanced to or in hands of officers or agents				0
12.5 Loans on personal security, endorsed or not				0
12.6				0
13. Electronic data processing equipment				
14. Federal income tax recoverable				
15.				
16.				
17. Life insurance premiums and annuity considerations deferred and uncollected on in force Dec. 31st of current year (less premiums on reinsurance ceded and less $_____ loading)				
18. Accident and health premiums due and unpaid				
19. Investment income due and accrued				
20. Net adjustment in assets and liabilities due to foreign exchange rates				
21. Receivable from parent, subsidiaries and affiliates				
22.				
23.				
24.				
25.				
26. TOTALS (Lines 1 to 25)				
27A. From Separate Accounts Statement				
27B. From Variable Life Insurance Separate Accounts Statement				
28. GRAND TOTAL (Lines 26 to 27B)				

U.S. Annual Statement pages copyright © John S. Swift Co., Inc. Reprinted with permission.

account in an amount equal to the excess book value. If an Investment Reserve account is used, its balance is shown in the Balance Sheet as a liability. When reducing, or *writing down,* the value of an asset, the debit portion of the journal entry is to an account such as Stocks Written Down. (The exact account title is worded to fit the appropriate asset classification.) For example, to indicate the writing down of a stock's book value from $1,500 to $1,200, a Canadian insurer's journal would show a $300 debit to Stocks Written Down and an equal credit to Stocks Owned:

> Stocks Written Down 300
>   Stocks Owned 300

As mentioned earlier, the credit portion of this entry could also have been to an Investment Reserve account.

Since assets are shown in the Canadian Balance Sheet at book value, no asset exhibit similar to U.S. Annual Statement Exhibit 13 is necessary. In addition, the terms *admitted asset* and *nonadmitted asset* are not used in the Canadian Annual Statement. These terms are, however, useful to indicate the nature of certain assets and are occasionally used in the remainder of this book. Assets of the type which are totally nonadmitted in the U.S. Annual Statement, such as furniture, most equipment, and amounts advanced to agents, are not shown in the Canadian Statement as assets. Instead, the costs of these types of items are treated as expenses.

Cash-basis accounting

In GAAP accounting, journal entries are made when income becomes receivable, as in the case of a sale on credit, or when an expense becomes payable, as in the case of merchandise purchased on credit. In contrast, many life and health insurance companies in the United States make a bookkeeping entry only when a cash transaction occurs.

Historically, almost all U.S. life and health insurance companies maintained their ledgers on a cash basis. Financial statements, however, were prepared on an accrual basis. Companies accomplished this accrual-basis financial reporting by entering adjustments from the cash basis to the accrual basis on working papers, not in the general ledger accounts. **Working papers,** or **work sheets,** are an informal tool that accountants use to adjust journal and general ledger information to the formats or valuations necessary for the preparation of formal financial statements such as the NAIC Blank. However, today's highly computerized accounting systems can maintain ledgers on an accrual basis in addition to a cash basis. Such systems virtually eliminate the need for working papers. By maintaining accrual-basis books, insurers can meet the need for more frequent and complete financial statements. Nonetheless, many life and health insurance companies continue to use cash-basis accounting for the following reasons:

1. *Life and health insurance companies do business on a cash basis.* In general, insurers do not buy or sell on credit. Insurance companies generally have a good cash flow and retain sufficient funds on hand to pay promptly any amounts owed.

Insurance premiums are payable in cash, except by specific agreements, and credit is not extended to policyowners. In order for a policyowner's insurance coverage to remain in effect, the premium must be paid, but the policyowner has no legal obligation to do so. Therefore, insurers do not know that they will receive premium income until it is actually remitted. Investment income, on the other hand, is legally collectible and usually has been earned by the due date, so recording investment income when it becomes due is generally justified. Premium income, however, typically represents the larger source of income for an insurer. The accounting process is based, therefore, on the conditions that surround the collection and recording of premium income. As a result, premium income entries are usually made in the ledger only when money is received, and accrual entries are made only when accrual-basis financial statements are required.

2. *Certain exhibits in the U.S. Annual Statement require showing cash-basis account balances.* Most income and expense account balances are entered on a cash basis in the exhibits of the U.S. Annual Statement. Cash-basis figures are also shown in an exhibit entitled "Reconciliation of Ledger Assets," which is Exhibit 12 in the U.S. Annual Statement. A **ledger asset** is an asset that is recorded on the insurer's books. The preparation of these exhibits is simplified if the ledger account balances show cash-basis figures. As mentioned earlier, however, some companies keep their books on an accrual basis. Such companies are allowed to prepare Exhibit 12 on an accrual basis. Some jurisdictions now allow companies with accrual-basis accounting procedures to delete Exhibit 12 from their Annual Statement.

Most Canadian companies keep their books on an accrual basis. Cash-basis figures are not shown in the Canadian Annual Statement or on a company's ledger. The Canadian Annual Statement thus does not include an exhibit equivalent to the U.S. Reconciliation of Ledger Assets exhibit.

3. *Use of cash-basis accounting does not impede the reporting process.* In a commercial company, valuation of merchandise or raw material on hand at the end of the accounting period may be necessary, but such valuation usually only requires a few days. Assets and liabilities in a non-insurance company are entered on the ledger because they are usually fixed in amount and do not change unless a cash transaction takes place. For example, when merchandise is purchased on credit, a liability of a fixed amount is created. When a payment is made, the liability is reduced

by the exact amount of the payment. To determine the total liability, an accountant need only examine the account balance. The trial balance can usually be prepared within a few days after the end of the reporting period, and statements are prepared shortly thereafter.

In a life insurance company, however, the valuation process is usually more time-consuming. For example, policy reserves, the largest liability classification in a life insurance company, are not fixed in amount but are constantly changing. A number of methods are used for valuing policy reserves, but each is quite detailed and time-consuming. The reserve for an individual policy varies according to the face amount of insurance, the plan of insurance, the age of the insured, and the number of years that the policy has been in force. Under one system for calculating policy reserves, amounts of insurance are summarized and multiplied by a factor for each plan, year of issue, and issue age to determine the total reserve for a group of policies. However, the number of calculations required to value a 10-year plan of insurance that the company has offered for ten years might be as many as 600 (10 years × 60 ages). The reserve values also differ according to each mortality or morbidity table and interest rate used in calculating the reserves.

With the advent of computers, the time required to value policy reserves, other policy liabilities, and the company's assets has decreased, but up to several weeks may still be required in a typical life and health insurance company. During this time, other accounting processes must continue. Therefore, to avoid complicating the valuation process, many life companies maintain cash-basis books, and the records of certain assets and liabilities are maintained on working papers separate from the company's ledger. These separate assets and liabilities are referred to as *nonledger accounts*.

Nonledger accounts. As we discussed earlier, because life insurance companies tend to maintain their general ledgers on a cash basis, adjustments need to be made to convert the general ledger accounts to an accrual basis for financial statement reporting. All accounts on a cash-basis accounting system are called *ledger accounts*. Investments such as bonds, stocks, mortgage loans, and real estate are ledger assets. Many of these investments are recorded on the books when cash is disbursed in payment for them. Only certain liabilities, often referred to as ledger liabilities, are recorded on a cash-basis set of books. Examples of ledger liabilities are amounts deducted from an employee's paycheck for taxes or amounts held by the company until they can be processed.

Accounts that are separate from the company's cash-basis ledger are called *nonledger accounts*. Generally, nonledger accounts are incorporated into the Balance Sheet, Summary of Operations, and other Annual Statement reports through the use of working papers. However, as mentioned earlier, some automated accounting systems make provisions for both ledger and nonledger accounts, and no working papers are necessary. The amounts contained in the nonledger accounts usually represent non-cash balances. For example, in the United States, the excess of an investment's market value over its book value is a form of nonledger asset. Income that is due or accrued on a company's investments is another example of a nonledger asset. The amount of policy reserves is an example of a nonledger liability.

In an accounting system that provides for both ledger and nonledger accounts, nonledger accounts are usually isolated from cash accounts in order to facilitate the preparation of certain pages of the Annual Statement. The term *nonledger assets* appears in the U.S. Annual Statement (Exhibit 13, Column 2), but the term nonledger liabilities does not. Neither term appears in the Canadian Annual Statement.

Balance account. The use of cash basis accounting also results in an unusual ledger account that may be called a **balance account** or **balancing account.** Other titles for the balance account are *ledger surplus,* the *general fund,* and *net ledger assets.* The balance account could be considered a composite of all of a company's nonledger accounts and nonadmitted assets. In its usual form, however, the balance account is simply a device for keeping the trial balance and ledger in balance at all times.

An example should demonstrate why the balance account is necessary. Assume that the accounting equation

$$\text{Assets} = \text{Liabilities} + \text{Capital}$$

for the Center Life Insurance Company had the following values:

$$\begin{aligned}\text{Assets} &= \$1{,}000{,}000 \\ \text{Liabilities} &= \$\ \ 800{,}000 \\ \text{Capital} &= \$\ \ 200{,}000\end{aligned}$$

The Balance Sheet equation for this company would then be

$$\$1{,}000{,}000 = \$800{,}000 + \$200{,}000$$

If the basic Balance Sheet equation is subdivided so that it shows both ledger and nonledger items, the equation becomes:

$$\begin{pmatrix}\text{ledger} \\ \text{assets}\end{pmatrix} + \begin{pmatrix}\text{nonledger} \\ \text{assets}\end{pmatrix} = \begin{pmatrix}\text{ledger} \\ \text{liabilities}\end{pmatrix} + \begin{pmatrix}\text{nonledger} \\ \text{liabilities}\end{pmatrix} + \begin{pmatrix}\text{ledger} \\ \text{capital}\end{pmatrix} + \begin{pmatrix}\text{nonledger} \\ \text{capital}\end{pmatrix}$$

If values are assigned to each portion of the equation for the Center Life Company, the result might appear as follows (000 omitted):

$$\$750 \begin{bmatrix} \text{ledger} \\ \text{assets} \end{bmatrix} + \$250 \begin{bmatrix} \text{nonledger} \\ \text{assets} \end{bmatrix} =$$

$$\$100 \begin{bmatrix} \text{ledger} \\ \text{liabilities} \end{bmatrix} + \$700 \begin{bmatrix} \text{nonledger} \\ \text{liabilities} \end{bmatrix} + \$80 \begin{bmatrix} \text{ledger} \\ \text{capital} \end{bmatrix} + \$120 \begin{bmatrix} \text{nonledger} \\ \text{capital} \end{bmatrix}$$

With nonledger items removed, the statement would read:

$$\$750 \begin{bmatrix} \text{ledger} \\ \text{assets} \end{bmatrix} \neq \$100 \begin{bmatrix} \text{ledger} \\ \text{liabilities} \end{bmatrix} + \$80 \begin{bmatrix} \text{ledger} \\ \text{capital} \end{bmatrix}$$

Because the two sides of the statement are not equal, the equation is no longer in balance. A balance account is required to put the equation back in balance. The difference between the two sides of the statement is the amount credited to the balance account. In this case, the equation is out of balance by $570 [$750 − ($100 + $80)], so the balance account is given a credit balance of $570. The balance account can thus be thought of as the difference between a company's ledger assets and its ledger liabilities. The ledger liabilities are made up of liability and capital accounts.

Companies that have an automated accounting system that contains all ledger, nonledger, and nonadmitted accounts do not need a balance account. A balance account is also generally not needed in Canadian companies because most Canadian companies record all assets and liabilities on the ledger at the end of the accounting period.

Other Types of Life Insurance Accounting

Thus far, this chapter has concentrated on statutory accounting—that is, accounting practices geared towards the completion of the insurer's Annual Statement. In addition to providing financial statements that conform to regulations promulgated by governmental insurance authorities, however, many life and health insurance companies perform other types of accounting and provide additional types of accounting information. The next section of this chapter discusses types of accounting besides statutory accounting.

GAAP (Generally Accepted Accounting Principles)

In 1972, the American Institute of Certified Public Accountants (AICPA) published an industry audit guide entitled *Audits of Stock Life Insurance Companies*.

This guide detailed the differences between an insurer's statutory accounting practices (SAP) and the generally accepted accounting principles (GAAP) that are used in the preparation of financial statements in non-insurance companies. As mentioned briefly earlier in the chapter, generally accepted accounting principles are based on concepts that are quite different from the concepts used in statutory accounting. However, insurers often use GAAP when preparing financial statements for internal management and outside parties other than state regulatory authorities. Students of life insurance accounting must therefore be familiar with GAAP as well as statutory accounting practices. Some of the differences between these two accounting "languages" are introduced here and are discussed in greater detail later in the text.

As you learned earlier, asset valuation in statutory accounting uses the liquidation concept, which is based on the assumption that the company is to be terminated on the date of the Balance Sheet. However, GAAP is based on the going-concern concept, which assumes that the company will continue to do business in the future. Asset values are generally higher under GAAP. As an example, for GAAP purposes, nonadmitted assets are restored to the Balance Sheet at their net realizable value.

Because of the conservative nature of statutory accounting, the earnings reported in a company's Annual Statement may not truly reflect the success or failure of the company's operations. For example, if a life insurance company issues a large number of policies in a certain year, the high costs of policy acquisition will cause the net gain from operations to decline even though sales have increased. Conversely, if a company issues very few policies, its net gain from operations will be higher, even though the company had a relatively poor year with regard to generating new business. GAAP accounting recognizes that the revenues associated with policy acquisition costs will be received in future years, often twenty or more years after issue. Therefore, under GAAP, the accountant sets up an asset account that records deferral of acquisition costs. These deferred acquisition costs are spread out over the life of the policy in relation to the anticipated premium revenues, thus achieving a matching of revenues with the related policy acquisition costs.

The calculation of future policy benefits is another area that differs between SAP and GAAP. Under SAP, the mortality and interest rates used in the calculation of reserves are prescribed by the regulatory authorities. However, GAAP reserves are based on conditions in effect when the policy was sold. For example, GAAP assumes an interest rate that approximates the company's anticipated investment yield, with some provision for conservation. Generally, reserves calculated for GAAP financial statements are lower than those calculated for the statutory Annual Statement.

GAAP for life and health insurance companies applies primarily to U.S. stock life and health insurance companies. Mutual companies do not report on a GAAP basis except perhaps for internal management purposes. In Canada, insurers follow the statutory accounting practices prescribed by the federal regulatory authorities. GAAP for life companies has not yet been adopted in Canada, but Canadian statutory accounting practices bear many similarities to U.S. GAAP.

Tax Accounting

Federal income taxation for life and health insurance companies is a highly complicated area. Because of the complexities and changes in tax law, companies devote a great deal of time to income tax planning and gathering financial information pertinent to taxes and the filing of federal and local tax returns. As with commercial companies, life and health insurance companies must also pay taxes such as property taxes and unemployment taxes. Accounting records and procedures must be maintained for each of these taxation fields. The primary objective of the tax accounting function is to pay all taxes that are due, but no additional taxes.

Managerial Accounting

SAP, GAAP, and tax accounting are all part of the larger field of accounting known as **financial accounting,** which is oriented primarily towards reporting financial information about a company to interested parties outside the company. However, another important field that is essential to the life and health insurance accounting function is managerial accounting. **Managerial accounting** is the field of accounting responsible for providing management with information that can be used in (1) formulating long- and short-term plans and (2) measuring the level of success achieved in carrying out these plans. For example, management may use accounting information when deciding whether to issue a new type of policy or phase out an unprofitable line of business. The internal system that provides reports and summaries for the use of management is the *managerial accounting system.*

Managerial accounting can take a number of different forms. Three aspects of managerial accounting activity are presented later in this text. Internal auditing and control of the company's procedures and accounts are essential aspects of proper company management. Planning and budgeting are also integral to an insurer's accounting function. Finally, the practice of cost accounting allows an insurance company's management to analyze the company's performance from a different perspective than that allowed by many financial accounting procedures.

Organization and Functions of a Life Accounting Department

Life and health insurance company accounting departments are generally organized to parallel the primary operations required of the accounting function. Among these functions are policy accounting, investment accounting, managerial accounting, tax accounting, and corporate accounting. Depending on the size of the company, each of these categories might be further subdivided with certain employees being responsible for one or more of the subdivisions. The following lists show the different aspects of each accounting function.

Policy accounting	Claim settlements
	Benefit settlements other than claims
	Annuity payments
	Premiums and considerations
	Commissions
Investment accounting	Bonds
	Stocks
	Mortgage loans
	Real estate
	Policy loans
Managerial accounting	Budgeting and financial planning
	Cost accounting
	Cash reporting
	Auditing and control
Tax accounting	Premium taxes
	Federal taxes
	Local taxes
	Unemployment taxes
Corporate accounting	Payroll
	Administration
	Accounting for general operating expenses
Financial reporting	Statutory Annual Statement
	GAAP financial statements
	Annual reports

Most of these functions are discussed in more detail in the chapters that follow.

Key Terms

solvency	statutory accounting
GAAP accounting	cash-basis accounting
going-concern concept	liquidation concept
admitted assets	nonadmitted assets
working papers	ledger accounts
ledger assets	ledger liabilities
nonledger accounts	balance account
financial accounting	managerial accounting

Review Questions and Exercises

1. Why is the accounting function important to insurers?
2. What information can be found in a company's Annual Statement?
3. Why are insurers solvency-oriented?
4. What are the two categories of nonadmitted assets?
5. What is cash-basis accounting? Why does cash-basis accounting often necessitate use of a balance account?
6. Aside from statutory accounting, what other fields of accounting are relevant to an insurer's accounting function?

2
An Overview of Financial Statements Used by Life and Health Insurance Companies

Learning Objectives

After reading this chapter, you should be able to:

- Understand the purposes of some of the different reports contained within the Annual Statement
- Explain the ways in which insurers are required to value various types of asset and liability classifications
- Describe the different capital and surplus items on the insurer's Balance Sheet
- Describe the primary uses of the Summary of Operations and the Analysis of Operations
- List the different sources of changes in an insurer's surplus
- Outline the basic construction of a U.S. insurer's statutory Cash Flow statement
- Describe some financial reports other than the Annual Statement

Introduction

Before studying specific life insurance accounting procedures, you should understand how life and health companies present a complete picture of their present financial condition and an analysis of their past operations. This chapter presents a general survey of insurance company financial statements, including the statutory Annual Statement, the annual report, the tax return, and statements that are generated for the use of company management. Some of the statements and reports listed above are produced in conformity with generally accepted accounting principles (GAAP). The primary focus of this chapter, however, will be on the Annual Statement and statutory accounting practices.

The Annual Statement

The first U.S. Annual Statement blank was adopted by the National Association of Insurance Commissioners (NAIC) in 1875. Like the Annual Statement in use today, the first Annual Statement emphasized the insurer's solvency. The 1875 Blank introduced the concepts of nonadmitted assets and nonledger accounts and was used, with minor revisions, until 1951. In that year, the NAIC adopted the basic form of the Annual Statement in use today. Periodic revisions to the Annual Statement Blank have been made since then. The Canadian Annual Statement was introduced in 1954 and significantly revised in 1959. As with the U.S. Annual Statement, periodic revisions to the Canadian Blank have been made. The U.S. and Canadian Annual Statements are basically compendiums of many different financial statements, reports, exhibits, and schedules that present a picture of a company's financial standing and performance. Among the sections of the Annual Statement described in this chapter are the Balance Sheet, the Summary of Operations, the Analysis of Operations, and the Cash Flow statement.

Balance Sheet

The purpose of the Annual Statement Balance Sheet is to show the degree of solvency of a company, that is, the amount of assets available to meet present and future claims and all other known liabilities. All assets and liabilities must be properly valued in order to measure properly the firm's solvency. As in commercial companies, the amount of a life and health insurance company's assets available in excess of its liabilities is considered to be the **capital** of the company. On an insurer's Balance Sheet, capital is represented by capital stock and surplus items. Thus, the basic accounting equation for an insurer could be adjusted to read

$$\text{Assets} = \text{Liabilities} + (\text{Capital Stock} + \text{Surplus})$$

In a mutual company or any other company that does not issue stock, the amount of capital stock is zero. Assets generally exceed liabilities plus capital stock unless the company is insolvent, but insolvency rarely occurs. When a company is insolvent, it is said to be operating at a deficit. A commercial company may be able to continue to operate—at least for a short period of time—when it has a deficit. However, if a life insurance company attempts to operate at a deficit, the company's operation is typically taken over by regulatory authorities who act to protect the interests of the company's policyowners.

The Balance Sheet on pages 2 and 3 of the U.S. and Canadian Annual Statements is not labeled "Balance Sheet." In both Blanks, the assets page of the Balance Sheet—the first Annual Statement page that contains financial data—is simply labeled *Assets*. The next page, the liabilities page, is labeled in the United States as *Liabilities, Surplus, and Other Funds,* and in the Canadian Statement as *Liabilities, Capital and Surplus*. (The Assets pages of the U.S. and Canadian Balance Sheets are presented in Figure 2-1.) All figures on the Balance Sheet are shown on an accrual basis.

Asset classifications and valuations

In general, assets fall into three primary classifications: (1) invested assets, (2) other admitted assets, and (3) deferred, due, and accrued income. Each of the asset classifications is discussed below.

Invested assets are those assets that produce income in the form of interest, rent, dividends, and capital gains. Most of this income is used to support the buildup of policy reserves, which are increased each year by the interest rate specified in the policies. The major portion of a life and health insurance company's investment holdings consists of bonds, mortgages, and other investments that promise payment of fixed amounts on specified dates. A smaller percentage of insurance company funds is invested in assets that are more subject to market fluctuations, such as stocks and real estate. Accounting for investments and investment income will be covered in Chapters 5 and 6. At this point, however, we will examine asset values shown for investments on the Balance Sheet.

Generally, bonds not in default are valued for Annual Statement purposes at their book values, which occasionally are amortized values. **Amortization** is the process by which the book value of an investment is periodically and systematically adjusted so that, on the maturity date, the book value equals that investment's par value. Bonds not eligible for amortization, along with common stocks, are carried at market prices on the statement date. Preferred stocks in good standing are generally valued at cost or amortized cost, if applicable. Real estate is normally admitted at its depreciated book value if this value is not greater than the property's market value. Because of the investment risk involved, the amount of a life and health insurance company's investments in stocks and real estate is often limited by law. For preparation of the U.S. Annual Statement, market values for investments are prescribed by the NAIC. In addition, the NAIC prescribes whether a preferred stock is in good standing and whether the security therefore can be carried at its purchase price (or cost), at cost adjusted for amortization, or at market value.

FIGURE 2-1
Assets page—U.S. Annual Statement.

ANNUAL STATEMENT FOR THE YEAR 1985 OF THE _____ Name

Form 1

	(1) Current Year	(2) Previous Year
ASSETS		
1. Bonds		
2. Stocks:		
2.1 Preferred stocks		
2.2 Common stocks		
3. Mortgage loans on real estate		
4. Real estate:		
4.1 Properties occupied by the company (less $_____ encumbrances)		
4.2 Properties acquired in satisfaction of debt (less $_____ encumbrances)		
4.3 Investment real estate (less $_____ encumbrances)		
5. Policy loans		
6. Premium notes, including $_____ for first year premiums		
7. Collateral loans		
8.1 Cash on hand and on deposit		
8.2 Short-term investments		
9.		
10. Other invested assets		
10A. Subtotals, cash and invested assets (Items 1 to 10)		
11. Reinsurance ceded:		
11.1 Amounts recoverable from reinsurers		
11.2 Commissions and expense allowances due		
11.3 Experience rating and other refunds due		
11.4		
12.		
13. Electronic data processing equipment		
14. Federal income tax recoverable		
15.		
16.		
17. Life insurance premiums and annuity considerations deferred and uncollected		
18. Accident and health premiums due and unpaid		
19. Investment income due and accrued		
20. Net adjustment in assets and liabilities due to foreign exchange rates		
21. Receivable from parent, subsidiaries and affiliates		
22.		
23.		
24.		
25.		
26. Subtotals (Items 10A to 25)		
27A. From Separate Accounts Statement		
27B. From Variable Life Insurance Separate Accounts Statement		
28. TOTALS (Items 26 to 27B)		

NOTE: The items on this page to agree with Exhibit 13, Col. 4.

The Notes to Financial Statements are an integral part of this statement.

FIGURE 2-1 (cont.)
Assets page—Canadian Annual Statement.

02

NAME OF COMPANY ▶

YEAR OF STATEMENT
19 _____

I. ASSETS ($'000)

		CURRENT YEAR 01	PREVIOUS YEAR 02
BONDS	01		
SHARES	02		
MORTGAGE LOANS	03		
REAL ESTATE, LESS ENCUMBRANCES OF $.......	04		
GROUND RENTS, LESS ENCUMBRANCES OF $.......	05		
POLICY LOANS	06		
TERM DEPOSITS AND GUARANTEED INVESTMENT CERTIFICATES	07		
CASH, INCLUDING DEMAND DEPOSITS	08		
OTHER INVESTMENTS	09		
INVESTMENTS IN SUBSIDIARIES	10		
INVESTMENT INCOME DUE & ACCRUED	11		
PREMIUMS OUTSTANDING	12		
AMOUNTS DUE FROM OTHER INSURERS	13		
MISCELLANEOUS ASSETS	14		
	15		
	16		
	17		
	18		
ASSETS IN SEGREGATED FUNDS (AT MARKET)	19		
TOTAL ASSETS	▶ 20		

NOTE: SECTION 48 OF THE CANADIAN AND BRITISH INSURANCE COMPANIES ACT REQUIRES THE MAINTENANCE OF SEPARATE FUNDS AND ACCOUNTS IN RESPECT OF LIFE AND OTHER THAN LIFE BUSINESS. THE REQUIRED DETAILS ARE REPORTED ON IN PAGES 05 TO 17 OF THIS STATEMENT.

Canadian insurance companies registered with the federal Department of Insurance may amortize only certain securities. These securities must not be in default and must be issued or guaranteed by the government of either Canada, the United Kingdom, or the United States. All other securities must be listed on the Annual Statement at their market value as determined by the federal Department of Insurance.

In the United States and Canada, mortgage loans are admitted at their book values unless the mortgage is delinquent as to interest and principal payments. Policy loans, which are considered investments, are admitted on the Balance Sheet at their book value. The book value of both mortgage loans and policy loans is the amount of unpaid principal on the loans.

Detailed information regarding an insurer's bonds, stocks, mortgages, and real estate is included in schedules and exhibits of the Annual Statement. These reports (which are introduced later in this chapter) show various values, changes in book values, and income received from each type of investment during the year. The schedule for mortgages, for example, reports on mortgages by type of security, type of mortgage, and by state and province.

Also listed in the invested asset section of the Balance Sheet are cash and short-term investments. These classifications include cash on hand, cash on deposit in checking accounts, and cash on deposit at interest in financial institutions. Insurers aggressively manage their cash on deposit to keep its total as low as possible, since comparatively low yields are earned on cash and service charges can often be incurred. The amount and location of an insurer's cash deposits and the amount of interest earned on these deposits are shown in U.S. Annual Statement Schedule E and Canadian Annual Statement Schedules F and G.

An insurer's *other admitted assets* include electronic data processing equipment, reinsurance ceded, federal income tax recoverable, and other items that can be established as necessary by the insurer. The reinsurance ceded asset includes amounts recoverable from reinsurers, commissions and expense allowances due from reinsurers, and experience ratings and other refunds due. The valuations of these assets are explained in Chapter 9 of this text.

Deferred, due, and accrued income is a Balance Sheet asset category that consists of (1) investment income due and accrued and (2) deferred and uncollected premiums on policies in force. *Deferred premiums* are premiums due after December 31 but before the next policy anniversary date. The deferred premium classification applies to premium payments made more frequently than annually. *Uncollected premiums* are life premiums and annuity considerations due and not received on or before the statement date. Deferred and uncollected premiums are also known as **premium assets.** Premium assets on *life* policies are admitted at their *net* premium values on the U.S. Balance Sheet. The **net premium value** is the gross premium minus the expense loading. For example, if the expense loading is 20 percent of the gross premium, the net premium value is 80 percent of the gross premium amount. Uncollected *health* insurance premiums, which are generally referred to as *due and unpaid,* are admitted on a *gross* premium basis if the premiums are due within 90 days. However, the cost of collecting these health insurance premiums, principally in the cost of commissions, is reflected as a liability.

Liability classifications

As mentioned in Chapter 1, most life insurance liabilities are reflected in nonledger accounts. These liabilities generally relate to policies currently in force or policies that have terminated with a remaining liability, as in the case of death claims incurred but unpaid or settlement amounts left on deposit with the company. A small percentage of a company's liabilities represents unpaid administrative, maintenance, and corporate costs. The liabilities pages of the U.S. and Canadian Balance Sheets are shown in Figure 2-2.

Policy reserves. The valuation of policy reserves in a life and health insurance company is the responsibility of a company's actuaries rather than its accountants. These reserves, therefore, are often called *actuarial reserves.* Because of the importance of these reserves in the Balance Sheet, however, you should have a general understanding of the valuation processes used. The reserve liability of a life and health insurance company for Annual Statement purposes is determined as of December 31 each year. Although policies are issued throughout the calendar year, actuaries assume that all policies are issued in the middle of the calendar year—June 30. Therefore, when the reserve liability is determined as of December 31, each policy may then be considered as having been in force for ½ year, 1½ years, 2½ years, etc., depending on the calendar year in which the policy was issued. Thus, the reserve liability as of December 31 for each policy can be approximated by taking the average of the reserve at the beginning of the policy year—the *initial reserve*—and the reserve at the end of the policy year—the *terminal reserve.* This average is known as the **mean reserve** and is expressed in the equation:

$$\text{Mean reserve} = \frac{(\text{Initial reserve}) + (\text{Terminal reserve})}{2}$$

The total reported for policy reserve liability in the Annual Statement is calculated assuming that all premiums are paid annually and have been received by the company. However, many premiums are paid on a monthly, quarterly, or semiannual basis, so that, on December 31, a portion of the year's premium income may not have been received. Thus, valuing the mean reserve on the Balance Sheet as of December 31 would overstate the amount of reserve liability unless an adjustment were made. In the U.S. Annual Statement, this overstatement is adjusted by reporting as assets both the amount of net deferred premiums

FIGURE 2-2
Liabilities page—U.S. Annual Statement.

Form 1 — ANNUAL STATEMENT FOR THE YEAR 1985 OF THE _____ Name — 3

	LIABILITIES, SURPLUS AND OTHER FUNDS	(1) Current Year	(2) Previous Year
1.	Aggregate reserve for life policies and contracts $............ (Exh. 8, Line H) less $............ included in Item 7.3		
2.	Aggregate reserve for accident and health policies (Exhibit 9, Line C, Col. 1)		
3.	Supplementary contracts without life contingencies (Exhibit 10, Line 7, Col. 5)		
4.	Policy and contract claims:		
4.1	Life (Exhibit 11, Part 1, Line 4d, Column 1 less sum of Columns 9, 10 and 11)		
4.2	Accident and health (Exhibit 11, Part 1, Line 4d, sum of Columns 9, 10 and 11)		
5.	Policyholders' dividend and coupon* accumulations (Exhibit 10, Line 7, Col. 6 plus Col. 7)		
6.	Policyholders' dividends $............ and coupons $............ due and unpaid (Exhibit 7, Line 10)		
7.	Provision for policyholders' dividends and coupons payable in following calendar year—estimated amounts:		
7.1	Dividends apportioned for payment to ...., 19...		
7.2	Dividends not yet apportioned		
7.3	Coupons and similar benefits		
8.	Amount provisionally held for deferred dividend policies not included in Item 7		
9.	Premiums and annuity considerations received in advance less $............ discount; including $............ accident and health premiums (Exhibit 1, Part 1, Col. 1, sum of Lines 4 and 14)		
10.	Liability for premium and other deposit funds		
11.	Policy and contract liabilities not included elsewhere:		
11.1	Surrender values on cancelled policies		
11.2	Provision for experience rating refunds		
11.3	Other amounts payable on reinsurance assumed		
11.4			
12.			
13.	Commissions to agents due or accrued-life and annuity $............ accident and health $............		
13A.	Commissions and expense allowances payable on reinsurance assumed		
14.	General expenses due or accrued (Exhibit 5, Line 12, Col. 4)		
14A.	Transfers to Separate Accounts due or accrued, excluding Variable Life Insurance (net)		
14B.	Transfers to Variable Life Insurance Separate Accounts due or accrued (net)		
15.	Taxes, licenses and fees due or accrued, excluding federal income taxes (Exhibit 6, Line 9, Col. 4)		
15A.	Federal income taxes due or accrued, including $............ on capital gains (excluding deferred taxes)		
16.	"Cost of collection" on premiums and annuity considerations deferred and uncollected in excess of total loading thereon		
17.	Unearned investment income (Exhibit 2, Line 10, Col. 2)		
18.	Amounts withheld or retained by company as agent or trustee		
19.	Amounts held for agents' account, including $............ agents' credit balances		
20.	Remittances and items not allocated		
21.	Net adjustment in assets and liabilities due to foreign exchange rates		
22.	Liability for benefits for employees and agents if not included above		
23.	Borrowed money $............ and interest thereon $............		
24.	Dividends to stockholders declared and unpaid		
25.	Miscellaneous liabilities (give items and amounts):		
25.1	Mandatory securities valuation reserve (Page 29A, final Item)		
25.2	Reinsurance in unauthorized companies		
25.3	Funds held under reinsurance treaties with unauthorized reinsurers		
25.4	Payable to parent, subsidiaries and affiliates		
25.5	Drafts outstanding		
25.6			
25.7			
25.8			
25.9			
25A.	From Separate Accounts Statement		
25B.	From Variable Life Insurance Separate Accounts Statement		
26.	TOTAL LIABILITIES (Items 1 to 25B)		
27A.	Common capital stock		
27B.	Preferred capital stock		
27C.			
28.	Gross paid in and contributed surplus (Page 3, Item 28, Col. 2 plus Page 4, Item 46a, Col. 1)		
29A.	Special surplus funds:		
(a)			
(b)			
(c)			
29B.	Unassigned funds (surplus)		
29C.	Less treasury stock, at cost:		
(1)	.... shares common (value included in Item 27A $............)		
(2)	.... shares preferred (value included in Item 27B $............)		
29D.	Surplus (total Items 27C + 28 + 29A + 29B − 29C)		
30.	Total of Items 27A, 27B and 29D (Page 4, Item 50)		
31.	TOTALS OF ITEMS 26 AND 30 (Page 2, Item 28)		

*Includes coupons, guaranteed annual pure endowments and similar benefits.

FIGURE 2-2 (cont.)
Liabilities page—Canadian Annual Statement.

03

NAME OF COMPANY ▶   YEAR OF STATEMENT
                                                                            19

II. LIABILITIES, CAPITAL AND SURPLUS ($'000)

		CURRENT YEAR 01	PREVIOUS YEAR 02
NET ACTUARIAL RESERVE	01		
OUTSTANDING CLAIMS AND PROVISION FOR UNREPORTED CLAIMS	02		
AMOUNTS ON DEPOSIT WITH THE COMPANY	03		
OTHER CONTRACT LIABILITIES	04		
PROVISION FOR DIVIDENDS AND EXPERIENCE RATING REFUNDS TO POLICYHOLDERS	05		
CURRENT INCOME TAXES, DUE AND ACCRUED	06		
OTHER TAXES, LICENCES AND FEES, DUE AND ACCRUED	07		
GENERAL AND INVESTMENT EXPENSES, DUE AND ACCRUED	08		
AMOUNTS DUE TO OTHER INSURANCE COMPANIES	09		
BANK OVERDRAFT AND BORROWED MONEY INCLUDING INTEREST DUE AND ACCRUED	10		
MISCELLANEOUS LIABILITIES	11		
	12		
	13		
	14		
STAFF PENSION AND INSURANCE FUNDS	15		
SEGREGATED FUND LIABILITIES	16		
TOTAL LIABILITIES (01 TO 16)	▶ 17		
DEFERRED INCOME TAXES	▶ 18		
CAPITAL, SURPLUS AND RESERVES: RESERVES REQUIRED BY THE DEPARTMENT	19		
RESERVES REQUIRED BY FOREIGN JURISDICTIONS	20		
ADDITIONAL RESERVES	21		
CAPITAL STOCK ISSUED AND PAID: COMMON STOCK	22		
: PREFERRED STOCK	23		
CONTRIBUTED SURPLUS	24		
UNAPPROPRIATED EARNED SURPLUS	25		
UNAPPROPRIATED SURPLUS (24+25)	▶ 26		
TOTAL CAPITAL, SURPLUS AND RESERVES (19 TO 25)	▶ 27		
TOTAL LIABILITIES, CAPITAL AND SURPLUS (17+18+27)	▶ 28		

and the amount of net uncollected premiums. In the Canadian Annual Statement, the amount of gross uncollected premiums less commissions and other costs of collection is reported as an asset. The amount of net deferred premiums, on the other hand, is deducted from actuarial reserves.

Policy reserves are assembled in exhibits in the Annual Statement blank, and only the totals are entered on the liability page of the Balance Sheet. Exhibit 8 in the U.S. Statement, Aggregate Reserve for Life Policies and Contracts, shows reserves by (1) type of coverage—life insurance, annuity, supplementary contracts with life contingencies, etc.; (2) mortality table, interest rate, and the valuation method used in calculating them; and (3) line of business. The lines of business for a life insurer are ordinary insurance, industrial insurance, and group insurance. Exhibit 9 in the U.S. Statement shows somewhat less detailed information on a company's accident and health insurance reserves. Reserves for supplementary contracts without life contingencies are shown in U.S. Annual Statement Exhibit 10. In the Canadian Annual Statement, policy reserve information is presented primarily in Exhibit 15, which distinguishes between a company's life, annuity, and accident and sickness business. Annual changes in the basis of a company's reserves are also presented in both countries' Annual Statements. These changes are made up of adjustments on the mortality and interest assumptions used.

Amounts held on deposit. The *amounts held on deposit* liability classification covers amounts left with the company to accumulate interest. This total includes amounts left in connection with death settlements, premiums paid sufficiently in advance that a discount has been allowed, and policy dividends left to accumulate at interest. Amounts applied towards supplementary contracts not involving life contingencies are also included in this classification. For Annual Statement purposes, the liability for amounts left on deposit is the amount as of the preceding policy anniversary plus estimated interest to the end of the year and new amounts added minus any payments made during the year.

Claims incurred but not yet paid. The *claims incurred but not yet paid* liability includes all types of claims that must be settled. Claim liabilities are usually entered in the Balance Sheet for the full amount of benefit claimed, even if the amount is in dispute. A liability for claims not yet reported must be estimated on the basis of the company's past experience.

Dividend liabilities. Both stockholder dividends and policy dividends are reflected as separate and distinct liabilities on the Annual Statement. The policy dividend liabilities classification includes a liability for all policy dividends that have been declared by a company's board of directors, but which are not yet payable. Most companies also include an amount for policy dividends that will become payable in the following calendar year, whether or not these dividends have been declared payable by the board. The amount of policy dividend liability must be approximated. Usually, policy dividends are contingent upon certain conditions such as the policy being in force on its anniversary or premiums being paid to a specified date. While an actuary can calculate the exact amount of liability on policies currently in force, some dividends may never become payable because the required conditions will not be met.

In addition to the liability for policy dividends on participating business in force, stock companies must also establish a liability for cash dividends that have been declared by the company's board, but which have not yet been paid to stockholders. Once the dividend is declared by the board, no change occurs regarding the amount of the liability.

Accrued expenses other than claims. This classification includes the liability for unpaid commissions; unpaid expenses, such as utilities, printing bills, and salaries accrued; taxes; and any other costs, except for policy claims, that are accrued or fully incurred.

Unearned income. The *unearned income* liability includes (1) investment income received in advance and any portion of investment income that has already been received but which may be allocable to the following calendar year and (2) advance premiums. **Advance premiums** are life insurance premiums that are due in the following year, but which were paid before December 31 of the current year. Some companies include premiums paid several years in advance, but these amounts are usually considered amounts held on deposit. Unearned premiums—the portion of health insurance premiums applicable to the following year—are not usually considered unearned income but instead are treated as policy reserves.

Amounts temporarily held for disposition. This liability classification covers only two items on the liability page of the Annual Statement but represents most of the liabilities that are normally entered on the company's ledger, i.e., those which result from cash transactions. The first statement item is *amounts withheld or retained by the company as agent or trustee.* This item includes (1) deposits by mortgagors that will be used to pay future taxes and property/casualty or hazard insurance premiums and (2) amounts withheld from wage and salary payments, such as withholding taxes or social security deductions. The second statement item is *remittances and items not allocated.* This total includes unallocated policy funds. Other amounts, such as amounts received and held in suspense accounts, are typically shown on a write-in line on the Annual Statement.

Capital stock and surplus

The following discussion relates generally to surplus as shown in the U.S. Annual Statement. The descriptions of capital stock and surplus items also apply to Canadian companies, but surplus is shown differently in the Canadian Balance Sheet.

The items *capital stock* and *surplus* appear on the liabilities page of an insurer's Balance Sheet. **Capital stock,** or legal capital, represents the par value of all shares of outstanding stock, i.e., issued stock that is not owned by the company. In the U.S. Annual Statement, this item is separated into *common capital stock* and *preferred capital stock*. In the Canadian Statement, the total is reported on a line entitled *capital stock paid*.

Surplus on the U.S. Statement is broken down into *contributed surplus, special surplus funds,* and *unassigned surplus*. When a stock life insurance company is first organized, its capital stock is generally sold for a price in excess of its par value. An amount equal to the par value of the stock multiplied by the number of stock shares sold is credited to the Capital Stock account, and the balance is credited to a Contributed Surplus account. The **contributed surplus** shown in the Balance Sheet is the amount in excess of par value paid in by stockholders minus the amount of stock dividends paid. **Special surplus funds** are reserves accumulated by some companies for the purpose of meeting general contingencies. Establishment of these reserves is optional. **Unassigned surplus** consists of all other surplus amounts, and it arises from operating earnings as well as from other sources. All cash dividends to stockholders or policyowners must be paid from unassigned surplus, and stock dividends also can be paid from this fund.

In the Canadian Annual Statement, **surplus** is divided into an amount set aside for stockholders, known as *surplus in shareholders funds*, and unassigned surplus in participating and nonparticipating funds, known as *surplus in insurance funds*. When a newly formed insurance company's cost of selling and issuing new business exceeds the premiums received, this cost and the company's fixed overhead expenses must be paid from contributed surplus until renewal premium volume reaches a sufficiently high level to pay expenses.

Summary of Operations

The Summary of Operations is the U.S. Annual Statement financial report that appears after the Balance Sheet. In Canada, this report is known as the Income Statement. (Figure 2-3 shows the reports used in both countries' Annual Statements.) Both reports are similar to the income and expense statement used in commercial companies. The Summary of Operations is used to determine the increase or decrease in surplus resulting from life and health insurance operations and to distinguish this amount from the increase or decrease resulting from other sources. Capital gains or losses, for example, are not considered part of the gain or loss from operations. Amounts paid out in dividends to policyowners and the amount of federal income taxes paid by the insurer are deducted before computing a final net gain (or loss) from operations.

The Summary of Operations can be divided into many different categories, some of which are discussed below:

1. *Income from insurance contracts* consists primarily of insurance premium income, annuity considerations, and policy proceeds retained under supplementary contracts.
2. *Net income from investments* consists of the total of interest, dividends, and rent derived from invested assets, less depreciation on real estate and all costs of servicing and accounting for investments and investment income. Net income from investments also includes amortization of discounts and premiums on securities. However, net income from investments does not include gains or losses from the sale of invested assets.
3. *Policy benefits* consists of all types of contractual policy payments. These payments include death claims, matured endowments, annuity payments, disability payments, surrender benefits, payments on health insurance policies, and payments on supplementary contracts.
4. *Increase in policy reserves* includes increases in reserves for policies both with and without life contingencies.

Other classifications included in the Summary of Operations are commissions, general expenses, taxes, policy dividends, and increases in loading. Many of these items are discussed later in this text.

Analysis of Operations

The Analysis of Operations by Line of Business appears on page 5 of the U.S. Annual Statement (see Figure 2-4). In this report, a company's net gain (or loss) is calculated for each line of business. A *line of business*—from an accounting standpoint—is a segment of the insurance market that has a cost pattern distinctively different from that of other segments. Differences in sales and servicing methods generally create these distinctive cost patterns. The Canadian report equivalent to the U.S. Analysis of Operations is called the Analysis of Income by Line of Business (see Figure 2-5). The items in the two analyses are similar, but some differences are present in the classifications for lines of business. The Canadian analysis shows the gains in each line of business separately

FIGURE 2-3
Summary of Operations—U.S. Annual Statement.

```
 4        ANNUAL STATEMENT FOR THE YEAR 1985 OF THE _____          Form 1
                                                              Name
                                                                    (1)              (2)
                                                              Current Year      Previous Year
                    SUMMARY OF OPERATIONS
                  (Excluding Capital Gains and Losses)
   1. Premiums and annuity considerations (Exhibit 1, Part 1, Line 20d, Col. 1) . . .
  1A. Annuity and other fund deposits . . . . . . . . . . . . . . . . . . . . . . .
   2. Considerations for supplementary contracts with life contingencies (Exhibit 12, Line 3) . . .
   3. Considerations for supplementary contracts without life contingencies and dividend accumulations
      (Exhibit 12, Lines 4 and 5) . . . . . . . . . . . . . . . . . . . . . . . .
  3A. Coupons left to accumulate at interest (Exhibit 12, Line 5A) . . . . . . . . .
   4. Net investment income (includes $............ equity in undistributed income or loss of subsidiaries) (Exhibit 2, Line 7) .
   5. Commissions and expense allowances on reinsurance ceded (Exhibit 1, Part 2, Line 26a, Col. 1) . . .
  5A. Reserve adjustments on reinsurance ceded (Exhibit 12, Line 10A) . . . . . . .
   6. _____
   7.         TOTALS  (Items 1 to 6) . . . . . . . . . . . . . . . . . . . . . .
   8. Death benefits . . . . . . . . . . . . . . . . . . . . . . . . . . . . . .
   9. Matured endowments (excluding guaranteed annual pure endowments) . . . .
  10. Annuity benefits (Exhibit 11, Part 2, Line 6d, Cols. 4 + 8) . . . . . . . . .
  11. Disability benefits and benefits under accident and health policies . . . . .
 11A. Coupons, guaranteed annual pure endowments and similar benefits (Exhibit 7, Line 15, Cols. 3 + 4) . . . .
  12. Surrender benefits . . . . . . . . . . . . . . . . . . . . . . . . . . . .
  13. Group conversions . . . . . . . . . . . . . . . . . . . . . . . . . . . .
  14. Interest on policy or contract funds . . . . . . . . . . . . . . . . . . . .
  15. Payments on supplementary contracts with life contingencies (Exhibit 12, Line 22.1) . .
  16. Payments on supplementary contracts without life contingencies and of dividend accumulations
      (Exhibit 12, Lines 22.2 + 23) . . . . . . . . . . . . . . . . . . . . . .
 16A. Accumulated coupon payments (Exhibit 12, Line 23A) . . . . . . . . . . .
  17. Increase in aggregate reserves for life and accident and health policies and contracts . . .
  18. Increase in reserve for supplementary contracts without life contingencies and for dividend and
      coupon accumulations . . . . . . . . . . . . . . . . . . . . . . . . . .
  19. _____
  20.         TOTALS (Items 8 to 19) . . . . . . . . . . . . . . . . . . . . . .
  21. Commissions on premiums and annuity considerations (direct business only) (Exhibit 1, Part 2, Line 30, Col. 1)
 21A. Commissions and expense allowances on reinsurance assumed (Exhibit 1, Part 2, Line 26b, Col. 1) . . .
  22. General insurance expenses (Exhibit 5, Line 10, Cols. 1 + 2) . . . . . . . .
  23. Insurance taxes, licenses and fees, excluding federal income taxes (Exhibit 6, Line 7, Cols. 1 and 2) . . .
  24. Increase in loading on and cost of collection in excess of loading on deferred and uncollected premiums . . .
 24A. Net transfers to (+) or from (−) Separate Accounts (excluding Variable Life Insurance) . . . . .
 24B. Net transfers to (+) or from (−) Variable Life Insurance Separate Accounts . . . . . . . . .
  25. _____
  26.         TOTALS (Items 20 to 25) . . . . . . . . . . . . . . . . . . . . .
  27. Net gain from operations before dividends to policyholders and federal income taxes (Item 7 minus Item 26) .
  28. Dividends to policyholders (Exhibit 7, Line 15, Cols. 1 and 2) . . . . . . . .
  29. Net gain from operations after dividends to policyholders and before federal income taxes (Item 27 minus Item 28) .
  30. Federal income taxes incurred (excluding tax on capital gains) . . . . . . . .
  31. NET GAIN FROM OPERATIONS AFTER DIVIDENDS TO POLICYHOLDERS AND FEDERAL INCOME TAXES (excluding tax on
      capital gains) (Item 29 minus Item 30) . . . . . . . . . . . . . . . . . .
```

for participating and nonparticipating business. While a few states now require companies to file one Analysis of Operations for participating business and another for nonparticipating business, this practice is not universal.

The U.S. Annual Statement instructions define the major and secondary lines of business for the allocation of receipts and expenses as:

FIGURE 2-3 (cont.)
Income Statement—Canadian Annual Statement.

04

NAME OF COMPANY ▶

YEAR OF STATEMENT
19

III. INCOME STATEMENT ($'000)

		CURRENT YEAR 01	PREVIOUS YEAR 02
PREMIUMS	01		
CONSIDERATIONS FOR SETTLEMENT ANNUITIES	02		
POLICY DIVIDENDS AND PROCEEDS OF CONTRACTS DEPOSITED IN SEGREGATED FUNDS	03		
NET INVESTMENT INCOME	04		
NET INVESTMENT GAIN (LOSS) ON SEGREGATED FUND ASSETS	05		
CONTRIBUTION TO STAFF PENSION AND INSURANCE FUNDS	06		
NET GAIN OR (LOSS) ON CURRENCY EXCHANGE TRANSACTIONS	07		
RESERVE ADJUSTMENT ON REINSURANCE CEDED	08		
	09		
	10		
SUBTOTAL (01 TO 10)	▶11		
CLAIMS INCURRED	12		
CLAIMS INCURRED PAID DIRECTLY FROM SEGREGATED FUNDS	13		
PAYMENTS UNDER SETTLEMENT ANNUITIES	14		
POLICY DIVIDENDS AND PROCEEDS OF CONTRACTS WITHDRAWN FROM SEGREGATED FUNDS	15		
NORMAL INCREASE IN ACTUARIAL RESERVES - MANDATORY PROVISION	16		
- ADDITIONAL PROVISION	17		
NORMAL INCREASE IN SEGREGATED FUNDS	18		
INCREASE IN STAFF PENSION AND INSURANCE FUNDS	19		
INTEREST INCURRED ON CLAIMS	20		
TAXES, LICENCES AND FEES, EXCLUDING INVESTMENT TAXES AND INCOME TAXES	21		
COMMISSIONS INCURRED (NET)	22		
GENERAL EXPENSES (EXCLUDING INVESTMENT EXPENSES)	23		
PAYMENTS FROM STAFF PENSION AND INSURANCE FUNDS	24		
DIVIDENDS TO POLICYHOLDERS	25		
INCREASE IN PROVISION FOR DIVIDENDS TO POLICYHOLDERS	26		
EXPERIENCE RATING REFUNDS	27		
INCREASE IN PROVISION FOR EXPERIENCE RATING REFUNDS	28		
INTEREST INCURRED ON AMOUNTS ON DEPOSIT	29		
	30		
	31		
INCOME TAXES - CURRENT	32		
- DEFERRED	33		
SUBTOTAL (12 TO 33)	▶34		
INCOME BEFORE UNUSUAL OR EXTRAORDINARY ITEMS (11 MINUS 34)	▶35		

FIGURE 2-3 (cont.)

	05	
NAME OF COMPANY ▶		YEAR OF STATEMENT 19

III. INCOME STATEMENT (CONTINUED) ($'000)

		CURRENT YEAR 01	PREVIOUS YEAR 02
INCOME BEFORE UNUSUAL OR EXTRAORDINARY ITEMS (CARRIED FORWARD FROM PAGE 04)	01		
UNUSUAL CHANGE IN ACTUARIAL RESERVE – LIFE	02		
– ACCIDENT & SICKNESS	03		
NON-AMORTIZABLE GAINS(LOSSES) IN RESPECT OF INVESTED ASSETS – LIFE	04		
GAIN(LOSS) DUE TO CHANGES IN BOOK RATES OF EXCHANGE	05		
INCOME BEFORE EXTRAORDINARY ITEMS AND INCOME TAXES ON UNUSUAL ITEMS (01 TO 05) ▶	06		
INCOME TAXES ON UNUSUAL ITEMS: CURRENT	07		
DEFERRED	08		
INCOME BEFORE EXTRAORDINARY ITEMS (06-07-08) ▶	09		
NET EXTRAORDINARY ITEMS (GIVE DETAILS ON PAGE 08)	10		
NET INCOME FROM INSURANCE OPERATIONS (09+10) ▶	11		
INCREASE(DECREASE) IN VALUE OF SECTION 64 AND 65 SUBSIDIARIES	12		
NET INCOME FROM ANCILLARY OPERATIONS	13		
NET INCOME CARRIED TO RECONCILIATION OF UNAPPROPRIATED EARNED SURPLUS (11+12+13) ▶	14		

- Industrial Life
- Ordinary—Life, Annuities, and Supplementary Contracts
- Credit Life—Group and Individual
- Group—Life and Annuities
- Accident and Health—Group, Credit, and Other

The Analysis of Operations is helpful to management in determining sources of gains (or losses) from insurance operations. The net gain for each line and the total gain can be an indication of the efficiency of personnel in managing that line of business. Comparison among companies based on figures shown for each line of business can be helpful in locating relative weaknesses in insurance operations. Most of the figures in the Summary of Operations and the Analysis of Operations are cross-referenced to other exhibits in the Annual Statement that provide considerable detail on the sources of income and cost items. With several exceptions, each item in the Summary of Operations is a total of certain account balances and nonledger items summarized in an exhibit or a section of an exhibit.

Some supplementary exhibits, such as those relating to premium income and policy benefits, show the same distribution by line of business as is shown in the Analysis. Exhibits covering expenses and taxes do not show this distribution, so

FIGURE 2-4
Analysis of Operations—U.S. Annual Statement.

ANNUAL STATEMENT FOR THE YEAR 1985 OF THE _____

ANALYSIS OF OPERATIONS BY LINES OF BUSINESS
(Gain and Loss Exhibit) (Excluding Capital Gains and Losses)

	(1) Total**	(2) Industrial Life	(3) Life Insurance	Ordinary (4) Individual Annuities	(5) Supplementary Contracts	(6) Credit Life* (Group and Individual)	Group (7) Life Insurance	(8) Annuities	(9) Group	Accident and Health (10) Credit* (Group and Individual)	(11) Other	
1. Premiums and annuity considerations			x	x	x	x	x	x	x	x	x	1.
1A. Annuity and other fund deposits												1A.
2. Considerations for supplementary contracts with life contingencies					x							2.
3. Considerations for supplementary contracts without life contingencies and dividend accumulations					x					x	x	3.
3A. Coupons* left to accumulate at interest												3A.
4. Net investment income												4.
5. Commissions and expense allowances on reinsurance ceded												5A.
5A. Reserve adjustments on reinsurance ceded												6.
6.												6.
7. Totals (Items 1 to 6)	x	x	x	x	x	x	x	x	x	x	x	7.
8. Death benefits			x			x	x					8.
9. Matured endowments (excluding guaranteed annual pure endowments)			x									9.
10. Annuity benefits				x				x				10.
11. Disability benefits and benefits under accident and health policies			x			x			x	x	x	11.
11A. Coupons, guaranteed annual pure endowments and similar benefits			x	x								11A.
12. Surrender benefits			x	x	x			x				12.
13. Group conversions			x				x					13.
13A. Transfers on account of group package policies and contracts							x	x	x	x	x	13A.
14. Interest on policy or contract funds			x	x	x							14.
15. Payments on supplementary contracts with life contingencies					x							15.
16. Payments on supplementary contracts without life contingencies and of dividend accumulations					x							16.
16A. Accumulated coupon* payments									x	x	x	16A.
17. Increase in aggregate reserves for life and accident and health policies and contracts							x					17.
18. Increase in reserve for supplementary contracts without life contingencies and for dividend and coupon* accumulations												18.
19.												19.
20. Totals (Items 8 to 19)												20.
21. Commissions on premiums and annuity considerations (direct business only)												21.
21A. Commissions and expense allowances on reinsurance assumed												21A.
22. General insurance expenses												22.
23. Insurance taxes, licenses and fees, excluding federal income taxes												23.
24. Increase in loading on and cost of collection in excess of loading on deferred and uncollected premiums												24.
24A. Net transfers to (+) or from (−) Separate Accounts (excluding Variable Life Insurance)												24A.
24B. Net transfers to (+) or from (−) Variable Life Insurance Separate Accounts												24B.
25.												25.
26. Totals (Items 20 to 25)												26.
27. Net gain from operations before dividends to policyholders and federal income taxes (Item 7 minus Item 26)												27.
28. Dividends to policyholders												28.
29. Net gain from operations after dividends to policyholders and before federal income taxes (Item 27 minus Item 28)												29.
30. Federal income taxes incurred (excluding tax on capital gains)												30.
31. Net gain from operations after dividends to policyholders and federal income taxes (excluding tax on capital gains) (Item 29 minus Item 30)												31.

*Business net exceeding 120 months duration.
†Includes the following amounts for FEGLI/SGLI: Item 1 _____ Item 8 _____

*Includes coupon, guaranteed annual pure endowments and similar benefits. Item 13 _____ Item 22 _____

**The items in this column to agree with Page 4, Column 1. Item 29 _____

FIGURE 2-5
Analysis of Income by Line of Business—Canadian Annual Statement.

17(LS)

NAME OF COMPANY ▶   YEAR OF STATEMENT
                                                                       19

XVI. ANALYSIS OF INCOME

		LIFE – PARTICIPATING			
		INDIVIDUAL		GROUP	
		INSURANCE	ANNUITY	INSURANCE	ANNUITY	TOTAL
		01	02	03	04	05
PREMIUMS	01					
CONSIDERATIONS FOR SETTLEMENT ANNUITIES	02					
NET INVESTMENT INCOME	03					
NET GAIN (LOSS) ON CURRENCY EXCHANGE TRANSACTIONS	04					
RESERVE ADJUSTMENT ON REINSURANCE CEDED	05					
	06					
	07					
	08					
NET TRANSFERS IN RESPECT OF MORTALITY, GENERAL EXPENSES AND TAXES FROM (TO) SEGREGATED FUNDS	09					
NET TRANSFER OF POLICY LIABILITIES TO SEGREGATED FUNDS	10					
INTER FUND TRANSFERS TO MEET LIABILITIES TRANSFERRED	11					
SUBTOTAL (ITEMS 01 TO 11)	▶ 12					
CLAIMS INCURRED	13					
PAYMENTS UNDER SETTLEMENT ANNUITIES	14					
NORMAL INCREASE IN ACTUARIAL RESERVES (TOTAL)	15					
INTEREST INCURRED ON CLAIMS	16					
TAXES, LICENCES AND FEES	17					
COMMISSIONS INCURRED (NET)	18					
GENERAL EXPENSES (EXCLUDING INVESTMENT EXPENSES)	19					
DIVIDENDS TO POLICYHOLDERS	20					
INCREASE IN PROVISION FOR DIVIDENDS TO POLICYHOLDERS	21					
EXPERIENCE RATING REFUNDS PAID	22					
INCREASE IN PROVISION FOR EXPERIENCE RATING REFUNDS	23					
	24					
	25					
	26					
	27					
INCOME TAXES – CURRENT	28					
– DEFERRED	29					
SUBTOTAL (ITEMS 13 TO 29)	▶ 30					
INCOME BEFORE UNUSUAL OR EXTRAORDINARY ITEMS (ITEM 12 MINUS 30)	▶ 31					

FIGURE 2-5 (cont.)

	17 (RS)								
	NAME OF COMPANY							YEAR OF STATEMENT 19___	
	BY LINE OF BUSINESS ($'000)								
	LIFE – NON-PARTICIPATING					ACCIDENT AND SICKNESS			
	INDIVIDUAL		GROUP						
	INSURANCE 06	ANNUITY 07	INSURANCE 08	ANNUITY 09	TOTAL 10	INDI-VIDUAL 11	GROUP 12	TOTAL 13	GRAND TOTAL 14
01									
02									
03									
04									
05									
06									
07									
08									
09									
10									
11									
▶12									
13									
14									
15									
16									
17									
18									
19									
20									
21									
22									
23									
24									
25									
26									
27									
28									
29									
▶30									
▶31									

these costs must be analyzed or assembled on separate working papers before entering them in the Analysis. These two exhibits, however, include a column for investment costs, which are deducted from investment income to produce a net investment income figure for the Summary. This deduction is made in an exhibit relating to investment income.

All items in the Summary and Analysis of Operations, as well as in the Balance Sheet, are shown net of reinsurance. For example, if the accrual-basis premium income is $306 million and the accrual-basis reinsurance premiums paid are $16 million, the premium income shown is $290 million. Claims and policy reserve increases are also shown net of reinsurance. The amount of reinsurance deductions is shown separately in each exhibit.

Capital and Surplus Account

In the accounting process, every business transaction must be recorded in terms of dollars received and spent. These transactions can be summarized and analyzed to determine the causes for increases and decreases in surplus during the year. Analyzing these changes provides useful decision-making information for management. The U.S. surplus account and the Canadian Reconciliation of Surplus are presented in a form that shows the surplus changes between the end of one year and the end of the next year.

Causes for changes in a life company's surplus are not limited to gains from operations, i.e., the total of insurance and investment income minus any insurance costs. Several other sources of surplus change may be referred to as *direct changes in surplus*. These changes are shown in a statement of surplus in the Annual Statement form. The principal sources of surplus change in a life insurance company are as follows:

1. Net gains from operations,
2. Capital gains and losses,
3. Changes in the Mandatory Securities Valuation Reserve (MSVR),
4. Dividends paid to stockholders,
5. Paid-in capital,
6. Changes in nonadmitted assets and related items,
7. Special surplus adjustments, and
8. Changes in the valuation basis of policy reserves.

Items 3 and 6 are not found in the Canadian surplus statement because these items are not applicable to Canadian insurance accounting practices.

Various exhibits and reports in the Annual Statement blank are used to summarize data relating to the types of surplus changes listed above. Short descriptions of each of these sources of change are as follows:

- *Net gain from operations* is determined in the Summary of Operations and was described earlier. The Canadian equivalent to net gain from operations is *balance carried to reconciliation of surplus,* which is calculated in the revenue account.
- *Capital gains and losses* are calculated from (1) the realized gain or loss on the sale of an asset and (2) the change in the admitted value of invested assets. Applicable federal income taxes are then subtracted from this amount.
- *The Mandatory Securities Valuation Reserve* is a reserve that is shown as a liability in the U.S. Annual Statement. This reserve is designed to absorb fluctuations in the market values of an insurer's stock and bond holdings.
- *Dividends paid to stockholders* is a distribution of surplus to stockholders and is not an operating cost. Dividends paid to policyowners, on the other hand, are not included in this reconciliation. Policy dividends are considered to be premium adjustments and not distributions of surplus. Therefore, policy dividends are treated as an insurance cost and are included in the Summary of Operations.
- *Changes in nonadmitted assets and related items* refers primarily to increases and decreases in the book values of assets—such as furniture and equipment—used in insurance operations. The amount of this item is taken from the Annual Statement exhibit that specifies which assets are to be nonadmitted. As mentioned earlier, this surplus change item is not found in the Canadian reconciliation of surplus. Most of the items equivalent to those included in the U.S. exhibit are treated as insurance expenses in the revenue account of the Canadian statement.

An increase in the book value of a nonadmitted asset decreases surplus. Similarly, a decrease in the value of these assets results in an increase in surplus. The following example explains this relationship. Assume that a company's basic accounting equation at a certain point in time is

$$\$2{,}000 \text{ (assets)} = \$1{,}300 \text{ (liabilities)} + \$700 \text{ (capital and surplus)}$$

Immediately after preparation of this statement, $200 is spent for furniture, a nonadmitted asset. As a result of this transaction, the furniture account is debited and Cash is credited for $200. An Annual Statement prepared after the furniture purchase must not admit the $200 furniture asset, so the amount of assets is decreased by the $200 in cash that was paid. Since the equation must be kept in balance, surplus must be reduced by $200 since, logically, no liability account is affected.

- The *special surplus adjustments* item reflects the increase or decrease in special contingency reserves. These adjustments are made to prevent undue fluctuation in unassigned surplus in years of adverse experience. Such reserves are established by transferring a portion of unassigned surplus to a special reserve account.
- *Change in the valuation basis of policy reserves* represents a change in policy reserves that is treated as a direct change in surplus. For example, such a change may take place when a company decides to value policy reserves on a more conservative basis, i.e., at a greater amount, than is required by law. This process of setting up additional policy reserves is known as **reserve strengthening.** Reductions of reserves in order to increase surplus also occur and are referred to as *reserve destrengthening.*

A more detailed consideration of many of the items in the Balance Sheet, the Summary of Operations, and other reports and reconciliations of the Annual Statement is included in later chapters of this book.

Cash Flow Statement

Beginning with the 1985 Annual Statement, U.S. insurers are required to file a Cash Flow statement on page 4A of the NAIC Blank. The Cash Flow statement (shown in Figure 2-6) replaces the Statement of Changes in Financial Position that had been used prior to 1985. The purpose of the Cash Flow statement is to show, for the period from the beginning of the reporting year to the end of the reporting year, where the company's cash came from, changes in the company's Cash account, and the purposes for which cash was used. Thus, the Cash Flow statement can be broken down into three sections: changes in the company's cash resulting from operations; changes in the company's cash because of investments sold, matured, or repaid; and a reconciliation between years of the company's cash and short-term investments.

Increases in a company's cash resulting from operations include premiums and annuity considerations as well as investment income received, excluding realized gains and losses and net of investment expenses. The total of these increases is then reduced by items such as payments of claims, surrenders, and other policy benefits; federal income taxes; commissions; and other operating expenses. Increases and decreases in the company's cash because of investments sold, matured, and repaid are then noted, as are other cash transactions. The final section of the Cash Flow statement shows the beginning-of-year and end-of-year totals of the company's cash and short-term investments.

In Canada, the Statement of Changes in Financial Position is still in use. This Statement appears on pages 6 and 7 of the Annual Statement (see Figure 2-7). While the changes in a company's cash appear in this statement, items not involving cash are also shown. Items not involving cash include due and accrued investment

FIGURE 2-6
Cash Flow exhibit—U.S. Annual Statement.

Form 1 ANNUAL STATEMENT FOR THE YEAR 1985 OF THE _____ 4A
                                                         Name

CASH FLOW

		Current Year	Previous Year*

1. Premiums and annuity considerations.
2. Annuity and other fund deposits.
3. Other premiums, considerations and deposits.
4. Allowances and reserve adjustments received on reinsurance ceded.
5. Investment income received (excluding realized gains/losses and net of investment expenses).
6. Other income received.
7. Total (Items 1 to 6).
8. Life and accident and health claims paid.
9. Surrender benefits paid.
10. Other benefits to policyholders paid.
11. Total (Items 8 to 10).
12. Commissions, other expenses and taxes paid (excluding FIT).
13. Net transfers to (+) or from (−) Separate Accounts (operational items only).
14. Total (Items 12 to 13).
15. Dividends to policyholders paid.
16. Federal income taxes paid (excluding tax on capital gains).
17. Net increase (+) or decrease (−) in policy loans and premium notes.
18. Other operating expenses paid.
19. Total (Items 15 to 18).
20. Net cash from operations (Item 7 minus Item 11 minus Item 14 minus Item 19).
21. Proceeds from investments sold, matured or repaid:
    - 21.1 Bonds.
    - 21.2 Stocks.
    - 21.3 Mortgage loans.
    - 21.4 Real estate.
    - 21.5 Collateral loans.
    - 21.6 Other invested assets.
    - 21.7 Net gains (+) or losses (−) on cash and short-term investments.
    - 21.8 Miscellaneous proceeds.
    - 21.9 Total investment proceeds (Items 21.1 to 21.8).
22. Tax on capital gains.
23. Total (Item 21.9 minus Item 22).
24. Other cash provided:
    - 24.1 Capital and surplus paid in.
    - 24.2 Borrowed money $_____ less amounts repaid $_____
    - 24.3 Other sources.
    - 24.4 Total other cash provided (Items 24.1 to 24.3).
25. Total (Item 20 plus Item 23 plus Item 24.4).
26. Cost of investments acquired (long-term only):
    - 26.1 Bonds.
    - 26.2 Stocks.
    - 26.3 Mortgage loans.
    - 26.4 Real estate.
    - 26.5 Collateral loans.
    - 26.6 Other invested assets.
    - 26.7 Miscellaneous applications.
    - 26.8 Total investments acquired (Items 26.1 to 26.7).
27. Other cash applied:
    - 27.1 Dividends to stockholders paid.
    - 27.2 Other applications (net).
    - 27.3 Total other cash applied (Items 27.1 and 27.2).
28. Total (Items 26.8 and 27.3).
29. Net change in cash and short-term investments (Item 25 minus Item 28).

RECONCILIATION

30. Cash and short-term investments:
    - 30.1 Beginning of year.
    - 30.2 End of year (Item 29 plus Item 30.1).

*Optional for 1985

FIGURE 2-7
Statement of Changes in Financial Position—Canadian Annual Statement.

06

NAME OF COMPANY ▶   YEAR OF STATEMENT
                     19

V. STATEMENT OF CHANGES IN FINANCIAL POSITION
(EXCLUDING SEGREGATED FUNDS)
($'000)

		LIFE		ACCIDENT & SICKNESS	
		CURRENT YEAR	PREVIOUS YEAR	CURRENT YEAR	PREVIOUS YEAR
A. SOURCES OF CASH:		01	02	03	04
I. OPERATIONS:					
NET INCOME CARRIED TO RECONCILIATION OF EARNED SURPLUS	01				
CHARGES (CREDITS) NOT INVOLVING CASH:					
NET CHANGES IN:					
NET ACTUARIAL RESERVES	02				
CLAIMS INCLUDING PROVISION FOR UNREPORTED CLAIMS	03				
PROVISION FOR DIVIDENDS AND E.R.Rs TO POLICYHOLDERS	04				
ADJUSTMENT FOR UNAMORTIZED GAIN OR LOSS ON BONDS/MORTGAGES	05				
FORMULA ADJUSTMENT IN RESPECT OF GAINS/LOSSES ON SHARES	06				
CURRENT TAXES PAYABLE	07				
DEFERRED TAXES	08				
ACCRUED COMMISSIONS, GENERAL AND INVESTMENT EXPENSES	09				
OTHER CONTRACTUAL OBLIGATIONS	10				
STAFF PENSION AND INSURANCE FUNDS	11				
REINSURANCE PAYABLE/RECEIVABLE TRANSACTIONS	12				
PREMIUMS RECEIVABLE	13				
INVESTMENT INCOME, DUE AND ACCRUED	14				
AMOUNTS ON DEPOSIT	15				
INTER-BRANCH RECEIVABLES	16				
DEPRECIATION ON REAL ESTATE	17				
DEPRECIATION/WRITE-DOWN OF MISCELLANEOUS ASSETS	18				
AMORTIZATION/ACCRUAL ON DEBT SECURITIES	19				
OTHER	20				
SUB-TOTAL: CASH GENERATED BY OPERATIONS (01 TO 20) ▶	21				
II. PRINCIPAL REPAYMENTS ON DISPOSITION OF INVESTED ASSETS:					
REDUCTION IN BOOK VALUES OF:					
BONDS	22				
SHARES	23				
MORTGAGES	24				
REAL ESTATE	25				
POLICY LOANS	26				
OTHER INVESTED ASSETS	27				
	28				
SUB-TOTAL (22 TO 28) ▶	29				

FIGURE 2-7 (cont.)

07

NAME OF COMPANY ▶   YEAR OF STATEMENT 19

V. STATEMENT OF CHANGES IN FINANCIAL POSITION
(EXCLUDING SEGREGATED FUNDS) - CONTINUED ($'000)

		LIFE		ACCIDENT & SICKNESS	
		CURRENT YEAR 01	PREVIOUS YEAR 02	CURRENT YEAR 03	PREVIOUS YEAR 04
III. OTHER SOURCES:					
CHANGES IN BORROWED MONEY	01				
CAPITAL AND CONTRIBUTIONS PAID IN DURING THE YEAR	02				
CHANGES IN INTER-FUND TRANSFERS DURING THE YEAR	03				
	04				
	05				
SUB-TOTAL - OTHER SOURCES (01 TO 05) ▶	06				
TOTAL FUNDS GENERATED (06 + PAGE 06, LINES 21+29) ▶	07				
B. APPLICATION OF FUNDS GENERATED:					
I. ACQUISITION OF INCOME PRODUCING ASSETS:					
BONDS	08				
SHARES	09				
MORTGAGE LOANS	10				
REAL ESTATE	11				
POLICY LOANS	12			▓▓▓	▓▓▓
OTHER INVESTED ASSETS	13				
	14				
SUB-TOTAL (08 TO 14) ▶	15				
II. OTHER DISPOSITIONS OF CASH:					
DIVIDENDS TO SHAREHOLDERS	16				
ACQUISITION OF MISCELLANEOUS ASSETS	17				
OTHER	18				
	19				
SUB-TOTAL OTHER DISPOSITIONS OF CASH (16 TO 19) ▶	20				
TOTAL FUNDS APPLIED (15+20) ▶	21				
NET CHANGE IN CASH (07-21) ▶	22				
C. RECONCILIATION OF CASH:					
CASH - BEGINNING OF YEAR	23				
- END OF YEAR (22+23) ▶	24				

income, premiums receivable, net actuarial reserves, taxes payable, and reductions in the book values of invested assets. Unlike the U.S. Cash Flow statement, the Canadian Statement of Changes in Financial Position is broken down into life business and accident and sickness business.

Five-Year Historical Data

Annual Statements in both the United States and Canada include a schedule of data for the past five years (see Figure 2-8). This schedule can be quite useful in identifying trends in a company's performance. The information available in the Five-Year Historical Data schedule in the U.S. Annual Statement includes

- the amount of life insurance in force by line of business,
- the amount of new business by line of business,
- the amount of premium income by line of business,
- the net gain (or loss) from operations by line of business,
- balances of various Balance Sheet items,
- totals of admitted and nonadmitted assets, and
- various operating ratios.

The Canadian Statement shows premiums and claims for accident and sickness insurance by line of business—cancellable, noncancellable, and group—as well as various items of financial data allocated between life insurance and accident and sickness insurance.

Analysis of Increase in Reserves during the Year

This schedule, which is typically prepared by a company's actuaries, classifies the change in a company's reserves (1) as either increases or decreases and (2) according to which line of business is affected. The corresponding schedule in the Canadian Annual Statement is called "Changes in Reserves." The Canadian Statement shows reserve totals by type of reserve—such as the investment valuation and currency reserve or the reserve for reinsurance ceded to unregistered reinsurers—allocated between life insurance and accident and sickness insurance. The balance for the end of the year and the balance for the beginning of the year are listed along with the increase or decrease in the reserve for the year.

Other Exhibits and Schedules

Life insurance company Annual Statements include many exhibits and schedules with extremely detailed supplementary data. Many of these exhibits and schedules pertain to investments, reserves, premiums, claims, and expenses.

In addition to these categories, which are discussed below, other information provided in the Annual Statement includes reinsurance amounts, amounts of resisted claims, policy dividend information, listings of depositories for company cash, and reconciliations of assets between years. The supplementary exhibits and schedules included in the U.S. and Canadian Statements are similar, but this discussion will note differences where they exist.

Investments

Both the U.S. and Canadian Annual Statements include detailed information about a company's investments. Investments are classified by type—bonds, stocks, mortgage loans, collateral loans, real estate, and other investments. Information presented for each type of investment is listed below, along with the exhibit or schedule for each investment classification.

- *Real estate*—Information includes a listing of each property owned and sold during the year along with the date on which the real estate was acquired, the name of the vendor, the property's cost and market value, any encumbrances on the property or improvements made during the year, and taxes paid on the real estate. This information is presented in Schedule A of the U.S. Statement and Schedule E of the Canadian Statement.
- *Mortgage loans*—Information includes a listing of loans held at the end of the year, the loans' outstanding principal balances and book values, any adjustments made in book value during the year, the amount of unpaid taxes, the value of mortgaged property, and a listing of overdue loans. This information is presented in Schedule B of the U.S. Statement and Schedules C, D, I, and J of the Canadian Statement.
- *Stocks and bonds*—Information includes a listing of all bonds and stocks owned at year's end along with their par value or number of shares owned, interest rate, book value, market value, interest or dividends, and adjustments made in book value during the year. This information is presented in Schedule D of the U.S. Statement and Schedules A, B, and I of the Canadian Statement.

Information on investment income includes (1) gross income by type of investment, (2) investment expenses, and (3) net investment income. In addition, capital gains and losses because of sales of investments and changes in investments' market values are reflected separately in the Annual Statement because, as mentioned earlier, they are not considered part of investment income. Exhibits 2 and 3 in the U.S. Statement reflect investment income, while Exhibit 4 shows capital gains and losses on investments. Canadian Exhibits 6 and 7 apply to investment income and Exhibit 8 records a company's capital gains and losses.

FIGURE 2-8
Five-Year Historical Data—U.S. Annual Statement.

14A ANNUAL STATEMENT FOR THE YEAR 1985 OF THE _____ Form 1
                                                              Name

FIVE-YEAR HISTORICAL DATA
All Figures Taken From or Developed From Annual
Statements of Corresponding Years

Show amounts in whole dollars only, no cents. Items from prior years should be included only if they are available from prior year's statements.

	(1) 1985	(2) 1984	(3) 1983	(4) 1982	(5) 1981
Life Insurance in Force (Page 15)					
1. Ordinary—Whole Life and Endowment (Line 31D)					
2. Ordinary—Term (Line 22, Col. 4, less Line 31D, Col. 4)					
3. Credit Life (Line 22, Col. 6)					
4. Group, excluding FEGLI/SGLI (Line 22, Col. 9 less Lines 38 & 39, Col. 4)					
5. Industrial (Line 22, Col. 2)					
6. FEGLI/SGLI (Lines 38 & 39, Col. 4)					
7. Total (Line 22, Col. 10)					
New Business Issued (Page 15)					
8. Ordinary—Whole Life and Endowment (Line 31D)					
9. Ordinary—Term (Line 2, Col. 4, less Line 31D)					
10. Credit Life (Line 2, Col. 6)					
11. Group (Line 2, Col. 9)					
12. Industrial (Line 2, Col. 2)					
13. Total (Line 2, Col. 10)					
Premium Income (Exhibit 1—Part 1)					
14. Ordinary and Industrial Life—First Year (Line 9d, Cols. 2 & 3)					
15. Ordinary and Industrial Life—Single and Renewal (Line 10d, Line 19d, Cols. 2 & 3)					
16. Other Life (Line 20d, Cols. 5 & 6)					
17. Annuity (Line 20d, Cols. 4 & 7)					
18. A & H (Line 20d, Cols. 8, 9 and 10)					
19. Total (Line 20d, Col. 1)					
Balance Sheet Items (Pages 2 & 3)					
20. Total admitted Assets Excluding Separate Account Business (Page 2, Item 26)					
21. Total Liabilities Excluding Separate Account Business (Page 3, Item 26 less Items 25A & 25B)					
22. Aggregate Life Reserves (Page 3, Item 1)					
23. Aggregate A & H Reserves (Page 3, Item 2)					
24. Mandatory Securities Valuation Reserve (Page 3, Item 25.1)					
25. Capital (Page 3, Items 27A and 27B)					
26. Surplus (Page 3, Item 29D)					
Percentage Distribution of Assets					
(Page 2) (Item No. ÷ Page 2, Item 10A) × 100.0					
27. Bonds (Item 1)					
28. Stocks (Items 2.1 and 2.2)					
29. Mortgage Loans on Real Estate (Item 3)					
30. Real Estate (Items 4.1, 4.2 and 4.3)					
31. Policy Loans (Item 5)					
32. Premium Notes (Item 6)					
33. Collateral Loans (Item 7)					
34. Cash and Short-term Investments (Items 8.1 and 8.2) (1981, Item 8)					
35. Other Invested Assets (Item 10)					
36. Cash and Invested Assets (Item 10A)	100.0	100.0	100.0	100.0	100.0

FIGURE 2-8 (cont.)

Form 1   ANNUAL STATEMENT FOR THE YEAR 1985 OF THE _____ 14B
                                                                                                              Name

FIVE-YEAR HISTORICAL DATA
(Continued)

	(1) 1985	(2) 1984	(3) 1983	(4) 1982	(5) 1981
Investments in Parent, Subsidiaries and Affiliates					
37. Affiliated Bonds (Page 29, Line 29, Col. 6)......					
38. Affiliated Preferred Stocks (Page 29, Line 47, Col. 3)...					
39. Affiliated Common Stocks (Page 29, Line 65, Col. 3)...					
40. Affiliated Short-term Investments (subtotal included in Schedule DA, Part 1, Col. 10)...					
41. Total of above Lines 37 to 40......					
Total Non-admitted and Admitted Assets					
42. Total Non-admitted Assets (Page 14, Line 26, Col. 3).....					
43. Total Admitted Assets (Page 14, Line 28, Col. 4)......					
Investment Data (Page 8)					
44. Ratio of Net Investment Income to Mean Assets (Exhibit 2, Line 8) (To 2 decimal places).......					
45. Net Investment Income (Exhibit 2, Line 7).....					
46. Realized Capital Gains (Losses) (Exhibit 4, Line 11, Col. 6)..					
47. Unrealized Capital Gains (Losses) (Exhibit 4, Line 12, Col. 6).					
48. Total of above Lines 45, 46 & 47......					
Benefits and Reserve Increases (Page 5)					
49. Total Policy Benefits — Life (Items 8, 9, 10, 11, 11A & 12, Col. 1, less Items 11 & 11A, Cols. 9, 10 & 11)......					
50. Total Policy Benefits — A & H (Items 11 & 11A, Cols. 9, 10 & 11)......					
51. Increase in Life Reserves — Other than Group and Annuities (Item 17, Cols. 2 and 3).....					
52. Increase in A & H Reserves (Item 17, Cols. 9, 10 & 11)...					
53. Dividends to Policyholders (Item 28, Col. 1)......					
Operating Ratios					
54. Insurance Expense Ratio (Page 5, Col. 1, Items 21, 21A & 22 less Item 5) ÷ (Page 5, Col. 1, Item 1 plus group annuity contribution funds) × 100.......					
55. Lapse Ratio (Ordinary Only) [(Page 15, Col. 4, Lines 14 & 15) × 100 ÷ ½ (Lines 1 & 22)].......					
56. A & H Loss Ratio (Schedule H, Part 1, Lines 3 and 4, Col. 1, %).......					
57. A & H Expense Ratio (Schedule H, Part 1, Line 8, Col. 1, %).					
A & H Claim Reserve Adequacy					
58. Incurred Losses on Prior Years' Claims — Group Health (Schedule H, Part 3, Line 3a, Col. 2)......					
59. Prior Years' Claim Liability and Reserve — Group Health (Schedule H, Part 3, Line 3b, Col. 2)......					
60. Incurred Losses on Prior Years' Claims — Health other than Group (Schedule H, Part 3, Line 3a, Col. 1 less Col. 2).					
61. Prior Years' Claim Liability and Reserve — Health other than Group (Schedule H, Part 3, Line 3b, Col. 1 less Col. 2).					
Net Gains From Operations After Federal Income Taxes by Lines of Business (Page 5, Item 31)					
62. Industrial Life (Col. 2)........					
63. Ordinary—Life (Col. 3)........					
64. Ordinary—Individual Annuities (Col. 4).....					
65. Ordinary—Supp. Contracts (Col. 5)......					
66. Credit Life (Col. 6).........					
67. Group Life (Col. 7).........					
68. Group Annuities (Col. 8)........					
69. A & H—Group (Col. 9)........					
70. A & H—Credit (Col. 10)........					
71. A & H—Other (Col. 11)........					
72. Total (Col. 1) (Page 5, Item 31, Col. 1).....					

FIGURE 2-8 (cont.)
Selected Data from 5 Years' Annual Statements—Canadian Annual Statement.

```
                                                   20
NAME OF COMPANY ▶                                                  YEAR OF STATEMENT
                                                                         19
```

XX. SELECTED DATA FROM 5 YEARS' ANNUAL STATEMENT ($'000)

		CURRENT YEAR 01	19 02	19 03	19 04	19 05
I. LIFE INSURANCE:						
A. IN FORCE (AMOUNTS-GROSS BASIS) DECEMBER 31:						
INDIVIDUAL - TERM	01					
- OTHER	02					
GROUP (INCL. PERMANENT)						
- EMPLOYEES	03					
- CREDIT	04					
- OTHER	05					
TOTAL INSURANCE IN FORCE ▶	06					
NO. OF INDIVIDUAL POLICIES IN FORCE (GROSS)	07					
B. NEW EFFECTED (AMOUNTS-GROSS BASIS)						
INDIVIDUAL - TERM	08					
- OTHER	09					
GROUP	10					
TOTAL NEW EFFECTED ▶	11					
C. PREMIUMS (NET) INSURANCE:						
INDIVIDUAL - RENEWAL	12					
- OTHER	13					
GROUP - RENEWAL	14					
- OTHER	15					
ANNUITIES - INDIVIDUAL	16					
- GROUP	17					
TOTAL PREMIUMS (NET) ▶	18					
D. FINANCIAL DATA:						
SEGREGATED FUND LIABILITIES	19					
TOTAL LIABILITIES	20					
RESERVES ALLOCATED	21					
CAPITAL & CONTRIBUTED SURPLUS	22					
UNAPPROPRIATED EARNED SURPLUS	23					
TOTAL ASSETS	24					

FIGURE 2-8 (cont.)

21

NAME OF COMPANY ▶ YEAR OF STATEMENT 19

XX. SELECTED DATA FROM 5 YEARS' ANNUAL STATEMENTS ($'000) - CONTINUED

		CURRENT YEAR 01	19 02	19 03	19 04	19 05
NET INCOME CARRIED TO SURPLUS	01					
NET INVESTMENT INCOME	02					
NET RATE OF RETURN ON INVESTMENTS	03					
GENERAL EXPENSES AND TAXES	04					
COMMISSIONS (NET)	05					
LIABILITIES OUT OF CANADA AS % OF TOTAL LIABILITIES	06					
ASSETS OUT OF CANADA AS % OF TOTAL ASSETS	07					
II. ACCIDENT AND SICKNESS:						
A. PREMIUMS AND CLAIMS:						
PREMIUMS EARNED (NET):						
- INDIVIDUAL CANCELLABLE	08					
- INDIVIDUAL NON-CANCELLABLE	09					
- GROUP	10					
TOTAL ▶	11					
PREMIUMS - DIRECT WRITTEN	12					
- NET WRITTEN	13					
CLAIMS INCURRED (NET):						
- INDIVIDUAL CANCELLABLE	14					
- INDIVIDUAL NON-CANCELLABLE	15					
- GROUP	16					
TOTAL ▶	17					
B. FINANCIAL DATA:						
TOTAL LIABILITIES	18					
RESERVES ALLOCATED	19					
CAPITAL & CONTRIBUTED SURPLUS	20					
ACCUMULATION OF AMOUNTS TRANSFERRED FROM/(TO) LIFE	21					
UNAPPROPRIATED EARNED SURPLUS	22					
TOTAL ASSETS	23					
NET INCOME CARRIED TO SURPLUS	24					
NET INVESTMENT INCOME	25					
NET RATE OF RETURN ON INVESTMENTS	26					
GENERAL EXPENSES (INCL. ADJUSTMENT EXPENSES) AND TAXES	27					
COMMISSIONS (NET)	28					
SECTION 103 MARGIN AVAILABLE	29					

Reserves

The schedules of reserves presented in the U.S. and Canadian Annual Statements differ somewhat for life reserves. The U.S. Statement presents the reserve amount by valuation basis—that is, by interest and mortality table—and the amounts are subdivided by lines of business. Exhibit 8A of the U.S. Blank also presents information on changes in the valuation basis of reserves if that basis changes from year to year. In addition to this information, the Canadian Annual Statement shows whether reserves are participating or nonparticipating as well as the amount of insurance in force.

In the U.S. Annual Statement, reserve information for accident and health policies includes reserves for group, credit, collectively renewable, noncancellable, guaranteed renewable, and nonrenewable policies. The Canadian Statement, on the other hand, shows categories for cancellable, noncancellable, and all other types of accident and sickness policies. Accident and health reserves are in Exhibit 9 of the U.S. Statement and Exhibit 15—Part 2 of the Canadian Statement. In addition to the above information, the Canadian Statement has an exhibit (Exhibit 16) to show unusual changes in the reserve produced by changes in the basis of valuation.

Premiums, expenses, and claims

Annual Statement premium exhibits show premium income by the categories of direct premiums received, premiums due and uncollected, and premiums assumed and ceded on reinsurance. The premiums are also detailed by line of business and by first year business versus renewal business. The premium schedules include schedules of dividends applied to premiums, reinsurance commissions, and commissions on direct business. Premium information is shown in Exhibit 1 of the U.S. Annual Statement and Exhibits 1, 3, and 12 of the Canadian Statement.

Schedules of expenses show a company's expenditures by type. Included among these expenditures are rent, salaries and wages, legal fees and expenses, taxes and licenses, travel expenses, and advertising costs. Expense information is allocated between insurance operations and investments. A separate schedule is provided for taxes, licenses, and fees. The U.S. exhibits for expenses are Exhibits 5 and 6, and Canadian expense exhibits are Exhibits 9 and 10.

Information presented for claims includes both claims incurred during the year and the liability for unpaid claims at the end of the year. As in most other schedules, the amounts are presented by line of business. Exhibit 11 in the U.S. Statement and Exhibits 2, 3, 4, and 5 in the Canadian Statement present information about claims.

Annual Reports

Until now, this chapter has presented an overview of the statutory Annual Statement that insurers are required to file with regulatory authorities. In addition to the Annual Statement, however, companies typically issue an annual report for other parties, such as stockholders, policyowners, potential investors, customers, and creditors, that may be interested in the company's financial performance. Annual reports include financial statements, such as the Balance Sheet, Income Statement, Cash Flow statement, and notes to the financial statements, but the figures in stock companies' annual reports generally differ from those provided in the Annual Statement. In mutual companies, the information in annual reports and the Annual Statement will generally be the same.

The financial statements included in published annual reports for U.S. stock companies are required by the Securities and Exchange Commission (SEC) to be prepared in conformity with generally accepted accounting principles (GAAP) as defined by the American Institute of Certified Public Accountants (AICPA) and the Financial Accounting Standards Board (FASB). Since GAAP more closely resembles commercial company accounting than do the statutory accounting practices (SAP) used in completing the Annual Statement, interested outside parties can, through examination of the annual report, better judge the performance of an insurance company against companies in other industries. Mutual company annual reports are based on SAP. The financial statements included in the annual report are usually audited by independent certified public accountants (CPAs)—in Canada, chartered accountants (CAs)—whose audit report is included in the annual report.

In addition to the financial statements and the auditor's report, an annual report usually includes other important information about the company, such as descriptions of the company and its subsidiaries as well as other industries in which the company operates. Also, highlights of company activities during the past year are presented, along with changes in management and plans for future operations. Usually, the annual report is produced by an insurance company's corporate communications or public relations department, although the accounting department provides the financial statements included in the report.

Other Reports

Aside from annual reports produced for creditors, potential investors, and others interested in the company's performance, many insurers are required to file reports with the Securities and Exchange Commission (SEC). Publicly held companies in the United States must file a *10-K report* on an annual basis and a *10-Q report* on a quarterly basis. The 10-K reports are available to stockholders and generally contain more detailed financial information than annual reports. The financial reports in the 10-K report are certified financial statements. On the other hand, the 10-Q report is an unaudited financial statement. Aside from the 10-K and 10-Q reports, insurers that offer certain types of interest-sensitive products must file additional financial statements with the SEC.

Tax Returns

Another type of insurance company financial statement is the company's tax return. Insurance companies prepare their federal income tax returns using the financial information set forth in the Annual Statement, but when calculating figures that will appear on tax returns, certain adjustments are made. For example, because of differences between the Annual Statement and the tax return, as well as the different requirements for each report, amounts shown on the tax return for various items of income and expense might not be identical to the amounts reported for those items in the statutory financial statements.

One adjustment in preparing the tax return concerns the accrual of bond discounts. When a company purchases a bond at a price below par and the amount of discount is amortized, the amount of discount involved is treated as accrued income in the Annual Statement. However, for the tax return, bond discount is not amortized and thus is not periodically recognized as income. For tax purposes, the discount is recognized as a lump sum capital gain at maturity—when the bond's par value is remitted to the insurer—or when the bond is sold. This treatment on the tax return not only defers tax recognition of discount as taxable income, but also results in taxation at the capital gains rate, which is lower than the rate for ordinary income.

Internal Financial Information

The function of managerial accounting generates numerous financial reports for use by a company's decision makers. Managerial accounting reports are many and vary from company to company. No two companies produce exactly the same reports for managerial use, but many companies produce variations of some basic types of reports. Two types of reports that many companies generate for internal use are cash flow statements and budgets.

An internal **cash flow statement** is similar to the Cash Flow statement that appears in the NAIC Blank, showing the sources and uses of a company's cash during a specified period of time—one week, one month, six months, etc. Through use of an internal cash flow statement, insurers can analyze their cash needs and their cash availability. These analyses can be particularly useful when choosing investment vehicles. Cash flow statements also allow management to study trends in various categories of receipts and disbursements so that operations can be managed in a more efficient manner. Management can also use cash flow statements to understand the changes in cash balances and to produce cash flow forecasts, cash budgets, and capital budgets.

A **budget** is a plan of financial operation for a future period. Budgets are expressed in monetary terms and are useful in setting objectives for performance. Actual results must be compared to the budget for the budget's usefulness to be maximized. A company may prepare more than one type of budget. Four types of budgets sometimes used in life and health insurance companies are

1. the *master budget,* which is an overall financial plan that can include estimates of the number of policies to be sold in a specific time period, projected expenses, and projected financial statements;
2. the *flexible budget,* which is a series of projections based on different levels of sales or claims activity;
3. the *capital budget,* which is a plan for purchases of major equipment extending up to five or ten years into the future; and
4. the *cash budget,* which projects cash receipts and disbursements and the resulting cash balances. Cash budgets can be useful in predicting cash shortages so that corrective action can be taken before shortages occur. Cash budgets are also helpful in predicting excess cash amounts so insurers can plan for investment of any excess cash.

Key Terms

amortization
net premium value
mean reserve
capital stock
line of business
10-K report
cash flow statement

premium assets
actuarial reserves
advance premiums
surplus
reserve strengthening
10-Q report
budget

Review Questions and Exercises

1. What are the three primary classifications of assets for an insurer?
2. What does the following fraction represent?

$$\frac{\text{Initial reserve} + \text{Terminal reserve}}{2}$$

3. Does your company have any capital stock? (If necessary, check your company's Annual Statement.) Why would an insurer not have capital stock?

4. Describe the different surplus classifications for an insurer.
5. For the purpose of allocating receipts and expenses, what are an insurer's major lines of business?
6. What is the purpose of the statutory Cash Flow statement?
7. What type of information is available in an insurer's Annual Statement regarding the following investments: (a) mortgage loans? (b) stocks and bonds? (c) real estate? Where in the United States and Canadian Annual Statements can this information be found?

3
Accounting Information Systems

Learning Objectives

After reading this chapter, you should be able to:

- Understand the importance of automation to the insurance accounting function
- Define a number of different data processing terms and concepts
- Differentiate between data and information
- Describe the purpose of the financial information system
- State the types of data maintained in an insurer's alpha system and in an investment accounting system

Introduction

Automated information systems pervade every aspect of the life and health insurance industry but are particularly important in the area of accounting. The first insurance company applications of automation typically involved the accounting functions. Automated systems are faster, more cost-effective, and more accurate than corresponding manual systems for processing large numbers of similar transactions. Moreover, the unique reporting requirements of the life insurance industry—as introduced in Chapters 1 and 2—require the rigorous control and easy retrieval of vast amounts of information. Automation is the most efficient manner of meeting these requirements.

Although automated systems are used in every area of insurance operations, accounting functions still make up the core of automated systems in insurance companies. Accounting information systems involve many more functional areas than the operations of the accounting department. Before discussing the current applications of automated accounting systems, we will study the development of automated systems in insurance companies.

Evolution of Automated Accounting Systems

The first automated systems used in insurance companies were introduced in the 1950s and 1960s. Early automation efforts were based on large mainframe computers, which were used to replace the manual aspects of repetitive accounting operations—such as payroll, accounts receivable, and accounts payable—that included large numbers of transactions. Premium billing systems were also early candidates for automation. In the 1970s, as computers and data processing became less expensive and more easily accessible to non-technically trained employees, more and more functions were automated. Automated systems were used not only to replace manual clerical processing, but also to provide better information to management, particularly for control and planning purposes.

In the 1980s, business entered the age of the microcomputer, a smaller type of computer whose size and ease of programming allows for more automated operations. The advent of the microcomputer has encouraged the use of information as a strategic resource that can be employed to improve individual productivity and company operations. For example, many agents now carry portable computers that can be used to prepare financial illustrations of the potential performance of flexible, interest-sensitive products. In order to identify prospects who fit a specific profile, marketing professionals use desktop computers or other types of terminals that are linked to mainframe data bases. Inquiries into policyowner status are carried out immediately by policyowner service staff using small computers.

In addition to policy-related transactions, computer systems in insurance companies are used to calculate and pay agent commissions, provide data needed to produce the Annual Statement and other financial reports, and provide various types of management information. In all of these examples, some aspect of an accounting information system is being used. In order to explain such systems more fully, however, we should first review some basic data processing terms and concepts.

Data Processing Terms and Concepts

One term that has already been used in this chapter is *system*. A **system** is a group of integrated elements that interact to achieve a desired end. In general, a system is composed of four elements: input, processing, output, and control. Figure 3-1 illustrates the relationship among these four elements. A **subsystem** is simply a system contained within a larger system. As will be seen later, a number of subsystems are included in the accounting information system.

A system does not necessarily have to be automated, and many systems are, in fact, manual. For the purposes of this text, however, unless otherwise noted, all systems referred to are automated. An **automated system** uses computers to perform one or more of the four basic tasks—input, processing, output, or control—that together form a system. The practical differences between manual and automated systems can be shown in a simple example. In a manual system, each new application received by a company would be recorded on one or more pieces of paper, and all new applications would be placed in a file drawer labelled *New Applicants*. Conceptually, an automated system works the same way as a manual system. However, in an automated system, the records take up only a small space on a magnetic tape or disk instead of a large amount of physical space in a file drawer, as would be necessary with a manual system.

Any representation of facts or figures can be referred to as **data**. Today's weather conditions, the color of one's automobile, and the name of an applicant for insurance are all examples of data. A data processing system takes data as an input, processes the data, and transforms it into output that is known as *information*. For this reason, a data processing system is also referred to as an *information processing system*. **Information** is data that has been processed and manipulated in various ways to make it meaningful and useful to interested parties.

In an insurance company, thousands of transactions take place every day. These transactions are the basic input to a company's data processing system. One of the prime purposes of a data processing system is to obtain and record the data generated by business transactions and to store and maintain that data so that it can be retrieved to meet the various informational needs of the organization.

FIGURE 3-1
The elements of a system.

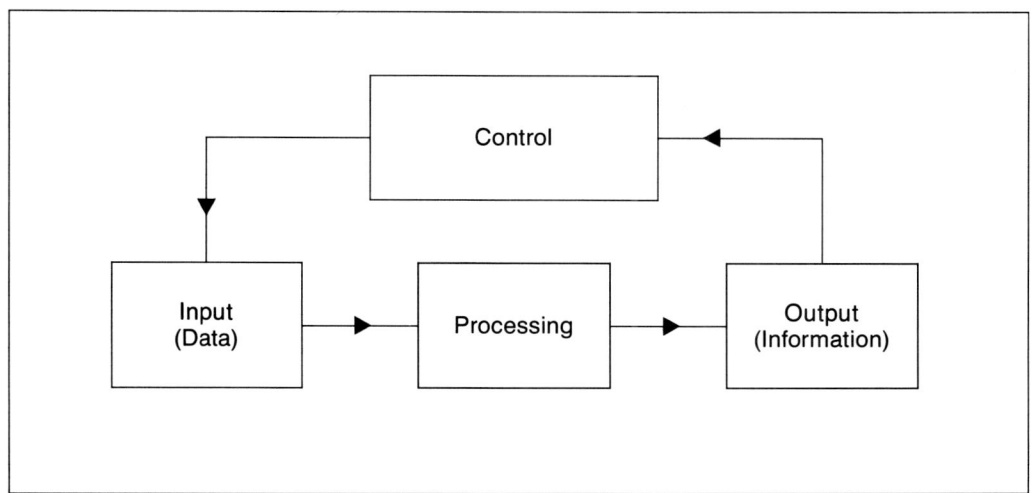

All of the information and input retained by a company constitute that company's *data base.* Most of the information in a data base comes from transactions that take place each day, but some of that data can come from outside the company as well. In the early days of automated systems, a great deal of redundant data existed. *Redundant data* is data that appears in more than one place in a data processing system. Such redundancy occurred because each computer program required its own data files. Therefore, whenever an item of data needed to be changed, the insurance company had to change that item in every file, greatly increasing the chance of error, since errors can occur each time a data base is manipulated. For example, if a policyowner's address was required for twenty different computer programs, under older systems, the address existed in twenty different places. Every time a policyowner changed his or her address, the insurance company had to change the address in twenty different files and thus had twenty chances to make an error.

As technology improved, however, this cumbersome and repetitive updating process was eliminated. Instead of each program drawing upon its own separate, but essentially identical, data base, each program can now draw upon one centralized data base. In the current generation of computers, a **data base** can be defined as a nonredundant collection of data that has been organized for easy access, update, and retrieval. Figure 3-2 illustrates the difference between the early approach to data bases and the contemporary, integrated approach to data bases.

All information processing systems require both hardware and software. **Hardware** consists of a computer system's physical component: the computer itself, the input/output devices, and the secondary storage devices used in conjunction with a computer system. **Software** consists of the instructions—the computer programs—given to a computer in order to make it perform a specific data processing task, produce information, or solve a particular problem. An **application program** consists of software that instructs the computer in how to perform one particular task or function. An example of an application program would be a computer program that instructs the computer to sort into alphabetical order all of one day's premium receipts from policyowners. **Integrated software** is the name given to computer programs that perform several different applications.

Software can be acquired in three ways: (1) it can be developed in-house by a professional staff of computer programmers and systems analysts; (2) the programming can be contracted to programmers outside of the company; and (3) general software packages—software developed by a vendor and intended for use in more than one company—can be purchased. For some large applications, all three methods might be used together.

A Financial and Managerial Accounting System

While each insurance company has computer systems tailored to its own operation, a core group of systems is common to most insurance companies. This section examines a typical, although hypothetical, financial and managerial accounting system and some of the subsystems that it includes. The financial and managerial accounting system discussed in the rest of this chapter covers all aspects of the company's insurance and investment operations and is both fully automated and completely integrated. The term *completely integrated* indicates (1) that the system uses a common data base and (2) that the components of the system communicate through this data base to record and classify financial transactions. These transactions can be based on either automatic or requested policy, investment, and administrative activities. While this type of system may not be used in every insurance company, from the standpoints of control of the company's finances and the effective use of personnel and other resources, management's goal is often to move toward this type of integrated system.

FIGURE 3-2
A comparison of early and modern data bases.

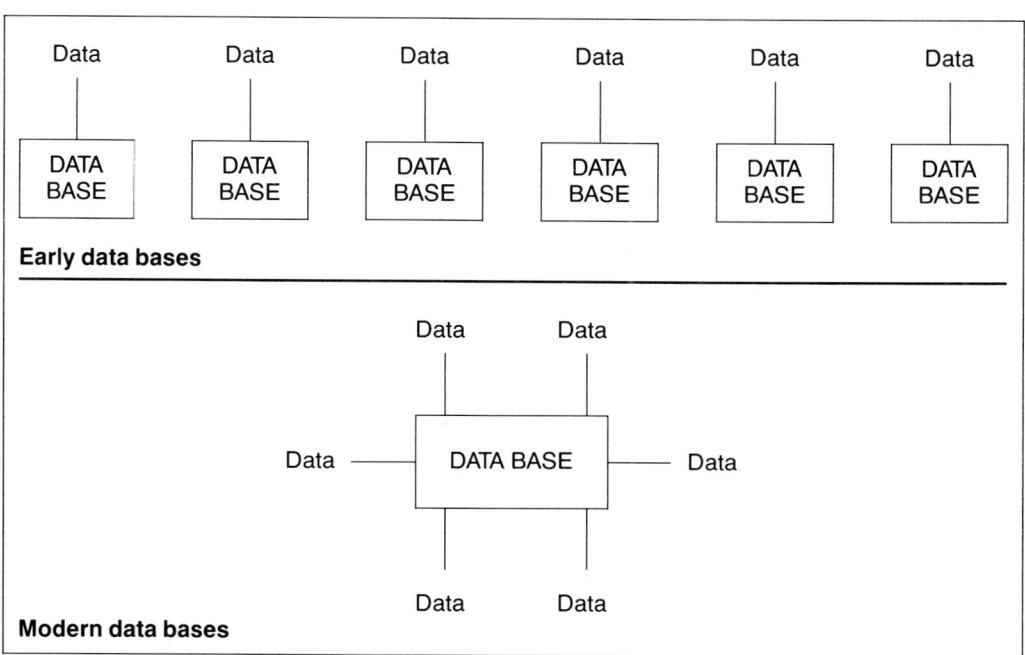

An insurer's accounting information system is one part of a larger financial information system (see Figure 3-3). The **financial information system** provides data on both the flow of money through the company and the ways in which the money is being used to achieve the company's objectives. As a result, this system supports company management in the planning, allocation, and control of the company's financial resources. The primary functions of the financial information system are to help identify future financial needs and future sources of funds, to control the company's use of funds, and to determine how effectively funds are being used. Information describing the company's flow of funds—both historical records and projections of future amounts—assists decision-makers from all of the company's functional areas in meeting their financial and budgetary responsibilities.

Transaction Processing

Although no two insurance companies are identical in the way that their systems are organized, the following operations are necessary for all major lines of insurance operations:

- prospecting and sales
- underwriting
- preparation of contracts
- premium billing and collection
- commission accounting
- policyowner service
- claims processing
- general ledger accounting
- management reporting

Many of these operations have some accounting ramifications. The relationships among these operations illustrate the interaction of the various elements of a typical accounting information system.

Typically, an insurer's accounting system processes thousands of daily transactions applicable to the operations listed above. Such transactions influence the financial performance of the company as well as the status of benefits for the company's insureds and policyowners. These transactions are processed by the following components of the financial and managerial accounting system:

- the general accounting system,
- the client/policy accounting system, and
- the investment accounting system.

In order to explain how these transactions are processed and how the information resulting from these transactions is used, we will describe each of the three subsystems of the financial and managerial accounting system in some detail.

FIGURE 3-3
A model of a financial information system.

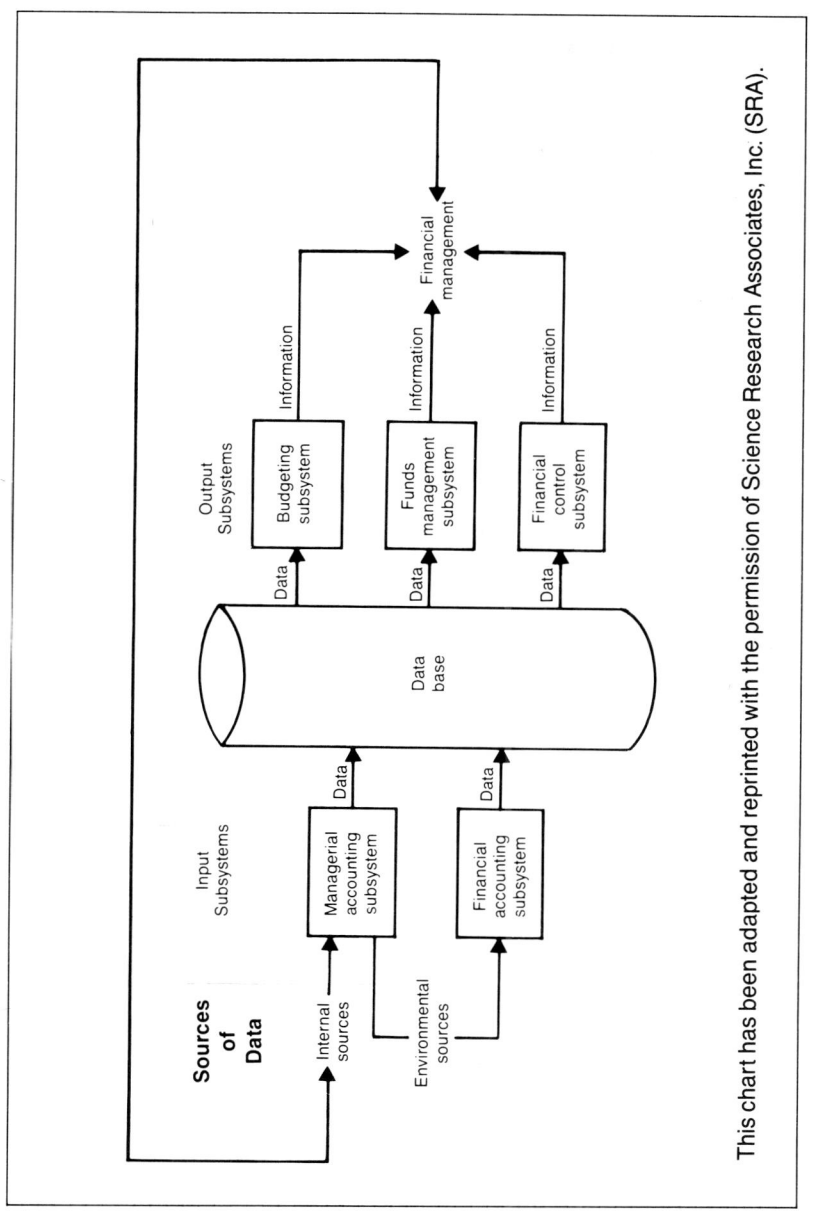

The General Accounting System

The **general accounting system** records and classifies the company's financial transactions from the other two accounting systems and from all areas of the company's operations. Sometimes, only summary information is supplied from the other accounting systems. The general accounting system is the principal source of financial information used to prepare the company's external and internal reports. The main component of the general accounting system's data base is a general ledger subsystem. The general ledger subsystem is typically based on a *chart of accounts* and is supported by a client/policy administrative system.

A life company's **chart of accounts** is a detailed listing of all of the accounts maintained in the company's accounting systems. Each account is typically given a distinct name and number. One way of numbering accounts is in accordance with page and line numbers of the statutory Annual Statement. For example, accounts that contain the number "0201" are reported on page 2, line 1 of the Annual Statement. Similarly, account numbers that include the numbers "0315" are reported on page 3, line 15 of the Annual Statement. Account numbers could also include digits that reflect other information, such as line of business. Another method of numbering accounts is categorization by type of account, e.g., 100-199 for Asset accounts, 200-299 for Liabilities, 300-399 for Capital and Surplus, 400-499 for Income, and 500-599 for Expenses. Account numbers can also be designed to indicate that the account balance is to be used for statutory reporting, GAAP reporting, or tax reporting.

In many cases, the totals shown on the Annual Statement reflect the total of many smaller accounts, as with the bond investments mentioned earlier. When companies invest in many different types of bonds, each type is often assigned a specific account name or number. The chart of accounts for an insurer's bond holdings could include the following titles:

- U.S. government bonds
- States', territories', and possessions' bonds
- Revenue bonds
- Railroad bonds
- Public utilities bonds
- Industrial and miscellaneous bonds
- Bond repurchase agreements
- Special revenue bonds

Depending on the company's accounting system, this listing could also be subclassified into long- and short-term bonds. While the different types of bond accounts are relatively limited, other types of accounts—such as agents' balances, premiums, or operating expenses—can each contain hundreds of subclassifications. Thus, the listing of a company's chart of accounts typically makes up quite a lengthy document. A single insurance company's system might contain thousands of accounts.

The general ledger subsystem

General ledger subsystems are used to maintain a company's accounts and to report on almost all of a company's financial transactions. These transactions can involve policy administration or accounting, investments, or other operational activities. Along with the general ledger subsystem, the company has several other specific accounting subsystems used for specialized financial transactions such as payment of income and premium taxes and calculation of agents' and brokers' advances and commissions. Subsystems are also maintained for accounts payable and receivable, check writing, check and bank reconciliations, personnel administration and payroll, and office supplies inventories. These specialized subsystems generally provide summary information to the general ledger subsystem.

In addition to the specialized subsystems, the general ledger subsystem provides for a variety of specialized subsidiary journals to support the entries made to the general ledger accounts. These subsidiary journals are defined by the accounting department. Typically, subsidiary journals are maintained for premiums and other income as well as claims and other disbursements. These special journals, specialized subsystems, and the general ledger subsystem make up the general accounting system.

The Client/Policy Accounting System

The **client/policy accounting system** handles all the activities that can occur automatically or by request for a given client or policy. This accounting system is the system most closely integrated with the general accounting system. In nearly all software that is designed to handle this client/policy accounting function, financial entries from the administration of client, policy, or benefit coverage records are transferred in detail to the general accounting system. Figure 3-4 shows the way in which one client/policy accounting system is constructed in order to receive all the necessary data and provide information for company use.

Policy and benefit accounting typically constitutes the largest volume of accounting activity in an insurance company. Even though some policy transactions, such as changes in address, are clearly not financial in nature, many other transactions affect the billing or in-force status of policies. Three principal functions performed by a client/policy accounting system are

1. the creation and maintenance of client and policy master files,
2. premium billing and receipt, and
3. other automatic or requested client and policy transactions.

Typical policy transactions can involve policy issue, premium billing and issuance of receipts, change of address, consolidation of billing, policy loans, calculation of periodic mortality and expense charges, declaration and payment of policy dividends, calculation of surrender charges, changes of policy benefits, termination of coverage, payment of agents' commissions, and claims settlement.

FIGURE 3-4
An example of a client/policy accounting system.

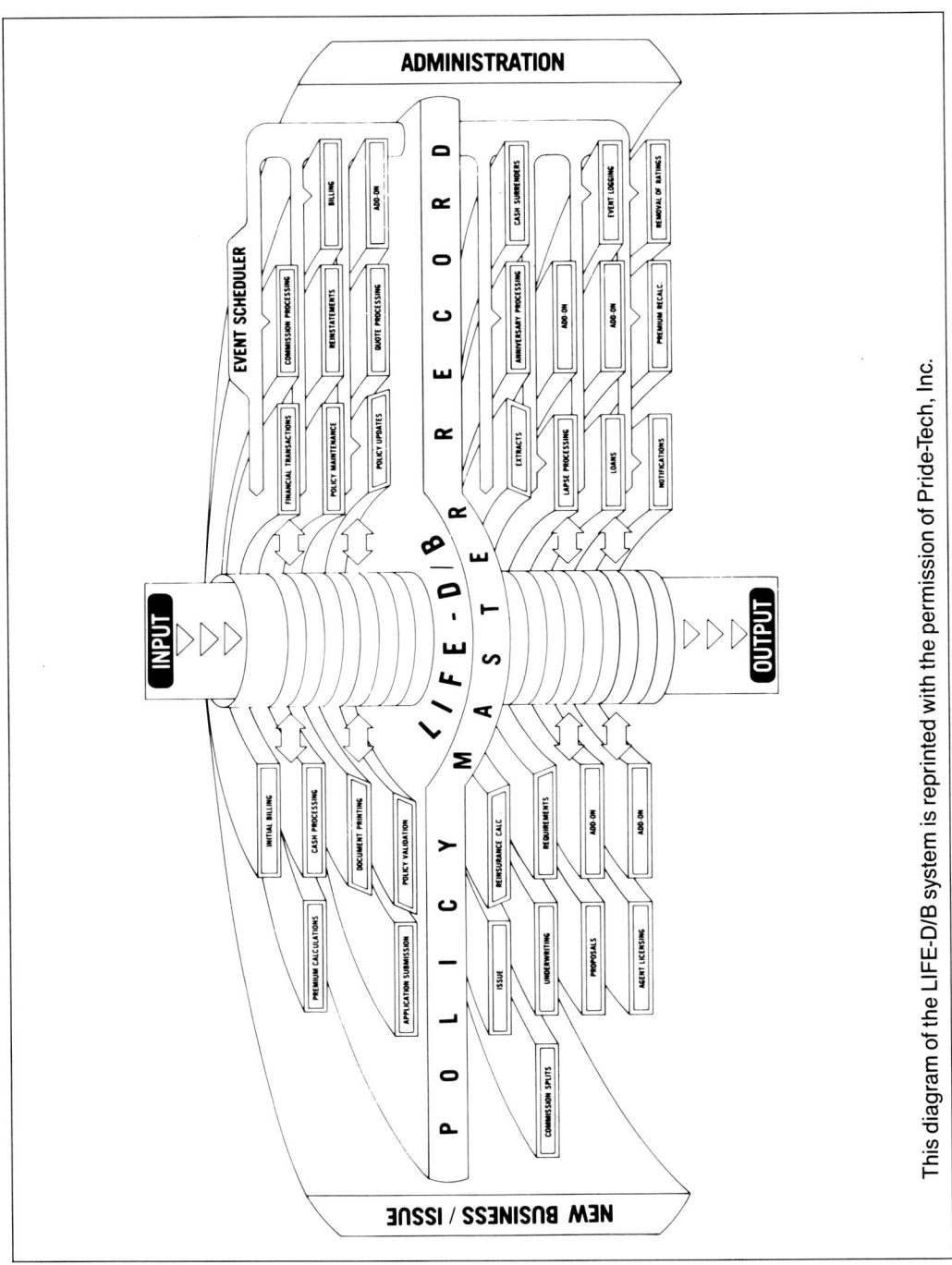

The client and policy master file

The data base that provides much of the data for accounting systems' computer programs is usually called the *client and policy master file*. Some of the business transactions that can cause the creation of client and policy master files are

- receipt of an application for insurance,
- receipt of an application for reinstatement of insurance, and
- receipt of policy ownership information.

The information that is carried in the client and policy master file is sufficient to identify both the policyowner and the specific coverages and benefits for that person's policy. For each *policyowner,* the information in the client and policy master file consists of a number of different data items:

- alphabetic name indexing
- name, address, and telephone number
- policy number indexing, including applied for but not issued, in-force, and terminated policies
- underwriting information, including Medical Information Bureau reports and consumer reports
- unapplied moneys received
- moneys held for disbursement
- beneficiary data
- ownership and assignment data
- billing control data, including method, frequency, and paid-to date (defined in Chapter 4)
- financial accumulations indexing and federal taxation information
- reinsurance data
- agent/broker data

Each master file also contains a large amount of data regarding specific policies. Some of the data relative to specific policies overlaps the data maintained for each policyowner. The *policy* data in the master file includes

- insurance coverage plan identification
- rider and benefit coverage plan identification
- insured's age, sex, and other pertinent data
- underwriting data
- reinsurance data
- claims history data for health coverages
- policy contract content
- premium data, including amount due, payment method, and payment frequency
- billing data, including the required pattern and dates of receipt
- agent/broker data

- financial accumulations such as dividends and unapplied nonforfeiture amounts
- automatic policy, rider, and benefit coverage transactions, including both dates and amounts
- cash surrender values and nonforfeiture amounts and values
- policy loan data
- mortality and expense charges, both actual and anticipated
- surrender charges and application rules
- reserve amounts

The following section describes the way in which much of the original information in the client and policy data base is created.

Processing insurance policy applications. After an agent has obtained a signed application from a prospect, the agent submits the application to the home office for underwriting. When the home office receives the application, its information is entered into the new business system. Application information can also be entered directly by the agent or by field office personnel. In either case, the prospect's name and date of birth are processed into an alphabetical index system, generally referred to as an alpha system.

An **alpha system** maintains data on (1) each person insured by the company, (2) recent applications that have been received and whether those applications have been accepted or declined, and (3) other records that the company has collected in doing business. The alpha system uses a number of identifiers—such as a person's name, age, and date of birth—to link these records. If an applicant has other insurance with the company, or has been declined recently by the company, the underwriter in the home office is alerted by the alpha system. In a large company, a typical alpha system contains records on millions of people.

Once an insurance application is approved, the file in the new business system is updated to reflect this transaction. The *new business system* (1) produces policy pages containing rates and values as they will apply to the policy as issued and (2) sends a master record to the administrative system. The **administrative system** maintains records and processes the daily transactions that involve insurance contracts. Premium billing and collection, policy changes, loans, and maturity and death claims are examples of the types of transactions processed by the administrative system. An administrative system usually has a large master record for each policy, and these individual master records are stored in the system's policy master file. The master record for each policy contains personal information about the insured—name and address, age, date of birth, and so on. In addition, this record contains data pertaining to the policy itself, such as the plan and amount of insurance as well as the existence of any riders, dividends on deposit, cash surrender value, and premiums payable. A third portion of the record usually contains actuarial data, such as the mortality table used when the policy was developed, the insured's risk classification, and cash value and dividend codes used for calculating the cash and dividend values. In general, the administrative system is able to do any processing necessary to keep the policy master record up to date. However, the most common function performed by the administrative system is premium billing and collection.

Premium billing and collection

The preparation of premium billings for each policyowner is a complex activity that is controlled by the calendar, certain client information, and policy billing data in the administrative system. Insurers regularly prepare and send bills or statements of amounts due so that policyowners can keep insurance benefits in force. Each day, the system scans client and policy data for those policies to be billed as well as for the method and frequency of billing.

Billing information resulting from this process is sent to the policyowner, or perhaps to the policyowner's bank or employer, in the form of a premium statement, loan payment notice, loan interest due notice, or bank draft. Later, the remittance received from the client is recorded with his or her policy information according to the specifications in the original billing notice or statement. Generally, the notice or statement is used directly in the data entry process when money is received. Actual data entry may take place in the agent's or broker's office, a regional office, or the home office.

Companies can often design their software to account for most, if not all, of the billing and payment methods used by the company and its policyowners. The following list provides examples of the types of billing and payment methods currently used:

Billing methods	**Payment methods**
direct billing	bank drafts
client consolidated bill	monthly government allotment
list bill or statement	post-dated check
agency bill	credit card charge
group bill	finance note
	payroll deduction
	preauthorized check
	policy loan
	electronic funds transfer
	cash

A variety of payment frequencies are also supported by billing software. These frequencies include the traditional annual, semi-annual, quarterly, monthly, and weekly modes as well as less common modes such as semi-monthly payments.

Automatic and requested transactions

In addition to billing and collection, other transactions are routinely processed against the client and policy data base. The frequency of other types of processing can vary from daily to annually. These transactions are either *automatic*—internally generated by the client and policy data base—or *requested*—externally generated by action on the part of the policyowner.

Automatic transactions originate because of contractual provisions within the client and policy data base. These transactions are usually generated by a search of stored data, either as part of regular system maintenance or through a special processing activity. Premium billing is one example of this kind of transaction. The other kinds of automatic transactions include

- lapse warnings and notices
- policy, rider, and supplemental benefit expiration notices
- policy maturity notices
- automatic premium loans
- transfers to extended term, reduced paid-up, or nonforfeiture status
- normal or advanced date paid-up notices
- periodic mortality and expense charges
- policy dividend notices
- contractual changes in benefits, coverages, and premiums

Requested transactions originate with the policyowner, assignee, or beneficiary. Such transactions are not generated by information in the client and policy data base although they may be affected by that information. The following is a list of some requested transactions:

- claims
- change of beneficiary
- change of address
- assignment
- requests for surrender or policy loan
- change of benefits or coverages
- request for nonforfeiture benefits other than surrender
- dividend option changes
- payment of premiums
- requests for policy value quotations

Agents' production, advances, and commissions subsystem. As premium collections, policy lapses, and other policy changes are processed, records are sent from the administrative system to a commission system. Such a system calculates commissions for each agent as well as compensation for field office managers. Of the specific accounting subsystems, the agents' and brokers' production, advances, and commissions subsystem (henceforth referred to as the agents' subsystem) is usually the most complex and is the subsystem integrated most closely with the client/policy accounting system. The calculation of compensation for the agent or broker and his or her manager cannot be accomplished without information from the client and policy data base. This particular data base typically contains policy status data as well as financial values on premiums.

The agents' subsystem contains information required to identify each agent's or broker's contractual and financial agreements with the company. The information in the client and policy data base is used in conjunction with the information in the agents' subsystem to determine the monetary amounts due to each agent or broker. From this information, periodic payments are made, as applicable, to the agent, broker, and manager. Typically, the design of this subsystem is highly individualized for each company.

The Investment Accounting System

The **investment accounting system** provides an inventory of all stocks, bonds, mortgage loans, real estate, and other investment assets. This investment data consists of information pertinent to the purchase and sale of these assets as well as the income received from them. This system is also used to record the values of a company's assets. Typically, these asset valuations are transferred to the general accounting system data base through summary entries to specific accounts. Any detailed reporting on specific invested assets or categories of assets is developed directly from the investment accounting system data base through either built-in reports or generalized report-writing software. With both of these methods of detailed reporting, companies can satisfy the specialized needs of investment accounting and also retain the flexibility to provide information for financial and managerial reports.

As with asset valuation, transactions regarding invested assets are transferred to the general accounting system. Records of the investment transactions—purchases, sales, maturities, income, amortizations, foreclosures, etc.—are carried in the data base of the investment accounting system. Totals of the amounts of these transactions can be transferred to the general accounting system through summary entries. In some companies, the investment accounting system is designed to transfer detailed investment information to the general accounting system.

Information Produced by Accounting Information Systems

As was discussed in Chapters 1 and 2, all insurance companies create financial statements and management information reports. These statements and reports often require different information, but all of them reflect the company's financial transactions. The source of all of the information used in these statements and reports is the company's accounting information system. Separate systems need not be maintained for the financial and managerial accounting subsystems. In fact, separate systems would be less efficient since the company data base would have to be maintained in more than one place. Such duplication of the data base complicates the control and verification of transactions.

Financial information and managerial information are used for different purposes. Financial accounting systems are designed primarily to provide information for reports to external parties. Managerial accounting systems are designed primarily to provide information for internal use. As was explained in the first two chapters, the information required for outside parties is often heavily regulated. The financial and other reporting that is done for internal management, on the other hand, is constrained only by the information available in the company's data base and by the needs and creativity of company management.

Many programs or subsystems are used to calculate the data necessary to produce the Annual Statement as well as other financial reports. For example, the administrative system provides actuarial programs or subsystems with the appropriate data to allow the actuaries to make all the necessary calculations of dividends and reserves. These subsystems often are quite detailed and can constitute some of the most complex processing done in an insurance company. The daily processing of various transactions also provides much of the data in the corporate data base. This data is used to create reports and provide management with the information needed to run the company efficiently.

Key Terms

system
automated system
information
redundant data
software
integrated software
general accounting system
client and policy master file
administrative system
requested transaction
investment accounting system

subsystem
data
data base
hardware
application program
financial information system
client/policy accounting system
alpha system
automatic transaction
agents' subsystem

Review Questions and Exercises

1. Do modern data bases depend on redundant data or nonredundant data? Explain your answer.
2. What is the significance of a *completely integrated* data processing system?

3. How does an insurer's management use the information in a financial information system?
4. Describe different ways that an insurance company can number its accounts for the chart of accounts. If possible, obtain a copy of your company's chart of accounts and see how it is constructed.
5. What is the function of a company's general ledger subsystem?
6. Distinguish between automatic and requested transactions. Give an example of each.
7. What types of information relative to individual policyowners are contained in the client and policy master file?

4
Premium and Commission Accounting

Learning Objectives

After reading this chapter, you should be able to:

- Describe the importance of the paid-to date in premium and commission accounting
- Understand the basic objectives of premium and commission accounting
- Record the journal entries relative to a number of different premium transactions
- List and describe the different premium classifications that insurers use
- Discuss the Annual Statement presentation of premium and commission information

Introduction

Premiums usually constitute the largest and most important source of revenue for a life insurer. Because many different individual policyowners and group policyholders remit premiums to an insurer, accounting for premiums is an especially intricate process. An insurer's premium accounting system encompasses a number of billing, collecting, and controlling operations. One function of the premium accounting system is to match premium income to the period in which the income was earned. Premium income must also be matched to the period over which the company will pay benefits and expenses related to that premium income. Another important function of the premium accounting system is accounting for agents' commissions.

Absolute accuracy in premium accounting must be achieved if business is to be conserved, if the goodwill of policyowners is to be retained, and if the requirements of regulatory authorities are to be fulfilled. This chapter explores premium and commission accounting as well as the Annual Statement treatment of premium and commission information.

Premium Control Process

When accounting for the receipt of premiums, an insurer's premium control process must ensure that each premium payment received is either the amount billed or a modified amount acceptable to the insurer. If a premium is not paid by the end of the grace period, the premium control process must either terminate the policy or change the policy record from premium-paying status to one of the nonforfeiture option classifications. In some cases, a policyowner may have requested that an automatic premium loan be made from the policy's cash surrender value or amounts on deposit with the company. The premium accounting system would record this loan when it is advanced. (Automatic premium loans are discussed more fully in Chapter 6.)

In an insurer's premium accounting system, premium control is accomplished through controls over the policyowners' master billing record. This record's most important bit of information for premium accounting is the **paid-to date,** which is the date to which a policyowner has paid his or her premium. The paid-to date of the master file is periodically monitored. When necessary, premium notices and past-due warnings are generated and changes from premium-paying to nonpremium-paying status are recorded.

Each premium received is also processed against the master file record in order to keep paid-to date information current. This process is initiated when the policyowner returns the premium notice and payment. Premium remittances will usually result in the generation of accounting entries and commission payments. (The premium and commission accounting processes for new business and renewal business are shown in Figures 4-1 and 4-2.) Premium remittances also influence informational reports such as cash flow statements.

Objectives of Premium Accounting

The premium accounting system of an insurance company must achieve certain objectives. These objectives can be stated as follows:

- A functional billing procedure must be established to assure that (1) premiums are billed prior to the due date with sufficient lead time between the billing and due dates; (2) no payment is applied against a currently due premium until all outstanding premiums have been received; (3) no premium is accepted after the expiration of the grace

FIGURE 4-1
An overview of premium and commission accounting for policy issue.

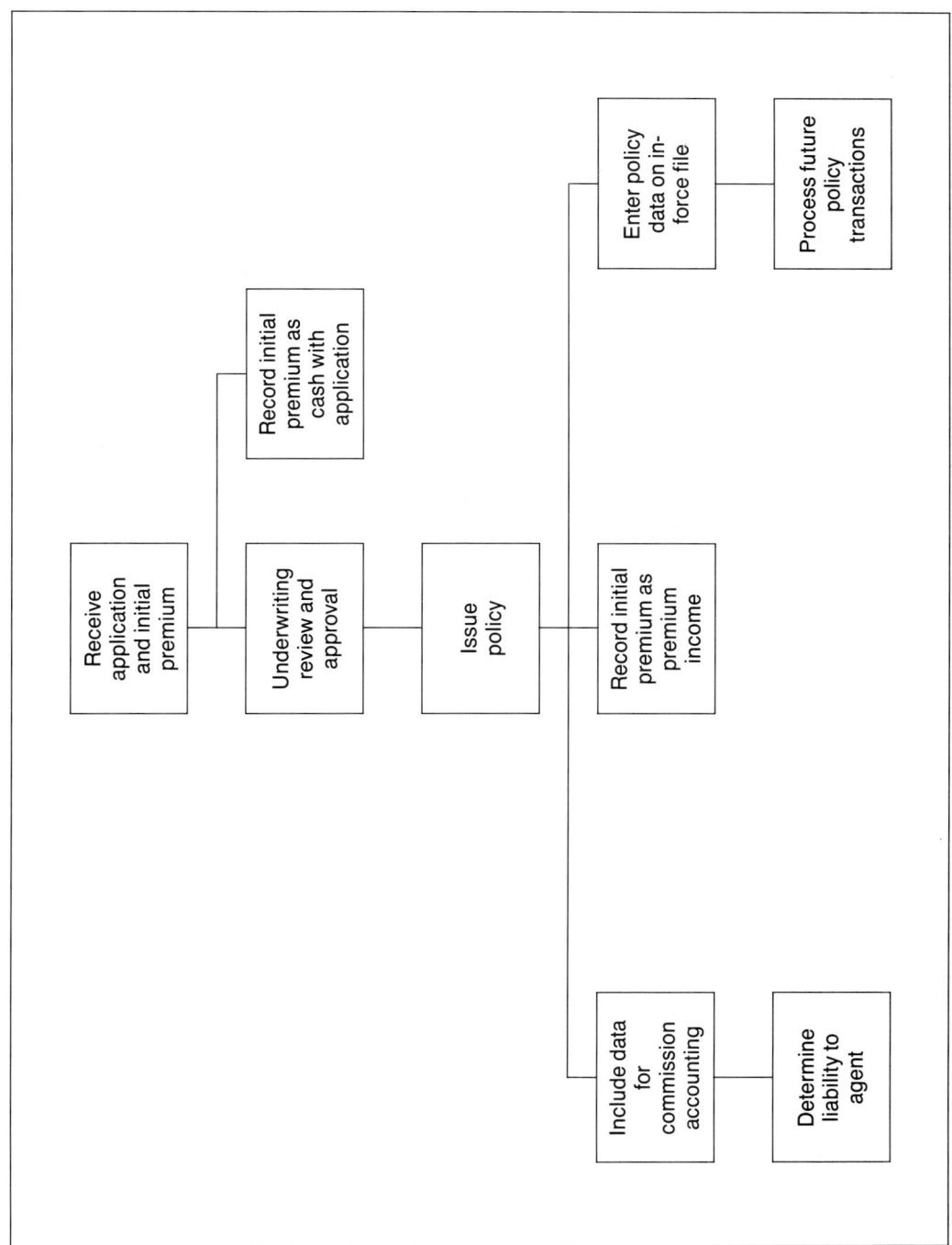

FIGURE 4-2
An overview of premium and commission accounting for renewal business.

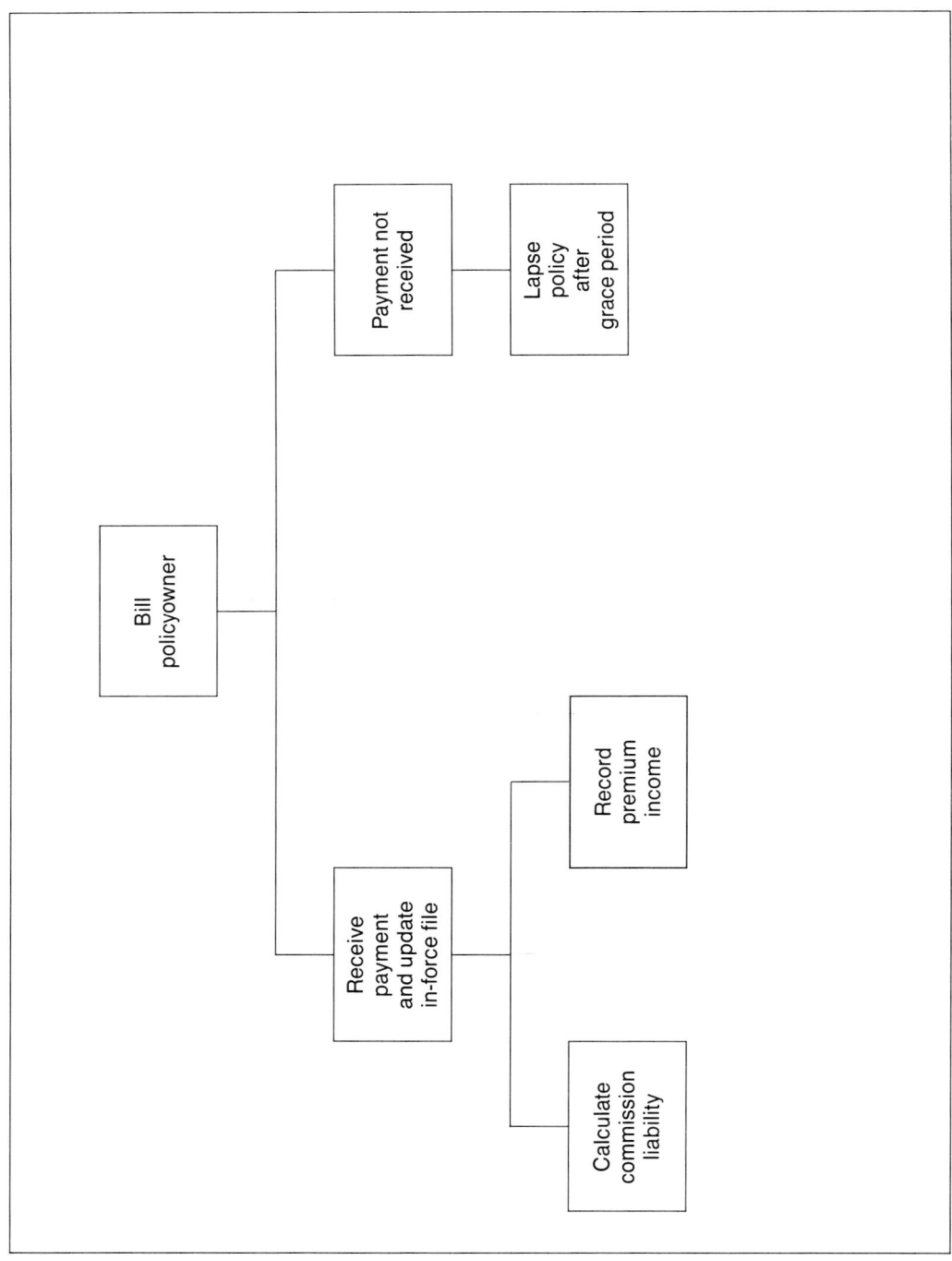

period, except under circumstances acceptable to the insurer; and (4) policies are either terminated or changed from premium-paying status to nonforfeiture status if no premium is paid or automatic premium loan is made upon expiration of the grace period.
- A comprehensive collection routine must be established to (1) promptly deposit payments in the insurer's account, (2) update the policyowner's master record for the amount received, and (3) change the paid-to date. The paid-to date is essential to both the **income recognition process** by which income is allocated to the period in which the income was earned and the valuation of premium asset and liability accounts for financial statement purposes.
- A detailed reporting method must be established in order (1) to record premium income by jurisdiction, for the purpose of premium tax assessments; by line of business; and by participating and nonparticipating classifications; and (2) to facilitate financial auditing of the following items:
  - the insurer's bank deposit in which a particular premium was included,
  - the journal entry in which that premium was recorded,
  - the policy record to which that premium was credited, and
  - the commission payment made in connection with receipt of the premium.

  These transactions will provide the audit trail to enable a state examiner or other auditor to begin from any one of the four items mentioned and trace the specific premium payment to the other reference points.
- Premiums must be identified, for statutory reporting purposes, as first-year premiums, renewal premiums, or single premiums.

In order to allocate premium income to its proper period, insurers must establish certain classifications for recording premiums. These classifications include (1) premium income, (2) premium suspense, (3) premium deposits, (4) unearned premiums, (5) advance premiums, and (6) uncollected premiums. Each of these classifications is discussed below.

Premium Income

The basic entry for a collected premium is:

  Cash xxx
    Premium Income xxx

The amount of premium received is credited to the Premium Income account unless the amount is held on deposit or in suspense. The basic premium income entry generally does not vary from product to product. However, premium income is typically credited to one of several Premium Income accounts that are differentiated according to the type of policy or year of payment. For example, when a policyowner remits a renewal premium for a life policy, the journal entry might show a credit to an account entitled Premium Renewal—Life.

If a policyowner pays a premium by check, and the check is not honored by the policyowner's bank, the original premium entry must be reversed:

> Premium Income xxx
>   Cash xxx

This entry reduces the total in the insurer's Premium Income and Cash accounts. Commission entries, which will be discussed later, also need to be reversed when a premium entry is reversed.

When a policyowner's check is not honored, some companies delay reversal of the premium entry until an effort has been made to collect on the check. Even in this case, a journal entry must be made to reflect the fact that the insurer actually received no money. This entry typically includes a debit to an accounts receivable asset account such as Returned Checks. A journal entry reflecting an insurer's attempt to collect on a policyowner's check could appear as:

> Returned Checks xxx
>   Cash xxx

When an amount is debited to a Returned Checks account, the amount has not yet been written off. If a returned check is honored upon a second attempt at collection, the journal entry that adjusts the debit balance in the accounts receivable account would typically appear as:

> Cash xxx
>   Returned Checks xxx

If, on the other hand, the policyowner's check is not honored upon subsequent attempts to deposit it, the following journal entry must be made to show that payment was never received:

> Premium Income xxx
>   Returned Checks xxx

This entry effectively removes the specific returned check item from the Returned Checks account and reduces the Premium Income account balance to the amount it totaled prior to the first premium entry for this particular check.

In many cases, the entry for recording receipt of a premium is a compound entry. This entry can reflect payment of policy loan principal and interest, deductions of policy dividends from the premium due amount, or other policy transactions. To illustrate, assume that the following dollar amounts apply to a person's life insurance policy:

> Premium due $100
> Policy loan interest due 25
> Policy dividend payable to policyowner 11

In such a case, the proper amount to be paid to the insurer would be $114 ($100 premium due + $25 interest due − $11 dividend payable). The entry to record receipt of this amount would be:

```
Cash .................................114
Dividends Applied to Premium ...............11
     Premium Income.............................100
     Interest on Policy Loans .......................25
```

The debit to a dividend account records the reduction of the insurer's debt to the policyowner. The credit to the interest account records the increased income for the insurer. If payment is made by check and the check is not honored, the dividend and interest accounts would have to be reversed along with the cash and premium accounts to reflect accurately the reinstatement of those amounts.

Premium Suspense

If a premium payment is received but the amount cannot be immediately credited to Premium Income, an entry would be made to the Premium Suspense account. The *premium suspense* classification is used to record amounts that are intended as premiums but that cannot be accepted as income until a particular event occurs. For example, initial premium payments submitted with a policy application may be credited to a Premium Suspense account pending approval and issuance of a policy. The entry to record an amount placed in suspense is:

```
Cash .................................xxx
     Premium Suspense ...........................xxx
```

When the reason for holding the premium in suspense no longer applies, the entry to apply the amount in suspense as an actual premium is:

```
Premium Suspense .......................xxx
     Premium Income............................xxx
```

If a policy is not approved and issued, the insurer must remit to the policyowner the amount held in suspense. The entry to record return of the premium would be:

```
Premium Suspense .......................xxx
     Cash ...................................xxx
```

The Premium Suspense account is a liability account. When a policyowner remits a premium in cash to an insurer, the insurer's asset total increases. However, when the money is put into Suspense, policy records are not updated. Thus, the policy record of the policyowner that remitted the premium still shows an uncollected premium, which is an asset for the insurer. As a result, when a premium is in Suspense, the amount is being counted as an asset twice: once as cash received by the insurer and again as an uncollected premium. By treating the amount in Suspense as a liability, the extra asset is offset and the proper totals are reflected in the insurer's books.

Premium Deposits

Premium deposits are amounts that are left on deposit with the insurer for the payment of future premiums. Premiums that are paid a certain amount of time in advance—typically, one year—and that are not credited to a premium income account are considered premium deposits and are credited to a special premium deposit account. The amount in the premium deposit account is not used to adjust premium income from the cash to the accrual basis. The deposits represent future premiums and are not considered premium payments for the current period.

Many insurers discount the amount of premium deposits to allow for the interest that will be earned on the amount while it is on deposit with the company. For example, assume that a policyowner wanted to pay the next two $100 annual premiums on a life insurance policy. The first premium is due in one month, just after the statement date. Receipt of that premium is credited to the Advance Premium account (which will be discussed later). The second premium, however, is not due for over a year. The insurer, in this case, may charge only $94.35 for the premium, if the insurer is anticipating a 6 percent return on premium deposits. At the end of the year, the $94.35 deposit will have accumulated, with interest, to roughly $100. The rate of interest that is granted on premium deposits is determined by the insurer's management. The interest earned on premium deposits can also vary by product type.

Most companies prefer to accept only discounted premiums as premium deposits, although some companies accept for deposit regular contributions that are unrelated to a policy's premiums. Such contributions can be made for the purpose of (1) accumulating an emergency fund that might be used for future premium payments or (2) accumulating an additional amount that can be withdrawn at some future date. As with premium suspense accounts, premium deposits are usually credited to a liability account and later applied to a premium income account. The interest paid as a result of the discount on these deposits, however, introduces a new element to premium accounting.

Assume that the renewal premiums on an ordinary policy are $100 per year, and that a policyowner has paid 10 years' premiums in advance at a discounted cost of $558.39. (Knowledge of the method of calculating the amounts of discounted premiums is not necessary for the purposes of this discussion.) The typical entry to record receipt of this $558.39 is:

```
Cash  . . . . . . . . . . . . . . . . . . . . . . . . . . . . .558.39
    Premium Deposits . . . . . . . . . . . . . . . . . . . . . . .458.39
    Premium Income  . . . . . . . . . . . . . . . . . . . . . . . 100.00
```

Note that the currently due premium is not credited to the Premium Deposit account, a liability account, but instead is credited directly to the Premium Income account. One year later when the next premium comes due, the amount of interest on the total principal of $458.39 is entered as a debit to an expense account, Interest Paid on Policy and Contract Funds. Assuming a 6 percent rate of return on premium deposits, the amount of interest for the first year of the deposit would be $27.50. The full amount of the second year's premium, $100, must be credited to the Premium Income account to record payment of that year's premium. The difference between the $100 premium and the $27.50 interest earned—$72.50—is transferred from the Premium Deposit account. The entry for this transaction would appear as:

```
Premium Deposits . . . . . . . . . . . . . . . . . . . . . . 72.50
Interest Paid on Policy and Contract Funds . . . 27.50
     Premium Income . . . . . . . . . . . . . . . . . . . . . . . . . . 100.00
```

This process is repeated each year until the amount held in the deposit account for this policy has been reduced to zero.

Unearned Premiums

The *unearned premium* classification is used to report the portion of a premium that is due or received before the Annual Statement date but which is applicable to the following reporting year. For example, if a quarterly premium payment of $24 is due on December 1, then $16 of that premium (two-thirds of $24) is applicable to the period from January 1 through February 28 of the following year. Thus, on the statement date of December 31, this premium has an unearned premium liability of $16. The unearned premium classification is usually applied to health insurance premiums, and not to life insurance premiums or annuity considerations.

Advance Premiums

A life insurance premium that is received before the statement date but which is not due until after that date is considered an **advance premium.** For example, a premium that is due on the policy anniversary date of January 2 but which is paid in the preceding December is considered an advance premium for statements prepared as of December 31. The definition for advance premiums may sound similar to the definition for premium deposits. However, advance premiums are typically due within the coming year, are recorded as premium income, and are not discounted. The amount of advance premiums on the statement date is used in adjusting premium income from a cash to an accrual basis and is recorded as a liability. In many companies, when an advance premium is received, the entry would be:

Cash xxx
    Premium Income xxx

A typical accounting entry to adjust for this advance premium in the Annual Statement would be:

Premium Income xxx
    Premiums Received in Advance xxx

Uncollected Premiums

Uncollected premiums are life insurance premiums and annuity considerations that are due on or before the statement date but which have not been received by that date. Accident and health premiums that are uncollected are identified separately and are generally referred to as *due and unpaid*. Uncollected premiums are an asset and are recorded as an accrual entry. The following example illustrates the entry for uncollected premiums. Assume that a life policy has an anniversary date of July 28, and that the monthly premiums are $10 each. If premiums have been paid through the October 28 due date, the premiums for November and December are uncollected premiums since they have not been received. The uncollected premiums for this policy thus total $20. The accounting entry to record the uncollected premiums is:

Uncollected Premiums 20
    Premium Income 20

If the premium is never collected, the entry to write off the amount of uncollected premium would be:

Premium Income 20
    Uncollected Premiums 20

Accounting for Commissions

The amount of commissions payable to an agent in connection with the sale or servicing of a life or health insurance policy is dependent on the amount of premiums received. Commission accounting processes must, therefore, be coordinated with the premium accounting system. In addition, the objectives of commission accounting are similar to those of premium accounting. These commission accounting objectives are

- accurately determining the amount of commission payable on each premium received;
- accurate recording of commission amounts payable to, or premiums due from, each agent;

- reporting earnings for each agent to tax authorities and forwarding all payroll and withholding taxes on those earnings; and
- establishing an audit trail from the premium payment on which the commission was calculated to the commission entry in the journal and to the commission entry in the agent's account.

Commission Accounting Basics

In accounting for agents' commissions, insurers generally establish an account in a subsidiary ledger for each agent as well as establishing a control account in the general ledger for the total of all agents' commissions. Each agent's account can either have a debit balance or a credit balance. The agent's account has a *debit* balance when the agent owes money to the company and the agent's account represents an account receivable. The agent's account has a *credit* balance when the company owes money to the agent and the agent's account represents an account payable. Either condition may exist from time to time, but both conditions cannot exist simultaneously for any one agent. For example, many companies advance commissions to a new agent during his or her first months with the company. During this period, the agent's account would have a debit balance, as does any other account receivable. When the agent repays the advanced money and the company owes commissions to the agent, his or her account will have a credit balance signifying an account payable. The crediting of earned commissions to an agent's subsidiary account provides a simple method of summarizing for tax purposes the amount of commissions earned by each agent.

Several types of accounting transactions occur frequently in connection with agents' commissions. These transactions include (1) recording in the general account the total of all commissions earned and paid, (2) crediting the agent's subsidiary ledger account with commissions earned, (3) disbursing the proper amounts to agents after deductions such as taxes, and (4) making special charges for services rendered or for premium adjustments.

If an insurer owes an agent commissions, the insurer's journal entry to show that these commissions were earned would typically appear as follows:

    Commissions Paid xxx
      Agents' Ledger Control xxx

When the amount of the commissions is actually paid, the journal entry would be:

    Agents' Ledger Control xxx
      Cash xxx

After both the earnings entry and this payment entry are posted, the control account balance becomes zero with reference to these particular commissions.

This zero balance indicates that the agent has been paid the full amount earned. The combined effect of the two transactions is the recording of an expense for commissions paid and a corresponding decrease in the Cash account.

As mentioned earlier in the chapter, insurers must occasionally refund premiums to policyowners. When a premium is refunded, the agent loses his or her commission earnings on that premium payment. Upon refund of the premium, the original commission entry must be reversed. The entry to reverse a prior commission entry would typically consist of a debit to Agents' Ledger Control and a credit to Commissions Paid. Reversal of a commission entry is also necessary when any other type of premium reversal takes place.

If a company chooses to pay commissions without first recording them in an agent's subsidiary ledger account, the journal entry in such a case would typically be:

  Commissions Paid xxx
    Cash xxx

When recording commissions in this manner, an insurer must maintain a supplemental record for tax purposes.

Accounting for taxes on agents' commissions

An insurer is required to deduct federal, state, local, and social security taxes from the earnings of those agents considered to be employees of the company. When the amount of taxes is deducted from an agent's commissions, accountants typically credit a liability account for the amount withheld for later payment to governmental authorities. For example, if an agent in the United States earns $100 in commissions on which $5 must be withheld for social security (FICA) payments, $10 must be withheld for federal income taxes, and $2 must be withheld for state taxes, the entry for this commission payment would appear in the general ledger as:

  Agents' Ledger Control 100
    Federal Income Taxes Withheld 10
    FICA Taxes Withheld 5
    State Income Taxes Withheld 2
    Cash 83

This entry reduces the record of commissions payable to the agent by $17 and increases the insurer's withholding tax liability account total by the same amount. Entries such as these are typically restricted to commissions payable to agents who, for tax purposes, are considered to be employees of the insurer. Most other agents are considered independent contractors, and commission payments to such agents are not subject to federal or state withholding.

Annual Statement Aspects—United States

Information regarding premiums is required throughout the Annual Statement. Two major reports relate to premium income:

(1) Exhibit 1—Part 1, in which premiums are illustrated on an accrual basis by line of business; and
(2) Schedule T, in which the premiums collected during the year are shown by the states and territories from which that income was received.

Items related to premiums are also included in the Balance Sheet, the Summary of Operations, and other Annual Statement reports. The following sections of this chapter discuss some of the premium-related aspects of the U.S. Annual Statement.

Exhibit 1

The main premium exhibit, Exhibit 1, is divided into two parts (see Figure 4-3). The first part presents the premiums and annuity considerations received by the company, while the second part of the exhibit records the following amounts:

- the amount of dividends and other benefits applied toward the payment of premiums,
- the amount of reinsurance commissions and expenses, and
- the amount of commissions incurred in the course of the company's direct business.

The presentation of premium income on an accrual basis, as mandated in Part 1 of Exhibit 1, requires the identification of premiums in terms of collected premiums, uncollected premiums, deferred premiums, and advance premiums. *Collected premiums* represent the amount of premium income *received* by the company during an accounting period. *Deferred premiums* are premiums that are due after the statement date but before the next policy anniversary. The following formula illustrates the mechanics of converting premium income from a cash to an accrual basis. An accrual-basis presentation shows the amount of premium income actually *earned* in the reporting year.

	Collected premiums
plus	Gross deferred and uncollected premiums at the end of the current period
minus	Gross deferred and uncollected premiums at the end of the previous period
minus	Advance premiums at the end of the current period
plus	Advance premiums at the end of the previous period
equals	Accrual-basis premium income

FIGURE 4-3
Exhibit 1—U.S. Annual Statement.

FIGURE 4-3 (cont.)

Form 1

ANNUAL STATEMENT FOR THE YEAR 1985 OF THE _____Name_____

EXHIBIT 1 — PART 2 — DIVIDENDS AND COUPONS* APPLIED, REINSURANCE COMMISSIONS AND EXPENSE ALLOWANCES AND COMMISSIONS INCURRED (direct business only)

	(1) TOTAL	(2) INDUSTRIAL LIFE	ORDINARY			GROUP		ACCIDENT AND HEALTH	
			(3) LIFE INSURANCE	(4) INDIVIDUAL ANNUITIES	(5) CREDIT LIFE* (Group and Individual)	(6) LIFE INSURANCE	(7) ANNUITIES	(8) GROUP	(9) CREDIT* (Group and Individual)	(10) OTHER

DIVIDENDS AND COUPONS* APPLIED (included in Part 1)

21. To pay renewal premiums (Exhibit 7, Line 1)
22. All other (Exhibit 7, Lines 2, 3 & 4)

REINSURANCE COMMISSIONS AND EXPENSE ALLOWANCES INCURRED

23. First year (other than single):
   a. Reinsurance ceded
   b. Reinsurance assumed
   c. Net ceded less assumed
24. Single:
   a. Reinsurance ceded
   b. Reinsurance assumed
   c. Net ceded less assumed
25. Renewal:
   a. Reinsurance ceded
   b. Reinsurance assumed
   c. Net ceded less assumed
26. Totals:
   a. Reinsurance ceded (Page 5, Item 5)
   b. Reinsurance assumed (Page 5, Item 21A)
   c. Net ceded less assumed

COMMISSIONS INCURRED (direct business only)

27. First year (other than single)
28. Single
29. Renewal
30. Totals (to agree with Page 5, Item 21)

*Business not exceeding 120 months duration.
*Includes coupons, guaranteed annual pure endowments and similar benefits.

The effect of this calculation, as with all adjustments of income to the accrual basis, is the determination of the amount of premium income that the insurer actually *earned* during the reporting period, regardless of whether that income was actually collected.

A number of comments should be made about Exhibit 1. First, in reporting premium income on the accrual basis, deferred and uncollected premiums are recorded at their gross totals, net of reinsurance. **Gross premiums** include the amount of loading, commissions, and other costs incurred in acceptance of the premium. Note also that premiums for the first policy year are shown separately from single premiums and renewal premiums (see Figure 4-3). This first-year information is useful to state insurance departments in determining whether the commissions or other first-year costs for the company's products are excessive. Only one line of Exhibit 1 is required for reporting single premiums, because due and advance premiums do not arise in connection with single premiums.

Column headings for all parts of the premium exhibit are the same as those used in the Analysis of Operations (Annual Statement page 5), except that the premium exhibit does not include a column for supplementary contracts. Supplementary contracts typically arise as a result of a death benefit that is not paid in a lump sum to a beneficiary. They are not considered new income for an insurer and are not taxable as part of premium revenue. (Supplementary contracts are discussed more fully in Chapter 8.)

Commissions

Annual Statement reporting of commissions incurred on an insurer's direct business is fairly simple. The total commissions incurred are classified as (1) first-year commissions other than on single premiums, (2) commissions on single premiums, and (3) commissions on renewal premiums. The total commissions incurred are then reported in the company's Analysis of Operations (Annual Statement page 5).

Schedule T

Schedule T of the U.S. Annual Statement shows the allocation by state and territory of premiums collected by the insurer during the reporting year. In Schedule T (see Figure 4-4), premiums are reported on a cash basis and therefore must agree with the amounts of *collected* premiums reported in Exhibit 1. The totals must also agree with the company's premium journals to prove that all premiums have been allocated to their proper jurisdiction. Columns are provided in Schedule T for classifying premium totals into the following categories: life insurance premiums, annuity considerations, and accident and health insurance premiums. As with the premium exhibit, supplementary contracts are not shown in Schedule T.

FIGURE 4-4
Schedule T—U.S. Annual Statement.

Form 1	ANNUAL STATEMENT FOR THE YEAR 1985 OF THE _____ Name			45
	SCHEDULE T — PREMIUMS AND ANNUITY CONSIDERATIONS Allocated by States and Territories			

(1) STATES, ETC.		(2) IS INSURER LICENSED? (Yes or No)	DIRECT BUSINESS ONLY		
			(3) LIFE INSURANCE PREMIUMS	(4) ANNUITY CONSIDERATIONS	(5) ACCIDENT AND HEALTH INSURANCE PREMIUMS, INCLUDING POLICY, MEMBERSHIP AND OTHER FEES
1	Alabama	AL			
2	Alaska	AK			
3	Arizona	AZ			
4	Arkansas	AR			
5	California	CA			
6	Colorado	CO			
7	Connecticut	CT			
8	Delaware	DE			
9	Dist. Columbia	DC			
10	Florida	FL			
11	Georgia	GA			
12	Hawaii	HI			
13	Idaho	ID			
14	Illinois	IL			
15	Indiana	IN			
16	Iowa	IA			
17	Kansas	KS			
18	Kentucky	KY			
19	Louisiana	LA			
20	Maine	ME			
21	Maryland	MD			
22	Massachusetts	MA			
23	Michigan	MI			
24	Minnesota	MN			
25	Mississippi	MS			
26	Missouri	MO			
27	Montana	MT			
28	Nebraska	NE			
29	Nevada	NV			
30	New Hampshire	NH			
31	New Jersey	NJ			
32	New Mexico	NM			
33	New York	NY			
34	No. Carolina	NC			
35	No. Dakota	ND			
36	Ohio	OH			
37	Oklahoma	OK			
38	Oregon	OR			
39	Pennsylvania	PA			
40	Rhode Island	RI			
41	So. Carolina	SC			
42	So. Dakota	SD			
43	Tennessee	TN			
44	Texas	TX			
45	Utah	UT			
46	Vermont	VT			
47	Virginia	VA			
48	Washington	WA			
49	West Virginia	WV			
50	Wisconsin	WI			
51	Wyoming	WY			
52	American Samoa	AS			
53	Guam	GU			
54	Puerto Rico	PR			
55	U.S. Virgin Is.	VI			
56	Canada	CN			
57	Other alien (itemize)***	OT			
90	Company contributions for employee benefit plans	X X X			
91	†Dividends applied to purchase paid-up additions and annuities	X X X			
92	†Dividends applied to shorten endowment or premium-paying period	X X X			
93	*Premium or annuity considerations waived under disability or other contract provisions	X X X			
94	TOTALS (Direct Business)	X X X			
95	Plus Reinsurance Assumed	X X X			
96	TOTALS (All Business)	X X X			
97	Less Reinsurance Ceded	X X X			
98	**Totals (All Business) less Reinsurance Ceded	††			

Explanation of basis of allocation by states, etc., of premiums and annuity considerations

†Dividend accumulations used to purchase paid-up additions and annuities, or to shorten endowment or premium-paying period, should not be included in this item but should be included in Columns 3 and 4 and distributed by states for those states which allowed the dividends to be deducted in calculating premium taxes. For other states, separate totals similar to those for dividends so applied may be shown. Dividends applied to pay renewal premiums and consideration for annuities must also be included in Columns 3 and 4 and distributed by states.
*Premium or annuity considerations waived under disability or other contract provisions should be shown here in one sum and not included in the distribution by states.
**The sum of Columns 3 and 4 should balance with Exhibit 1, Lines 6d, 10d and 16d, Col. 1, less Cols. 8, 9 and 10. Column 5 should balance with Exhibit 1, Lines 6d, 10d and 16d, Cols. 8, 9 and 10, or with Schedule H, Part 1, Line 1; indicate which _____
***All U.S. business must be allocated by state regardless of license status.   ††Insert the number of yes responses except for Canada and Other alien.

State insurance departments refer to Schedule T to verify premium totals for taxation purposes. Because of this function of Schedule T, spaces are provided for deducting the amounts of nontaxable premiums. Premiums waived because of disability are nontaxable, and, in most states, dividends deducted from premiums are nontaxable.

Health Insurance Premiums and Commissions

While summary totals of an insurer's accident and health business are reported in Exhibit 1, columns 8-10 (see Figure 4-3, page 84), a more detailed record of a company's accident and health business is presented in Schedule H (see Figure 4-5). Due health insurance premiums are admitted on the Annual Statement at their gross amount if they are due within 90 days. Within certain guidelines, premiums that are due after 90 days are nonadmitted for Annual Statement purposes. Related commissions and estimated costs of collection are included with commission liabilities and are used to adjust commissions from the cash to the accrual basis.

Balance Sheet Information

Advance premiums and premium deposits are shown as separate liabilities on the Balance Sheet. If a discount was allowed when the premiums were received, the liability amount for premium deposits is the present value on December 31 of the future premiums. Amounts held in suspense pending issue or reinstatement of a policy are also liabilities and are shown on the Balance Sheet under the title, *remittances and items not allocated.* In companies that use a Returned Check account for premium payments made by checks that are not honored, the amount in this account is treated as a nonadmitted asset.

Net deferred and uncollected life insurance premiums are treated as assets on an insurer's Balance Sheet. Accident and health premiums that are due within three months of the statement date are also included on the assets page of the Balance Sheet. When an insurer treats unearned health insurance premiums as policy reserves, the premiums are included on the liability page of the insurer's Balance Sheet as a part of the *aggregate reserve for accident and health policies.*

Annual Statement Aspects—Canada

A number of exhibits in the Canadian Annual Statement relate to premium income and commission payments. Exhibit 1 reports on the premiums, commissions, and dividends for a company's life insurance business. Exhibit 3 records information on accident and sickness premiums, and Exhibit 12 displays information on the premiums owed to the insurer. Canadian insurers must also

FIGURE 4-5
Schedule H—U.S. Annual Statement.

Form 12

ANNUAL STATEMENT FOR THE YEAR 1985 OF THE 35
Name

SCHEDULE H—ACCIDENT AND HEALTH EXHIBIT

	(1) TOTAL		(2) GROUP ACCIDENT AND HEALTH		(3) CREDIT* (Group and Individual)		(4) COLLECTIVELY RENEWABLE		OTHER INDIVIDUAL POLICIES (5) NON-CANCELLABLE		(6) GUARANTEED RENEWABLE		(7) NON-RENEWABLE FOR STATED REASONS ONLY		(8) OTHER ACCIDENT ONLY		(9) ALL OTHER	
	Amount	%†	Amount	%†	Amount	%†	Amount	%†	Amount	%†	Amount	%†	Amount	%†	Amount	%†	Amount	%†
PART 1. ANALYSIS OF UNDERWRITING OPERATIONS																		
1. Premiums written																		
2. Premiums earned (see note b)																		
3. Incurred claims																		
4. Increase in policy reserves																		
5. Commissions*																		
6. General insurance expenses																		
7. Taxes, licenses and fees																		
8. Total expenses incurred																		
9. Gain from underwriting before dividends to policyholders																		
10. Dividends to policyholders																		
11. Gain from underwriting after dividends to policyholders																		
PART 2. RESERVES AND LIABILITIES																		
A. PREMIUM RESERVES:																		
1. Unearned premiums																		
2. Advance premiums																		
3. Reserve for rate credits																		
4. Total premium reserves, current year																		
5. Total premium reserves, previous year																		
6. Increase in total premium reserves																		
B. POLICY RESERVES:																		
1. Additional reserves																		
2. Reserve for future contingent benefits (deferred maternity and other similar benefits)**																		
3. Total policy reserves, current year																		
4. Total policy reserves, previous year																		
5. Increase in policy reserves																		
C. CLAIM RESERVES AND LIABILITIES:																		
1. Total current year																		
2. Total previous year																		
3. Increase																		
PART 3. TEST OF PREVIOUS YEAR'S CLAIM RESERVES AND LIABILITIES																		
1. CLAIMS PAID DURING THE YEAR:																		
a. On claims incurred prior to current year																		
b. On claims incurred during current year																		
2. CLAIM RESERVES AND LIABILITIES, DEC. 31, CURRENT YEAR:																		
a. On claims incurred prior to current year																		
b. On claims incurred during current year																		
3. TEST:																		
a. Line 1a and 2a																		
b. Claim reserves and liabilities, Dec. 31, previous year																		
c. Line a minus Line b																		
PART 4. REINSURANCE																		
A. REINSURANCE ASSUMED:																		
1. Premiums written																		
2. Premiums earned (see note b)																		
3. Incurred claims																		
4. Commissions																		
B. REINSURANCE CEDED:																		
1. Premiums written																		
2. Premiums earned (see note b)																		
3. Incurred claims																		
4. Commissions																		

* Business not exceeding 120 months duration.
† In each column of Part 1, show the percentages of Line 2 for Lines 3 through 11 inclusive.

*Includes $.................reported as "Policy, membership and other fees retained by agents."
**If not included in claim reserves.
(b) Premiums earned are before adjustment for the increase in policy reserves which has been treated as a separate deduction.

FIGURE 4-6
Exhibit 1—Canadian Annual Statement.

```
                                    22(LS)

NAME OF COMPANY ▶                              YEAR OF STATEMENT
                                                      19
EXHIBIT 1:                                     PREMIUMS, COMMISSIONS AND
```

		PARTICIPATING			
		INDIVIDUAL		GROUP	
		INSURANCE	ANNUITY	INSURANCE	ANNUITY
PART 1: PREMIUMS		01	02	03	04
DIRECT:					
SINGLE	01				
FIRST YEAR	02				
RENEWAL	03				
SUB TOTAL DIRECT	▶ 04				
ASSUMED:					
SINGLE	05				
FIRST YEAR	06				
RENEWAL	07				
SUB TOTAL ASSUMED	▶ 08				
CEDED:					
SINGLE	09				
FIRST YEAR	10				
RENEWAL	11				
SUB TOTAL CEDED	▶ 12				
TOTAL NET OF CEDED (04+08-12)	▶ 13				
PART 2 - COMMISSIONS					
DIRECT:					
SINGLE	14				
FIRST YEAR	15				
RENEWAL	16				
COMMISSIONS INCURRED ON REINSURANCE ASSUMED	17				
COMMISSIONS AND ALLOWANCES RECEIVED ON REINSURANCE CEDED	18				
TOTAL COMMISSIONS INCURRED (NET)	▶ 19				
PART 3: DIVIDENDS TO POLICYHOLDERS*					
DIRECT:					
PAID OR PAYABLE IN CASH	20				
LEFT WITH COMPANY AT INTEREST	21				
DEPOSITED IN SEGREGATED FUNDS	22				
APPLIED AS SINGLE PREMIUMS FOR: PAID-UP ADDITIONS	23				
REDUCING PREMIUMS	24				
OTHER	25				
	26				
SUB TOTAL DIRECT	▶ 27				
INCURRED ON REINSURANCE ACCEPTED	28				
RECEIVED ON REINSURANCE CEDED	29				
TOTAL NET OF CEDED (27+28-29)	▶ 30				

*INCLUDING EXPERIENCE RATING REFUNDS UNDER GROUP CONTRACTS

FIGURE 4-6 (cont.)

22 (RS)

NAME OF COMPANY ▶ _____   YEAR OF STATEMENT
                                                        19____

DIVIDENDS - LIFE ($'000)

	NON-PARTICIPATING				SUBTOTALS		
	INDIVIDUAL		GROUP		PARTIC-IPATING	NON-PARTIC-IPATING	TOTAL
	INSURANCE	ANNUITY	INSURANCE	ANNUITY			
	05	06	07	08	09	10	11
01							
02							
03							
▶ 04							
05							
06							
07							
▶ 08							
09							
10							
11							
▶ 12							
▶ 13							
14							
15							
16							
17							
18							
▶ 19							
20							
21							
22							
23							
24							
25							
26							
▶ 27							
28							
29							
▶ 30							

complete Exhibits 1 and 3 with information pertaining exclusively to business transacted outside of Canada. In addition, summary information regarding premiums can be found in the company's basic financial statements such as the Balance Sheet and the Income Statement.

Exhibit 1

Exhibit 1 is entitled "Premiums, Commissions, and Dividends—Life" (see Figure 4-6). The Canadian premium exhibit is divided into three parts— (1) premiums, (2) commissions, and (3) dividends to policyholders. For each of these divisions, insurers are required to record the dollar amounts in various classifications: participating and nonparticipating business, individual and group coverage, insurance premiums, and annuity considerations. As with the U.S. Statement, amounts are also shown separately for single premiums, first-year premiums, and renewal premiums. The dollar totals that are reported in this exhibit are all shown net of reinsurance. In the Canadian premium exhibit, only accrual-basis figures are shown. Thus, unlike U.S. Annual Statement Exhibit 1, neither cash-basis figures nor adjustments from cash to accrual basis are included.

Exhibit 3

Exhibit 3, "Premiums and Claims—Accident and Sickness," records accounting data on health insurance premiums and claims by major classifications of coverage. The Canadian accident and sickness premium exhibit differs from the Canadian life premiums and considerations exhibit in that both the amount of earned premiums and the total amount of premiums received are reported. Thus, the amount of unearned premiums for health insurance can be determined by subtracting the total premiums earned from the total amount of premiums received.

Exhibit 12

Details relating to the outstanding premium asset for a company's life, annuity, and accident and sickness business are shown in Exhibit 12, which is entitled "Outstanding Premiums (Net of Reinsurance Ceded)." Outstanding premiums are the Canadian equivalent of due and uncollected premiums in the United States. In this Exhibit, the value of the company's gross outstanding premiums is reduced by the estimated costs of collection and commission payments. Dollar totals in Exhibit 12 must be recorded by line of business and broken down into individual and group coverages. The resulting total of outstanding premiums net of reinsurance is then recorded on the Balance Sheet assets page as the company's total amount of premiums outstanding.

Miscellaneous

The third column of Exhibit 11, "Amounts on Deposit with the Company" (Annual Statement page 33), is used to record the amount of premium deposits received by the insurer for the payment of future life insurance premiums. This premium deposit amount is one of the items included in the total of *amounts on deposit with the company* reported on the Liabilities, Capital and Surplus page of the insurer's statutory Balance Sheet. The amount of interest accumulated on these deposits is reported in the Income Statement (Annual Statement page 4).

Key Terms

paid-to date
premium suspense
unearned premium
uncollected premium
deferred premium
outstanding premium

income recognition process
premium deposit
advance premium
collected premium
gross premium

Review Questions and Exercises

1. What are the functions of an insurer's premium reporting process?
2. What could the following journal entry represent as it applies to premium accounting?

    Returned Checks 40
    Cash 40

3. Under what circumstances would money remitted to an insurance company be classified as Premium Suspense? Is Premium Suspense an asset or liability account? Explain your answer.
4. Why do insurers discount the amount of premium deposits?
5. If a policyowner sent an insurer $650, with $150 to be applied to the current premium and $500 to be applied to premium deposits, what would the insurer's journal entry be to reflect receipt of this money?
6. What is the difference between advance premiums and premium deposits?
7. State the formula that U.S. insurers use for calculating accrual-basis premium income.

5
Accounting for Bond and Stock Investments

Learning Objectives

After reading this chapter, you should be able to:
- Understand the reasons for and the methods involved in determining an insurer's accrual-basis income for a reporting year
- Distinguish between the collected, unearned, accrued, due, and nonadmitted income classifications
- List the type of information included in the subsidiary ledger for bonds
- Distinguish between realized and unrealized capital gains
- Make the appropriate journal entries for the purchase and sale of bonds and stocks issued by other companies
- Explain why an insurer would purchase a bond at a discount or premium
- Describe the Annual Statement presentation and valuation of an insurer's bond and stock investments

Introduction

Investments play an integral role in the financial operations of life and health insurance companies. In calculating both the premium rates that a company should charge and the reserves that will be needed for the payment of future policy benefits, actuaries assume that a certain rate of return will be earned on the company's investments. If the actual rate of return falls short of the assumed rate, the company may experience a surplus drain that could prove harmful to operations.

Investments also represent the major asset owned by life and health insurance companies. In recent years, investments have constituted more than 90 percent of the assets of the life and health insurance industry. For life and health insurers, investments usually represent the second largest source of income after premium income. In some companies, investment income exceeds premium income. Funds available for investment can be used to acquire bonds, stocks, mortgage loans, and real estate. These funds can also be used for making policy loans and collateral loans as well as for investing in subsidiary companies. Because of (1) the number of investment alternatives available, (2) the number of investment transactions made by insurers, and (3) the legal restrictions placed on investing, a thorough understanding of investment accounting is important to the study of life and health insurance accounting. This chapter introduces the accounting principles used in determining investment income, the specific valuation methods used for bond and stock investments, and the reporting requirements for investment income.

Accounting for Investment Income

Investment income consists primarily of interest but can also include dividends and rental income. For the purpose of the United States Annual Statement, this income is recognized on an accrual basis rather than on a cash basis. Accrual-basis accounting attributes income and expenses to the period in which the income is earned or the expenses are incurred rather than when the cash is received or paid out. When financial statements are prepared on an accrual basis, a number of adjustments in account balances must be made at the time of financial reporting in order to match income and expenses to their proper reporting period. The accrual-basis amount of gross investment income represents the amount of income actually earned during the reporting year. This amount is calculated from the totals of various income classifications and is recorded in column 7 of U.S. Annual Statement Exhibit 3 (see Figure 5-1). Note that these calculations must be made for all types of investments.

The income classifications needed for determining accrual-basis income are collected income, unearned income, due income, accrued income, and nonadmitted income. Each type of investment does not necessarily result in each of these types of income. Definitions of these income classifications are as follows (the examples that accompany each definition assume that the reporting period is from January 1 of one year to December 31 of the same year and that the financial reporting date is December 31):

- **Income collected during the year,** or **collected income,** is the amount of income actually received in cash during a reporting period, including

FIGURE 5-1
Exhibit 3—U.S. Annual Statement.

	(1) COLLECTED DURING YEAR	CURRENT YEAR				(6) PREVIOUS YEAR (3) + (4) — (2) — (5)	(7) EARNED DURING YEAR (1) — (2) + (3) + (4) — (5) — (6)
		(2) UNEARNED	(3) DUE	(4) ACCRUED	(5) NON ADMITTED		

EXHIBIT 3 — GROSS INVESTMENT INCOME

1. U.S. government bonds .... *
1.1 Bonds exempt from U.S. tax . . . . . . *
1.2 Other bonds (unaffiliated). . . . . . . *
1.3 Bonds of affiliates. . . . . *
2.1 Preferred stocks (unaffiliated) . . . . . ‡
2.11 Preferred stocks of affiliates. . . . . . ‡
2.2 Common stocks (unaffiliated) . . . . .
2.21 Common stocks of affiliates . . . . .
3. Mortgage loans. . . . . **
4. Real estate . . . . §
5. Premium notes, policy loans and liens . .
6. Collateral loans. . . . .
7.1 Cash on hand and on deposit. . . . . .
7.2 Short-term investments. . . . . †
8. Other invested assets . . . .
9. ....
9.1 Financial options and futures . . . . .
10. Totals . . . .

*Includes $............accrual of discount less $............amortization of premium and less $............paid for accrued interest on purchases.
‡Excludes $............paid for accrued dividends on purchases.
**Includes $............accrual of discount less $............amortization of premium and less $............paid for accrued interest on purchases.
§Includes $............for company's occupancy of its own buildings; and excludes $............interest on encumbrances.
†Includes $............accrual of discount less $............amortization of premium and less $............paid for accrued interest on purchases.

certain adjustments for amortization as well as interest paid on home office purchase and occupancy (included in the footnotes to Exhibit 3). Thus, for the reporting period from January 1 to December 31, income received between these dates constitutes collected income.

- **Unearned income** is a subset of collected income. Unearned income is income that was collected by the insurer during the reporting period but that will not be earned until a later period and is applicable to the later period. For example, if interest is collected in December of the reporting year but was not scheduled for payment until the following year, then the amount of interest applicable to the following year is considered unearned income.
- **Due income** is income that was scheduled for payment prior to the financial reporting date, but which has not been received by the insurer as of the reporting date. For example, assume that interest on an investment is payable semiannually on June 1 and December 1. The interest payment scheduled for December 1 would be considered due income if it has not been received by December 31.
- **Accrued income** is comprised of income earned but not receivable until a specified date in the next reporting period. Using the dates

introduced in the example for due income, interest earned during December but not receivable until the following June would constitute accrued income.
- **Nonadmitted income** is comprised of due income that is overdue for more than a certain period—anywhere from three months to two years—as prescribed by state insurance laws. In classifying income as nonadmitted income, an insurer is implicitly stating that collection of this income is uncertain.

These income classifications are not mutually exclusive. As we stated above, unearned income is a subset of collected income. Therefore, some income items might be both unearned and collected. Similarly, certain income may be due and accrued if that income has both been earned and scheduled for payment prior to the reporting date. Other income might be accrued but not due if it has been earned but is not scheduled for payment until after the reporting date.

The determination of an insurer's accrual-basis investment income for a given reporting year includes an adjustment for the previous year's income. The calculation includes deducting the net of the previous year's due and accrued income minus the previous year's unearned and nonadmitted income. These totals must be obtained from the previous year's Annual Statement. By including this previous year adjustment, each item of income in the calculation is counted only once for the purpose of determining accrual-basis income.

Earned income is calculated using the totals of the five income classifications mentioned above and the previous year's adjustment. Through this calculation, an insurer determines the amount of income actually earned during a reporting period, as opposed to the amount that has been received during that period. To calculate the amount of **earned income,** or accrual-basis income, for a given year, the total of due and accrued income for the current year is added to the amount of interest actually collected during that year. From this total, three figures are subtracted: (1) unearned income for the current year; (2) nonadmitted income for the current year; and (3) the previous year adjustment, net of accrued, unearned, and nonadmitted income from the previous year.

For example, assume that the ABC Life Insurance Company's bond investments yielded the following interest income amounts as shown in Exhibit 3 of the U.S. Annual Statement:

Collected income (Column 1)	$90,000,000
Unearned income (Column 2)	6,000
Due income (Column 3)	300,000
Accrued income (Column 4)	30,000,000
Nonadmitted income (Column 5)	50,000
Previous-year adjustment (Column 6)	28,000,000

For the ABC Life Company, then, gross investment income for bonds for the current year would be calculated as

	$90,000,000	(Collected income)
+	300,000	(Due income)
+	30,000,000	(Accrued income)
−	6,000	(Unearned income)
−	50,000	(Nonadmitted income)
−	28,000,000	(Previous-year adjustment)
=	$92,244,000	(Gross investment income)

Canada

Canadian insurers also show investment income on an accrual basis. However, a Canadian insurer's accrual-basis or earned income need not be calculated on the Annual Statement itself. All Canadian insurers keep their books on an accrual basis and thus the amount of earned income can simply be reported in columns 1 and 3 of Exhibit 6 (see Figure 5-2). Due and accrued income is also reported in Exhibit 6, but no column is included for unearned investment income. Unearned income is, however, accounted for on the Liabilities, Capital and Surplus page of the insurer's Balance Sheet.

Accounting for Bonds and Stocks

Bonds

Bonds are certificates of indebtedness issued by corporations, governmental units, and other legal entities. These certificates are normally secured by the assets or the general credit of the issuing party. Although bonds are bought and sold like stocks, a bond does not give the holder any ownership interest in the issuing company, as a stock does. A bond is actually a contract in which the issuer of the bond agrees (1) to repay on a specified future date or dates the amount of money borrowed from the bond purchaser and (2) to pay a specified rate of interest on the borrowed amount while the indebtedness is outstanding. The amount borrowed is generally known as the **principal, par value, face value,** or **maturity value** of the bond. The date on which the principal is to be repaid or the last principal payment is to be made is the **maturity date.**

Bonds can be classified as either public offerings or private placements. **Public offerings** are bonds offered for sale to the general public. Such bonds must be registered with government agencies. **Private placements** are bonds offered by the bond issuer directly to specific financial institutions. Such bonds

FIGURE 5-2
Exhibit 6—Canadian Annual Statement.

28

NAME OF COMPANY ▶			YEAR OF STATEMENT 19	
EXHIBIT 6 - INVESTMENT INCOME (EXCLUDING SEGREGATED FUNDS) ($'000)				
	LIFE		ACCIDENT & SICKNESS	
	EARNED 01	DUE AND ACCRUED 02	EARNED 03	DUE AND ACCRUED 04
BONDS: INTEREST 01				
AMORTIZATION OF PREMIUM AND ACCRUAL OF DISCOUNT 02				
AMORTIZATION OF NET REALIZED GAINS AND LOSSES IN LIFE BRANCH 03		▓	▓	▓
SHARES: DIVIDENDS 04				
AMORTIZATION OF REALIZED AND UNREALIZED GAINS AND LOSSES IN LIFE BRANCH 05		▓		
MORTGAGE LOANS: INTEREST 06				
AMORTIZATION OF PREMIUM AND ACCRUAL OF DISCOUNT 07				
AMORTIZATION OF NET REALIZED GAINS AND LOSSES IN LIFE BRANCH 08		▓	▓	▓
INCOME FROM REAL ESTATE INCLUDING $ FOR COMPANY'S OCCUPANCY OF ITS OWN BUILDINGS 09				
INCOME FROM GROUND RENTS 10				
INTEREST ON POLICY LOANS 11			▓	▓
INTEREST ON TERM DEPOSITS AND GUARANTEED INVESTMENT CERTIFICATES 12				
INTEREST ON BANK DEPOSITS 13				
INTEREST ON OVERDUE PREMIUMS 14				
INCOME FROM OTHER INVESTMENTS 15				
CAPITAL GAINS & LOSSES ON INVESTED ASSETS - ACCIDENT & SICKNESS 16	▓	▓		
TOTALS: GROSS INVESTMENT INCOME ▶ 17				
INVESTMENT AND REAL ESTATE EXPENSES INCLUDING INTEREST INCURRED ON BORROWED MONEY 18				
INVESTMENT TAXES 19				
REGULAR ANNUAL DEPRECIATION OF REAL ESTATE 20				
TOTAL: INVESTMENT EXPENSES, INVESTMENT TAXES & DEPRECIATION (ITEMS 18 TO 20) ▶ 21				
NET INVESTMENT INCOME (ITEMS 17-21) ▶ 22				

need not be registered with government agencies. The terms of privately placed bonds are negotiable between the seller and the investor.

For each bond owned, insurers typically establish a subsidiary ledger account that contains all the information necessary to identify the bond. Such information can include the principal amount, interest rate, interest payment dates, issuer, issue date, and maturity date of the bond, as well as any debit and credit transactions affecting the ledger balance. As subsidiary ledgers are created for each individual investment, control accounts are maintained in the general ledger for each investment classification—short-term bonds, long-term bonds, etc. The total of the subsidiary ledger account balances for a specific investment classification must always be equal to the control account balance for that investment classification.

Certain information about a bond, including its interest rate and maturity date, is printed on the bond certificate that is issued to the bond owner. Bond interest is typically payable semiannually. Thus, the owner of a $1,000 par value bond paying an annual interest rate of 10 percent is entitled to a $50 interest payment twice each year ($1,000 par value × 10 percent rate of interest ÷ 2 payments each year). The rate of interest specified on the bond certificate is known as the **coupon rate,** the **stated rate,** or the **nominal rate.** The regular interest rate payments are sometimes referred to as *coupon payments.*

Bonds are a major investment vehicle for insurance companies. In 1985, bonds comprised approximately 51 percent of the assets of U.S. life and health insurance companies and approximately 44 percent of the assets of Canadian life and health insurance companies. As mentioned earlier, insurers must be reasonably certain that their investments provide the return necessary to meet future obligations such as the payment of death claims, medical benefits, annuities, and matured endowments. Since bonds offer a predictable amount of income in the form of interest, insurers can be reasonably certain that their bond investments will provide the necessary investment return. Insurers typically invest in bonds issued by corporations rather than those issued by governments since the former usually provide a higher rate of interest. Some companies, however, traditionally invest in government bonds rather than corporate bonds. Insurers must use discretion in choosing the types and issuers of bonds for investment since the safety of the principal must be assured.

Corporations and governmental authorities that issue bonds use a variety of means to secure the safety of an investor's principal amount. A corporation issuing bonds generally promises that, in the case of the issuing company's default, property or assets pledged by the issuer may be sold in order to pay off the claims of the bond owners. A bond is said to be *secured* by such property or assets. For example, corporations issue **mortgage bonds,** which are secured by land and buildings owned by the bond issuer, and **collateral trust bonds,** which are secured by negotiable securities owned by the bond issuer.

Governments also issue a number of types of bonds. Municipal bonds may be classified as either general obligation bonds or special obligation bonds. **General obligation bonds** are secured by the general taxing power of the issuing governmental unit, and **special obligation bonds,** or **revenue bonds,** are secured by revenue from a restricted source such as a toll bridge or a water system, or by a special tax source such as gasoline taxes or special property taxes. Bonds that are secured by the full faith and credit of the issuing governmental unit are also sold by the U.S. and Canadian federal governments as well as state and provincial governments.

Accounting for the purchase and sale of bonds

When bonds are purchased, they are recorded on an insurer's books at cost. Insurers generally record the purchase of a $1,000 bond at par value by debiting an investment asset account, such as Bonds Owned, and crediting Cash for the cost—in this case, the face value—of the purchased bond. Thus, an entry to record the purchase of a $1,000 bond at par value is:

    Bonds Owned 1,000
        Cash 1,000

Bond investments may result in capital gains or losses for an insurer. For accounting purposes, these gains and losses are categorized in the United States as either realized or unrealized. (For Canadian insurers, no distinction is made between realized and unrealized capital gains or losses. This aspect of Canadian investment accounting is discussed later in this chapter.) In the United States, a **realized** capital gain or loss would generally result only from the sale of a bond or other asset. The amount of realized gain or loss from the sale of an asset is the difference between that asset's sale price and its book value or amortized cost (to be discussed later in this chapter). If the asset's sale price is greater than its book value or amortized cost, the sale results in a gain that is referred to on the Annual Statement as *profit on sale or maturity.* Similarly, if the asset's book value or amortized cost exceeds the sale price, a loss results that is referred to on the Annual Statement as *loss on sale or maturity.*

Unrealized capital gains and losses, on the other hand, do not result from the sale of an asset. For certain invested assets—stocks, certain bonds, and mortgages with nonadmitted values—these gains and losses reflect the difference between the asset's book value and its market value. An asset's **market value** is the price that the asset would command if it were offered for sale instead of being retained in the insurer's portfolio. For insurers in the United States, unrealized capital gains and losses are reported in columns 1, 3, and 5 of Annual Statement Exhibit 4 (see Figure 5-3). Unrealized capital gains and losses apply primarily to common stocks.

FIGURE 5-3
Exhibit 4—U.S. Annual Statement.

	EXHIBIT 4 — CAPITAL GAINS AND LOSSES ON INVESTMENTS					
	(1) INCREASE IN BOOK VALUE	(2) PROFIT ON SALE OR MATURITY	(3) DECREASE IN BOOK VALUE	(4) LOSS ON SALE OR MATURITY	(5) NET GAIN (+) OR LOSS (−) FROM CHANGE IN DIFFERENCE BETWEEN BOOK AND ADMITTED VALUES	(6) NET GAINS (+) OR LOSSES (−) (1) + (2) − (3) − (4) + (5)
1. U.S. government bonds						
1.1 Bonds exempt from U.S. tax						
1.2 Other bonds (unaffiliated)						
1.3 Bonds of affiliates						
2.1 Preferred stocks (unaffiliated)						
2.11 Preferred stocks of affiliates						
2.2 Common stocks (unaffiliated)						
2.21 Common stocks of affiliates						
3. Mortgage loans						
4. Real estate			**			
5. Premium notes, policy loans and liens						
6. Collateral loans						
7.1 Cash on hand and on deposit						
7.2 Short-term investments						
8. Other invested assets			**			
9. Foreign exchange	x x x	x x x	x x x	x x x		
9.1 Financial options and futures						
9.2						
10. Totals						

10.1 Less federal income taxes incurred on capital gains
10.2 Balance to Surplus Account, Page 4, Item 34
   Distribution of Line 10.2, Col. 6. (Attach statement or memorandum explaining basis of division.)
11. Net realized capital gains (+) or losses (−) on assets disposed of during the year $............... less $............... reflected in previous years' statements and less $............... federal income tax incurred on capital gains
12. Net unrealized capital gains (+) or losses (−) of the year

*Adjustments due to amortization to be reported in Exhibit 3.
**Excluding $............... depreciation on real estate and $............... depreciation on other invested assets included in Exhibit 2, Line 4.

To determine whether a capital gain or loss has resulted from the sale of an asset, an accountant must know the value of the asset being sold. In accounting for the sale of a bond, both the bond's sale price and its purchase price are recorded on a net basis. This net basis reflects adjustments for expenses incurred in the purchase and sale of bonds. These expenses are largely made up of commissions paid to brokers. Expenses incurred in *purchasing* a bond are *added* to the purchase price, while expenses incurred in *selling* a bond are *subtracted* from the sale price. To illustrate, if the purchase price of a bond is $1,000 and the commission paid to a broker on this purchase is $50, the bond's cost that is recorded on the insurer's books is $1,050 ($1,000 purchase price + $50 commission). Thus, an appropriate journal entry to record such a bond purchase is:

> Bonds Owned 1,050
>   Cash 1,050

If this same bond is subsequently sold for $1,150, after a deduction for broker's commissions, the sale would result in a $100 *realized* capital gain for the insurer ($1,150 sale price − $1,050 purchase price). An appropriate journal entry to record this bond sale is:

> Cash 1,150
>   Bonds Owned 1,050
>   Profit on Sale of Bonds 100

The $1,150 debit to Cash represents the net proceeds of the bond sale.

When interest on a bond is received, the journal entry used to record receipt of that bond interest consists of a debit to Cash and a credit to an income account such as Interest Income on Bonds. Thus, the journal entry to record receipt of $100 of bond interest would be:

> Cash 100
>   Interest Income on Bonds 100

Accrued bond interest income. Accrued bond interest income is the amount of interest on a particular bond that has been earned but that is not yet payable. If a bond is sold between interest payments, the new owner will receive any accrued interest income as part of the next interest payment, even though such interest was actually earned by the seller. To compensate the seller for lost interest, the bond's purchase price must include an amount equal to the interest income that has accrued up to the purchase date.

The journal entries showing the purchase of a bond with accrued interest income can be illustrated with an example. If a $1,000 bond with a 10 percent interest rate is purchased at par with $20 interest accrued as of the purchase date, the journal entry on the purchaser's books would be:

> Bonds Owned 1,000
> Interest Income on Bonds 20
>   Cash 1,020

The debit to Interest Income on Bonds serves two purposes. It demonstrates that the additional $20 paid to the bond's seller above the face value is attributable to interest income that the seller would have received had the bond not been sold. In addition, when the next semiannual interest payment is received by the bond's new owner, the debit to Interest Income on Bonds will record a decrease in the new owner's income from this bond. When the next interest payment of $50 is received, the entry to record receipt of the payment is:

```
            Cash ..................................50
                  Interest Income on Bonds ......................50
```

The $20 debit to Interest Income on Bonds at the time of purchase and the $50 credit to that account at the time the interest is received result in a credit balance of $30. Since the semiannual interest payment on this bond equals $50, and the previous owner earned $20 of this amount, the credit balance of $30 in the Interest Income on Bonds account reflects the correct amount of interest earned by the new owner.

Some insurance companies debit accrued interest on bond purchases to an account created specifically for payment of such interest. By creating such an account, a total of the accrued interest payments made by an insurer can be easily obtained. Insurers are required to provide this information in a footnote to U.S. Annual Statement Exhibit 3. Canadian insurers are not required to report separately the amount of accrued interest on purchases.

Bond discount and premium

As mentioned earlier, the annual amount of interest paid on a bond is a fixed amount that is determined by multiplying the par value of the bond by the bond's stated rate of interest. This amount is payable to the bond owner regardless of the actual price paid for the bond. If a price other than par is paid, the actual rate of return—known as the **effective rate** or **yield**—on the amount paid for the bond will differ from the stated rate of return.

The difference between the price paid for a bond (disregarding any accrued interest) and the bond's par value is known as a **discount** if the price paid for the bond is lower than par, and as a **premium** if the price paid for the bond is higher than par. As a general rule, when a bond is purchased at a discount, the effective rate of return will exceed the stated rate of return. Conversely, when a bond is purchased at a premium, the effective rate of return will be lower than the stated rate of return.

An insurer would purchase a bond at a discount or premium in order to achieve a desirable rate of return on a particular investment. For example, assume that the current interest rate available on newly issued bonds is 12 percent. On any of its bond investments, the insurer generally would want to receive at least the 12 percent rate of return that could be realized in the current bond market. To realize this rate of return, the insurer could buy a bond with a stated rate of 12 percent. However, 12 percent bonds may not be available for purchase at that time. In such a case, the insurer could purchase, at a discount, a bond with a lower stated rate of return. Alternatively, the insurer could pay a premium for a bond with a higher stated rate of return. In either case, the insurer's investment could yield the rate of return currently available on similar investments.

To illustrate, assume that the ABC Life Company is buying a $1,000 par value 8 percent bond that matures in one year. In the case of ABC's bond purchase, however, the insurer hopes to realize a 10 percent effective rate of return. To realize this 10 percent rate of return, the insurer would pay $982—an amount less than the bond's par value—to the bond owner. By buying the bond for $982, the insurer has purchased the bond at an $18 discount. Upon maturity of the bond, the insurer will have collected $1,080 ($1,000 maturity value plus $80 interest income)—a 10 percent return on the $982 investment.

Assume, on the other hand, that when the bond market interest rate is 10 percent, the only bonds available for purchase are previously issued $1,000 par value bonds that mature in one year with a 12 percent stated rate of interest. Since the owner of these bonds is presently earning 2 percent more interest than is available in the current market, the insurer would have to pay an amount in excess of the $1,000 par value to make the sale of the 12 percent bonds worthwhile to the current owner. By paying a premium for the bonds, the insurer will realize an effective rate of return lower than the stated rate of return.

For example, assume that an insurer wishes to purchase a $1,000 par value 12 percent bond that matures in one year in order to realize a 10 percent rate of return. (While an insurer might want to earn 12 percent on the investment, in a market dominated by 10 percent interest rates, a bond owner would not likely be relinquishing an investment at a price that yielded 12 percent. The money received from such a sale could only be reinvested at the current 10 percent rate, assuming a similar investment vehicle. In exchanging a 12 percent rate of return for a 10 percent rate of return, the bondowner making the exchange would be, in effect, accepting a loss of potential income.) To achieve the desired 10 percent rate of return, the insurer would have to pay the bondowner $1,018 for the $1,000 par value bond. Upon maturity of the bond, the insurer will have collected $1,120 for its investment ($1,000 maturity value + $120 coupon income), a 10 percent effective rate of return on its $1,018 investment.

The price that an investor is willing to pay for a bond is the bond's *market value*. A bond's market value is equal to the present value, at the effective rate of interest, of (1) the amount due at maturity of the bond and (2) the annual interest payments. For example, assume that a $1,000 eight percent 10-year bond is purchased one year after the issue date to yield a 10 percent effective rate of return. The present values—at the 10 percent effective rate of return—of the $1,000 maturity value and the $720 interest income (8 percent × $1,000 × 9 years) result in a market value for that bond of $885. (Knowledge of the exact method of calculating present values is not necessary for this discussion.) The entry to record the purchase of a $1,000 par value bond at a $115 discount ($1,000 − $885), assuming no purchase expenses, consists of an $885 debit to Bonds Owned and a credit to Cash for the same amount.

Amortization of premium or discount. On bonds that are purchased at a discount or premium, an amortization entry is made to those bonds' accounts during each accounting period. **Amortization** is the accounting process by which the book value of an investment is periodically and systematically adjusted so that, on the maturity date, the book value equals that investment's par value. Amortization is necessary because it allocates the amount of discount or premium to the full period of the insurer's ownership of the bond. Such allocation serves to match the correct amount of interest income to the period in which the income will be earned. The amortization process is demonstrated in the following example.

Assume that a 5-year $10,000 par value bond has a stated interest rate of 8 percent, and an insurer has purchased one of these bonds eighteen months after the issue date. The bond has been purchased to yield an effective rate of 10 percent. Based on the formula introduced earlier (present value at the effective rate of interest of both the par value and the unmatured interest income), the purchase price would be $9,421 (rounded to the nearest dollar). The entry to record the purchase of this bond is:

> Bonds Owned 9,421
>   Cash 9,421

When the bond owner receives the first semiannual interest payment of $400 ($10,000 par value × 8 percent interest rate × ½ year), the receipt of the interest payment is recorded on the insurer's books as a debit to Cash and a credit to Interest Income on Bonds. The entry is:

> Cash 400
>   Interest Income on Bonds 400

An amortization entry must also be made at this time. The cost of the bonds ($9,421) multiplied by the bonds' effective rate for one-half year (10 percent × ½) equals $471. An additional $71 ($471 − $400) is credited to the income account to reflect the additional amount of investment income. A debit to Bonds Owned for $71 serves to increase the book value of the bonds. The amortization entry is:

> Bonds Owned 71
>   Interest Income on Bonds 71

(Some U.S. insurers record the entries for accrual of discount or amortization of premium in a separate interest account since this information is required for completion of U.S. Annual Statement Exhibit 3.) This entry increases the interest income on the insurer's books to $471 for the six months and also increases the book value of these bonds to $9,492. To determine the amortization entry for the next half-year period, $9,492 must be multiplied by one-half of 10 percent at the end of the year. The result of this calculation is $475. Subsequently, the amortization entry for this half-year period will be for $75 ($475 − $400 stated interest). The amortization process is continued each six months until the maturity date when the book value of the bonds is equal to their par value. Figure 5-4 shows the amortization process over the life of this bond.

If a bond is purchased at a premium, the amortization entry is the reverse of that described for bonds purchased at a discount. For bonds purchased at a premium, the effective rate of interest is lower than the stated rate. As a result, the income account must be debited to decrease earned income and the asset account must be credited to reduce the book value of the bonds.

For example, assume that the ABC Life Insurance Company has purchased a 5-year $1,000 bond with an 8 percent stated rate of interest. If, because of current market rates, ABC desired a 6 percent effective rate of return, the insurer would pay $1,085.30—a premium of $85.30—for this bond. The amortization amount for the first six months is $7.44 ($40 at the stated rate minus $32.56 at the effective rate). The amortization entry is:

    Interest Income on Bonds 7.44
        Bonds Owned 7.44

Upon recording this entry, the book value of the bond is reduced to $1,077.86. This amount is used to determine the amortization entry for the next interest

FIGURE 5-4
A discount amortization table.

	(1) Book Value	(2) Interest at Stated Rate	(3) Interest at Effective Rate	(4) Amortization Amount	(5) Adjusted Book Value
1	9,421.00	400.00	471.00	71.00	9,492.00
2	9,492.00	400.00	475.00	75.00	9,567.00
3	9,567.00	400.00	478.00	78.00	9,645.00
4	9,645.00	400.00	482.00	82.00	9,727.00
5	9,727.00	400.00	486.00	86.00	9,813.00
6	9,813.00	400.00	491.00	91.00	9,904.00
7	9,904.00	400.00	496.00	96.00	10,000.00

Note that column (3) minus column (4) (interest at the effective rate minus the amortization amount) always results in the amount in column (2)—the stated interest rate amount.

period. As with bonds purchased at a discount, this amortization process is continued each six months until the bond's maturity date when the book value of the bond is equal to its par value. Figure 5-5 shows the complete amortization process for a bond purchased at a premium.

In an alternative method of accounting for bonds purchased at a discount or premium, a separate account is established for the discount or premium, and the bond is carried on the owner's books at par value. For Annual Statement valuation, the statement value of a bond recorded on the books in this manner is still the par value adjusted for the premium or discount as applicable. (Annual Statement valuation is discussed later in this chapter.) With the alternate method of bond accounting, the entry for a $1,000 bond purchased for $950 on the first day of an interest period is:

        Bonds Owned 1,000
            Unaccrued Discount on Bonds 50
            Cash 950

When each interest installment is received, the amortization entry would be recorded as:

        Unaccrued Discount on Bonds xxx
            Interest Income on Bonds xxx

FIGURE 5-5
A premium amortization table.

	(1) Book Value	(2) Interest at Stated Rate	(3) Interest at Effective Rate	(4) Amortization Amount	(5) Adjusted Book Value
1	1,085.30	40.00	32.56	−7.44	1,077.86
2	1,077.86	40.00	32.34	−7.66	1,070.19
3	1,070.19	40.00	32.11	−7.89	1,062.30
4	1,062.30	40.00	31.87	−8.13	1,054.17
5	1,054.17	40.00	31.63	−8.37	1,045.79
6	1,045.79	40.00	31.37	−8.63	1,037.17
7	1,037.17	40.00	31.12	−8.88	1,028.28
8	1,028.28	40.00	30.85	−9.15	1,019.13
9	1,019.13	40.00	30.57	−9.43	1,009.71
10	1,009.71	40.00	30.29	−9.71	1,000.00

Note that column (3) minus column (4) (interest at the effective rate minus the amortization amount) always results in the amount in column (2)—the stated interest rate amount.

(The totals for these amortization entries depend, as mentioned earlier, on the effective rate and the stated rate of interest of the bond in question.) If this bond is resold before its maturity date, the Unaccrued Discount on Bonds account would be debited with an amount that would bring that account's balance to zero.

Under this alternative method of accounting for the purchase of bonds, if a premium is paid, then the purchase amount is debited to an Unamortized Premium on Bonds account at the time of purchase. Amortization amounts are subsequently credited to the Unamortized Premium on Bonds account and debited to Interest Income on Bonds.

Stocks

Shares of capital stock represent units of ownership in a corporation. An investor who purchases stock in a corporation is issued a stock certificate that indicates the number of shares of the corporation's stock owned by that investor. Investment income resulting from stock ownership generally is in the form of cash dividends paid to the stock owner. Dividends are occasionally paid in the form of additional shares of the corporation's stock and, in this case, are known as stock dividends.

Capital stock is generally assigned a par value that is printed on each stock certificate. The par value of a stock, however, has no effect on the stockholder's accounting for the purchase or sale of stock, nor does the par value have any impact on the market value of the stock. The market value of a single share of stock is the amount that a buyer would pay for that one share on any given day. Dividends may be expressed as a percentage of the par value, but more commonly they are expressed in terms of dollars per share.

Life and health companies invest in stocks to diversify and to provide a higher long-term average rate of return than other investments. The two major classes of capital stock are **common stock** and **preferred stock**. Common stocks have greater investment risk for life companies than bonds or preferred stocks since, unlike those investments, the rate of return on common stocks (1) is rarely guaranteed and (2) is more strongly influenced by market and economic conditions. Since life and health insurance companies must meet or exceed the rate of return assumed by actuaries for the establishment of both policy premium rates and the future policy benefit reserves, insurers should exercise considerable caution when choosing common stock for investment purposes. Most jurisdictions limit the amount of common stock that an insurer can own.

The Stocks Owned account referred to throughout the following examples is a general ledger account. A subsidiary ledger is kept for each specific block of stock owned. The subsidiary ledger for a particular stock typically includes the date and amount of the transaction, the number of shares owned, and a description of the issuing company. In addition, the market value per share of each stock owned on December 31 is noted in the stock's subsidiary record to facilitate the preparation of the Annual Statement and to determine any gain or loss that may result from sale of the stock.

Accounting for the purchase and sale of stock

Accounting principles for the purchase and sale of stock are similar to the accounting principles for the purchase and sale of bonds. The stockholder records stock purchases at cost. For example, if an insurance company purchases 100 shares of XYZ Corporation stock for $89 per share, the transaction is recorded by debiting the cost of the stock to the Stocks Owned asset account and crediting Cash for the same amount. The entry is:

    Stocks Owned 8,900
        Cash 8,900

If commission costs or other costs of purchase are incurred, they generally are *not* recorded separately in the journal entry, but the totals of these expenses are included in the Stocks Owned and Cash entries. If $600 in expenses were incurred in this purchase, the entry for the purchase would be:

    Stocks Owned 9,500
        Cash 9,500

When an insurer sells stock that it owns in another corporation, the Cash account is credited for the number of shares sold multiplied by the market price per share at the time of sale. Assume that the insurer in the above example sold the XYZ stock that was purchased for $9,500 at a price of $7,500. In such a case, the journal entry to record the stock sale would be:

    Cash 7,500
    Loss on the Sale of Stock 2,000
        Stocks Owned 9,500

Accounting for stock dividends. When a company declares a stock dividend, stockholders receive additional shares of the company's stock rather than cash. A stock dividend is declared as a percentage of outstanding stock. Consequently, the amount of stock received is based on the amount of stock owned by the stockholder at the time. If an insurer owns stock in a company that declares a stock dividend, no journal entry is required in the insurer's general ledger account to record the dividend. Since no change in the total cost of the stock is involved, a journal entry could not, in fact, be made. The number of shares received as a dividend, however, is noted on the subsidiary account for that stock so that the correct cost per share can be calculated in determining appropriate gains or losses if the stock is sold.

For example, assume that an insurance company owns 100 shares of XYZ Corporation stock that was purchased at a cost of $9,000. If XYZ declares a 50 percent stock dividend, holders of XYZ stock are entitled to a 50 percent increase in the number of shares owned. Hence, the number of shares of XYZ stock that the insurer owns would increase to 150. On the insurer's books, the $9,000 cost of the stock remains unaffected, but the book value per share in this case is lowered in the subsidiary account from $90 ($9,000 cost ÷ 100 shares) to $60 ($9,000 cost ÷ 150 shares).

If the insurer sells any of this stock, the gain or loss on the sale is measured as the difference between the sale price and the adjusted cost of $60 per share. Thus, if the insurance company sells 50 shares of the XYZ stock for $65 per share (after expenses of sale), the profit on that sale is $250 [($65 selling price − $60 cost per share) × 50 shares]. The entry to record the sale is a debit to Cash for $3,250 ($65 × 50 shares), a credit to Stocks Owned for $3,000 ($60 cost per share × 50 shares), and a credit to a capital gain account for the realized gain of $250. The entry is:

```
Cash . . . . . . . . . . . . . . . . . . . . . . . . . . . . . . . 3,250
    Stocks Owned . . . . . . . . . . . . . . . . . . . . . . . . . . . 3,000
    Gain on Sale of Stock . . . . . . . . . . . . . . . . . . . . . 250
```

As another example, if all 150 shares had been sold at $70 per share, the entry would have been:

```
Cash . . . . . . . . . . . . . . . . . . . . . . . . . . . . . . . 10,500
    Stocks Owned . . . . . . . . . . . . . . . . . . . . . . . . . . . 9,000
    Gain on Sale of Stock . . . . . . . . . . . . . . . . . . . . . 1,500
```

On the other hand, stock sold after a dividend has been declared can also result in capital losses. If all 150 shares of stock in the previous example were sold for $55 per share, the insurer would have a realized capital loss of $750 [($60 − $55) × 150 shares]. The amount received on the sale would be $8,250 ($55 × 150 shares), and a capital loss account, Loss on the Sale of Stock, would be debited for the difference between the cost and the sale price of the stock. The entry is:

```
Cash . . . . . . . . . . . . . . . . . . . . . . . . . . . . . . . 8,250
Loss on Sale of Stock . . . . . . . . . . . . . . . . . . . . . 750
    Stocks Owned . . . . . . . . . . . . . . . . . . . . . . . . . . . 9,000
```

Accounting for cash dividends. Cash dividends are considered income for stockholders on the date the dividends are received. The entry for a $1 per share cash dividend received for 200 shares of stock owned is:

```
Cash . . . . . . . . . . . . . . . . . . . . . . . . . . . . . . . 200
    Dividends Received . . . . . . . . . . . . . . . . . . . . . . . . 200
```

If the cash dividend has been declared before a reporting date and is payable after that date, the amount of the dividend is recorded on the Annual Statement as accrued income, provided the insurer held the stock as of the ex-dividend date. The **ex-dividend date,** or **ex-date,** is the date that determines whether the stockholder is eligible to receive the declared dividend.

Annual Statement Aspects of Bond and Stock Investments—United States

Insurers must account for their investments in many sections of the NAIC Annual Statement. Specific information on most of an insurer's bond and stock investments are reported in detail in Schedule D of the Annual Statement. Short-term bond investments are reported in Schedule D-A. From the information reported in Schedule D and Schedule D-A, insurers construct various exhibits that detail many aspects of the status and performance of that insurer's invested assets. A brief overview of the major Annual Statement investment exhibits follows.

Exhibit 4—Capital Gains and Losses on Investments, introduced in reference to bond accounting, shows the amount of gains and losses on an insurer's investments. Although changes in the book values of assets do not contribute to realized gains or losses, these changes do result in unrealized gains and losses for an insurer. Exhibit 4 includes columns for recording information in the changes in book values since the changes must be accounted for when determining the *net* capital gains and losses for a reporting year.

Exhibit 3—Gross Investment Income was presented in the discussion of accounting for investment income. The information recorded in Exhibit 3 is essential for determining the net investment income calculated in Annual Statement Exhibit 2. **Net investment income** can be described as the total of gross investment income minus any expenses, taxes, and depreciation recorded or incurred during the reporting year. In Exhibit 2, the ratio of net investment income to mean assets is also presented.

Exhibit 13—Assets includes columns for recording ledger assets, nonledger assets, and nonadmitted assets. The book values of an insurer's investments are recorded in the column for ledger assets. Nonledger assets relating to bond and stock investments generally refer to common stock values. For common stock investments, nonledger assets would be the excess of market value over book value. However, if the book value of stocks owned is greater than the stocks' market value, the difference is considered an unrealized capital loss. For bonds, nonadmitted assets generally refer to the values of bonds that are in default or not in good standing.

Annual Statement Valuation of Bonds and Stocks

Each year, the NAIC publishes a Valuation of Securities manual that insurers in the United States are required to use when preparing their Annual Statements. This manual prescribes the procedures for valuing bond and stock assets. The values of the securities listed on an insurer's Annual Statement are considered to reflect their value as of December 31 of the reporting year.

Bonds

On an insurer's Annual Statement, bonds are recorded at their admitted value, or statement value, which is generally the bonds' amortized cost. The **amortized cost** of a bond is the amount originally paid for the bond, adjusted for amortization of the bond premium or discount as applicable. Some bonds, however, are considered by the NAIC to be unamortizable or valued at less than their cost because they are in default or are considered to be poor investment risks. For the purposes of the U.S. Annual Statement, unamortizable bonds are valued at their market values, which are assumed to be less than the amortized cost. Even though U.S. insurers do not typically adjust the book value of bonds to show their market value, on December 31, most insurers note the market value of such investments on the subsidiary ledgers for those investments.

The NAIC Annual Statement requires that an insurer group its bond investments by the type of organization that issued the bonds. The types of issuing organizations are listed in Schedule D as follows (see Figure 5-6): (1) federal governments; (2) states, territories, and possessions; (3) political subdivisions of states, territories, and possessions; (4) revenue and special assessment obligations of governments and their political subdivisions; (5) railroads; (6) public utilities; (7) industrial and miscellaneous sources; and (8) parents, subsidiaries, and affiliates.

Stocks

Most common stocks owned by an insurer are listed on the U.S. Annual Statement at their market value as of the statement date. Two exceptions, however, should be noted. First, the NAIC determines the statement values of common stocks that are not publicly traded. Second, the common stock of an insurer's subsidiary or affiliated companies and other companies controlled by the insurer can be valued by any of a number of methods prescribed by the NAIC. Regardless of the method used, insurers must make sure that the valuation basis used and the resultant values are appropriate to the circumstances. The common stock of all subsidiary, controlled, and affiliated companies need not be valued on the same basis.

FIGURE 5-6
Schedule D, Part 1—U.S. Annual Statement.

30

Bonds to be grouped in the following manner and each group arranged alphabetically.
(The listing in Groups 2, 3 and 4 should be alphabetical by State.) Show sub-totals for each group

Form 1249
1. Governments (including all obligations guaranteed by governments).
2. States, Territories and Possessions (direct and guaranteed).
3. Political Subdivisions of States, Territories and Possessions (direct and guaranteed).
4. Special revenue and special assessment obligations and all non-guaranteed obligations of agencies and authorities of governments and their political subdivisions.
5. Railroads. (unaffiliated)
6. Public Utilities. (unaffiliated)
7. Industrial and Miscellaneous. (unaffiliated)
8. Parent, Subsidiaries and Affiliates.

ANNUAL STATEMENT FOR THE YEAR 1985 OF THE ....
Name

SCHEDULE D — Part 1

Showing all Long-term BONDS Owned December 31 of Current Year

Supplemental columns for data concerning Amortization. SEE NOTE

(1) **DESCRIPTION		(2) INTEREST		(3) DATE OF				(4)	(5)	(6)	(7)	(8)	INTEREST		(10)	(11)	(12)	(13)	(14)	(15)	(16)	(17)	(18)
CUSIP Identification ***	Give complete and accurate description of all bonds owned, including the location of all street railway and miscellaneous companies. If bonds are "serial" issues give amount maturing each year.	Rate of	*How Paid	Maturity		††Option		BOOK VALUE	PAR VALUE	Rate Used to Obtain Market Value	§§MARKET VALUE (excluding accrued interest)	ACTUAL COST (excluding accrued interest)	(9.1) Amount Due and Accrued Dec. 31 of Current Year on bonds not in default	(9.2) Gross Am't Received During Year	Increase by Adjustment in Book Value During Year	Decrease by Adjustment in Book Value During Year	Amount of Interest due and accrued Dec. 31, current year, on bonds in default as to principal or interest	§NAIC Designation	Year Acquired	Effective Rate of Interest at Which Purchase Was Made	†Amortized or Investment Value Dec. 31 of Current Year	‡Increase in Amortized Value During Year	‡Decrease in Amortized Value During Year
				Year	Month	Year	Call Price																

§§Where a market value is published in the NAIC Valuation of Securities Manual, it must be entered in Column 7. Where amortized value or any other value is used, insert a symbol alongside the amount reported.

*Insert initial letters of months in which interest is payable.

**Where a bond is payable in a foreign currency the par value and purchase price in that currency should be included as a part of the description.

***From entry in the previous year's Annual Statement if owned at that time; from the purchase confirmation (or certificate) if purchased subsequently. Leave blank for private placements.

†Perpetual bonds, bonds in default as to principal or interest and bonds not amply secured, are to be entered in this column at market value.

‡Companies which use "Amortized Values" as "Book Values" may omit entering figures in these columns, and provide the following footnote:
"The increases and decreases in amortized values are the same as those shown in columns for 'Increase and Decrease by Adjustment in Book Value,' excepting as otherwise indicated."

§Insert the NAIC designation for such security printed in the NAIC Valuation of Securities Manual.

NOTE—This supplemental information, required of all Companies which amortize their bonds, is not to be used as a substitute for the information required in the preceding columns but in addition thereto.

††Show year and call price pertaining to option, if any, on which amortization is based. On bonds purchased at a premium, the maturity date or call feature producing lowest amortized value should be used.

Most preferred stock in good standing is valued at its cost. Preferred stock not in good standing is valued at the lower of cost or market values as quoted by the NAIC. For preferred stocks not listed by the NAIC, insurers report the stocks' market value or other applicable value as of December 31 of the reporting year. As with bonds, Schedule D of the Annual Statement (see Figure 5-7) groups stocks owned into certain classifications. For stocks, the groupings are: (1) railroads; (2) public utilities; (3) banks, trusts, and insurance companies; (4) industrial and miscellaneous companies; and (5) parents, subsidiaries, and affiliates.

Annual Statement Aspects of Bond and Stock Investments—Canada

Capital gains and losses for a Canadian insurer are reported in Exhibit 8 of the Canadian Annual Statement. Two primary differences exist between the Canadian capital gains exhibit and Exhibit 4 of the U.S. Annual Statement. First, the terminology differs slightly between the two statements. In Canada, the "writing up" and "writing down" of an investment's book value is equivalent to an increase or decrease in the book value of investments in the United States. Second, the Canadian exhibit makes no reference to the admitted values of an insurer's investment assets. In Canada, the book value of an investment asset is that investment's admitted value. Exhibit 6 of the Canadian Annual Statement is the equivalent of Exhibits 2 and 3 of the U.S. Statement in which investment income items are reported. As mentioned earlier, unlike in the United States, adjustments to an accrual basis are not shown in the Canadian Annual Statement since accrual-basis income is already reflected in the company's accounts. Exhibit 7 is used for calculating the net rate of return on the company's cash and invested assets.

Bonds

An insurer's bond investments are presented in Schedule A of the Canadian Annual Statement. Bonds issued by the Canadian federal government, Canadian provinces, the Treasury Department of the United States, and the government of the United Kingdom are valued on an amortized basis. All other bonds are valued in accordance with market values published annually by the Standing Committee on Valuation of Securities of the Association of Superintendents of Insurance of the Provinces of Canada. Unlike the U.S. Annual Statement, the Canadian Annual Statement does not show individual purchases and sales of bonds and stocks, although Canadian life and health companies are required to file semi-annual reports regarding these purchases and sales.

FIGURE 5-7
Schedule D, Part 2—U.S. Annual Statement.

Form 14

Stocks to be grouped in following order and each group arranged alphabetically:
- Railroads. (unaffiliated)
- Public Utilities. (unaffiliated)
- Banks, Trust and Insurance Companies. (unaffiliated)
- Industrial and Miscellaneous. (unaffiliated)
- Parent, Subsidiaries and Affiliates.

Show sub-totals for each group.

ANNUAL STATEMENT FOR THE YEAR 1985 OF THE ....

Name

SCHEDULE D – Part 2 – Section 1

Showing all PREFERRED STOCKS *Owned December 31 of Current Year*

	(1) DESCRIPTION	(2)	(3)	(4)	(5)	(6)	(6A)	(6B)	(7)	DIVIDENDS		(9)	(10)	(11)	(12)
CUSIP Identification ***	Give complete and accurate description of all preferred stocks owned, including redeemable options, if any, and location of all street railway, bank, trust and miscellaneous companies.	NO. OF SHARES	PAR VALUE PER SHARE	BOOK VALUE	*RATE PER SHARE	STATEMENT VALUE	RATE PER SHARE USED TO OBTAIN MARKET VALUE	MARKET VALUE	ACTUAL COST	(8 1) DECLARED BUT UNPAID	(8 2) AMOUNT RECEIVED DURING YEAR	INCREASE BY ADJUSTMENT IN BOOK VALUE DURING YEAR	DECREASE BY ADJUSTMENT IN BOOK VALUE DURING YEAR	§NAIC DESIG-NATION	YEAR ACQUIRED

*Insert the word "cost" for preferred stocks in good standing valued at cost. If the company elects to value stocks purchased prior to 1965 at 1964 Annual Statement Values, enter the rate shown in the 1964 Annual Statement with a symbol alongside the figure. Insert the market rate for preferred stocks not in good standing.

***From entry in the previous years's Annual Statement if owned at that time; from the purchase confirmation (or certificate) if purchased subsequently. Leave blank for private placements.

NOTES: Complete information must be furnished in connection with any holding of preferred or common stock on the statement date which is optioned or restricted in any way as to its sale by the insurer. Identify all such securities by the symbol "R" to be inserted beside the figure shown as the rate per share to obtain market value.
Transferable shares only, of Savings and Loan or Building and Loan Associations to be reported herein.
§Insert the NAIC designation for such security printed in the NAIC Valuation of Securities Manual.

30A

FIGURE 5-8
Schedule B—Canadian Annual Statement.

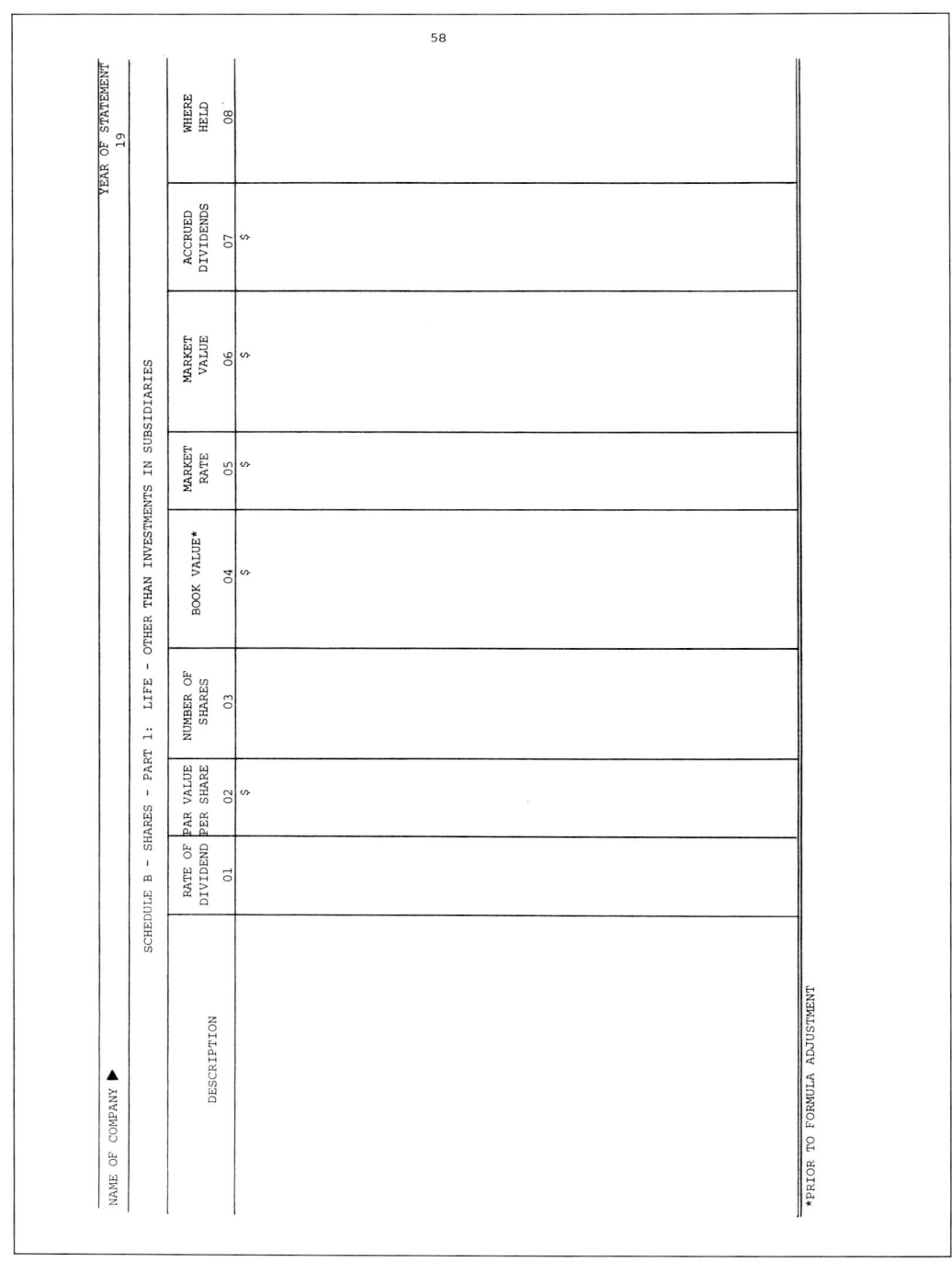

Stocks

Stocks owned by Canadian life and health insurers are presented in Schedule B of the Annual Statement (see Figure 5-8). Canadian insurers are required to value stocks on a more conservative basis than are U.S. insurers. In Canada, the book value of a stock is reported in all instances, but a stock's book value may be increased or decreased only with the specific approval of the Superintendent of Insurance in the province in which the insurer has its home office.

Key Terms

collected income	unearned income
due income	accrued income
nonadmitted income	earned income
par value	face value
maturity value	maturity date
public offering	private placement
mortgage bond	collateral trust bond
general obligation bond	special obligation bond
effective rate	yield
bond discount	bond premium
realized capital gain (or loss)	unrealized capital gain (or loss)
market value	amortization
ex-date	net investment income

Review Questions and Exercises

1. What are the five income classifications used for determining accrual-basis, or earned, income?
2. Distinguish between public offerings and private placements.
3. If an insurer profits from the sale of a bond, is the Profit on Sale of Bonds account debited or credited to record this profit?
4. What would the journal entry be to record the purchase at par of a $5,000 bond with $100 accrued interest as of the purchase date?
5. Under what circumstances would an insurer purchase a bond with a stated rate of 12 percent for the purpose of achieving a 10 percent yield on the investment?

6. How are the following types of stock valued for the purposes of the U.S. Annual Statement:
    (a) publicly traded common stock
    (b) common stock of an insurer's affiliated companies
    (c) preferred stock in good standing
    (d) preferred stock not in good standing

   How does the Annual Statement valuation of stocks differ in the United States and Canada?

6

Accounting for Other Investments

Learning Objectives

After reading this chapter, you should be able to:

- Describe types of insurance company investments other than bonds and stocks
- State the difference between a first mortgage and a second mortgage
- List the types of information in subsidiary ledger accounts for mortgage loans and escrow balances
- Record a number of journal entries pertaining to mortgage loans, real estate, and policy loans
- Calculate the capital gain or loss on the sale of real estate
- Discuss the Annual Statement presentation of mortgage loans, real estate, and policy loans

Introduction

A life insurance company's investment possibilities are not limited to bonds and stocks. Other investment possibilities for an insurer include mortgage loans, real estate, policy loans, and any other type of investment permitted by state law. In this chapter, the accounting principles for mortgage loans, real estate, and policy loans are presented.

Mortgage Loans

In 1985, mortgage loans comprised approximately 21 percent of the U.S. life and health insurance industry's total assets. In Canada, mortgages represented approximately 30 percent of the industry's total assets. Under the terms of a **real estate mortgage loan,** a person, business, or other entity borrows money from a lender and offers some specific piece of real estate, such as a house, farm, or office building, to the lender as collateral. If the borrower fails to (1) make the required periodic payments of interest and principal, (2) pay taxes on the property promptly, or (3) maintain and insure the property adequately, the lender may foreclose the mortgage. **Foreclosure** is a legal procedure by which a lender recovers the unpaid loan balance by gaining title to the real estate offered as collateral if the borrower defaults in the obligation to meet the terms of the loan.

The same piece of real estate can be used as collateral for more than one mortgage loan. The original mortgage secured by a piece of real estate is called the **first mortgage.** The difference between the market value of the property and the amount of mortgage loan outstanding is the **owner's equity** in the property. In some cases, if the owner's equity is large enough, a **second mortgage** loan to the property owner can be made. Most jurisdictions limit insurance companies from investing in second mortgages because such mortgages pose a greater risk for the lender. By definition, first mortgages have a prior claim to second mortgages. If the holder of a second mortgage is forced to foreclose because the borrower has not made the agreed-upon payments, the holder of the second mortgage must assume the first mortgage in order to collect on the loan.

Insurance laws generally restrict the amount or number of first-mortgage loans in excess of 75 percent (in some states, 66⅔ percent) of the appraisal or market value of a piece of property, though exceptions can be made if the loan is guaranteed by a governmental agency. For example, the U.S. Federal Housing Authority (FHA) and the Veterans Administration (VA) agree to purchase mortgage loans insured by the FHA or guaranteed by the VA, respectively, in the event of default on the part of the borrower. Some loans that are guaranteed by government agencies can be made for up to 100 percent of the appraised value of the property. Mortgage loans not insured or guaranteed by a government agency are called **conventional mortgage loans.** Most insurers today only issue conventional mortgages on commercial properties, though some insurers do grant conventional residential mortgage loans.

Mortgages can be for any number of years, but on a government-backed loan, the term is usually a multiple of 5 years up to a maximum of 35 years. On conventional residential mortgages, the term is generally for 15 to 30 years in the United States and 15 to 35 years in Canada. On conventional commercial mortgages, the term is generally for 15 to 30 years in the United States and 5 to 15 years in Canada.

Life and health insurance companies invest in mortgage loans for several reasons. First, mortgage loans are well suited to an insurer's need for a guaranteed rate of return over a long period of time. Even variable rate mortgages, in which the rate of interest payable on the loan principal varies according to market conditions, have a minimum guaranteed rate of return. Second, mortgage loans provide a high degree of safety for an insurer's investment funds. The safety of an insurer's investment is provided by the insurer's right to foreclose the mortgage. In addition, the gross rate of return on mortgage loans can often be higher than the rate of return on investments such as bonds. Mortgage loans that are made to businesses can provide not only for a fixed rate of interest, but also for other potential income, such as a percentage of the gross revenues or net income earned by the borrower during use of the property.

Accounting for Mortgage Loans

When a life and health insurance company issues a mortgage loan, a subsidiary ledger account is established that indicates the characteristics of the mortgage loan. The characteristics listed in the subsidiary ledger include

- due date
- amount due
- interest rate
- location of property
- principal value
- borrower identification—name, address, etc.
- property's appraisal value
- type of loan—farm, non-farm, commercial, FHA, VA, etc.

To account for the mortgage loan, the insurance company debits a Mortgage Loans asset account and credits Cash for the amount of the loan. Generally, the borrower pays closing costs, but if any expenses are paid by the lender, an expense account is debited and Cash is credited for the amount of the expenses. For example, assume that the Sage Insurance Company granted a $40,000 mortgage loan to a borrower and that the insurer paid $2,500 in closing costs. The entry on the insurer's books to record this transaction would be:

```
Mortgage Loans . . . . . . . . . . . . . . . . . . . . . . . 40,000
Mortgage Expenses Paid  . . . . . . . . . . . . . . .  2,500
     Cash . . . . . . . . . . . . . . . . . . . . . . . . . . . . . . . . . . . . 42,500
```

The borrower is sometimes required to pay to the lender an amount that will be held in escrow, or trust, for payment of property taxes, hazard insurance premiums, and other expenses that may arise. The amount held in escrow is credited by the lender to a liability account. If $900 is required for escrow at the time the loan is made, the entry on the insurer's books to record the borrower's remittance of these funds is:

```
Cash ................................. 900
    Escrow Funds—Mortgages ..................... 900
```

Escrow entries for each mortgage are posted to an escrow account within each mortgage loan subsidiary ledger account. Since escrow entries do not affect mortgage loan balances on the Annual Statement, some companies prefer to keep escrow entries in a separate subsidiary ledger account. Subsidiary ledger accounts for escrow balances typically include

- payee name
- escrow identification
- type of escrow fund
- loan identification
- amount due
- due date

The subsidiary ledger escrow accounts are monitored by a general ledger control account established specifically for escrow deposits.

Most mortgage loans are repayable in monthly installments. Insurers have no legal obligation to notify borrowers of the due dates of mortgage payments, though many insurers send a payment due notice shortly before the due date. Some insurers provide the borrower with a book of dated coupons that are to be detached and submitted to the insurer along with a loan payment when payment is due. Other insurers use a preauthorized check system. If a borrower is late in making a mortgage payment, the borrower may be assessed a penalty. Penalty charges for late payment generally are credited to Interest Income on Mortgages or to Miscellaneous Investment Income.

The monthly payment made by the borrower includes elements of principal, interest, and, in many cases, an amount to be placed in escrow. Typically, the borrower pays the same *total* amount to cover interest and principal each month. The portion of each monthly mortgage payment applicable to interest, however, is slightly smaller each month because each monthly principal repayment reduces the amount of the loan on which interest is payable. As the interest portion is lessened, the percentage of each mortgage payment applicable to principal increases correspondingly. The amount to be placed in escrow remains the same each month until a change in taxes, insurance premiums, or other expenses necessitates a change in the amount required to be in escrow.

To illustrate, a $10,000 12 percent 20-year mortgage loan requires a monthly repayment from the borrower (exclusive of escrow items) of $110.11. The interest income for the first month is $100 ($10,000 × 12 percent ÷ 12), which is credited to an income account. The remaining $10.11 reduces the loan balance. If the total monthly payment including real estate taxes is $145.11, the amount to be credited to the escrow account is $35 ($145.11 − $110.11). A journal entry made for the first monthly payment would be:

    Cash 145.11
        Mortgage Loans 10.11
        Interest Income on Mortgages 100.00
        Escrow Funds—Mortgages 35.00

When taxes or insurance premiums are paid on the borrower's property, the escrow account is debited in an amount equal to the amount paid, and Cash is credited for that amount.

A mortgage may be paid off prior to the end of its term, either by the original borrower or as part of resale of the property. For example, if a mortgage loan has a debit balance of $6,500 and the property securing this loan is being sold, a credit entry for $6,500 would be required to clear the Mortgage Loan account with respect to that particular loan. If this $6,500 loan has $32 in accrued interest and an escrow account with a $61 credit balance, the borrower must remit $6,471 ($6,500 loan + $32 accrued interest − $61 escrow) to pay off the outstanding mortgage loan. The entry to record the payoff of the mortgage would be:

    Cash 6,471
    Escrow Funds—Mortgages 61
        Mortgage Loans 6,500
        Interest Income on Mortgages 32

The credit to the interest account and the debit to the escrow account serve to clear these accounts with regard to this particular loan. In some cases, the borrower will be assessed charges for early payment of the mortgage. For addition of prepayment charges to the amount that is received by the insurer, Cash would be debited and Mortgage Prepayment Income would be credited for the amount.

If a mortgaged property is sold to a third party before the mortgage is paid off, and if the new owner assumes the mortgage (i.e., takes responsibility for its payments), no journal entry is required on the lender's books. However, the subsidiary ledger account is changed to indicate the new owner of the property.

Many mortgage loans made by insurance companies are made through real estate firms or mortgage brokers that service such loans for a fee—usually a percentage of the unpaid loan balance. These servicing firms are called **mortgage correspondents,** and on an insurer's books, fees paid to mortgage correspondents are debited to Mortgage Service Fees Paid, an expense account.

Accounting for the purchase of mortgage loans

In addition to granting mortgage loans to borrowers, insurance companies can invest in mortgages by purchasing them. Depending on the circumstances, an insurance company may purchase a mortgage loan for an amount equal to the balance of the loan, or at a premium or a discount depending on the market interest rate. In some cases, the borrower may be unaware that such a sale has been made, because the seller of the mortgage continues to service the loan and receive the regular monthly payments. These regular payments are then remitted to the insurer for repayment of the mortgage loan.

An insurer would purchase a mortgage loan at a discount or premium for the same reasons that an insurer would purchase a bond at a discount or premium—to achieve a desirable rate of return on a particular investment. For example, assume that the current mortgage interest rate is 12 percent. If an insurer is purchasing a 10 percent mortgage loan, the insurer generally would want to receive the 12 percent rate of return that could be realized in the current mortgage loan market. In order to yield this 12 percent effective rate of return, the seller would have to sell the mortgage loan to the insurer at a cost lower than the loan principal amount. In this case, the insurer's investment could yield the rate of return currently available on similar investments.

The amortization amount is determined periodically. If the mortgage loan was purchased at a discount, the addition to interest earned that results from amortization is debited to Unamortized Discount on Mortgages and credited to Interest Income on Mortgages. The entry made to amortize $1,000 of mortgage discount is:

Unamortized Discount on Mortgages 1,000
    Interest Income on Mortgages 1,000

If the mortgage loan has been purchased at a premium, the amortization entry serves to reduce the amount of interest earned. Thus, to record the amortization of a mortgage loan purchased at a premium, the insurer debits Interest Income on Mortgages and credits Unamortized Premium on Mortgages for the amortization amount.

Some companies prefer to record the adjustment to income resulting from the amortization of a discount or premium in a subdivision of the Interest Income on Mortgages account. Recording these transactions directly to an interest income account facilitates preparation of Annual Statements since the annual amortization relating to mortgage loans must be reported.

Foreclosure

Occasionally, an insurance company must foreclose a mortgage. On the date the insurer forecloses the mortgage, the unpaid balance of the loan plus any accrued interest, foreclosure costs, and unpaid property taxes are recorded in the insurer's books as the value of a real estate asset acquired, assuming this value does not exceed the appraisal value at foreclosure. The essence of this transaction is the conversion of a *mortgage loan* asset into a *real estate foreclosed* asset. The following example illustrates some elements of a foreclosure.

Assume that an insurer forecloses a mortgage to which the following dollar amounts apply:

Appraised property value	$10,000
Unpaid loan balance	$ 7,290
Accrued interest	$ 710
Legal fees for foreclosure	$ 300

Upon foreclosure, the book value of this property is debited to a Real Estate Foreclosed account in the amount of $8,300—the total of the loan balance, accrued interest, and foreclosure costs. The appraised value of the property has no impact on the insurer's journal entry, although the book value of the property cannot exceed that appraised value. A mortgage interest income account is credited to record the accrued interest. Mortgage Suspense, a liability account, is credited to record the foreclosure expenses owed by the company. The entry is:

Real Estate Foreclosed	8,300	
Mortgage Loans		7,290
Accrued Interest Income on Mortgages		710
Mortgage Suspense		300

When the insurer issues a check for payment of the legal expenses, the balance of the Mortgage Suspense account is brought to zero with reference to this particular liability by the following entry:

Mortgage Suspense	300	
Cash		300

Some companies do not include the accrued interest on a foreclosed property for purposes of valuing the foreclosure, since collection of this interest is sometimes doubtful. Some companies also do not use a Mortgage Suspense account to record the expenses owed by the insurer. In these companies, accountants credit an accounts payable account instead of Mortgage Suspense.

Real Estate

Real estate investments generally constitute a small but growing percentage of the investments of most U.S. life insurance companies. In 1985, real estate investments comprised between 3 and 4 percent of the assets of U.S. life companies. In Canada, 5 percent of life company assets were in real estate in 1985. Most companies own three types of real estate: (1) home and regional office buildings, (2) investment properties, and (3) real estate obtained through foreclosure. Accounting for real estate is a specialized topic. This text presents only a general overview of accounting for real estate investments in life and health insurance companies.

Accounting for Real Estate

The cost of real estate purchased by an insurer is recorded on the insurer's books as an asset. The cost of a piece of real estate equals the purchase price of that real estate plus any acquisition costs, such as title insurance premiums and legal fees, incurred during the purchase. Thus, if real estate is purchased for $50,000, and $8,000 in acquisition costs are incurred, the insurer would debit Real Estate Owned and credit Cash for $58,000, the total cost of the real estate.

When an insurer owns real estate, the cost of that real estate (exclusive of land) is depreciated over the useful economic life of the property. A real estate depreciation entry on an insurer's books would appear as a debit to Depreciation on Real Estate (an expense account) and a credit to Accumulated Depreciation on Real Estate (a contra asset account). Using this type of entry, an insurer can record the depreciation of the property while maintaining on the books the original cost of the property. The Real Estate Owned account is not affected by the depreciation entry. Keeping the depreciation amounts separate also facilitates preparation of Annual Statement schedules relative to real estate.

Sale of real estate

When an insurer sells a piece of real estate, both the asset account for that property and the appropriate accumulated depreciation account in the subsidiary ledger must be closed. For example, assume that an insurer sells for $105,000 property that cost $100,000. Accumulated depreciation to date totals $15,000. The entry to record the sale of this property would be:

```
Cash . . . . . . . . . . . . . . . . . . . . . . . . . . . . 105,000
Accumulated Depreciation on Real Estate . .  15,000
    Real Estate Owned . . . . . . . . . . . . . . . . . . . . . 100,000
    Profit on Sale of Real Estate . . . . . . . . . . . . . . . . 20,000
```

The debit to Accumulated Depreciation on Real Estate and the credit to Real Estate Owned serve to close out those accounts for this particular property. The capital gain or loss on the sale is determined by subtracting from the sale price the property's cost minus any accumulated depreciation. In equation form,

Capital Gain (or Loss) = Sale Price − (Cost − Accumulated Depreciation)

Thus, in the example above,

$$\begin{aligned} \text{Capital Gain (or Loss)} &= 105{,}000 - (100{,}000 - 15{,}000) \\ &= 105{,}000 - 85{,}000 \\ &= 20{,}000 \end{aligned}$$

Since the amount is positive, the insurer had a realized capital gain of $20,000, resulting in the credit to Profit on Sale of Real Estate. If any costs had been incurred during the sale, they would have been subtracted from the sale price when determining the capital gain or loss on the sale. The types of costs typically incurred in the sale of real estate include commissions and closing costs.

If the insurer in the above example had sold this same property for $80,000, the insurer would have realized a $5,000 capital loss [$80,000 sale price − ($100,000 cost − $15,000 accumulated depreciation)]. While the debit to Cash in this case would be for $80,000 and Loss on the Sale of Real Estate would be debited $5,000, the entries to Accumulated Depreciation on Real Estate and Real Estate Owned would remain the same in order to close out those accounts for the particular piece of property sold. The entry would appear as:

```
Cash ................................. 80,000
Accumulated Depreciation on Real Estate ... 15,000
Loss on Sale of Real Estate ............. 5,000
    Real Estate Owned ........................ 100,000
```

Property taxes

Property taxes are typically charged when real estate is purchased. These taxes are usually not included in the asset account balance for real estate owned. Instead, they are recorded as an investment expense, except when the property has been acquired through foreclosure. Taxes are generally payable in advance at specified times during the year. When real estate is bought or sold, taxes are considered to accrue between tax payment dates. If an insurer purchases property after the seller has paid the taxes for the current tax period, the insurer must return to the seller the amount of tax applicable to the remainder of the tax period. For example, assume that an insurer is purchasing a piece of real estate to which the following dollar amounts apply:

Purchase price	$100,000
Title insurance premium	$ 1,000
Legal fees of purchase	$ 1,500
Taxes paid by seller at outset of tax period	$ 1,200

If two-thirds of the tax period has passed when the insurer purchases this property, then the insurer must return $400 to the seller. This $400 amount represents the amount of tax applicable to the period of time that the insurer will own the property during that tax period. To record this real estate purchase, the insurer would (1) debit the Real Estate Owned account for the cost of the purchase ($100,000 purchase price + $1,000 title insurance premium + $1,500 legal fees = $102,500), (2) debit the Real Estate Taxes Paid expense account for $400 (the amount paid to the seller), and (3) credit Cash for the total of the debits. The entry is:

    Real Estate Owned .102,500
    Real Estate Taxes Paid .400
        Cash 102,900

In some cases, an insurer purchases real estate on which taxes have *not* been paid in advance. When such a purchase is made, the seller of the real estate must either (1) pay to the purchaser the amount of any accrued and unpaid taxes or (2) reduce the purchase price by that same amount. Using the dollar amounts from the previous example but assuming that *no* taxes had been paid on the property, if $800 in taxes had accrued at the time of purchase, this $800 would be credited on the insurer's books to the Real Estate Taxes Paid expense account. The entry is:

    Real Estate Owned .102,500
        Real Estate Taxes Paid 800
        Cash 101,700

When the insurer pays the property tax of $1,200 on the tax payment date, the Real Estate Taxes Paid account is debited for $1,200. The $1,200 debit gives that account (assuming a zero balance at the outset of the transaction) a debit balance of $400, the amount of tax applicable to the part of the tax period during which the insurer owned the property. Some insurers, rather than credit an expense account for the taxes paid by the seller, credit a liability account for Real Estate Taxes Payable.

Property taxes and foreclosure. An insurer has two options when it obtains property through foreclosure: (1) hold the property for resale or (2) rent the property in order to produce additional investment income. When real estate obtained through foreclosure is being held for resale, property taxes on that real estate are usually capitalized. To **capitalize** means to record an expense as an asset. In this case, the amount of property taxes is added to the cost of the property. Thus, if ABC Life has foreclosed on property and is carrying that property on its books at $60,000, the payment of a $500 property tax assessment on that property would increase the cost of the property on the insurer's books to $60,500. The entry to record the payment of $500 in taxes on foreclosed property is:

    Real Estate Foreclosed .500
        Cash 500

Property taxes are treated differently if an insurer has obtained property through foreclosure, has completed the foreclosure proceedings, and is renting the property to produce additional income. After completion of the foreclosure proceedings, the property taxes paid by the insurer on that property must be treated as an operating expense and cannot be capitalized.

When foreclosed property is sold, any amount that the insurer receives for prepaid taxes is added to the sale price when determining capital gains or losses. Similarly, any amount that the insurer pays for accrued taxes or expenses is deducted from the sale price when determining capital gains or losses. Some companies treat the sale of foreclosed property in a different manner. Amounts received for prepaid taxes would be offset against a Prepaid Rent account. Amounts paid by the insurer for accrued taxes would be debited to the Real Estate Taxes account.

Rental income and expense

In order to show the proper amount of investment income and expense in the Annual Statement, the accounting principles of many life and health insurance companies require that the insurer charge rent to itself for occupancy of the home office building. In such a case, the journal entry for this rental charge consists of a debit to Rental Expense and a credit to Rental Income for the rent amount. The amount of rent that a company charges to itself can be based on either (1) an estimate of the current market rental value of the property or (2) a figure determined by the amount of expenses, taxes, and depreciation on the property plus an amount representing interest on the investment in the home office building. Rent that an insurer pays to itself generally has no effect on that company's net income or surplus.

When an insurer rents property to another entity, the entry to record income received for rental of that real estate consists of a debit to Cash and a credit to Rental Income. Expense transactions regarding rental properties are shown in the journal as a debit to Rental Property Expense and a credit to Cash.

Policy Loans

A person who owns a life insurance policy that builds a cash surrender value can borrow from the insurer a **policy loan** to be secured by the policy's cash surrender value. Compared to investments such as bonds, stocks, and mortgage loans, insurers have little control over their policy loan investments as they are a contractual right of the policyowner.

Policy loans differ from other types of investments in a number of ways. First, policy loans are not handled by an insurer's investment department even though such loans are, in fact, investments and the interest received on policy loans is treated as investment income. Second, in contrast to other loans, policy loans do not have maturity dates. Third, systematic repayment plans are not required, and a policyowner need not pay interest on a policy loan if his or her policy has sufficient cash surrender value to secure the loan plus any accrued interest. Policy loan interest not paid by the policyowner is added to the amount of the policy loan. If the total of an outstanding loan and its accrued interest exceeds the policy's cash surrender value, however, the policy will terminate without further value, and the insurance contract will no longer be in force. Therefore, many companies encourage systematic repayment of the principal, and most companies bill for interest annually.

Ordinary life policies and many of the newer insurance products such as universal life and variable life contain a provision granting the policyowner the right to request a policy loan. Policy conditions vary, but a policyowner usually can borrow any amount up to the net cash value of the policy minus one year's interest on the loan. The **net cash value** is equal to the cash surrender value of both the policy and any paid-up additions minus any existing indebtedness and accrued interest on that debt.

Policy loans are usually calculated so that interest on the loan is payable on the policy anniversary date. Some companies charge interest on policy loans at the end of the policy year, and others charge interest in advance. Assuming the same stated rate of interest, interest charged in advance results in a higher effective rate of return for an insurer than interest charged at the end of the year.

Two types of policy loans are widely used: conventional policy loans and automatic premium loans. A *conventional policy loan* is made to a policyowner when he or she assigns the policy to the insurer as security for the loan. The policyowner may be required to submit the policy to the insurer for an endorsement showing that the assignment has taken place. This endorsement protects banks and other loan sources if the policyowner tries to offer the policy as security for another loan. An *automatic premium loan (APL)* is designed to pay the premium on a policy if the premium has not been paid by the end of the premium payment grace period. A special loan agreement is not required for this type of policy loan. An APL is generally provided for in a policy provision agreed upon by the policyowner and the insurer at the time the insurance contract was formed.

Accounting for Policy Loans

To account for the granting of policy loans, insurers generally establish a Policy Loans control account in the general ledger and an account in a subsidiary ledger for each individual loan. If a policy loan is made to (1) produce $100 cash for the policyowner, (2) pay a premium due of $25, and (3) pay six months' interest in advance up to the next policy anniversary date at the rate of 8 percent per year (a total of $5), the journal entry for this policy loan would be:

```
    Policy Loans  . . . . . . . . . . . . . . . . . . . . . . . . . . . 130
        Renewal Premiums  . . . . . . . . . . . . . . . . . . . . . . . . 25
        Interest on Policy Loans  . . . . . . . . . . . . . . . . . . . . . 5
        Cash  . . . . . . . . . . . . . . . . . . . . . . . . . . . . . . 100
```

Assume that three months later, this policyowner borrows another $100. The interest on this additional amount up to the next policy anniversary date is $2. Three accounts are affected by this second loan:

(1) Cash is credited to account for the payment of the $100 policy loan.
(2) Interest on Policy Loans is credited to record the increase in interest income.
(3) Policy Loans is adjusted so that the insurer's books show a single policy loan outstanding for this policyowner rather than two separate outstanding policy loans. A $130 credit to Policy Loans decreases the account balance in the amount of the first loan, and a $232 debit to Policy Loans records the total amount of policy loan outstanding for this policyowner (previous $130 loan + new $100 loan + $2 interest).

The entry to reflect the second policy loan would appear as:

```
Policy Loans ............................232
    Policy Loans ................................130
    Interest on Policy Loans .........................2
    Cash ........................................100
```

While the amount of the second policy loan could simply be debited to Policy Loans, the method described above permits easier auditing and control for the insurer.

If an automatic premium loan is used to pay for a delinquent premium payment, the debit can be made to a special loan account, Automatic Premium Loans. Separate subsidiary ledger accounts can be maintained for an automatic premium loan and a conventional policy loan made to the same policyowner, or the two loans can be consolidated into one account. This consolidation is often preferable if the insurer sends to the policyowner a single interest bill that reflects both loans. Consolidation of policy loans is also preferable for maintaining subsidiary ledger accounts and for calculating net cash value amounts.

Policy loan interest

On policies that have a policy loan outstanding, a bill for policy loan interest usually accompanies the policy's premium notice or is shown directly on the premium notice itself. An exception to this billing procedure occurs (1) when the premiums on a policy are being paid on a date other than the policy anniversary date, (2) when a policy is paid up, or (3) when premiums are paid by a special plan, such as a preauthorized check plan. Although policy loans may be taken out at any time during the policy year, interest is usually calculated based on the policy's anniversary date.

The entry on an insurer's books when $100 in policy loan interest is received is:

```
Cash ................................100
    Policy Loans ...........................100
```

Policy Loan Interest is not credited since the amount of interest accruing has been recorded in accrual entries over the life of the loan and has been capitalized as part of the asset.

If policy loan interest payable at the end of a year has not been paid when due and if that policy's cash surrender value is sufficient to cover the interest due, the amount of interest due is automatically added to the policy loan. Whenever the amount of a loan plus any accrued policy loan interest becomes equal to or greater than the cash surrender value of the policy, the policyowner must pay some or all of the interest due to avoid cancellation of his or her insurance policy. In effect, repayment of the interest is repayment of the loan principal.

A policyowner is generally entitled to a refund or credit of prepaid interest if interest on a policy loan has been paid in advance and a loan payment is made prior to the next interest date. A prepaid interest refund can reduce the amount required to pay off the loan. For example, assume that a policyowner has paid, in advance, one year's worth of 6 percent interest on a $200 loan, and that the loan is repaid three months before the next interest due date. In such a case, the entry on the insurer's books to reflect the $200 loan repayment is:

```
Cash ................................197
Interest on Policy Loans ...................3
    Policy Loans ...........................200
```

The $3 debit to Interest on Policy Loans reduces the interest income for the insurer from the $12 collected to the correct amount of interest, $9, for the period during which this policy loan was outstanding.

If *no* interest has been paid in advance, the policyowner must pay the accrued interest at the time the principal of the loan is repaid. For example, when a $200 6 percent policy loan is paid off three months before the policy's next anniversary date, the company must collect nine months' worth of accrued interest in addition to the loan principal. Assuming the company had not been recording accruing interest on the company's books, the entry to record the repayment of the $200 loan plus payment of $9 in accrued interest is:

```
Cash ................................209
    Interest on Policy Loans .......................9
    Policy Loans ...........................200
```

Annual Statement Aspects of Other Investments—United States

Mortgage Loans

Mortgage loans are typically recorded at their book value for Annual Statement purposes. If, however, a loan exceeds the amount permitted by law, then the excess is reported as a nonadmitted asset. For mortgage loans, the legal limit is generally expressed as a percentage of the appraised value of the real estate. Mortgages that are delinquent in payments and those that are in the process of foreclosure are also admitted at book value if this value does not exceed the maximum prescribed by law. Generally, states allow the inclusion of second mortgages among an insurer's admitted assets but require disclosure of the amounts.

Mortgage loans are summarized in Schedule B of the Annual Statement according to type, geographic location, and status of payment—e.g., current, delinquent more than three months, and in process of foreclosure. Four sections of U.S. Annual Statement Schedule B are shown in Figure 6-1. *Type of loan* may refer to the following groupings: farm, non-farm, FHA insured, VA guaranteed, conventional, and purchase money. A **purchase money mortgage** is a mortgage in which the seller of the property grants credit to the purchaser, and the purchaser uses the real estate being purchased as collateral for the loan.

Only large mortgages, i.e., those that (1) exceed one million dollars or (2) comprise one-half of one percent of the insurer's admitted assets, are listed separately in the U.S. Annual Statement. Schedule B of the Annual Statement includes a Verification Between Years section that shows the increases and decreases in the mortgage account from the beginning of the reporting year to the end of that year.

Real Estate

The value of real estate owned by an insurer is reported on the Annual Statement as the real estate's book value or appraised value, whichever is lower. For Annual Statement purposes, the book value of a piece of real estate equals the cost of that real estate minus the amounts of accumulated depreciation and any encumbrances—i.e., mortgages payable to others—that may exist on the property. If the capitalization of taxes, however, brings the book value of the real estate to more than its appraised value, then the insurer must either report this excess as a nonadmitted asset or reduce the real estate book value so that it equals the appraised value. A reduction of the book value of a real estate asset would appear on an insurer's books as a debit to a capital loss account, such as Decrease by Adjustment in Book Value, and a credit to Real Estate Owned. Depreciation on real estate is considered an investment expense item for Annual Statement purposes. Such depreciation is deducted from gross investment income to determine net investment income in Annual Statement Exhibit 2.

FIGURE 6-1
Schedule B—U.S. Annual Statement.

Form 1 — ANNUAL STATEMENT FOR THE YEAR 1985 OF THE .... (Name) — 21

SCHEDULE B - Part 1 — Section 1

Summary of Long-term Mortgage Loans (including foreclosed liens subject to redemption) owned at December 31 of Current Year and changes therein during the year

	FARM MORTGAGES		OTHER THAN FARM MORTGAGES			(6) TOTAL	
	(1) Purchase Money**	(2) Other	(3) Insured or Guaranteed under F.H.A., N.H.A. or V.A.	(4) Purchase Money**	(5) All Other		
1. Book value of mortgages owned, December 31st of previous year							1.
2. Loans in cash or granted on disposal of real estate							2.
3. Cost of mortgages, insured and other, purchased							3.
4. Additional cash loaned on $ .... of refunded mortgages*							4.
5. Interest covered by increase in, or refunding of, mortgages							5.
6. Taxes covered by increase in, or refunding of, mortgages							6.
7. Other items covered by increase in, or refunding of, mortgages							7.
8. Accrual of discount on mortgages purchased							8.
9. Transfers							9.
10.							10.
11.							11.
12. TOTALS							12.
13. Payments on principal including cash on mortgages refunded							13.
14. Mortgages foreclosed and transferred to real estate							14.
15. Mortgages on properties acquired by deed, in lieu of foreclosure, and transferred to real estate							15.
16. Decrease in book value of mortgages refunded or by adjustment in book value of mortgages							16.
17. Amortization of premium on mortgages purchased							17.
18. Transfers							18.
19.							19.
20.							20.
21. TOTAL DEDUCTIONS							21.
22.							22.
23. Book value of mortgages owned, end of year, per Exhibit 13, Line 3, Col. 1							23.

*Where refunding or extension involves the advance of no additional cash, no entries should be made.

SCHEDULE B - Part 1 — Section 2

Summary of Long-term Mortgage Loans (including foreclosed liens subject to redemption) owned at December 31 of Current Year in each State and Foreign Country

(1) STATE OR FOREIGN COUNTRY	FARM MORTGAGES						OTHER THAN FARM MORTGAGES										(10) GRAND TOTAL	
	(2) Purchase Money**		(3) Other		(4) Total Farm		(5) Insured or Guaranteed by Federal Housing Administration or under National Housing Act (Canada)		(6) Insured or Guaranteed by Veterans Administration (exclusive of any portion insured by F.H.A.)		(7) Purchase Money**		(8) All Other		(9) Total Other than Farm			
	No.	Amount	No.	Amount	No.	Amount	No.	Amount	No.	Amount	No.	Amount	No.	Amount	No.	Amount	No.	Amount
TOTALS																		

**A purchase money mortgage is understood to be one which represents a part of the consideration received on sale of property owned by the company (Mortgagee).

GENERAL INTERROGATORY

1. Are any investments other than mortgage loans, such as ground rents, included in Schedule B? Answer: ....

FIGURE 6-1 (cont.)

ANNUAL STATEMENT FOR THE YEAR 1985 OF THE _____

Long-term Mortgages owned at December 31 of Current Year upon which interest is not overdue more than three months, which are not in process of foreclosure or in course of voluntary conveyance to the Company. Show individually those which exceed $1,000,000 or 1/2% of admitted assets December 31 preceding year, whichever is smaller, and others upon which taxes, assessments or other liens are delinquent more than one year, and, with appropriate comment, those where mortgagor is an officer, director, parent, subsidiary or affiliate, classified by States in each sub-section. All others may be summarized.

SCHEDULE B - Part 2 — Section 1

(1) NUMBER	(2) STATE AND COUNTY OR CITY	(3) YEAR GIVEN	(4) AMOUNT OF PRINCIPAL INDEBTEDNESS AT END OF YEAR	(5) BOOK VALUE	(6) INCREASE BY ADJUSTMENT IN BOOK VALUE DURING YEAR	(7) DECREASE BY ADJUSTMENT IN BOOK VALUE DURING YEAR	(8) INTEREST DUE AND UNPAID**	(9) UNPAID TAXES*	(10) VALUE OF LAND AND BUILDINGS	(11) COMMENT

*Report ALL taxes unpaid by mortgagor, if any taxes are unpaid more than one year from date when penalty attaches.
**Show grand total only.

FIGURE 6-2
Schedule E—Canadian Annual Statement.

NAME OF COMPANY ▲					SCHEDULE E - REAL ESTATE - PART 1: LIFE						YEAR OF STATEMENT 19
DESCRIPTION AND LOCATION OF PROPERTY	FARM OR OTHER	DATE ACQUIRED	ENCUM- BRANCES	ACTUAL COST	BOOK VALUE, LESS ENCUMBRANCES	MARKET VALUE, LESS ENCUMBRANCES	EXPENDED ON CAPITAL ACCOUNT	OPERATIONS DURING YEAR OF ACCOUNT			NET INCOME
								GROSS INCOME	NON- CAPITAL EX- PENDITURE	REGULAR ANNUAL DE- PRECIATION	
	01	02	03 $	04 $	05 $	06 $	07 $	08 $	09 $	10 $	11 $

Each item of real estate owned by an insurer is described in Annual Statement Schedule A. Items acquired during the reporting year are listed separately from those acquired in previous years. Within these separate listings, real estate assets are further subdivided into (1) items owned at the end of the year and (2) items sold during the year. Other portions of Schedule A include a reconciliation of the previous year-end and current year-end real estate account balances, an analysis of the book values of real estate obtained through foreclosure (i.e., "acquired in satisfaction of mortgage indebtedness"), and summaries of real estate owned by location.

Policy Loans

Policy loans are admitted at their book value, which for policy loans is cost minus principal repayments. However, if a policy loan exceeds the cash value of the relevant policy, the excess of the loan over the cash value of the policy is considered a nonadmitted asset. The Annual Statement does not include a schedule for policy loans.

Annual Statement Aspects of Other Investments—Canada

Mortgage loans, policy loans, and real estate are generally included in the Canadian Annual Statement at their book values. Any investment in default or not amply secured may require an adjustment in book value. An adjustment in the book value of an investment may also be required for (1) any asset with a market value below that asset's book value or (2) real estate with an appraised value below the property's book value. Schedules C and D of the Canadian Annual Statement are used to record information about an insurer's mortgage loans, though few details about specific mortgage loans are required in the Schedule itself. A separate detailed list of each mortgage loan is provided to support Schedule C. A Canadian insurer's real estate investments are listed in some detail in Annual Statement Schedule E. In many cases, Schedule E presents summary information only (see Figure 6-2) and refers regulators to an attached report for a detailed listing of the company's real estate holdings.

Key Terms

foreclosure
second mortgage
conventional policy loan
net cash value

first mortgage
conventional mortgage loan
automatic premium loan
purchase money mortgage

Review Questions and Exercises

1. Why do states limit the amount or number of second mortgage loans owned by an insurer?
2. Given the following dollar amounts, calculate the capital gain or loss on this sale of real estate:

    Cost of real estate = $120,000
    Accumulated depreciation on real estate = 50,000
    Sale price of real estate = 180,000

    What journal entry could properly record this sale?
3. For what purposes are amounts held in escrow?
4. What are the three classifications of real estate owned by an insurer?
5. What transaction could the following journal entry represent?

    Policy Loans 220
        Renewal Premiums 30
        Interest on Policy Loans 5
        Cash 185

6. How must insurers value their mortgage loan and real estate investments for purposes of the Annual Statement?

7
Policy Benefit Settlements

Learning Objectives

After reading this chapter, you should be able to:

- Understand the objectives of policy benefit accounting
- Describe the types of information included in the master dividend record
- List the three classifications of dividend liabilities
- Make the journal entries required for different policy dividend transactions
- Describe the accounting methods for various nonforfeiture options
- Understand the Annual Statement treatment of policy benefit settlements

Introduction

Most of the income of life insurance companies is assigned to meet current and future obligations to policyowners. These obligations include payment of both policy benefits and supplementary contract benefits as well as the establishment of policy reserves. Policy and contract benefits can be divided into the following categories:

- policy dividends
- nonforfeiture benefits
- claim settlements
- annuity and supplementary contract payments

Accounting methods for policy dividends and nonforfeiture benefits, as well as the Annual Statement treatment of such benefits, are presented in this chapter. Chapter 8 discusses both claim settlements and supplementary contract payments.

Objectives of Policy Benefit Accounting

In general, the objectives of proper accounting for policy benefit payments are:

1. To record the payment of claims, annuity payments, or other policy benefits only upon proper authorization of the payment;
2. To maintain a historical record of all policy benefit payments;
3. To provide an audit trail from the point of disbursement authorization to entry to the general ledger account and the relevant policy record; and
4. To provide data from which unpaid policy liabilities—pending policy dividends, dividend accumulations, etc.—can be calculated.

In addition, proper internal control procedures require that, as a security measure, someone outside the accounting department authorize every disbursement. This procedure is especially important in handling benefit payments because such payments can sometimes be for large amounts.

Historical records of all types of policy disbursements must be maintained for governmental purposes, statistical analyses, and policyowner inquiries. Regulatory authorities, through the statutory Annual Statement, require a great deal of information about claims and benefit payments. In addition, analysis of claim and benefit payment statistics is useful in determining adequate rates to be charged for insurance coverage in the future. Although such analysis is not typically an accounting function, claim and benefit accounting systems must be designed to facilitate such statistical studies. Finally, the ability to answer policyowner inquiries is especially important if the principal policy or contract remains in force after a payment is made.

Methods of achieving these accounting objectives are somewhat different for each benefit classification. These methods are, therefore, discussed for each dividend and policy benefit category.

Policy Dividends

When an insurer sets premium rates for participating life and health insurance policies, the company's actuaries determine the premiums to be charged based on conservative assumptions of expenses, mortality or morbidity, and the interest rates to be earned on the company's premium income. Since actual experience in these areas often does not match the actuaries' conservative assumptions, insurers can refund money to policyowners in the form of dividends when conditions are favorable. Dividends are thus often referred to as "returns of premiums."

Annual dividends on participating policies are generally payable on policy anniversaries after a policy has been in force for one or more years. After annual dividends on individual policies are actuarially determined, the aggregate dividends must be approved by the company's board of directors. The board's resolution authorizing the payment of dividends usually applies to policies that reach policy anniversaries within a certain calendar period. As a result, the total amount of dividends payable is necessarily an estimate, contingent upon the number of policies still in force on their anniversary dates.

When a manual accounting system is used, dividends are manually calculated and then dividend notices are prepared and filed by the policies' anniversary dates. In an electronic data processing system, a dividend file is created as part of the master file system or as a separate file. Regardless of the method used, the file is reviewed daily or weekly for policies that have an anniversary date falling on a defined future day. As these dates approach, policy dividends are paid as necessary.

Dividend Records

Dividend amounts are relatively small when compared to premium amounts and must be calculated and processed as economically as possible. Dividends are calculated on a mass basis at least once per year through the use of dividend schedules. Entries to record the payment of dividends are also made on a mass basis whenever practical. Such entries, however, are generally made on a monthly basis or when payments are made.

In every life insurance company that sells participating insurance, a master dividend record for each participating policy is included in the accounting or administrative records. The following table summarizes the types and uses of data usually included in each master dividend record:

Types of Data Included in Master Dividend Record	Use of Data
1. Dividend calculation data—including plan, issue age, amount, and duration of the policy.	Computing the dividend payable each year.
2. Dividend payment data—including policy number, name of policyowner, dividend option elected, amount of dividend, and amount of paid-up additions available.	Preparing checks, accounting entries, and dividend notices to the policyowner.

Types of Data Included in Master Dividend Record (cont.)	Use of Data (cont.)
3. Balances held under each option.	Policy status and liability determination.
4. History of dividends paid or applied under each option.	Policyowner inquiries and maintenance of audit trails.

Shortly before the date that a dividend becomes payable, the master dividend record is used to produce both the dividend notice and a current dividend transaction record for each policy. With automation, the dividend information generated is simultaneously processed against individual policy master records. Companies that keep accumulated dividends on the ledger make journal entries at this time. If necessary, journal entries are also made to the general ledger. The amount of each entry is the total dollar amount of all dividends being applied under the particular option. After a dividend is paid or applied under an option, the master dividend record is updated to reflect the payments or applications.

As each list is prepared, the transaction records are saved to provide a detailed history of the dividend transactions. This file is used later to (1) prepare summaries of dividend transactions by state and province for Annual Statement purposes, (2) prepare listings by policy numbers and branch offices for tracing dividend disbursements in case a policyowner should question whether he or she was sent a dividend, (3) facilitate audits by supervisory authorities, and (4) report interest credited for income tax purposes.

Dividend Liabilities

Once a dividend is designated by the company's board of directors, the total dividend amount becomes a liability to the company. The types of liabilities related to dividends include dividends due and unpaid, dividends payable in the following year, and dividend accumulations. Each type of dividend liability is discussed below:

- *Dividends due and unpaid* have been declared by the company's board but have not been paid or applied as of the financial statement date. Even if a premium is due at the financial statement date, and the dividends could potentially be applied toward the premium due amount, an asset for the due premium is recorded and a liability for the dividend is established. A liability for unpaid dividends is always required, regardless of the dividend option selected by the policyowner.
- *Dividends payable in the following year* represent the estimated amount of all dividends that have been declared by the company's board, but that are not payable until the next year.

- *Dividend accumulations* result from a policyowner's election to leave the dividends owed to him or her on deposit with the company. The company must also record an appropriate liability for dividend accumulations.

Dividend Payment Options

Policyowners can elect a number of different methods of receiving their dividends. In general, policy dividends can be

1. paid in cash,
2. applied to reduce the current premium due on the policy,
3. left with the company to accumulate at interest,
4. applied to purchase paid-up additions to the policy, or
5. applied to purchase one-year term insurance.

The fifth option is less common than the other four. The insurance coverage provided under the fifth dividend option is frequently limited to an amount not in excess of the cash surrender value of the policy. The fifth dividend option can also be used to increase the value of term insurance. In Canada, applications of the fourth and fifth dividend options are known as **bonus additions.** If any portion of the policyowner's dividend remains after it has been applied to one option, the balance of the dividend can be applied to another option.

When a dividend is paid in cash, the dividend file is updated and the entries are recorded in a dividend journal, which can be the source for preparing checks to send to the individual policyowners. When a dividend is used to reduce a policyowner's premium, the dividend amount is deducted from the billed premium and shown on the billing notice mailed to the policyowner. The actual recording of the application of dividends towards premiums is generally done when the insurer records receipt of the premium payment. If the dividend equals or exceeds the premium, the entry is recorded on the policy anniversary date. Any excess of dividend over premium can be paid in cash or applied to another dividend option.

If dividends are left to accumulate at interest, the individual policyowner's record and the dividend file are adjusted for the current dividend and the amount of interest accrued since the dividend was declared. Interest on policy dividends accrues at a rate stipulated in the policy, plus any additional rate that the company may determine. When a dividend is used to purchase paid-up insurance or one-year term insurance, the amount of additional insurance purchased is determined by dividing the dividend by the appropriate net single premium. A rider to the basic policy record is occasionally added to reflect the additional insurance coverage. Paid-up insurance can also be treated as a separate policy rather than as a rider to the basic coverage.

Dividend Entries

Accounting procedures for policy dividends differ from those for dividends on capital stock. As mentioned earlier, in some companies, no journal entry is made for policy dividends at the time that they are declared, but a nonledger liability is created in the amount of estimated dividends payable. In these companies, journal entries are made for policy dividends only when they are paid in cash or when they are applied under an option. These entries may be made daily, but some companies make the entries less frequently in order to utilize more efficiently the company's data processing equipment in the preparation of checks, notices, and lists. Different accounts are used for each dividend option.

Dividends paid in cash

The journal entry to record dividends paid in cash is a debit to Policy Dividends Paid, an expense account for policyowner benefits, and a credit to Cash in the amount of the dividends paid. Thus, the entry to record the payment of $500 in policy dividends would appear as:

    Policy Dividends Paid 500
        Cash 500

Some companies pay terminal policy dividends upon the termination of a policy. A **terminal policy dividend** is a substantial extra dividend or pro-rata dividend covering the period between the last policy anniversary date and the termination date of the policy. When a policy matures, becomes a final claim, or is surrendered, terminal dividends are payable in cash. If a policy lapses and is placed under a nonforfeiture option, that policy's terminal dividend can generally be used to increase the values applied under the option. Entries for these dividend settlements are made as a part of the policy settlement entry and are covered in other sections of this chapter and Chapter 8.

Dividends applied to pay premiums

To record dividends applied to pay premiums due, the journal entry is a debit to Policy Dividends Applied to Premiums and a credit to Premium Income. These entries are made daily as the premiums are recorded. Sometimes a dividend applied to pay a premium is greater than the premium itself. In such a case, as may happen in connection with a monthly premium, the difference is generally paid in cash and the cash portion of the payment is recorded as for a cash dividend. For example, assume that a policyowner had a monthly $100 premium and the insurer had declared a $120 dividend that became payable at the time the policyowner's premium came due. If the policyowner wanted to apply the dividend to pay the premium and receive the balance of the dividend payment in cash, the following journal entry would be required:

    Policy Dividends Applied to Premiums 100
    Policy Dividends Paid 20
        Premium Income 100
        Cash 20

Each journal entry should indicate any partial dividends paid or applied in order to provide a clear audit trail.

When a dividend is larger than a policy's premium, policyowners can also apply the unused portion of the dividend to pay subsequent premiums, instead of receiving the balance as a cash payment. If the policyowner described above wanted to use the extra $20 to pay a portion of the next month's premium, the entries for the two months would be:

Month 1
    Dividends Applied to Premiums 100
        Premium Income 100

Month 2
    Dividends Applied to Premiums 20
    Cash 80
        Premium Income 100

Another alternative would be to apportion the original $120 dividend to a total year's premiums. If the policyowner wanted to apply $10 per month of the $120 dividend to each of the next year's premiums, the monthly entry for this policyowner's premium payment would be:

    Dividends Applied to Premium 10
    Cash 90
        Premium Income 100

If a policy lapses while a dividend is being held for application under a premium payment option, the dividend is usually applied under a nonforfeiture option in the same manner as a cash dividend. Nonforfeiture options are discussed later in this chapter.

Other entries

When current dividends are left on deposit with the insurer, interest accrued on previous deposits since the last anniversary date is commonly added to the dividend deposit total. Many companies make the entry on the anniversary date on which the dividend becomes payable, provided that premiums are paid to that date. Some companies record the journal entry when the premium payment is received. A typical entry to record dividends left to accumulate at interest is:

        Dividends on Deposit xxx
            Dividend Accumulations xxx

The Dividend Accumulations account is an income account for the insurer and is identified separately from the other dividend accounts. Dividends on Deposit is an expense account.

The entry to record dividends applied to buy paid-up additions is:

> Dividends to Purchase Paid-Up Additions (PUA) . . xxx
> Single Premiums for PUA xxx

Note that the credit for a purchase of paid-up additions is to a premium income account. Payments for paid-up additions and other options that provide insurance are usually recorded on the ledger in separate single premium accounts. By recording the premiums for paid-up additions in a separate account, accumulation of data for taxation and Annual Statement purposes is made easier.

Premiums for paid-up additions are exempt from premium tax in most states and in all Canadian provinces. The premium tax exemption for policyowner dividends is justified since taxes have already been paid on the full policy premium. In addition, the premium used to purchase the additional paid-up insurance is classified as a return of premiums because of favorable experience during the previous year. Since some of the premium is being returned, the premium tax levied on the insurer's previous-year premium income is excessive for the amount of income eventually realized. By not levying a tax on dividends applied to purchase insurance, this excessive tax burden is alleviated.

A simplified diagram for the process of recording and paying policy dividends is presented in Figure 7-1.

Disbursements of Dividends Held under an Option

Under a number of different circumstances, dividends that have been applied under an option must be paid out to a policyowner or beneficiary. These circumstances include (1) withdrawal of dividend accumulations by the policyowner, (2) surrender of paid-up additions for their cash surrender value, and (3) termination of the policy by surrender, by death, or as a paid matured endowment.

Entries are made regularly for the payment of accumulated dividends held under an option as well as the cash surrender values of paid-up additions. These transactions involve cash, and the total in an insurer's Cash account must always be current. The transaction for each of these disbursements must be recorded so that an audit trail from the payment to the dividend record is maintained. The balance in the master dividend record must also be concurrently adjusted to reflect the revised balance. If the policy terminates by death or as a paid matured endowment, the master dividend record for that policy must also be placed in a terminated status to prevent generation of further dividend transactions.

To record the payment of accumulated dividends held under an option, the following entry would typically be made:

> Dividend Accumulations xxx
> Cash xxx

FIGURE 7-1
The accounting process for recording and paying dividends.

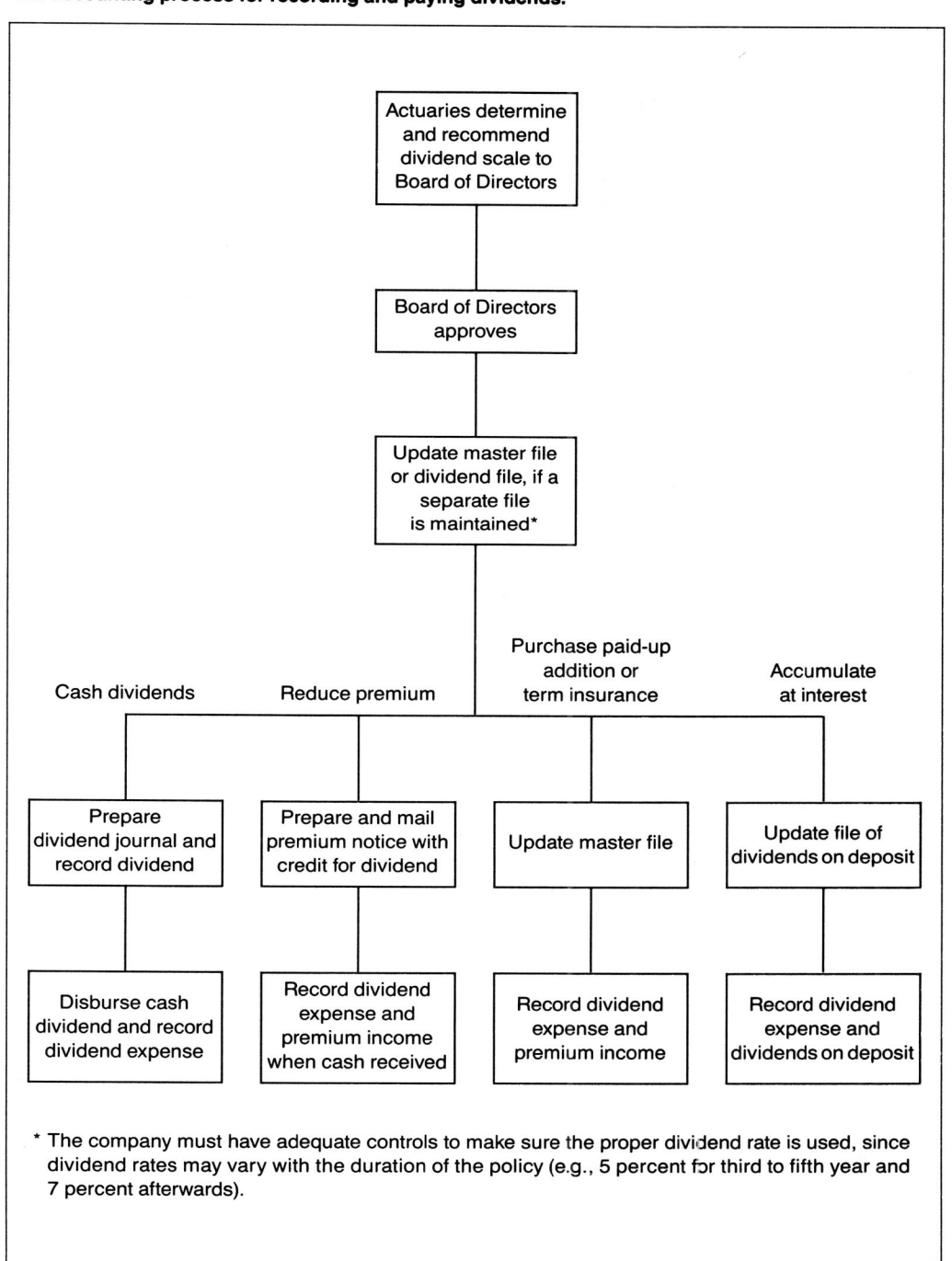

The amount reflected in the entry would typically include any interest accrued on the accumulations.

To record the surrender of paid-up additions for which the cash surrender value is $300, the following journal entry would be used:

    Surrenders Paid (or Surrenders Paid on PUA) . . . 300
        Cash 300

Entries for dividend accumulations paid in connection with a death claim or matured endowment are presented in the next chapter.

Nonforfeiture Options

When a policy lapses, the basic insurance contract is terminated, except for those rights that the policyowner has under nonforfeiture options. **Nonforfeiture options** are the choices available to a policyowner concerning the methods under which he or she can apply the policy's cash surrender value when the policy expires. Nonforfeiture values may be taken in one of three forms: (1) cash surrender, (2) reduced paid-up insurance, or (3) extended term insurance. The following sections present the accounting procedures for each of these nonforfeiture options.

Cash Surrender

When a policyowner decides to terminate his or her policy and has elected the cash surrender value option, insurance protection stops and the cash surrender value owed to the policyowner is calculated. This amount is then remitted to the policyowner, and the company has no further obligation under the policy.

When a policy is surrendered for cash, the basic journal entry to record the surrender is:

    Surrenders Paid xxx
        Cash xxx

The debit to the Surrenders Paid account records a decrease in the company's surplus. However, a change in the liability for policy reserves occurs simultaneously with the decrease in surplus. As a result, the net effect on surplus is very small because the decrease in surplus is offset by the increase in surplus resulting from a reserve released. The phrase **reserve released** refers to a policy reserve, established in connection with an in-force policy, that is no longer required. When such a reserve is no longer needed, it is "released" and reclassified as surplus. If a policy with a cash surrender value of $3,200 is surrendered, and the reserve released for this policy totals $3,400, then the net effect on surplus would be a $200 increase in surplus. The decrease in liability occurs when reserve liabilities are calculated at the end of the reporting period.

If a policy loan is outstanding on the policy, the amount of the loan plus any accrued interest to the date of lapse must be deducted from the settlement, and the cash payment must be reduced accordingly. The Policy Loans account is credited to close out this account with reference to the particular loan. The Policy Loan Interest account is either credited for accrued interest, which is earned interest for the company, or debited when interest paid in advance is being refunded. As an example of the payment of interest accrued on a policy loan, assume that the following amounts applied to a life insurance policy and that the policyowner wants to withdraw the surrender value of her policy:

> Cash surrender value = $500
> Policy loan outstanding = $115
> Policy loan interest accrued = $ 15

To reflect payment of the amount due to the policyowner, the insurer's journal entry would be:

> Surrenders Paid 500
>   Cash 370
>   Policy Loans 115
>   Policy Loan Interest 15

The Cash account reflects the proper amount payable to the policyowner under these circumstances.

If dividend accumulations are on deposit, the amount payable to the policyowner in the event of surrender is the cash surrender value plus the amount on deposit and accrued interest, if any. The Dividends on Deposit account is debited as if these deposits were being paid out independently of the cash surrender. If terminal dividends are payable, they are also added to the settlement and the Policy Dividends Paid account is debited. Current dividends are paid out prior to the lapse date and thus are not ordinarily included with policy surrender payments. If paid-up additions have been purchased for a policy that is being surrendered, the surrender value of these additions is added to the surrender value of the policy.

Many transactions regarding policies surrendered for their cash surrender value are affected by policy loans, dividends, and paid-up additions. For an example of an entry reflecting such a transaction, consider the following example. Assume that the surrender value of a policyowner's ordinary policy is $3,200, the surrender value of $100 in paid-up additions is $60, dividend accumulations are $532, and a $2,000 policy loan is outstanding with $10 interest having been paid by the policyowner in advance. The total amount payable to this policyowner upon surrender of the policy is calculated as follows:

	Cash surrender value of the policy	$3,200
plus	Cash surrender value of the paid-up additions	60
plus	Dividend deposits	532
plus	Loan interest refund	10
	Total	$3,802
minus	Policy loan	2,000
	Net payable	$1,802

The entry to record this payment would be:

```
Surrenders Paid ........................ 3,260
Dividend Accumulations .................. 532
Policy Loan Interest ...................... 10
    Policy Loans .............................. 2,000
    Cash ...................................... 1,802
```

Note that this entry debits the Policy Loan Interest account. The debit to Policy Loan Interest reflects the return of $10 in interest that had been paid by the policyowner in advance.

Reduced Paid-Up and Extended Term Insurance

When applying the reduced paid-up or extended term insurance nonforfeiture options, a settlement of the net cash surrender value is being made. Instead of receiving cash, however, the policyowner receives an equivalent value in the form of paid-up term or extended term insurance, paid-up whole life insurance, or paid-up endowment insurance.

When a policy is to be continued under one of these options and no dividend accumulations or loans are outstanding, no accounting entry is required. The transaction is simply a transfer of the policy's reserve liability from a premium-paying classification to a paid-up insurance classification. Bookkeeping entries are required only if dividend accumulations are on deposit at the time of lapse or if a policy loan is outstanding.

For example, if an ordinary policy has a $2,000 cash surrender value, dividend accumulations of $250, and a $750 policy loan outstanding with $40 interest due at the time of lapse, the entry to record the repayment of the policy loan and the purchase of paid-up or extended term insurance would be:

```
Dividend Accumulations .................. 250
Surrenders Paid ......................... 540
    Policy Loans .............................. 750
    Policy Loan Interest ....................... 40
```

With this entry, the dividend and policy loan accounts relative to this policy are closed out before the term insurance is purchased. In this example, the total cash surrender value that will be applied to the nonforfeiture option is $1,460 ($2,000 cash surrender value minus $540 applied to the repayment of the policy loan and interest). No entry is required for the application of the $1,460 towards establishment of a reserve.

Concurrently with the entries for nonforfeiture transactions, the following record changes take place: (1) the in-force policy record is changed from premium-paying status to paid-up status; (2) the paid-up insurance record for the respective policyowner is established; and (3) the dollar control on due premiums, if any, is adjusted to indicate that the premium is no longer due. **Dollar control** is a process for continuously maintaining a total of separate amounts in a particular file while amounts are being added to and deleted from the file.

If a lapsed policy is reinstated, entries made at the time of lapse are reversed. Thus, accounts that were credited at the time of lapse are debited for the same amount, and accounts that were debited at the time of lapse are credited for the same amount.

A simplified flowchart showing the procedure for recording nonforfeiture benefits is presented in Figure 7-2.

Annual Statement Aspects—United States

Five items on the U.S. Annual Statement Balance Sheet liability page (page 3) are partially or wholly concerned with dividend liabilities:

1. The liability for dividend accumulations is calculated by totaling the dividend deposit amounts of the master records. These records show the liability as of each policy anniversary. The total of dividend deposits is then increased for interest that has accrued up to December 31. The combined liability for dividend accumulations and accrued interest is included in the exhibit for supplementary contracts not involving life contingencies (Annual Statement Exhibit 10).
2. The *policyowners' dividends due and unpaid* line reports dividends that have been declared by the company's board of directors but which have not yet been paid or applied toward the payment of premiums. Dividends to be applied under other options might also be included with this liability. Since some premiums are unpaid by the policyowners at the end of the year, any policy dividends contingent upon payment of those premiums will be unpaid by the company.
3. The amount of policyowners' dividends payable in the following calendar year is estimated and reported as another separate item on the liability page. This category covers all dividends that have been declared and that will become payable if the policies are in force on their anniversaries

FIGURE 7-2
The accounting process for recording nonforfeiture benefits.

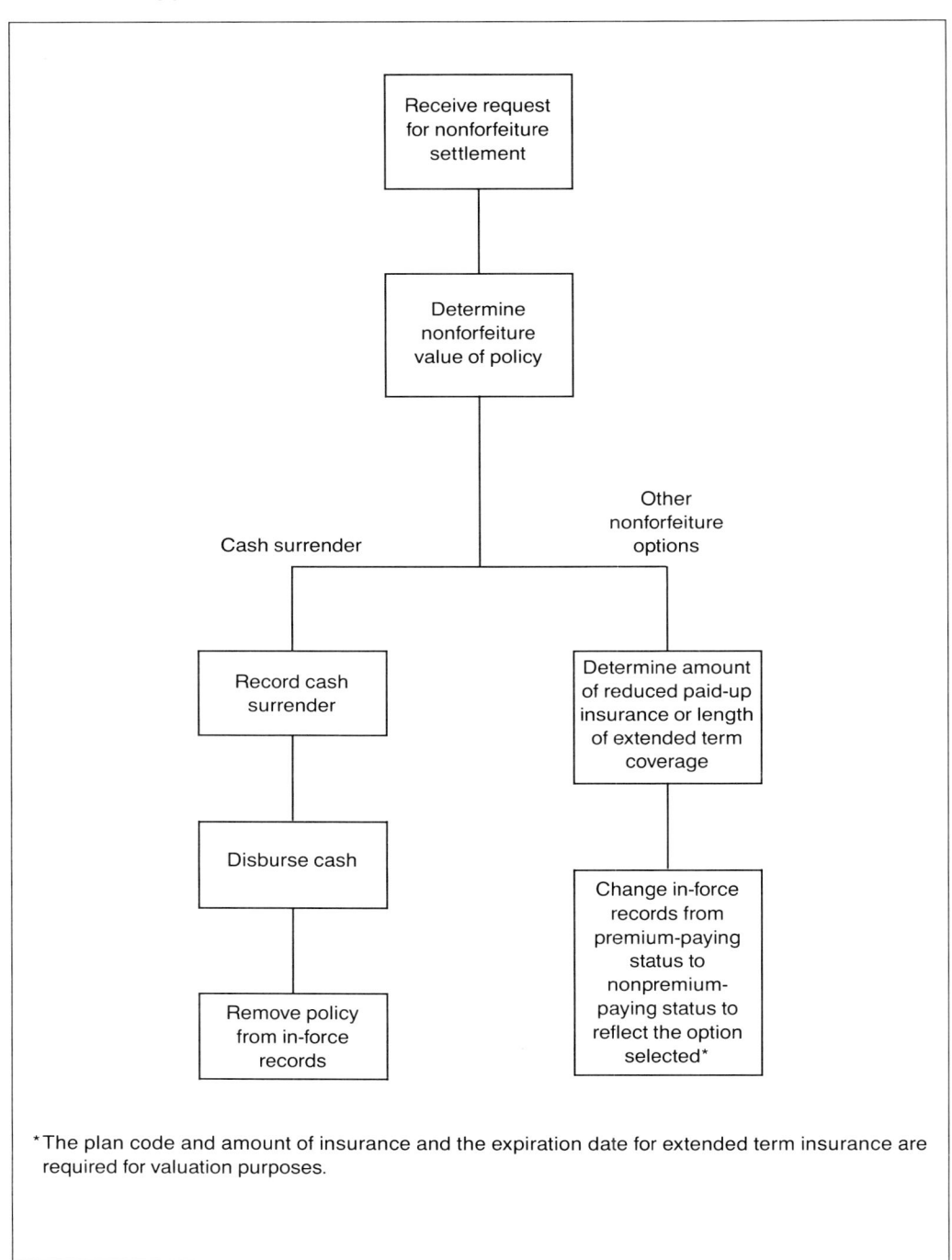

*The plan code and amount of insurance and the expiration date for extended term insurance are required for valuation purposes.

during the following year. Customarily, an estimate of the full year's liability for dividends is reported, even though the dividends for a part of the following year have not yet been declared. Establishing a liability for dividends not yet declared is an optional practice in most states and provinces.

4. The estimated liability for deferred dividend policies is also a separate item on the insurer's Balance Sheet. Companies with deferred dividend policies usually set up a liability for a portion of the deferred dividend each year, even though the dividend is not yet payable. For example, if the deferred dividends are payable on every fifth anniversary, a fifth of the anticipated dividend on each policy is added to this liability each year until the dividend is paid.

5. The liability for paid-up additions is included as part of the Balance Sheet's total for life insurance policy reserves. This liability is not shown as a separate item on either the liability page or in the policy reserve exhibit (Exhibit 8).

Increases in dividend liabilities from one year-end to the next are included in the Summary of Operations (page 4) as follows:

1. The change from the beginning-of-year balance to the end-of-year balance for (a) policyowners' dividends due and unpaid, (b) dividends payable in the following year, and (c) amount held for deferred dividend policies are all included in the dividend exhibit (Exhibit 7—see Figure 7-3). Exhibit 7 adjusts cash-basis figures for dividend liabilities to an accrual basis. The adjusted amount included in the Exhibit 7 total is carried to the Summary of Operations as *Dividends to policyholders.*

2. The change in dividend accumulations is included on the line entitled *Increase in reserve for supplementary contracts without life contingencies and for dividend and coupon accumulations.*

3. The increase in reserve on paid-up additions is included with the increase in life insurance policy reserves.

Schedule T of the U.S. Annual Statement shows premiums and annuity considerations allocated by states and territories. This schedule requires that dividends which are used to reduce premiums be reported along with premium income. However, some states allow all policy dividends to be deducted from premiums for premium tax purposes. A special report for each state in which the Annual Statement is filed requires in addition that all dividends applied to policies on residents of that state be shown by dividend option and by major line of insurance. This distribution by state is generally prepared from the dividend transaction records.

FIGURE 7-3
Exhibit 7—U.S. Annual Statement.

EXHIBIT 7 — DIVIDENDS AND COUPONS* TO POLICYHOLDERS

	DIVIDENDS		COUPONS	
	(1) LIFE	(2) ACCIDENT AND HEALTH	(3) LIFE	(4) ACCIDENT AND HEALTH
1. Applied to pay renewal premiums				
2. Applied to shorten the endowment or premium-paying period				
3. Applied to provide paid-up additions				
4. Applied to provide paid-up annuities				
5. TOTAL LINES 1-4				
6. Paid in cash				
7. Left on deposit with the company				
8.				
9. TOTAL LINES 5-8				
10. Amount due and unpaid (Item 6, Page 3)				
11. Provision for annual dividend and coupon policies (Item 7, Page 3, in part)				
11A. Terminal dividends (Item 7, Page 3, in part)				
12. Provision for deferred dividend policies (Item 7, Page 3, in part)				
12A. Amount provisionally held for deferred dividend policies not included in line 12 (Item 8, Page 3)				
13. TOTAL LINES 10-12A				
14. Line 13 of previous year				
15. TOTAL DIVIDENDS AND COUPONS TO POLICYHOLDERS (LINES 9+13-14)	(To Page 4, Item 28)		(To Page 4, Item 11A)	

*Includes coupons, guaranteed annual pure endowments and similar benefits.

Annual Statement Aspects—Canada

As with the Annual Statement used in the United States, much information about dividends and nonforfeiture options is required in the Canadian Annual Statement. On the liabilities page of the Balance Sheet used by Canadian insurers, three lines are used to report amounts on deposit with the company, other contract liabilities, and provisions for dividends and experience-rating refunds to policyowners. Details of each of these amounts are presented in Exhibits 11, 17, and 18, respectively.

Exhibit 11—Amounts on Deposit with the Company (Annual Statement page 33) is used to reconcile the past year-end total of a company's deposit liabilities, including dividends, with the current year-end total. Four items essential to such reconciliation are reported in this exhibit. The following three items are added to the past year-end total: (1) adjustments because of changes in book rates of exchange, (2) deposits made during the year, and (3) interest credited, which is entered as a cost in the insurer's income account. The fourth item, the amount of money withdrawn during the year, is deducted from the past year's total.

Exhibit 17—Other Contract Liabilities (Annual Statement page 40) reports on the amounts of dividends and experience rating refunds due and unpaid. Provisions for dividends and experience rating refunds payable in the coming year are reported in Exhibit 18 (page 40).

7 Policy Benefit Settlements

FIGURE 7-4
Exhibit 1, Part 3—Canadian Annual Statement.

PART 3: DIVIDENDS TO POLICYHOLDERS*

DIRECT:

PAID OR PAYABLE IN CASH	20
LEFT WITH COMPANY AT INTEREST	21
DEPOSITED IN SEGREGATED FUNDS	22
APPLIED AS SINGLE PREMIUMS FOR: PAID-UP ADDITIONS	23
REDUCING PREMIUMS	24
OTHER	25
	26
SUB TOTAL DIRECT	▲ 27
INCURRED ON REINSURANCE ACCEPTED	28
RECEIVED ON REINSURANCE CEDED	29
TOTAL NET OF CEDED (27+28-29)	▲ 30

*INCLUDING EXPERIENCE RATING REFUNDS UNDER GROUP CONTRACTS

Canadian insurers report summary information regarding dividends to policyowners in Part 3 of Exhibit 1: Premiums, Commissions, and Dividends—Life (Annual Statement page 22—see Figure 7-4). Columns are constructed for the presentation of dividend information for insurance and annuity products sold to both individual policyowners and group policyholders. As with the U.S. Annual Statement, the different dividend options are represented on different lines of the exhibit.

In this Exhibit, dividends that have been paid or are payable in cash include dividends that policyowners have applied towards (1) the payment of due premiums, (2) the payment of a loan granted by the insurer, and (3) the purchase of any benefit outside the provisions of the policy.

Dividends that policyowners have left on deposit with the company to accumulate interest are also reported in Exhibit 1. The interest that accumulates on dividends left on deposit is not included in this exhibit but, as mentioned above, should be reported in Exhibit 11. Another line of Exhibit 1 reports the amount of current dividends applied to purchase units in segregated funds. A **segregated fund** is an asset account that stands apart from a company's general account. Segregated funds are used in accounting for those investments that do not arise from money collected from sales of a company's guaranteed life insurance products.

Exhibit 1 also presents the amount of dividends applied as single premiums (1) for paid-up additions and (2) towards a reduction in premiums. The amount reported for dividends applied as single premiums is included in the total of single premiums presented in Part 1 of Exhibit 1. The *reducing premiums* line is used to record only those dividends that have been applied to purchase a reduction of premiums over a period of years. For the purposes of this calculation, dividends applied (a) towards the payment of the next premium only or (b) to reduce the number of premium payments during the next year are not considered to be purchases of premium reductions.

Key Terms

dividends due and unpaid
dividend accumulations
bonus additions
reserve released

dividends payable in the following year
terminal policy dividend
dollar control
segregated fund

Review Questions and Exercises

1. What are the uses of the different types of data in the master dividend record?
2. List and describe the various dividend liability classifications.
3. Define *terminal policy dividend*.
4. What transaction could the following journal entry represent?

    Policy Dividends Applied to Premiums 350
    Policy Dividends Paid 80
        Premium Income 350
        Cash 80

5. Given the following dollar totals for an individual policy, determine the amount payable to the policyowner on surrender of the policy.

    Cash surrender value of the policy $6,000
    Cash surrender value of the paid-up additions 400
    Dividend deposits 1,200
    Loan interest refund 30
    Policy loan outstanding 1,000

    What would the journal entry be for payment of this amount?

8
Claim and Contract Settlement

Learning Objectives

After reading this chapter, you should be able to:

- Describe the different journal entries used for reporting payment of death claims, disability claims, matured endowment claims, and annuities
- List items that can be deducted from or added to the face amount of a life insurance policy before payment of the death benefit is made
- Describe the effect of reinsurance benefits on accounting entries
- List reasons that a claim settlement may not be made until long after the claim is reported
- Describe the four types of unpaid claim liabilities reported in the U.S. Annual Statement Balance Sheet
- Understand the overall Annual Statement presentation of claims

Introduction

Claims are defined as requests for payments under the terms and conditions of life and health insurance policies. Payments on annuities and supplementary contracts are known as **contract payments.** This chapter discusses the accounting and Annual Statement aspects of both claim settlements and the contract payment liabilities associated with life and health insurance policies.

Since the amounts of both claims and contract payments are often quite large, requests for these payments must be examined carefully and approved by a qualified person before money is paid. (An overview of the claim settlement process is shown in Figure 8-1.) The responsibility for authorizing payments and accounting entries in connection with claim settlements is assigned to a claim examiner. The claim examiner is a specialist in investigating claims and should be thoroughly familiar with various policy and contract provisions. When the company makes claim and contract settlements, cooperation between the insurance company's claim examiners and the accounting department helps control the company's settlement process. (Internal controls are discussed more fully in Chapter 13.)

In many companies, journal entries for claim settlements are made when a claim is approved. No entry is made prior to the approval date of the claim even though the company may have previously known the exact amount payable to the beneficiary. If a check is issued, the entry is made in connection with issuance of the check. If the proceeds are left with the company under one of the settlement options, the entry is made as soon as the amounts and conditions of the settlement contract are established. On the other hand, some companies establish a liability for a claim when notice of the claim is received. Many Canadian companies also make journal entries for claims as they are reported. Canadian companies might also simultaneously establish an asset, if applicable, for amounts due from reinsurance companies.

Claim payment entries are quite simple if no policy loans, premiums, or dividend values are outstanding. In companies that record claim settlements only when they are approved, the entry consists of a debit to an insurance benefit account that identifies the type of claim being paid, such as Death Claims Paid—Ordinary, and a credit to Cash. (Throughout this chapter, the journal entries should be considered, unless otherwise stated, to refer to ordinary insurance.)

If an insured dies accidentally while insured under an accidental death rider or provision, the amount of the accidental death benefit payable is debited to a separate account to provide necessary Annual Statement information. For example, assume that Jim Miller purchased from the Lighthouse Insurance Company a life insurance policy on his own life. The policy had a $50,000 death benefit and a $50,000 accidental death benefit. If Mr. Miller dies and the claim examiner determines that his beneficiary is entitled to the face value of the policy as well as the accidental death benefit, the journal entry that Lighthouse's accountant would record upon payment of Mr. Miller's accidental death claim would be:

    Death Claims Paid 50,000
    Accidental Death Claims Paid 50,000
        Cash 100,000

Accounting controls and records are required for calculating claim liability amounts at the end of each year and for controlling claim payments made in installments. These controls vary according to claim classifications and are,

8 Claim and Contract Settlement

FIGURE 8-1
An overview of the claim settlement process.

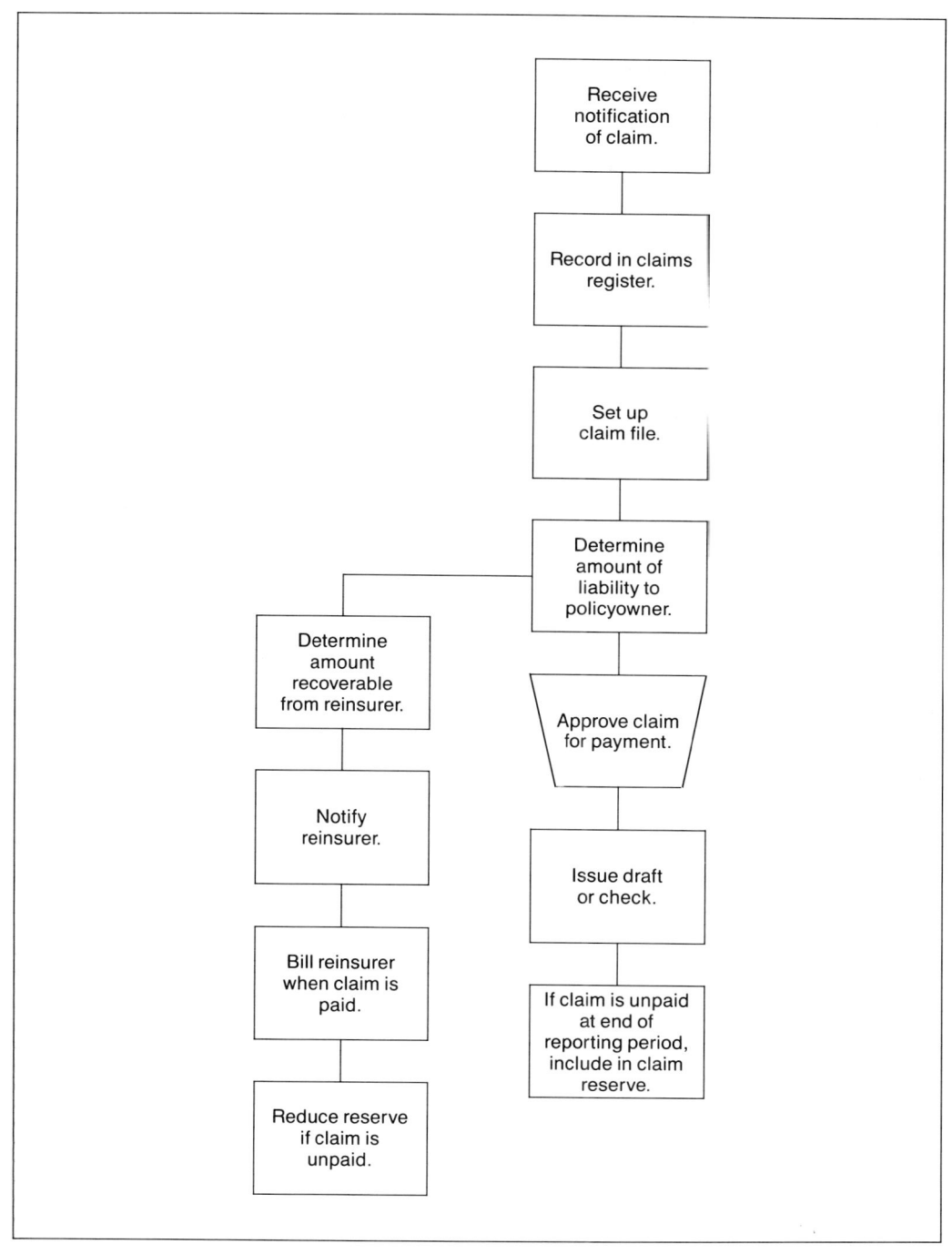

therefore, discussed after the classifications themselves. The two principal claim classifications are life insurance claims, including matured endowments, and health insurance claims.

Life Insurance Claims

Most life insurance policies provide for payment of the policy's face amount in the event of the insured's death. Some universal life products provide for payment of more than the face amount of the policy. In addition, numerous other adjustments can typically be made to the amount payable to the beneficiary. As a result, the actual amount of death benefit payable can be more or less than the policy's face amount. In the insurer's books, the claim account will usually reflect the gross amount of all claims, while debits and credits to other accounts will reflect adjustments to the gross amount. Examples of the various types of adjustments that could affect the amount of proceeds payable under a death claim are presented below.

Items that may be *added to* the death benefit include

- return of premiums that have been paid in advance for periods beyond the next policy anniversary,
- return of the balance on deposit in a premium deposit fund,
- paid-up additions that have been purchased by the policyowner,
- return of premiums paid for the balance of the policy year from the date of the insured's death,
- policy dividends currently payable but not yet paid,
- dividends left with the company to accumulate at interest,
- unearned interest on a policy loan paid beyond the date of death, and
- interest paid on delayed claims.

The final item listed above reflects a recent practice in which companies are required to pay interest on delayed claims. The interest accumulates between the date on which the policy should have originally been settled and the date of final settlement. The interest is accrued in each year as an expense for delaying claim payment and is paid out to the claimant along with the policy proceeds.

Items that may be *deducted from* the death benefit include

- outstanding policy loans,
- accrued policy loan interest at the date of death,
- premiums due and unpaid if death occurs during the grace period, and
- deferred premiums (deducted by some companies).

To show the effect of such additions and deductions on the basic journal entry for claim settlement, assume that a person insured under a $10,000 ordinary insurance policy died in an automobile accident and that his policy provided for an accidental death benefit equal to the face amount. Assume also that

- dividend accumulations with interest totaled $532 at the date of death,
- a $2,000 loan against the policy existed on the date of death, and
- $10 interest on the policy loan had been paid in advance.

The compound entry to record the settlement of this policy would be:

```
Death Claims Paid . . . . . . . . . . . . . . . . . . . . . 10,000
Accidental Death Claims Paid . . . . . . . . . . . . 10,000
Dividends on Deposit . . . . . . . . . . . . . . . . . . . . 532
Policy Loan Interest . . . . . . . . . . . . . . . . . . . . . . 10
    Policy Loans . . . . . . . . . . . . . . . . . . . . . . . . . . . . . 2,000
    Cash . . . . . . . . . . . . . . . . . . . . . . . . . . . . . . . . . . 18,542
```

The $18,542 paid in cash represents the company's total liability to the beneficiary ($20,000 in death benefits plus $542 in dividend deposits and policy loan interest paid in advance) minus the amount of policy loan still owed to the insurer ($2,000). Note that the dividend accumulations payable are entered separately from the amount of the death claim paid.

The policy's premium payment status can also affect the benefit payable and the entries made when the claim is settled. If the insured died during the grace period and if a premium was due and unpaid, the claim payment entry must include a credit to Premium Income since premium payments must be up-to-date before claims can be settled. The credit to Cash is subsequently reduced by the amount of the premium due. In case of death during the grace period, the full premium due is usually deducted from the death benefit, but some companies deduct only a pro-rata fractional premium. For example, if a quarterly premium is due, many companies deduct a quarterly premium from the death benefit. Others deduct only enough to pay for one month's coverage during the grace period. Many companies refund any portion of the premium paid beyond the date of death. In such a case, the premium account is debited for the amount of the refund.

Adjustments to the face amount of a policy are not always reflected in the accounting entries. A reduction in the face amount payable to correct a misstatement of age on the application requires no separate entry. Also, no separate entry is required for the settlement of paid-up additions. Both of these adjustments usually are made directly to the amount payable and are included in the debit to Death Claims Paid. However, although a separate claim account is not required for the paid-up additions, some companies may use a different account to maintain better control of records relating to changes in paid-up additions. To demonstrate the effect of adjustments to the face amount payable, assume that a $5,000 death claim was incurred on an ordinary policy during the grace period. An age adjustment reduced the amount payable to $4,750. The policy had paid-up additions of $100. A terminal cash dividend of $50 was payable, and the current monthly premium due at the time of death was $15. The entry to record payment of this claim would be:

    Death Claims Paid 4,850
    Dividends Paid 50
        Premium Renewal 15
        Cash 4,885

Note that the debit to Death Claims Paid reflects both the amount of the age-corrected death claim and the amount of paid-up additions purchased on the policy.

A number of other situations exist in which the death claim paid is different from the policy's face amount. If the amount of death benefit settlement is adjusted because of the suicide of the insured within the exclusion period, the amount of the entry is an adjusted death benefit amount. For example, if an insured commits suicide soon after paying $150 as an initial premium and the policy provides that the company's liability in such a case shall be limited to an amount equal to the premiums paid, the entry is:

    Death Claims Paid 150
        Cash 150

Some companies, though, treat the return of the premium amount in the case of the insured's suicide as a reversal of the premium received entry. Assuming the policy had been in force for more than one year, the entry would be:

    Premium Renewal 150
        Cash 150

If a claim presented during the contestable period is denied because of misrepresentation or fraud in the policy application, the policy is deemed to be void from its inception. In such a case, a refund of all premiums must be made. As with some companies' payments in case of the insured's suicide, the entry is treated as a premium refund. Assuming the policy was in its first year and the premium paid was $200, the entry would appear as:

    Premiums—First Year 200
        Cash 200

Sometimes, a policyowner may have obtained an insurance policy by misrepresenting the state of the insured's health, yet the insurer wishes to avoid a lawsuit. In such a case, the company might make a compromise settlement. The entry for a compromise settlement is no different from the entry for the payment of a full death benefit. To record a $2,000 check paid as a compromise settlement of a $5,000 claim, the entry is:

    Death Claims Paid 2,000
        Cash 2,000

Matured Endowment Payments

When an endowment insurance policy reaches maturity, the entry is the same as for a death claim except that the account debited to record the claim payment is Matured Endowments Paid. Assume that the following figures apply to a matured endowment insurance policy with a face amount of $10,000:

- a policy dividend of $113 was payable on the maturity date,
- the policyowner had $500 in dividend accumulations and $800 of paid-up additions,
- a $5,320 policy loan is outstanding against the policy, and
- policy loan interest of $116 is due.

The entry to record the settlement of this policy would be:

```
Matured Endowments Paid  . . . . . . . . . . . . . 10,800
Policy Dividends Paid  . . . . . . . . . . . . . . . . . . 113
Dividends on Deposit  . . . . . . . . . . . . . . . . . . 500
    Policy Loans . . . . . . . . . . . . . . . . . . . . . . . . . . . . . . 5,320
    Policy Loan Interest . . . . . . . . . . . . . . . . . . . . . . . . 116
    Cash . . . . . . . . . . . . . . . . . . . . . . . . . . . . . . . . . . . 5,977
```

The $5,977 total results from the deduction of the policy loan and interest due to the company from the total payable to the policyowner. The Dividends on Deposit account is a liability account.

A few policies provide a series of small annual endowments payable to policyowners. These annual endowments frequently are in the form of coupons attached to policies and may be applied under the same options as dividends. Coupons differ from dividends, however, in that both the frequency and the amount of payment for coupons are guaranteed. When these coupons, or endowment amounts, are paid, a matured endowment account is debited and Cash is credited. When they are applied to purchase additional insurance, an entry may not be required because the company merely transfers the reserve from one form of insurance to another. A company might make an entry, though, if the policyowner uses the endowment to purchase an annuity. The entry would be made in order to record the change in the type of business. Nonetheless, many companies make entries regarding these endowments in order to provide necessary financial data. The recording of such entries also helps maintain the accuracy of the company's inforce statistics.

Effects of Life Insurance Claim Settlements on Surplus

Amounts debited to the Death Claims Paid account result in a decrease in surplus. However, policy reserves are released when a claim is reported and pending, so that the effect on surplus is less than the amount paid for the death benefit. Assume, for example, that a death claim payment on a policy totals $5,000. If the reserve on the policy is $2,100, the claim will reduce surplus by $2,900 ($5,000 − $2,100). Payment of a claim for accidental death, however, reduces surplus almost to the full extent of that claim because reserves released on accidental death claims are relatively small. Smaller reserves are set aside for accidental death claims since the incidence of such claims is low. Group insurance certificates are usually term insurance with little or no reserve released at the time of an insured's death. Therefore, a group claim has a greater impact on surplus than an ordinary claim of the same size.

Surplus is not affected by a matured endowment settlement because, with an endowment policy, the combined reserve of the policy and paid-up additions (if any) on the maturity date is exactly equal to the total amount of the policy plus additions. As in the case of a death claim, this reserve is released when the payment is made.

Health Insurance Claims

As used in this text, "health insurance" refers to the type of insurance known in the U.S. Annual Statement as "accident and health insurance" and in the Canadian Annual Statement as "accident and sickness insurance." Health insurance claims vary depending on the type of coverage and the company issuing the policy, but they fall into two major categories: disability claims and medical expense claims.

Insurers typically offer two types of disability insurance. **Disability income insurance** is a form of health insurance that provides a monthly income benefit should the insured become disabled as defined in the policy. The other type of disability insurance commonly offered is a **waiver-of-premium benefit** which specifies that the insurer will not require premium payments as long as the insured is disabled. Disability insurance benefits continue until the insured recovers or dies, or until the policy benefit limit is reached.

Medical expense insurance pays for the cost of hospital room and board, miscellaneous hospital expenses, surgical expenses, and medical care as set forth in the policy. Major medical insurance, one form of medical expense insurance, provides for a high overall maximum limit on all covered expenses and usually requires that the insured pay a deductible amount and a percentage of the remaining expenses.

Health insurance policies state the conditions under which the company may refuse to accept further premiums, thereby cancelling insurance coverage. These renewability conditions can be categorized as (1) renewable at the option of the company, (2) guaranteed renewable, (3) collectively renewable, and (4) guaranteed renewable and noncancellable. The company cannot refuse to continue a guaranteed renewable policy but can increase premium rates for all policies in a particular premium class. If a policy is guaranteed renewable and noncancellable, the company cannot cancel insurance, refuse to renew coverage, or increase premium rates.

U.S. companies are required to show individual health insurance premiums in the Annual Statement by each of these classifications. Premiums for accident-only coverages are also shown separately. Therefore, accounts are usually maintained for claims paid within each of the renewability classifications and within the principal health insurance classifications of disability claims and medical expense claims. Accounts may also be further subdivided, for example, into hospital benefits and surgical benefits.

The accounting entries for health insurance claims are similar to entries for life insurance claims. The processes for controlling claim payments are somewhat different, however, because the policy usually remains in force after a claim has been paid.

Disability Claims

When an insured becomes disabled as defined by the company in a disability income policy, he or she becomes eligible for a series of payments that will continue until death or recovery from the disability or until the policy benefit limit is reached. A claim examiner is responsible for determining that the insured is still disabled before each payment is made, although the examiner may investigate the claim only once per year if recovery seems unlikely. A typical entry for a $400 monthly disability payment is:

>   Disability Claims Paid 400
>   Cash 400

Many life policies contain a rider or policy provision stating that the insurance company will waive the policy's premium payments for as long as the insured is disabled. Ordinary life insurance premiums that are waived because of the insured's disability are considered *claims* against the disability subline of business and *premium income* to the life insurance line of business. The amount of the journal entry for a premium waiver is the amount of the gross premium waived. In a U.S. life and health company, a typical entry to record the waiver of a $110 life insurance premium because of disability is:

>   Premiums Waived—Disability 110
>   Premium Renewal—Life 110

Premiums applicable to supplemental coverages, such as premiums for accidental death benefits, are also waived under the disability waiver provision. If, in the example just given, the policyowner also owed a $5 accidental death benefit premium, the amount of this supplemental coverage premium would be added to the debit and credit entries. Thus, with the waiver of the additional $5 premium, the entry would appear as:

    Premiums Waived—Disability 115
        Premium Renewal—Life 115

The premium record must be posted as though the premium had been paid in cash, but the premium taxes and commissions are not payable since the premium was not actually received by the company. Some companies use a special income account to facilitate premium tax reporting and financial statement preparation.

Canadian companies are not required to make entries for premiums waived because of disability since the Annual Statement excludes these amounts from premium income. However, this information is shown in a special disability exhibit. A company might, therefore, prefer to make entries and then offset these two nominal accounts against each other when the Annual Statement is prepared.

In the case of health insurance provided by an individual policy, no entry is required for waiver of premium because both the income and the disbursement are in the same line of business. Many companies, however, do make such an entry to facilitate claim studies. A typical entry for health insurance waiver would be the same as for ordinary insurance, with only a change of line of business in the account titles. For example, assume that Tom Shepherd owned an individual health insurance policy that provided for a waiver of the $75 premium in the case of his disability as defined in the policy. The entry to record this premium waiver would be:

    Premiums Waived—Disability—Health 75
        Premium Renewal—Health 75

Medical Expense Claims

Medical expense insurance is usually referred to as *hospital insurance*. This term is a misnomer, however, since medical expense insurance provides different types of coverages that pay the cost of hospital room, board, and other expenses; surgical expenses; and the cost of limited medical care. These various coverages are known as *basic coverages*. A limit for each coverage may be stated in the policy as the maximum number of days the benefit will be payable or as the maximum amount payable.

Major medical insurance is a form of medical expense insurance and is characterized by a high overall maximum limit on all covered expenses rather than by limits on different types of expenses. However, some limits for particular types of expenses are included within the maximum limit. The maximum may be as high as $100,000 or $1,000,000 for a single illness within a calendar year or policy year. Normally, these policies pay less than the total costs incurred by the insured. For example, on a $1,000 hospital care bill, the insured may be required to pay the first $200 and 20 percent of the remainder. The amount paid by the insurer in such a case would be $640 (80 percent of [$1,000 − $200]).

A typical journal entry recording a medical expense claim on a group insurance policy would show a debit to Hospital Benefits Paid—Group and a credit to Cash. For recording a payment to a surgeon, the debit would be to Surgical Claims Paid—Group. Many companies, however, prior to actual payment of a medical expense claim, establish reserves for claims incurred but not yet reported and claims in the process of settlement. The journal entries for the establishment of these reserves are reversed when actual payment is made.

Effect of disability claims on reserves

Payments under a disability claim can continue far into the future. Since insurers do not know what the total disability claim amount might be, a company's accountants or actuaries usually create a claim reserve liability that is the present value of all amounts that are predicted to become payable while the insured is disabled. This amount is determined in accordance with morbidity tables and interest rates used by the company for this purpose. Reserves of this type are frequently called **disabled life reserves**.

Morbidity tables allow for the determination of the probable occurrence and duration of disability or sickness. The longer a disability claim exists, the longer the claim is likely to continue into the future. For example, at age 45, a disability that has existed for one year is likely to continue for three additional years, whereas a disability that has existed for two years is likely to continue for four more years. To adjust for this pattern of morbidity, the reserve liability for a disability claim continues to increase with the passage of time even though claim payments are being made regularly. As the end of the claim period approaches, the reserve liability begins to decrease.

When an insured person recovers from a disability and is able to return to work, the disabled life reserve is released. Some insureds recover quickly, allowing reserves to be released early, while other insureds' disability periods are longer, necessitating increased reserves. No ledger entry is made to record changes in disability claim reserve liabilities since the reserves are usually treated as non-ledger liabilities.

Annuity and Supplementary Contract Payments

Annuity payments are periodic payments of a fixed or variable amount that are made during a fixed period or for the lifetime of one or more people. Annuity contracts are purchased primarily to furnish income to one or more people, known as the annuitant(s). Payments from supplementary contracts, also known as settlement contracts, arise from an insurance policy's provisions that allow the insured or beneficiary to select the method of disbursing the proceeds of a life insurance policy. If the proceeds are held at interest or paid in installments over a specified period, the contract is called a **supplementary contract without life contingencies** (referred to in many companies as **WOLC**). When the duration of the payment period depends on the lifetime of the beneficiary, the contract is referred to as a **supplementary contract with life contingencies (WLC)**. A supplementary contract may be a combination of the two types, such as when an insured elects payment for the beneficiary's life with a specified number of years guaranteed.

Recording of Supplementary Contracts and Annuities

When a supplementary contract goes into effect, a new set of records is generally prepared. The contract is given an identification number different from that of the terminated policy. Companies usually maintain a register in which the initial information on supplementary contracts is recorded. This register is a control device, enabling the company to determine which supplementary contracts are outstanding and, therefore, which ones should be valued as liabilities.

An annuity payment record is similar to a supplementary contract record. Both of these records usually do not show an outstanding balance but instead describe the contract and the payments that have been made or are to be made. The record gives the amount of each installment, the name of the payee, the payment dates, and the period of the installments. A balance is normally maintained only when settlement proceeds are left on deposit at interest and are subject to withdrawal.

Settlement of Supplementary Contracts and Annuities

If the proceeds of a life insurance claim settlement are left with the insurer under a supplementary contract, an income account is typically credited for the portion of the settlement to be applied under the chosen settlement option. Account names for these income accounts might be Consideration for Supplementary Contracts with Life Contingencies (WLC) or Consideration for Supplementary Contracts without Life Contingencies (WOLC), according to the circumstances of the case. The complete entry for settlement of a supplementary contract is shown in the following example.

Using the situation presented on pages 163 and 165 for payment of an accidental death benefit, assume that the company agreed to pay $10,542 and to hold the remaining $8,000 of the settlement to provide a monthly income for 10 years certain and for life thereafter. The entry for this particular settlement would be:

```
Death Claims Paid .................... 10,000
Accidental Death Claims Paid ........... 10,000
Dividends on Deposit .................... 532
Policy Loan Interest ...................... 10
    Policy Loans............................... 2,000
    Consideration for
        Supplementary Contracts WLC .............. 8,000
    Cash ..................................... 10,542
```

The consideration for the supplementary contract is simply deducted from the Cash account and credited to the appropriate liability account.

Recording payments of annuities is relatively simple. An account for Annuity Benefits is debited and Cash is credited in the amount of the payment to the annuitant or beneficiary.

Reinsurance Benefit Entries

If a claim is presented on a policy that has been reinsured, the claim history for that policy is not considered complete until the reimbursement check is received from the reinsurance company. Each reinsurance claim in connection with ordinary insurance is usually paid individually. Reinsurance on group life insurance or health insurance may be settled either individually or on a periodic payment plan, such as once each month. A typical entry when the reimbursement check is received from the reinsurance company is:

```
Cash ................................... xxx
    Reinsurance Benefits Received ................. xxx
```

If an accidental death benefit was reinsured, a credit to Reinsurance Benefits Received—Accidental Death would be added to the entry, with a corresponding increase in the debit to Cash.

The accounting entries for reinsurance benefits received are affected by the type of reinsurance agreement in effect between the insurer and the reinsurer. In the case of coinsurance, the amount of the credit entry for the life portion of the reinsurance is the face amount reinsured. If the reinsurance is yearly renewable term, the reserve on the reinsured portion of the principal policy is deducted from the face amount of the reinsurance, with the debit to Cash adjusted accordingly. The reinsurance accounts credited are income accounts.

Claim Records and Controls

Claim disbursements may be classified by their effect on policy status. Classifications of this type are useful in discussing claim accounting records and control processes as well as the effect that a particular type of claim has on the company's claim liability. The classifications for different claim disbursements are (1) single claim payments that terminate the policy liability, as in the case of death claims or matured endowments; (2) single claim payments, such as medical expense claims, that do not terminate the policy; and (3) continuous periodic payments, such as installments or payments made under supplementary contracts or disability income provisions, that are made after the filing of a single original claim.

Payments made under the third classification can be terminated by death or special compromise settlements. The settlement on a particular policy might involve both the first and third classifications. For example, a death claim might be settled by issuing a supplementary contract, in which case the initial claim settlement would fall under the first classification and the payments under the supplementary contract would fall under the third.

Except for matured endowments on which the payment of the policy benefit is initiated by the company, claim reporting is generally initiated by the policyowner, the insured, the policy beneficiary, or, in the case of group insurance, by the employer. A notice of sickness, injury, or death is sent either directly to the company or to the policyowner's agent or broker. Notification of a claim includes the

- notice of death, injury, or sickness;
- cause of death or nature of injury or sickness;
- date of occurrence; and
- insured's name and policy number.

When the home office is notified that a claim has been filed, the policy records are assembled and an entry is made in a claim register. The purposes of this process are

1. to control the processing of claims from the time the first notice is received until payment is made and the reinsurance, if any, is collected;
2. to enable the company to determine for Annual Statement purposes the liability for claims incurred but not yet paid at the end of the year; and
3. to enable a company that maintains all items on the ledger to report the asset total for amounts recoverable from reinsurers.

The pertinent policy information and all currently available information about the claim are entered in the register. Major steps in processing the claim are recorded in the register as they occur. If the claim is not valid because of misrepresentation or fraud in obtaining the policy, that fact is also recorded in the claim register. In case of death claims, if an amount different from the policy's face amount is payable as a result of a suicide, age correction, or for any other reason, such facts are also entered in the register.

In the case of claims that do not cause the policy to terminate, a separate claim number is customarily assigned to each claim. This number provides an audit trail from the claim register to the policy record, the claim papers, and the disbursement check. When claim numbers are assigned, companies typically establish a separate file for each claim to prevent undue cluttering of the principal policy record since many claims may exist on a single policy. With disability claims, claim examiners typically maintain a control that indicates when the next payment is payable or when the next premium is to be waived. A simple record of payment data serves this purpose.

Many companies do not use claim numbers or claim control records if a claim terminates the policy, as happens with a death claim. In these cases, all records related to the claim and the disbursement are filed in the principal record for the particular policy. If proceeds are left with the company for later disbursement under a supplementary contract, a new file and record are prepared under a new contract number.

Drafts

Some insurers issue drafts in payment of claims. These drafts are similar in appearance to checks, but the drafts are not automatically charged by the bank against the company's bank account. Instead, the bank notifies the company each day of drafts received. After approval of the draft, the company either issues a check to the bank in the amount of the draft or allows the bank to charge the company's account. The bank sends a charge notice to serve as the basis for any entry in the books and for use in bank statement reconciliation. The person presenting the draft is typically reimbursed in the same manner as if he or she were presenting a check.

Companies issue drafts because they allow for quick payment of claims without issuance of checks. Drafts are a better way to provide control of the company's funds than checks. Drafts drawn improperly or drawn to pay an amount not properly payable may be refused by the insurance company, but such refusal may not be available for a check written on the company's accounts. In addition to this advantage, drafts create less paperwork than do checks.

Drafts are recorded by one of two methods:

1. Under the "controlled as issued" method, drafts are recorded immediately as paid losses. The draft copy is used to record (1) a reduction in the claim reserve, (2) an increase in the losses paid in the subsidiary

loss records, and (3) the increase of paid losses in the general ledger. When the drafts that have been presented for payment are honored by the insurer, the transaction is shown as a debit to a liability account for drafts and a credit to the Cash account.
2. Under the "controlled as paid" method, drafts are recorded only when honored. The draft copy is used to record the loss payment after the copy has been matched with the cleared draft. When drafts are issued by independent or field adjusters, a system is needed to control both the original draft and the copy because either can be received by the company first. Suspense accounts are normally used for this type of control. The Suspense account is debited when the draft is honored by the bank and credited when the draft copy is received.

Claim Liabilities

The amount payable on claims being investigated can be approximated quite accurately at the end of each year by examining the company's claim registers and then totaling the unpaid claims. However, estimates are also made of other claim liabilities that have been incurred but not yet reported to the company. These estimates must be made carefully because large amounts may be involved and every dollar of claim liability reduces the company's surplus.

Claim settlements frequently are not made until many months after the claims are reported or incurred. Reasons for this delay include the following:

- Time is required to investigate and determine whether a claim is covered by the policy. This investigation is particularly necessary in the case of a contested claim or in the case of a restricted coverage such as accidental death coverage.
- Determining the proper payee or ascertaining the amount payable may be difficult.
- An insured person might not file a claim until some time after the claim is first incurred, particularly in the case of a disability.
- Releases from state inheritance or federal estate tax offices are often required.

The date a claim is incurred determines whether or not a claim liability should be set up. The incurred date determines the beginning of the insurer's liability even though the policyowner or insured may wait months before filing his or her claim. In the case of a death claim, a claim liability is incurred upon the death of the insured. Assuming no special circumstances, the beneficiary is due the proceeds upon the insured's death.

In the case of health insurance, unless the policy provides otherwise, a claim may be incurred on the day the sickness or injury first manifests itself if the policy was in force on that date. If a medical expense policy provides that coverage must be in force when the insured enters the hospital, the claim is incurred on the date of entry. Many disability policies include a waiting period provision which states that payments will not start until after the disability has continued for six months. In such a case, two significant dates for establishing the company's liability exist: (1) the date when disability actually began and (2) the date when the waiting period restriction is satisfied. A liability of an indefinite amount is created as of the first date. The insurer knows this date only after it has passed. This indefinite liability is often not recorded in the general ledger. On the second date, a definite liability equal to the present value of future payments is established.

For inclusion in the U.S. Annual Statement, liabilities for unpaid claims are divided into four parts:

1. claims in the course of settlement
2. due and unpaid claims
3. incurred but unreported claims
4. resisted claims

These four liabilities are reported on the U.S. Annual Statement liability page. Two additional types of claim liabilities that occur only in connection with health insurance claims are (1) the present value of amounts not yet due on claims and (2) the reserve for future contingent benefits. These health insurance claim liabilities are called **claim reserves** and are not treated as unpaid claims. Instead, they are treated as health insurance reserves, and are reported on a different line of the U.S. Annual Statement liability page.

Claims in the course of settlement are those claims that have been reported to the company and which are being investigated. The amount of claims in the course of settlement is calculated through an examination of claim registers and claim files. The full amount claimed is usually set up as a liability even though some claims have not yet been approved. On disability policies, the liability for claims in the course of settlement is often reported as the amount of claim that would be payable if the claimant recovered from the disability on the valuation date.

Due and unpaid claims are those claims that have been approved by the company but which have not been paid. Claims typically remain due and unpaid because of delays in the disbursement routine, delays in arranging settlement contracts, the time required to clarify beneficiary rights, or other factors that do not affect the amount of the liability. Only the amount that would have been payable prior to the end of a specific accounting period is included in the due and unpaid claims classification. For example, if the insured became disabled in December as defined by policy provisions, only the December payment is included as an unpaid claim. The present value of future payments is treated, as mentioned before, as claim reserves.

Incurred but unreported claims are those claims that were incurred in the accounting reporting period, but which had not been reported to the company as of the Annual Statement date. Companies rarely complete the Statement until some weeks have elapsed in the new year, so some of this claim liability can be determined by reviewing entries made in the claim registers in the new year. The liability for unreported death claims is the estimated difference between the face amount of each claim and the reserve that will be released to surplus when that claim is paid. Estimates must be used since the company does not know which insured persons died, nor the size or number of policies that will be affected.

Companies generally determine the incurred but unreported claim reserve by one of two methods:

1. Relying on past experience modified for current conditions, such as a change in the amount of insurance in force, a change in the cut-off date for estimating unreported claims, or changes in the economic environment; or
2. Determining the actual claims subsequently reported up to some point in time—such as thirty days after the Balance Sheet date—and estimating the claims yet to be reported beyond that date. Because claims are usually reported quickly, the adequacy of their reserve can generally be determined by reviewing actual claims reported before the completion and filing of the Annual Statement.

Resisted claims are claims that the company has refused to pay, but which may be paid in the future. Included in this classification are claims for benefits not clearly covered by a policy and claims that are connected with lawsuits pending against the company. The full benefit claimed—not the amount the company expects to pay—is established as the pending claim liability.

The **present value of amounts not yet due on claims** is an amount set aside as a reserve for future payments on claims currently being paid in installments, as in the case of disability income coverages and waiver-of-premium benefits. The reserve for disability income insurance and waivers of premiums provided by riders attached to life policies is described in the reserve exhibit of the U.S. Annual Statement as *reserves on disabled lives.*

The **reserve for future contingent benefits** is an amount established as a reserve for deferred maternity benefits and for any other claims that may have already been incurred, but which may be contingent upon a future event or circumstances beyond the company's control. Some companies treat deferred maternity benefits as an unearned premium liability on the assumption that a portion of the premium paid is set aside for these claims.

Annual Statement Aspects—United States

The U.S. Annual Statement blank contains two policy claim exhibits in which the claims data is assembled for reporting in the Summary of Operations, the Analysis of Operations, and on the Balance Sheet. Exhibit 11 relates to all life and health claims and is referred to here as the *general claim exhibit*. Exhibit 9, on the other hand, contains information regarding health insurance claims only.

The general claim exhibit, which appears on pages 12 and 12A of the Annual Statement, is entitled "Policy and Contract Claims" (see Figure 8-2). The exhibit is divided into two parts with columns that coincide with those in the Analysis of Operations. Lines in the first part of the general claim exhibit show the total claim liability in the following categories: (1) due and unpaid; (2) in course of settlement, divided into "resisted" and "other"; and (3) incurred but unreported, less reinsurance. These three categories can be referred to collectively as *incurred and unpaid claims*. The type of claim, such as death claim or matured endowment, is not shown in this exhibit, but the column headings provide an approximate classification by general claim categories of ordinary, group, and accident and health. Matured endowments are included with death claims, but the amounts of matured endowments, both cash basis and accrual basis, are shown in footnotes.

Part 2 of Exhibit 11 shows amounts, including reinsurance benefits, used to arrive at a company's net incurred claims. This net amount is subdivided by line of insurance when entered in the Summary of Operations and Analysis of Operations even though the net amount is not subdivided in the general claim exhibit.

The liability for supplementary contracts with life contingencies is calculated in Exhibit 8 of the Annual Statement, which covers reserves on life policies. Therefore, the reserves on supplementary contracts with life contingencies become a part of the life reserve on the liability page of the Annual Statement. The reserves for supplementary contracts without life contingencies and the liability for dividends left with the company to accumulate at interest are shown in Exhibit 10 with a separate line for each valuation rate and the rate guaranteed in the contract. Companies are permitted to value these supplementary contracts and dividend deposits using an interest rate other than that specified in the contract if the valuation produces a greater liability amount. The rate used is usually the guaranteed rate plus the excess interest rate. The column in Exhibit 10 headed Amounts Left on Deposit covers only policy proceeds and dividends left on deposit, not premiums left on deposit.

The Annual Statement blank filed in each state requires data on health insurance claims incurred and paid in that state by type of renewability clause and by method of settlement. In addition, claims of all types are presented on page 46 of the U.S. Annual Statement. Because of the information required for the many claims exhibits and schedules in the Annual Statement, each company must keep

180 Accounting in Life and Health Insurance Companies

FIGURE 8-2
Exhibit 11, Part 1—U.S. Annual Statement.

ANNUAL STATEMENT FOR THE YEAR 1985 OF THE _____ Name

EXHIBIT 11—POLICY AND CONTRACT CLAIMS

PART 1—Liability End of Current Year

	(1) TOTAL	(2) INDUSTRIAL LIFE	ORDINARY				GROUP		ACCIDENT AND HEALTH		
			(3) LIFE INSURANCE	(4) INDIVIDUAL ANNUITIES	(5) SUPPLEMENTARY CONTRACTS	(6) CREDIT LIFE* (Group and Individual)	(7) LIFE INSURANCE	(8) ANNUITIES	(9) GROUP	(10) CREDIT* (Group and Individual)	(11) OTHER
1. Due and unpaid:											
a. Direct											1. a.
b. Reinsurance assumed											b.
c. Reinsurance ceded											c.
d. Net											d.
2. In course of settlement:											2.
2.1 Resisted:											2.1
a. Direct									X X X	X X X	X X X a.
b. Reinsurance assumed									X X X	X X X	X X X b.
c. Reinsurance ceded									X X X	X X X	X X X c.
d. Net									X X X	X X X	X X X d.
2.2 Other:											2.2a.
a. Direct				†	†	†					b.
b. Reinsurance assumed				†	†	†					c.
c. Reinsurance ceded				†	†	†					d.
d. Net											
3. Incurred but unreported — net as to reinsurance				†		†	†		†	†	3.
4. Totals:											4.
a. Direct											a.
b. Reinsurance assumed											b.
c. Reinsurance ceded											c.
d. Net		•					•				d.

*Including matured endowments (but not guaranteed annual pure endowments) unpaid amounting to $ _____ in Column 2, $ _____ in Column 3 and $ _____ in Column 7.
†Include only portion of disability and accident and health claim liabilities applicable to assumed "accrued" benefits Reserves (including reinsurance assumed and net of reinsurance ceded) for unaccrued benefits for Ordinary Life Insurance $ _____ and Group Life $ _____ are included in Page 3, Item 1. (See Exhibit 8, Section F); and for Group Accident and Health $ _____
Individual Annuities $ _____ Credit Life (Group and Individual) $ _____ and Other Accident and Health $ _____ are included in Page 3, Item 2 (See Exhibit 9, Section B)
Credit (Group and Individual) Accident and Health $ _____
*Business not exceeding 120 months duration.

Form 1

a statistical record of each claim paid during the year and reconcile the total shown on the records to the general ledger accounts. Companies must also value separately the incurred but unpaid claim liabilities for each state, as well as determine an incurred total for each state in which the company is licensed. Health insurance claims and premiums must be reported to each state annually on an incurred basis for each principal plan of health insurance in force. This report is made separately from the Annual Statement.

Two claim reserve liabilities are included in a special health insurance reserve exhibit entitled Exhibit 9—Aggregate Reserve for Accident and Health policies. This exhibit consists of two parts: "A. Active Life Reserve" and "B. Claim Reserve." Columns are included for individual policies, group health insurance reserves, and for various renewability classifications.

On the liability page of the Annual Statement Balance Sheet, the total liability for unpaid life insurance claims is entered on a separate line from unpaid health insurance claims. Unpaid settlement contract installments and unpaid disability benefits provided by life policies are included with the life insurance claim liability.

In Annual Statement Schedule H, premiums, claims, and other insurance costs for health insurance are adjusted from the cash basis to the incurred basis. A company can then arrive at (1) incurred claim ratios and other significant percentages and (2) the total "gain from underwriting after dividends to policyholders." This gain is the result of deducting incurred claims, expenses, and taxes from earned premiums. The increase in the present value of future benefits and the increase in reserve for future contingent benefits are treated as part of claim costs in arriving at losses incurred in the current year as shown in this exhibit.

Annual Statement Aspects—Canada

Canadian Annual Statement Exhibit 2 (see Figure 8-3) provides an analysis of claims incurred and outstanding for a company's life business. Part 2 of this exhibit presents outstanding claims, including a provision for unreported claims. The exhibit, which is divided into participating and nonparticipating business, offers information on a company's claim experience for the categories of individual insurance, individual annuities, group insurance, and group annuities. The amounts are reflected net of reinsurance ceded as is typical throughout the Canadian Statement.

Incurred claims are displayed as death claims, accidental death claims, disability claims, matured endowments, annuity payments, and surrender values. Space is provided for other categories as defined by each insurer. A line is shown at the bottom of the exhibit to indicate the amount of reinsurance ceded in the types of business listed above. Unreported death claims are included with outstanding claims for the purpose of computing the incurred claims during the

FIGURE 8-3
Exhibit 2—Canadian Annual Statement.

23(LS)

NAME OF COMPANY ▶ YEAR OF STATEMENT 19___

EXHIBIT 2: CLAIMS INCURRED AND

		PARTICIPATING			
		INDIVIDUAL		GROUP	
		INSURANCE 01	ANNUITY 02	INSURANCE 03	ANNUITY 04

PART 1 - CLAIMS

NET OF REINSURANCE CEDED:					
DEATH CLAIMS	01				
ACCIDENTAL DEATH CLAIMS	02				
DISABILITY CLAIMS	03				
MATURED ENDOWMENTS	04		▓		▓
ANNUITY PAYMENTS	05	▓		▓	
SURRENDER VALUES	06				
	07				
	08				
TOTAL ▶	09				
REINSURANCE CEDED	10				

PART 2 - OUTSTANDING CLAIMS INCLUDING

NET OF REINSURANCE CEDED:					
DEATH CLAIMS	11				
ACCIDENTAL DEATH CLAIMS	12				
DISABILITY CLAIMS	13				
MATURED ENDOWMENTS	14		▓		▓
ANNUITY PAYMENTS	15	▓		▓	
SURRENDER VALUES	16				
	17				
	18				
PROVISION FOR UNREPORTED DEATH CLAIMS	19				
TOTAL ▶	20				
DUE FROM OTHER COMPANIES ON REINSURED CONTRACTS FOR CLAIMS PAID	21				

8 Claim and Contract Settlement

FIGURE 8-3 (cont.)

```
                                  23(RS)
```

| NAME OF COMPANY ▶ | YEAR OF STATEMENT 19 |

OUTSTANDING - LIFE ($'000)

NON-PARTICIPATING				SUBTOTALS		
INDIVIDUAL		GROUP		PARTIC- IPATING	NON- PARTIC- IPATING	TOTAL
INSURANCE 05	ANNUITY 06	INSURANCE 07	ANNUITY 08	09	10	11

INCURRED

01						
02						
03						
04	▓▓		▓▓			
05	▓▓		▓▓			
06						
07						
08						
▶09						
10						

PROVISION FOR UNREPORTED CLAIMS

11						
12						
13						
14	▓▓		▓▓			
15	▓▓		▓▓			
16						
17						
18						
19						
▶20						
21						

FIGURE 8-4
Exhibit 3—Canadian Annual Statement.

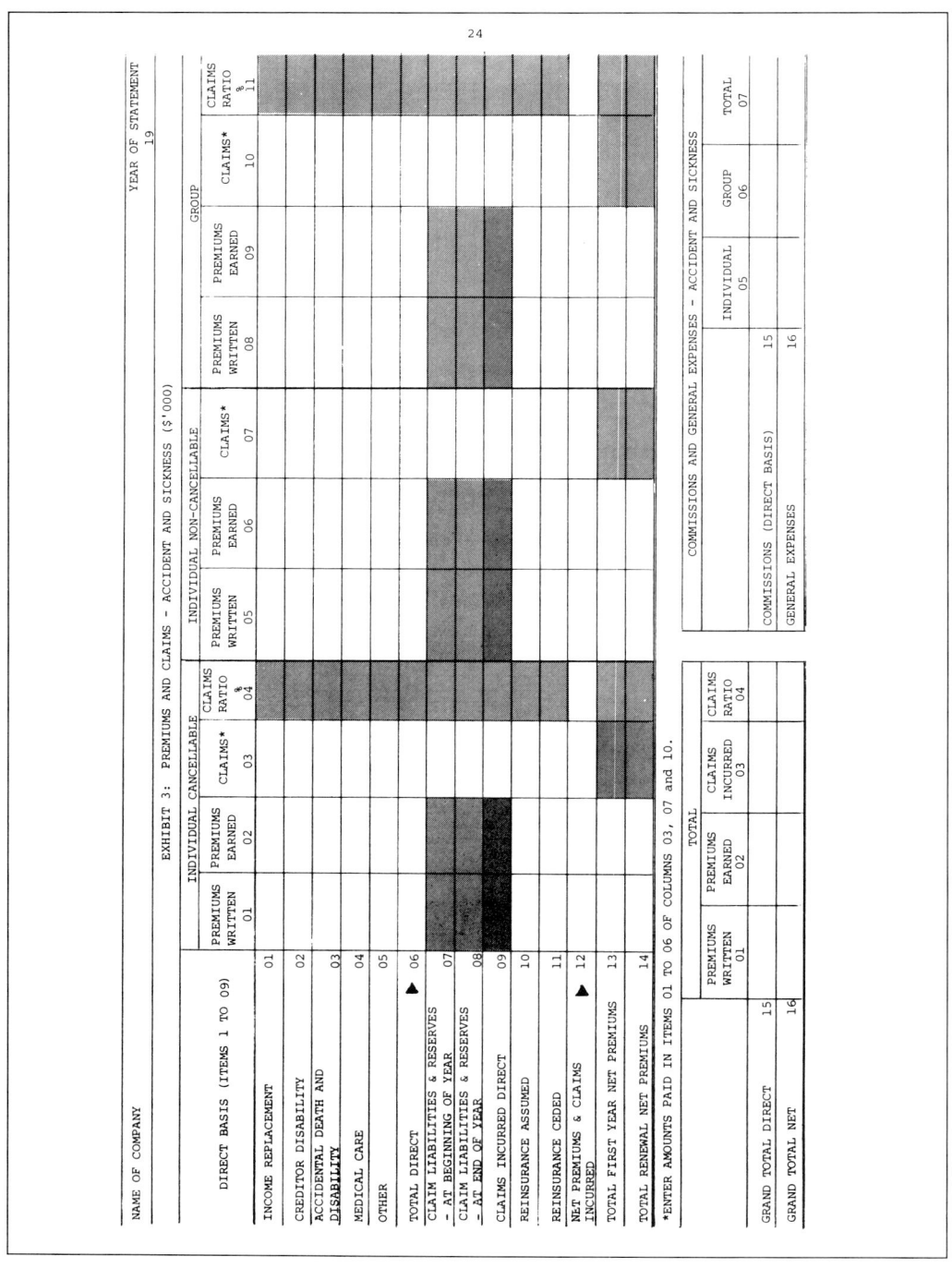

FIGURE 8-4 (cont.)
Exhibit 4—Canadian Annual Statement.

EXHIBIT 4 - CLAIM LIABILITIES (OTHER THAN INSTALMENT CLAIMS)* - ACCIDENT & SICKNESS ($'000)

NAME OF COMPANY ▲

YEAR OF STATEMENT 19__

	DIRECT			REINSURANCE ASSUMED			REINSURANCE CEDED			NET			
		INDIVIDUAL			INDIVIDUAL			INDIVIDUAL			INDIVIDUAL		
	GROUP	CANCEL-LABLE	NON CAN-CELLABLE	GROUP	CANCEL-LABLE	NON CAN-CELLABLE	GROUP	CANCEL-LABLE	NON CAN-CELLABLE	GROUP	CANCEL-LABLE	NON CAN-CELLABLE	TOTAL
	01	02	03	04	05	06	07	08	09	10	11	12	13
AMOUNTS DUE ON REPORTED CLAIMS 01													
AMOUNTS NOT YET DUE ON REPORTED CLAIMS 02													
PROVISION FOR INCURRED BUT NOT REPORTED CLAIMS 03													
PROVISION FOR ADJUSTMENT EXPENSES 04													
05													
06													
OTHER 07													
TOTAL ▲ 08													

*PROVISION FOR INSTALMENT CLAIMS IS INCLUDED IN EXHIBIT 15 PART 2

25

reporting year. The outstanding claims portion of the exhibit uses the same columns and lines of information as the incurred claims portion of the exhibit. An additional line is provided for unreported death claims, as well as amounts due from reinsurers.

The disability claim line in these exhibits reflects only disability claim payments that fell due during the year but which were not paid by the end of the year. Unreported disability claims are displayed in the actuarial exhibit and are not shown in the claims exhibit. Complete information regarding disability claims is presented in Exhibits 3 and 4 (Figure 8-4).

Key Terms

claims
disability income insurance
medical expense insurance
supplementary contracts
  without life contingencies
draft
resisted claims

contract payments
waiver-of-premium benefit
basic coverages
supplementary contracts
  with life contingencies
claim reserves
disabled life reserves

Review Questions and Exercises

1. Distinguish between claims and contract payments.
2. What journal entry would you make in order to record a cash payment of a $30,000 death benefit and a $15,000 accidental death benefit?
3. Which of these claims has the greatest impact on reserves relative to the amount payable in the death claim: an accidental death claim or a matured endowment claim?
4. What are *disabled life reserves?*
5. What are the two methods of recording drafts? How do they differ?
6. From the information available in the following journal entry, determine the death benefit payable:

    Death Claims Paid 5,000
    Accidental Death Claims Paid 7,500
    Dividends on Deposit 750
    Policy Loan Interest. 60
        Policy Loans. 1,000
        Consideration for
          Supplementary Contracts WLC 4,310
        Cash 8,000

9
Other Assets, Other Liabilities, and Separate Accounts

Learning Objectives

After reading this chapter, you should be able to:

- Identify and describe additional categories of assets and liabilities
- Understand the categorization of electronic data processing equipment as an admitted asset
- Make the journal entries necessary to adjust paid expenses from a cash basis to an accrual basis
- Give the reasons for establishing separate accounts

Introduction

In previous chapters, we have discussed the major assets and liabilities that appear on an insurer's Balance Sheet. Typically, an insurer's assets are made up primarily of investments, and its liabilities apply mainly to policy and contract provisions. This chapter includes a discussion of assets other than investments and liabilities not related to policy and contract provisions. The other assets and liabilities that are included on the Canadian Annual Statement are not significantly different than those on the U.S. Annual Statement and thus are not specifically discussed in this chapter. This chapter also includes a discussion of the assets and liabilities that appear on the Balance Sheet for a U.S. insurer's separate accounts, generally known as segregated funds or segregated accounts for Canadian insurers.

Other Assets

The insurance laws in most states specify certain assets that may be admitted when determining the total amount of a company's statutory unassigned surplus. Certain other assets, while not specifically authorized, are admitted because of their relationship to the operations of the company. This section deals with miscellaneous assets not relating to investments.

Electronic Data Processing Equipment

Unlike furniture and equipment, which are nonadmitted assets, most electronic data processing (EDP) equipment is considered an admitted asset for statutory reporting purposes in most states. A number of different reasons exist for admitting EDP equipment and not admitting other equipment and furniture. EDP equipment generally has a higher resale value than these other types of assets. Also, by treating EDP equipment as an admitted asset, regulators are allowing insurers to amortize the typically high cost of the equipment over a number of years. If EDP equipment were considered a nonadmitted asset, the equipment's full cost would have to be charged against surplus when purchased. With such a negative impact on surplus, some insurers might be reluctant to purchase computers and other data processing necessities. In the United States, insurers are typically permitted to amortize the cost of equipment when the initial cost exceeds $100,000. In Canada, only mainframe computers (as described in Chapter 3) can be capitalized, and the cost of this hardware must exceed $1,000,000 to be eligible for capitalization.

Many states have established guidelines for determining the Annual Statement values of electronic data processing equipment. When valuing such equipment, the following factors are typically considered:

- *minimum cost requirements.* Equipment with a cost under a certain dollar amount may not be admissible.
- *maximum cost limits.* Limits on the dollar value of the equipment may be imposed, such as "2 percent of total admitted assets."
- *rate of amortization,* which may be set by statute.
- *usage.* The equipment must be currently in use for processing the company's transactions.

Reinsurance Ceded

Reinsurance is a type of insurance transaction between insurers, in which companies buy, sell, or exchange risks on certain policies in order to reduce potential losses on certain insurance risks. The "reinsurance ceded" category is used to record amounts owed to the reporting company as a result of reinsurance transactions. The following subcategories are included in the current version of the U.S. Annual Statement:

- amounts recoverable from reinsurers,
- commissions and expense allowances due, and
- experience rating and other refunds due.

Each subcategory is discussed below.

Amounts recoverable from reinsurers

When an insurer obtains reinsurance on a policy, all or part of that policy's risk is assumed by a reinsurer. Consequently, the reinsurer is obligated to pay some portion of the policy benefits. The original insurer, also called the ceding company, must pay any benefits payable in connection with its reinsured policies. However, part or all of the benefits paid—depending on the reinsurance agreement—are recoverable from the reinsuring, or assuming, company. This amount is recorded as an account receivable by the ceding company using the following entry:

>Amounts Recoverable from Reinsurers xxx
>   Death Claims Paid xxx

(This entry assumes that a life insurance policy has been reinsured. A different account would be credited if health reinsurance had been purchased.) Death Claims Paid is credited since the amounts to be received represent a reduction in the death claim paid by the ceding company to the beneficiaries.

For example, assume that the Centrist Life Insurance Company issued a life insurance policy with a $250,000 death benefit. Since Centrist Life's **retention limit**—that is, the highest amount of risk that Centrist will assume on a single policy without reinsurance—is $200,000, the company reinsured $50,000 of the policy. After Centrist arranged for the $50,000 of reinsurance coverage through Parker Reinsurance, the insured died and the beneficiary was found to be entitled to the full death benefit. To reflect payment of the death benefit to the beneficiary, the entry on Centrist's books (as discussed in Chapter 8) would be:

>Death Claims Paid 250,000
>   Cash 250,000

Upon the death of this insured, Parker Reinsurance owes Centrist $50,000. Centrist's accountants would make the following journal entry to record the amount receivable:

>Amounts Recoverable from Reinsurers 50,000
>   Death Claims Paid 50,000

When Parker pays the $50,000, Centrist's accountants would record the following entry:

```
Cash ............................. 50,000
    Amounts Recoverable from Reinsurers .......... 50,000
```

This entry shows that Parker's liability to Centrist has been paid. The $50,000 increase in the company's Cash account also adjusts the books to show that Centrist paid $200,000 from its reserves in this settlement.

Generally speaking, the reinsurer must be licensed to write business in the domiciliary, or home, state of the ceding company in order for the amounts to be admitted on the Annual Statement. If the reinsurer is not licensed in that state, the ceding company must obtain some collateral, usually in the form of letters of credit, in order for the amounts to be admitted. However, the ceding company must establish on its books a liability account for Reinsurance in Unauthorized Companies (discussed later in this chapter and in Chapter 10). In addition, a liability account, Funds Withheld from Unauthorized Companies, must also be established to reflect the ceding company's possession of the reinsurer's collateral.

Commissions and expense allowances due

As part of the agreements between the companies involved in reinsurance transactions, certain allowances are made for expenses such as commissions and policy issue costs incurred by the ceding company in writing the direct business. The reinsurer generally reimburses the ceding company for an appropriate share of these expenses. The unpaid portion of the reimbursable amount is accumulated in the Commissions and Expense Allowances Due account on the ceding company's books.

Experience rating and other refunds due

When setting reinsurance premium rates, the reinsurer builds an element of profit into the premium assessed the ceding company. This profit is based on an estimate of the claims the reinsurer expects to pay. Many reinsurers provide for a partial premium refund if the actual claims experience is better than the claims experience projected when the premium was established. When refunds to the ceding company are due, the unpaid portion of the reimbursable amount is accumulated in the ceding company's Experience Rating and Other Refunds Due account. As in the case of amounts recoverable from reinsurers, the reinsurer must be licensed in the ceding company's home state in order for the amount of any refund to be admitted.

Net Adjustment in Assets and Liabilities due to Foreign Exchange Rates

Some insurers have operations or investments in foreign countries. As with any business, certain assets and liabilities will relate primarily to those foreign countries. In order to ease maintenance of records for preparation of the U.S. Annual Statement, these transactions are recorded in U.S. dollars at the rate of exchange at the time the transaction occurs. Adjustments for differences in exchange rates are made in year-end adjusting entries.

For example, assume that the Gentry Life Insurance Company, a U.S. insurer, wants to purchase $1,000,000 in Canadian bonds and that the exchange rate is as follows: $1 (Can.) = $.90 (U.S.). That is, one Canadian dollar is the equivalent of 90 U.S. cents. Gentry would first transfer to Canada $900,000 (U.S.) for the bond purchase. The journal entry to reflect the transfer and the subsequent conversion of the U.S. currency into Canadian currency would be:

```
Canadian Cash  . . . . . . . . . . . . . . . . . 1,000,000
    U.S. Cash . . . . . . . . . . . . . . . . . . . . . . . . . . . 900,000
    Gain on Foreign Exchange . . . . . . . . . . . . . . . . 100,000
```

The Gain on Foreign Exchange amount is included in Exhibit 4 (Capital Gains and Losses) of the U.S. Annual Statement as *cash on hand and on deposit*. When Gentry purchases the bonds, the entry would be:

```
Bonds Owned . . . . . . . . . . . . . . . . . . 1,000,000
    Canadian Cash  . . . . . . . . . . . . . . . . . . . . . . 1,000,000
```

A year-end work sheet adjusting entry is required to adjust the statement value of the bonds to reflect the actual foreign exchange value of $900,000 (U.S.), assuming that the exchange rate had not changed at the time of Annual Statement preparation. In this situation, an unrealized loss account would be debited to reflect the exchange rate difference. The entry on the work sheet would be:

```
Unrealized Loss on Foreign Exchange . . 100,000
    Foreign Exchange Liability . . . . . . . . . . . . . . . . 100,000
```

This loss offsets the gain reflected at the time of purchase. The unrealized loss appears in the Capital Gains and Losses exhibit, and the liability for foreign exchange appears on the Balance Sheet.

If, at the time of the reporting date, the exchange rate had dropped to $1 (Can.) = $.85 (U.S.), then the $1,000,000 in Canadian bonds would be worth $850,000 (U.S.). In such a case, the U.S. insurer has an unrealized loss of $50,000. This loss is present because an asset that had been worth $900,000

(U.S.) would now have a value of $850,000 (U.S.). Unlike the loss described above, however, the loss on a change in the exchange rate at the time of financial statement preparation is charged directly to surplus.

Other Liabilities

This section of the chapter includes liabilities that are generally unrelated to policy and contract provisions. Companies that maintain nonledger assets and liabilities keep many of these following liabilities off the ledger. In such cases, their totals are determined by an inventory process at the end of the accounting period.

General Expenses Due or Accrued

The liability for general expenses due or accrued is established for goods or services that have been received by the company but which have not been paid for at the end of the year. A considerable amount of judgment must be used in determining the amount of the company's liability. To determine this amount, all unpaid invoices dated prior to the end of the year are totaled. In addition, unfilled purchase orders are reviewed to determine the approximate cost of all items ordered but not yet received. Finally, an insurer may add an additional "adjustment factor" to the sum of the first two totals in order to account for any other miscellaneous expenses not previously identified.

Salaries and wages are usually partially incurred at the time the Annual Statement is prepared, and a liability for the salaries and wages incurred but unpaid is created. An existing liability for expenses due and accrued from contributions to employee benefit plans, professional and service fees, utility services used, and investment expenses is also reported in the Annual Statement.

Since medical examinations and inspection reports can be ordered by agents as well as home office personnel, all expenditures for these items are not made centrally in the home office. Therefore, the total of this general expense liability requires estimation by somewhat inexact methods. Reasonably accurate estimates can be made shortly after the end of the accounting period by reviewing charges made for these services during the first few weeks of the next accounting period.

To adjust paid expenses from a cash to an accrual basis, accountants must (1) add the amount of expenses payable at the end of the current year and (2) subtract the amount of expenses that were accrued at the end of the previous year. To illustrate, assume that expenses paid during the year total $1,000, unpaid expenses at the end of the current year are $150, and unpaid expenses at the end of the previous year were $100. The entries to adjust the ledger are as follows:

Entry #1

Expenses 150
    Accrued Expenses 150

Entry #2

Accrued Expenses 100
    Expenses 100

Expenses is an account whose total is reported on the company's Income Statement. Accrued Expenses, on the other hand, is a Balance Sheet liability account. The first entry above records the current year's liability for accrued expenses and the second entry reverses the prior year's liability. The combination of the two entries produces the proper adjusted incurred expense amount for the reporting year of $1,050 ($1,000 + $150 − $100).

Agent Commissions Due and Accrued

A commission is considered due or accrued when a premium is received too late in the year to process the commission payment. Commissions are generally accrued only on premiums actually received. This commission liability is usually a nonledger item in companies that maintain nonledger accounts. The liability is determined by an inventory process at the end of the accounting period.

Taxes, Licenses, and Fees Due or Accrued, Excluding Federal Income Taxes

The liability for *taxes, licenses, and fees due or accrued* includes (1) items billed but not yet paid, such as licenses; (2) amounts payable but not yet billed, such as real estate taxes; and (3) estimates of amounts still owed for premium taxes on premiums collected during the year. Most of the items in this liability classification can be determined by an inventory process. Some liability amounts have to be estimates, but many of them can be calculated. For example, for premium taxes, the total premiums received from policyowners in a given state in the reporting year can be multiplied by the state's premium tax rate and reduced by any prepayments or possible offsets (see Chapter 12) to determine the unpaid liability.

Amounts Retained by the Company as Agent or Trustee

In the normal course of business, life insurance companies will act as agents or trustees and retain or keep on deposit funds that will ultimately be paid to others, but which are not related to reserves or policy benefits. Two of the more common types of funds that fall into the category of amounts retained by the company as agent or trustee are:

1. payroll deductions for federal and state income taxes, social security taxes, pension plan contributions, and health insurance premiums. These deductions are ledger liabilities at the time the salaries are paid.
2. escrow balances relating to mortgage loans held by the company. The balances are maintained for the payment of property taxes and hazard insurance on the real estate securing the loan.

These amounts are ledger liabilities, and usually no adjustments or estimates are needed to report these liabilities accurately.

Remittances and Items not Allocated

Cash receipts generally are deposited when received. This practice not only provides for good accounting control but also makes the funds received available for investment. However, in many instances, the credit entry to offset the debit to Cash cannot be determined. In such cases, the credit is posted to a liability account referred to as a *suspense account*. Suspense transactions are usually recorded under the following circumstances:

1. Premium remittances are received with insurance applications and the recording of premium income is contingent on the company's acceptance of the risk.
2. Premium payments are received for amounts different than the amount billed by the company.
3. Premiums or other remittances are received with insufficient information for proper accounting distribution (for example, the absence of a policy number or name on the check).

When the proper accounting treatment is determined, Suspense is debited, and the credit is posted to the appropriate account. The Suspense accounts are ledger liabilities. As a result, estimation of the total amount in suspense is not necessary because the actual amount is known.

Establishing suspense accounts also helps to avoid the situation of asset duplication—i.e., recording assets twice on the company's financial statements. For example, if a renewal premium is not fully processed at year-end, the premium could appear twice on the Balance Sheet's asset page—once as Cash and once as a Deferred and Uncollected Premium. Use of a suspense account generally offsets the asset's appearance under the Deferred and Uncollected Premium classification.

Borrowed Money

The *borrowed money* liability includes any amounts borrowed plus the accrued and unpaid interest on those amounts. The loan itself is a ledger liability that is calculated at the end of the accounting period. Borrowed money, however, does not include mortgage loans payable. Historically, most life insurance companies do not borrow money. Thus, an amount for this liability does not appear often on insurers' financial statements. However, the increasing complexity of the financial marketplace may result in more insurers borrowing money.

Dividends to Stockholders Declared and Unpaid

In addition to the liability for policy dividends on participating business, stock companies must also establish a liability for cash dividends to stockholders as of the date that the dividends have been declared by the board. Dividends to stockholders are charged directly to surplus and are not treated as an operating expense. The accounting entry to record the dividend liability would be:

```
Dividends to Stockholders . . . . . . . . . . . . . . . . . . xxx
     Dividends to Stockholders
        Declared and Unpaid . . . . . . . . . . . . . . . . . . . . . . . . xxx
```

When the dividend is paid, a debit entry to Dividends to Stockholders Declared and Unpaid and a credit entry to Cash would be made.

Reinsurance in Unauthorized Companies

The ceding company in a reinsurance agreement is permitted to reduce its policy and contract liabilities for that portion of the risk reinsured. However, if the reinsurer is not licensed or authorized in the home state of the ceding company, the ceding company must set up a liability for the reserve credits taken, minus any funds due the reinsurer but held by the ceding company. Since the home state does not "recognize" or supervise the unauthorized reinsurer, the receivable on the ceding company's books is treated as a liability and not considered collectible. This liability for reinsurance in unauthorized companies is, for certain companies, a nonledger liability.

Mandatory Securities Valuation Reserve

Because of the nature of the life insurance business, U.S. insurers are required to guard their surplus against fluctuations in the values of their investments in bonds, preferred stocks, and common stocks. For this purpose, the NAIC requires the establishment of a liability account known as the **Mandatory Securities Valuation Reserve (MSVR)**. The MSVR is established primarily to protect policyowners from the effects of wide fluctuations in an insurer's surplus. Though considered a liability account, the MSVR is not actually a liability in the sense that it represents a debt to another party. This reserve is designed to absorb, within certain specified limits, realized and unrealized capital gains and losses resulting from the company's investments. Insurers can establish voluntary reserves similar to the MSVR for other investments, such as real estate or mortgage loans.

The change in the market value of stocks and bonds and the periodic adjustment of the MSVR are calculated on working papers and reported in a life company's financial statements. The amount of the MSVR each year consists of

1. the balance of the previous year's MSVR, plus
2. the net of capital gains and capital losses for the current year, plus
3. an additional amount added each year in accordance with requirements established by the NAIC, plus
4. any voluntary contributions to the MSVR by the insurance company.

A formula determines the required maximum amount of each insurer's MSVR. The maximum MSVR and subsequent adjustments to this maximum are calculated by multiplying by specified percentages the admitted values of each of several different types of bonds or stocks. (The exact method of calculation is lengthy and is presented in Figure 9-1.)

Formerly, all of an insurer's capital gains went directly to the MSVR until the maximum MSVR was reached. Similarly, all capital losses went directly to the MSVR until the MSVR was reduced to zero. Until these limits were reached, capital gains and losses had no effect on surplus. The MSVR rules have been changed, however, so that insurers have the option of designating capital gains (or losses) to surplus before the maximum MSVR (or zero) is reached. The effect of the different rules for attributing capital gains or losses to surplus and the MSVR is shown in Figure 9-2. After the maximum MSVR is reached, capital gains directly increase surplus. If the MSVR balance becomes zero, subsequent capital losses directly decrease surplus.

Separate Accounts

Until the 1960s, insurers were required by statutory accounting practices to pool all of their accounts into a single, general account. With the advent of nonguaranteed insurance products, though, insurers obtained permission to establish *separate accounts,* generally known in Canada as *segregated accounts.* These separate or segregated accounts are maintained apart from the company's

9 Other Assets, Other Liabilities, and Separate Accounts

FIGURE 9-1
Mandatory Securities Valuation Reserve calculation—U.S. Annual Statement.

FIGURE 9-2
Two methods of attributing gains or losses to the MSVR and surplus.

Assume that the following dollar totals apply to the Basic Life Insurance Company:

Surplus	=	$4,000,000
Current MSVR total	=	$ 55,000
Capital gains for the year	=	$ 65,000
Maximum MSVR allowed	=	$ 100,000

Method 1 (applicable under old regulations)	Method 2 (applicable under new regulations)
Under the **old rules,** capital gains had to be allocated to the MSVR until the maximum MSVR was reached. The balance of the capital gains amount was assigned to surplus.	Under the **new rules,** capital gains can be allocated to surplus before the maximum MSVR is reached. Amounts can still be allocated to the MSVR as long as the maximum is not exceeded.
Thus, using the figures above, under the old rules, $45,000 of the $65,000 in capital gains had to be allocated to the MSVR so that its maximum amount could be reached. The balance of the capital gains amount, $20,000, would be assigned to surplus.	Thus, using the figures above, under the new rules, $40,000 of the $65,000 in capital gains could be allocated to surplus before any amount is assigned to the MSVR. The balance of the capital gains amount, $25,000, would then be assigned to the MSVR.
Under the old rules, the new figures for the company would be: Surplus = $4,020,000 Current MSVR = $ 100,000	Under the new rules, the figures for the company could be: Surplus = $4,040,000 Current MSVR = $ 80,000

Note that the total of MSVR and surplus in both cases equals $4,120,000.

general accounts for the purpose of managing the funds used for nonguaranteed insurance products. By maintaining a separate account, an insurer can use more aggressive investment strategies without jeopardizing the funds in its general account.

Insurers can have more than one separate account. Such accounts are subdivided into those for variable life insurance and those for all other types of insurance products that are funded by separate accounts. The number of separate accounts that a company maintains is dictated by the degree of asset segregation that is required by the nature of the company's products. An Annual Statement is filed for the aggregate of all variable life separate accounts, and, in most cases, a separate Annual Statement is filed for the aggregate of all other separate accounts.

The Annual Statement for an insurer's separate account focuses primarily on the investment activities of that separate account and on the flow of funds to and from the general account. The assets of a separate account typically consist of bond, stock, and real estate investments; dividends receivable; and accrued interest relative to investments, cash, and amounts receivable. Separate account liabilities generally consist of amounts owed to brokers, amounts owed to the organization administering the separate account (if applicable), and surplus.

Although the totals of the assets and liabilities in an insurer's separate accounts are reported on the general account Balance Sheet, detailed information regarding an insurer's separate accounts is presented in the Annual Statement that applies specifically to the insurer's separate accounts. This Statement is generally presented after the complete general account Annual Statement or, depending on the size of the separate account Statement, in a different volume that pertains only to the company's separate accounts. The Balance Sheet for the U.S. separate account Annual Statement is shown in Figure 9-3.

Note that the assets page of the separate account Annual Statement resembles a shortened version of the company's general account Annual Statement assets page. *Receivables for investments sold* is the only asset in the separate account Balance Sheet that does not appear on the general account Blank. Similarly, the separate account's liabilities page contains primarily the same items as the general account Balance Sheet liabilities page, and those items that differ apply almost exclusively to investment-related expenses (see Figure 9-3). The following totals appear on the liabilities page of the separate account Annual Statement and not on the general account Blank: charges for investment management administration and contract guarantees due or accrued; investment taxes, licenses, and fees due or accrued, excluding federal income taxes; and payable for investments purchased. The total *Reserve for federal income taxes* also appears only on the separate accounts Balance Sheet.

FIGURE 9-3
Separate Accounts Balance Sheet—United States.

ANNUAL STATEMENT FOR THE YEAR 1985
OF THE SEPARATE ACCOUNTS OF THE _____
Name   Form 1-S

	(1) Current Year	(2) Previous Year
ASSETS		
1. Long-term bonds (Schedule D)		
2. Stocks (Schedule D):		
2.1 Preferred stocks		
2.2 Common stocks		
3. Mortgage loans on real estate (Schedule B)		
4. Real estate (Schedule A):		
4.1 Properties acquired in satisfaction of debt (less $_____ encumbrances)		
4.2 Investment real estate (less $_____ encumbrances)		
5. _____		
6. _____		
7.1 Cash on deposit (Schedule E)		
7.2 Short-term investments (Schedule DA)		
8. Other invested assets (Schedule BA)		
8A. Subtotals—Cash and invested assets (Items 1 to 8)		
9. Investment income due and accrued		
10. Receivable for investments sold		
11. Net adjustment in assets and liabilities due to foreign exchange rates		
12. _____		
13. _____		
14. Totals (Items 8A to 13)		

State basis of valuation:

FIGURE 9-3 (cont.)

```
                    ANNUAL STATEMENT FOR THE YEAR 1985
    Form 1-S      OF THE SEPARATE ACCOUNTS OF THE ..................................................   $
                                                      Name
```

	(1) Current Year	(2) Previous Year
LIABILITIES AND SURPLUS		
1. Aggregate reserve for contracts with life contingencies (Exhibit 6, Column 2, Grand Total)		
2. Supplementary contracts without life contingencies (Exhibit 7, Line 5)		
3. Liability for annuity and other deposit funds		
4.		
5.		
6. Charges for investment management, administration and contract guarantees due or accrued		
7. Investment expenses due or accrued (Exhibit 4, Line 11)		
8. Investment taxes, licenses and fees due or accrued, excluding federal income taxes (Exhibit 5, Line 8)		
9. Federal income taxes due or accrued (excluding deferred taxes)		
10. Reserve for future federal income taxes		
11. Unearned investment income (Exhibit 2, Col. 2, Line 10)		
12. Other transfers to general account due or accrued (net)		
13. Remittances and items not allocated		
14. Payable for investments purchased		
15. Net adjustment in assets and liabilities due to foreign exchange rates		
16.		
17.		
18. Total Liabilities (including $.................... due or accrued net transfers to (+) or from (−) the general account)		
19. Special surplus funds:		
19.1		
19.2		
19.3		
20. Unassigned surplus		
21. Surplus (Items 19 and 20)		
22. Totals		

The total amount of assets and liabilities on a separate account Balance Sheet is often equal. As a result, an insurer's separate account Annual Statement occasionally shows no surplus amount. If a surplus amount is reported, the amount can reflect a number of different factors, such as money invested by the company when the separate account was established.

A number of activities that relate to the administration of the separate account are, for the purposes of financial reporting, considered distinct from the operation of the separate accounts and thus are recorded in the general account Annual Statement. Examples of such activities are

- underwriting and contract administration
- premium collection
- the payment of claims, benefits, and premium taxes

Expenses related to these activities are also reported in the general account Statement and not in the separate account Statement. As a result, benefit payments relating to variable annuities (one product for which a separate account is created) appear in the general account Statement's policy and contract claims exhibit (Exhibit 11) and considerations for such products are reported in the premium and annuity consideration exhibit of the general account Statement (Exhibit 1—Part 1).

One aspect of the separate account Annual Statement that makes it different from the general account Annual Statement is that the terms *admitted asset* and *nonadmitted asset* do not appear in the separate account Statement. Unlike the general account Annual Statement, fair market values are assigned to every asset in the separate account Statement, even if an asset's value is zero.

Key Terms

reinsurance
assuming company
asset duplication
separate accounts
segregated accounts

ceding company
suspense account
Mandatory Securities Valuation Reserve (MSVR)

Review Questions and Exercises

1. Why is EDP equipment considered an admitted asset when furniture and equipment are not?
2. What are three factors used in valuing EDP equipment for Annual Statement purposes?

3. What transactions or events could the following journal entries represent?
    (a) Amounts Recoverable from Reinsurers.......40,000
            Death Claims Paid............................40,000
    (b) Unrealized Loss on Foreign Exchange........25,000
            Foreign Exchange Liability....................25,000
4. What is the Mandatory Securities Valuation Reserve (MSVR) and what is its purpose?
5. How many separate accounts can an insurer create? How many separate account Statements can an insurer file? Has your company established any separate accounts?
6. What is an unauthorized reinsurance company? For accounting purposes, how is reinsurance with such a company handled?

10
Capital and Surplus

Learning Objectives

After reading this chapter, you should be able to:

- Describe the different elements of capital and surplus for life and health insurers
- Make proper journal entries for a number of capital and surplus transactions
- Identify the different surplus classifications used in the United States and Canada
- Understand why accurate calculation of surplus is important to an insurer's operations
- List the items that can increase or decrease an insurer's surplus

Introduction

An understanding of capital and surplus is necessary for any student of life and health insurance accounting. Such an understanding is necessary because (1) virtually every accounting transaction made by an insurer affects surplus either directly or indirectly; (2) insurance company management considers the year's change in surplus when measuring the results of the company's operations; and (3) persons interested in the financial soundness of an insurer often look at the company's ratio of capital and surplus to assets. This chapter explores the Surplus and Other Funds section of a U.S. insurer's statutory Balance Sheet, the Capital and Surplus Account of the U.S. Annual Statement, and the Canadian equivalents of these reports. Before discussing these topics, however, a review of the basic accounting equation as it applies to life and health insurers may be helpful.

The basis for financial accounting in all companies is the Balance Sheet equation:

$$\text{Assets} = \text{Liabilities} + \text{Owners' Equity}$$

This equation, which must always be in balance, is used to show a company's financial position at a given time. Two differences between the Balance Sheet of a life and health insurer and that of a non-insurance company, however, must be reiterated. First, life and health insurance accounting modifies the Balance Sheet equation by deducting nonadmitted assets from the basic accounting equation. Second, the elements of owners' equity are capital and surplus in life insurance accounting, rather than capital and retained earnings, as is the case in commercial or GAAP accounting. **Capital** is the amount of money invested in the company by its owners or stockholders. **Retained earnings,** in GAAP accounting, consists of the net change in owners' equity resulting from gains or losses in the company's operations as well as any dividends paid to the stockholders. In life and health insurance accounting, however, the second element of owners' equity is known as surplus. *Surplus,* in life insurance accounting, is thus similar to *retained earnings* in commercial or GAAP accounting. In mutual companies, surplus also includes elements of policyowner ownership interests. Using the terminology introduced above, the basic accounting equation for life and health insurance companies can be restated as

$$\text{Assets} = \text{Liabilities} + \text{Capital} + \text{Surplus}$$

Capital and surplus as part of an insurer's Balance Sheet are reported on page 3 of both the U.S. and Canadian Annual Statements (see Figures 10-1 and 10-2).

Capital

Stock Companies

An insurance company that sells stock in the company to obtain funds for starting and continuing its operations is known as a **stock company.** An insurer is required to declare a par value or stated value for any stock that is issued. The **par value** of stock is the designated legal value assigned to each outstanding share of stock. The number of outstanding shares of an insurer's stock—i.e., the number of shares owned by outside investors—multiplied by the stock's par value constitutes that insurer's *capital,* referred to in the United States as **capital paid up.** Capital paid up is shown on the *common capital stock* and *preferred capital stock* lines of the U.S. Annual Statement. In Canada, capital paid up is referred to as **capital stock issued and paid** or **capital stock paid.**

10 Capital and Surplus

FIGURE 10-1
Capital items on the U.S. Annual Statement Balance Sheet.

	(1) Current Year	(2) Previous Year
27A. Common capital stock.		
27B. Preferred capital stock.		
27C.		
28. Gross paid in and contributed surplus (Page 3, Item 28, Col. 2 plus Page 4, Item 46a, Col. 1).		
29A. Special surplus funds:		
(a)		
(b)		
(c)		
29B. Unassigned funds (surplus).		
29C. Less treasury stock, at cost:		
(1) .... shares common (value included in Item 27A $......)		
(2) .... shares preferred (value included in Item 27B $......)		
29D. Surplus (total Items 27C + 28 + 29A + 29B − 29C).		
30. Total of Items 27A, 27B and 29D (Page 4, Item 50).		
31. TOTALS OF ITEMS 26 AND 30 (Page 2, Item 28).		

*Includes coupons, guaranteed annual pure endowments and similar benefits.

FIGURE 10-2
Capital items on the Canadian Annual Statement Balance Sheet.

		CURRENT YEAR 01	PREVIOUS YEAR 02
CAPITAL, SURPLUS AND RESERVES:			
RESERVES REQUIRED BY THE DEPARTMENT	19		
RESERVES REQUIRED BY FOREIGN JURISDICTIONS	20		
ADDITIONAL RESERVES	21		
CAPITAL STOCK ISSUED AND PAID: COMMON STOCK	22		
: PREFERRED STOCK	23		
CONTRIBUTED SURPLUS	24		
UNAPPROPRIATED EARNED SURPLUS	25		
UNAPPROPRIATED SURPLUS (24+25)	▶ 26		
TOTAL CAPITAL, SURPLUS AND RESERVES (19 TO 25)	▶ 27		
TOTAL LIABILITIES, CAPITAL AND SURPLUS (17+18+27)	▶ 28		

To illustrate the calculation of capital paid up (U.S.) or capital stock paid (Canada), assume that a newly forming U.S. insurer sells, at its par value, all 1,000 shares of its $2 par value stock. The journal entry to record this sale would be:

```
Cash ............................ 2,000
    Capital Paid Up ............................ 2,000
```

This $2,000 amount would be shown on the appropriate Annual Statement line for capital paid up.

Stocks are typically sold for a price in excess of par value, however. The excess of the price paid for the stock over its par value, multiplied by the number of outstanding shares, is described in the U.S. Annual Statement as **gross paid in and contributed surplus.** If the $2 par value stock of the newly forming company mentioned earlier was sold for $10 per share, the journal entry to record the transaction would be:

```
Cash ............................ 10,000
    Capital Paid Up ............................ 2,000
    Gross Paid In and Contributed Surplus .......... 8,000
```

The amount of gross paid in and contributed surplus also reflects any expenses or commissions associated with issuing the stock. In Canada, the excess of a stock's purchase price over that stock's par value is reported to **contributed surplus.**

Sometimes a company repurchases shares of its own stock. Repurchased stock is considered to be **treasury stock** of the issuing company. The value of an insurer's treasury stock is deducted from the other capital and surplus funds when determining the insurer's amount. The journal entry to record an insurer's repurchase of its own stock consists of a debit to Treasury Stock and a credit to Cash for the number of shares repurchased multiplied by the price paid for those shares. The total of an insurer's treasury stock is also reported on page 3 of the U.S. Annual Statement.

Adjustments to capital

One way in which an existing stock company can increase its capital is by issuing additional stock. When a company issues additional stock, the effect on capital is the same as when the company's stock was originally introduced. The number of shares sold multiplied by the stock's par value equals the amount by which capital paid up or capital stock paid is increased.

A company can also issue additional stock through a stock dividend, in which stockholders receive additional shares of a company's stock at no charge. Upon declaration of a stock dividend, a stock's par or outstanding book value does not change, but the number of outstanding shares of the company's stock increases. As a result, capital paid up is increased by the number of new shares issued for the dividend multiplied by the par value of each share. Unassigned surplus, which will be discussed more fully later in this chapter, is decreased by this amount to keep the Balance Sheet equation in balance. Thus, the total value of the company's capital and surplus does not change, but some money is reclassified from one portion of owners' equity to another.

For example, if a newly formed insurance company with 1,000 outstanding shares of $2 par value stock declared a 25 percent stock dividend, then the insurer would issue 250 additional shares (25 percent of 1,000 shares outstanding) of $2 par value stock. The company's capital paid up or capital stock paid would subsequently increase by $500 (250 shares × $2 par value) and unassigned surplus would decrease by the same amount. The entry in the insurer's journal would be:

    Unassigned Surplus........................500
        Capital Paid Up 500

Another method of increasing capital is to increase the par value of the stock. The entry for increasing from $2 to $3 the par value of 1,000 shares of outstanding stock is:

    Gross Paid In and Contributed Surplus 1,000
        Capital Paid Up..............................1,000

As with stock dividends, this type of transaction does not affect the total of capital and surplus but is only a reclassification of amounts within the owners' equity accounts. Such a transaction does not change the number of outstanding shares, only the stock's par value.

While increases in the capital of a stock insurer are fairly common, reductions in the capital of a stock life company are not as common. A number of financial transactions, however, can reduce the amount of an insurer's capital account. Such transactions include

(1) *repurchase of the company's own stock.* This type of transaction, i.e., the purchase of treasury stock, was discussed earlier.
(2) *retirement of treasury stock.* To retire treasury stock, an insurer would make the following entry:

        Capital Paid Up xxx
        Gross Paid In and Contributed Surplus xxx
            Treasury Stock...........................xxx

The amount to be recorded against Capital Paid Up should be the par value of the retired stock multiplied by the number of shares retired. This transaction allows for retirement of a portion of outstanding stock.

(3) *mutualization.* **Mutualization** is the process of converting a stock life company into a mutual life company. In order to mutualize a stock life insurance company, an insurer must repurchase and retire *all* outstanding

shares of its stock. Upon mutualization, an insurer will have no capital paid up or gross paid in and contributed surplus. Any gain or loss realized from mutualization is reported directly to surplus.

(4) *liquidation of the company's assets.* **Liquidation** involves the selling of a company's assets and the termination of the company's operations. Naturally, liquidation of a life insurance company would reduce that company's capital to zero. The reduction in capital is accomplished through payments to stockholders.

Mutual Companies

For Annual Statement purposes, a mutual life and health company has no capital since such a company issues no stock. The funds needed to begin the operations of a mutual company are provided by the policyowners' premium payments. All capital and surplus entries in a mutual company's Annual Statement are thus recorded on lines designated specifically for surplus.

Surplus

Calculation of Total Surplus

Earlier in this chapter, we defined the basic accounting equation for life and health insurers as

$$\text{Assets} = \text{Liabilities} + \text{Capital} + \text{Surplus},$$

because *owners' equity* for an insurer equals *capital* plus *surplus*. To determine the amount of surplus, the basic accounting equation can be further modified to read:

$$\text{Surplus} = \text{Assets} - (\text{Liabilities} + \text{Capital})$$

or

$$\text{Surplus} = \text{Assets} - \text{Liabilities} - \text{Capital}$$

When an insurer calculates its surplus using this equation, the proper valuation of assets and liabilities is most important to the accuracy of the surplus total. For example, if an insurer includes the value of certain nonadmitted assets on the statutory Balance Sheet, the amount of surplus will be overstated since such assets should not be included on the Balance Sheet nor in the surplus calculations. Legal requirements generally prescribe the types and proper valuations of assets and liabilities that should be included for the purposes of determining surplus.

Accurate calculation of an insurer's surplus is necessary not only for proper financial reporting, but also because the amount of surplus plays an important role in an insurance company's operations. First, the surplus of an insurance company is used to provide a cushion against unexpected events that could prevent a company from meeting its future financial obligations. Such events include large fluctuations in morbidity and mortality rates, excessive losses from capital investments, or underwriting losses from unpredictable catastrophes. Second, surplus is designed to provide an insurer with additional funds both for investment and for expenses that are often incurred during expansion of a company's operations. Insurance company management, as a result, must have a conservative reporting of the company's surplus in order to plan the company's actions properly.

To illustrate the determination of surplus for a life insurer, assume that the ABC Life Company reported the following dollar amounts on its statutory Balance Sheet:

Total assets
  (U.S. and Canadian Annual Statement page 2) $50,000,000
Total liabilities
  (U.S. and Canadian Annual Statement page 3) $40,000,000
Capital
  (U.S. and Canadian Annual Statement page 3) $ 2,000,000

Using the modified basic accounting equation introduced earlier, the amount of ABC Life Company surplus can be found:

Surplus = Assets − (Liabilities + Capital)
Surplus = $50,000,000 − ($40,000,000 + $2,000,000)
Surplus = $50,000,000 − $42,000,000
Surplus = $8,000,000

After determining its surplus amount, a U.S. insurer should classify its surplus in one of three ways:

(1) as *gross paid in and contributed surplus* (discussed in the section on capital),
(2) as *special surplus funds,* or
(3) as *unassigned funds (surplus).*

The allocation of surplus for a Canadian insurer is described later in this chapter.

Special surplus funds

Special surplus funds, or **special surplus,** consist of surplus that a life company's board of directors has segregated for the purpose of (1) meeting unforeseen contingencies such as those described earlier in this chapter or (2) paying for certain extraordinary expenses that may arise. Special surplus is also known as *assigned surplus, appropriated surplus, earmarked surplus,* and *contingency reserves.* The contents of a special surplus fund may not be used for any purposes other than those specified at the time of the fund's creation. Some of the types of special surplus funds that insurers create are presented in Figure 10-3.

If surplus set aside for a particular contingency has not been used, then the company's board of directors can vote to redesignate that amount of surplus for another contingency or to another surplus account. Life companies are not generally required to set aside any surplus for special surplus funds. However, regulatory authorities can, in certain cases, mandate the creation and amount of special surplus funds. According to the NAIC, these special surplus funds should be used only for voluntary and general contingency reserves. Examples of such mandated surplus funds are special reserves for aviation reinsurance and separate account business. Mutual companies sometimes designate a certain amount to a special surplus fund to help ensure that the company's surplus does not fall below a required minimum.

Unassigned surplus funds

Outside of the insurance industry, unassigned surplus is referred to as *retained earnings* since it represents the accumulation of operating income not paid out in dividends. For insurance companies, **unassigned surplus** is the amount of surplus remaining after the creation of any special surplus funds. On the Annual Statement, unassigned surplus is referred to as *unassigned surplus funds.* Unlike special surplus, which is available only for specific contingencies, unassigned surplus is available to meet any contingency that may arise. Unassigned surplus can also be used to satisfy a contingency for which a special surplus fund has been created and exhausted. In addition, unassigned surplus is available to pay for any operating expenses, especially when a company experiences an operating loss during a year.

The primary difference between unassigned surplus and other types of surplus is the importance that unassigned surplus has for a stock life company. When a stock company declares dividends for its stockholders, the amount of dividend that the company can declare is based on the amount of that company's unassigned surplus. Laws in an insurer's state of incorporation determine the amount of unassigned surplus available for dividends. Two primary factors in the amount of unassigned surplus available for distribution to shareholders are

(1) the amount of business that the company writes, and
(2) contractual agreements that the company may have—e.g., loan agreements—that might affect the company's future financial situation.

FIGURE 10-3
Types of special surplus funds.

Reserve for aviation reinsurance

Group life contingency reserve

Real estate reserve

Reserve for home office remodeling

Asset fluctuation reserve

Currency exchange reserve

Negative actuarial reserve

Cash value deficiency reserves

Another difference between unassigned surplus and other types of surplus is that unassigned surplus can appear as a negative amount on an insurer's Balance Sheet. A negative amount of unassigned surplus can occur, for example, on a new life company's Balance Sheet. The amount of money required for starting operations and establishing necessary reserves may cause a net loss from operations that would result in negative unassigned surplus. When this situation occurs because of new business written, whether for a new or existing company, the effect is known as *issue strain*.

Allocation of Balance Sheet surplus—Canada

On a Canadian insurer's Balance Sheet, surplus is distributed among the following classifications:

- Required reserves
- Additional reserves
- Contributed surplus
- Unappropriated earned surplus

(Figure 10-4 shows the U.S. equivalents of each of these classifications.) *Required reserves* are allocated to (1) reserves required by the insurance department of the province in which an insurer operates and (2) reserves required by foreign jurisdictions. A life company can set aside *additional reserves* as necessary in order to meet future obligations or provide for unforeseen contingencies. These reserve amounts are similar in function to a U.S. insurer's special surplus funds. *Contributed surplus* was discussed in the section on capital earlier in this chapter. *Unappropriated earned surplus,* like unassigned surplus funds on the U.S. Statement, constitutes the amount of an insurer's surplus remaining after determination of an insurer's reserve, capital, and other surplus amounts.

FIGURE 10-4
A comparison of surplus terminology in the U.S. and Canada.

United States	Canada
Special Surplus Funds	Required Reserves
	Additional Reserves
Gross Paid In and Contributed Surplus	Contributed Surplus
Unassigned Surplus Funds	Unappropriated Earned Surplus

Accounting for Changes in Surplus—United States

Unlike the amount of an insurer's capital, the surplus of a stock or mutual insurer can change daily as a result of the company's operations. U.S. insurers are required to report their annual change in surplus in the Capital and Surplus Account on page 4 of the Annual Statement. The causes of change in an insurer's surplus are not limited to gains from the company's operations. Other sources of change can also influence an insurer's surplus total. The Capital and Surplus Account (see Figure 10-5) specifies many types of surplus change, attributable both to operations and to direct changes in surplus. These types of surplus change are discussed later in this chapter.

To calculate the net annual change in a company's surplus, the total of the previous year's surplus is adjusted for the factors listed in the Annual Statement's Capital and Surplus Account. Some of these factors increase an insurer's surplus amount, while others decrease that amount. After all of the factors affecting an insurer's previous year-end surplus are determined, an insurer can then calculate its current year-end surplus total.

To ascertain the accuracy of the totals used in calculating an insurer's net annual change in surplus, the insurer can compare the amount of surplus for the current reporting year (reported on Annual Statement page 4) to the total of the current year's surplus as calculated from the basic accounting equation, Surplus = Assets − (Liabilities + Capital). If the insurer's calculations are correct and the valuation of the insurer's assets and liabilities is consistent and accurate, the total of capital and surplus on the insurer's statutory Balance Sheet will match the current year-end capital and surplus total reported on the final line of the Capital and Surplus Account. As mentioned earlier, this year-end surplus total is a function of numerous changes in the previous year's surplus total. The sources of these changes are described below.

Net gain

The primary source of change in an insurer's surplus is the gain or loss from insurance operations, which includes net investment income. In the Capital and Surplus Account, this gain or loss is recorded on a *net basis,* i.e., after deductions for dividends and taxes. Thus, a **net gain** could be defined as the total of an insurer's income minus the total of the insurer's (1) expenses, (2) benefit payments, (3) federal income taxes, and (4) dividends to policyholders. Sources of an insurer's income include premiums and net investment income, and an insurer's expenses typically include commissions, taxes, and general insurance-related expenditures.

Calculation of net gain or loss

Income (premiums + net investment income)
-   expenses (commissions, taxes, other expenditures)
-   benefit payments
-   federal income taxes
-   policyowner dividends

=   **Net gain** (if the amount is positive)

—or—

Net loss (if the amount is negative)

FIGURE 10-5
Capital and Surplus Account—U.S. Annual Statement.

```
                    CAPITAL AND SURPLUS ACCOUNT                        Current Year   Previous Year
32. Capital and surplus, December 31, previous year (Page 3, Item 30, Col. 2) . . . . . .
33. Net gain (Item 31) . . . . . . . . . . . . . . . . . . . . . . . . . . . . . . . . . .
34. Net capital gains (Exhibit 4, Line 10.2) . . . . . . . . . . . . . . . . . . . . . . .
35. Change in non-admitted assets and related items (Exhibit 14, Line 13, Col. 3) . . . .
36. Change in liability for reinsurance in unauthorized companies, increase (–) or decrease (+)
    (Page 3, Item 25.2, Col. 1 minus 2) . . . . . . . . . . . . . . . . . . . . . . . . .
37. Change in reserve on account of change in valuation basis, increase (–) or decrease (+)
    (Exh. 8A, Line 7, Col. 4) . . . . . . . . . . . . . . . . . . . . . . . . . . . . . .
38. Change in mandatory securities valuation reserve, increase (–) or decrease (+)
    (Page 3, Item 25.1, Col. 1 minus 2) . . . . . . . . . . . . . . . . . . . . . . . . .
39. ............................................................................
40. ............................................................................
41. Change in treasury stock, increase (–) or decrease (+) (Page 3, Items 29C (1) & (2), Col. 1 minus 2) . . . .
42. ............................................................................
43. Change in surplus in Separate Accounts Statement. . . . . . . . . . . . . . . . . . .
44. Change in surplus in Variable Life Insurance Separate Accounts Statement . . . . . .
45. Capital changes:
    (a) Paid in . . . . . . . . . . . . . . . . . . . . . . . . . . . . . . . . . . . . .
    (b) Transferred from surplus (Stock Dividend) . . . . . . . . . . . . . . . . . . . .
    (c) Transferred to surplus (Exhibit 12, Line 29) . . . . . . . . . . . . . . . . . .
46. Surplus adjustments:
    (a) Paid in . . . . . . . . . . . . . . . . . . . . . . . . . . . . . . . . . . . . .
    (b) Transferred to capital (Stock Dividend) (Exhibit 12, Line 30, inside amount for stock $) . . . . .
    (c) Transferred from capital (Exhibit 12, Line 29) . . . . . . . . . . . . . . . . .
47. Dividends to stockholders . . . . . . . . . . . . . . . . . . . . . . . . . . . . . .
48. ............................................................................
49. Net change in capital and surplus for the year (Items 33 through 48) . . . . . . . .
50. Capital and surplus, December 31, current year (Items 32 + 49) (Page 3, Item 30) . .

NOTE: Items 1 to 31 to agree with Page 5, Col. 1, Items 1 to 31.
```

If an insurer's income is *less* than the total of its expenses, benefit payments, federal income taxes, and policyowner dividends, the insurer has experienced a **net loss**. Net gains increase an insurer's surplus, and net losses decrease an insurer's surplus. Net gains or losses from operations, however, do not include *capital* gains or losses on investments. Capital gains or losses are recorded separately on another line of the Capital and Surplus Account.

Net capital gains

This reconciliation line in the Capital and Surplus Account records the difference between an insurer's (1) realized and unrealized capital gains—net of any capital gains taxes—and (2) realized and unrealized capital losses that resulted that year from the insurer's investments. A **net capital gain** occurs if the amount of realized and unrealized capital gains exceeds the amount of realized and unrealized capital losses. Conversely, a **net capital loss** occurs if realized and unrealized capital losses exceed realized and unrealized capital gains for a reporting year. Unless offset by a change in the MSVR (Mandatory Securities Valuation Reserve, which was discussed in Chapter 9), net capital gains directly increase surplus, and net capital losses directly decrease surplus. The amount reported for net capital gains in the Capital and Surplus Account is obtained from the insurer's current-year exhibit for capital gains and losses on investments (Exhibit 4, page 8 of the U.S. Annual Statement).

Change in nonadmitted assets and related items

This line of the Capital and Surplus Account records the change in the values of an insurer's nonadmitted assets reported in U.S. Exhibit 14. Such assets include furniture and most equipment; supplies, stationery, and printed matter; and cash advanced to company officers or agents. The change in an insurer's nonadmitted asset value is calculated in U.S. Annual Statement Exhibit 14 (Analysis of Nonadmitted Assets and Related Values). In the reporting of an insurer's annual change in surplus, an increase in the insurer's nonadmitted asset value decreases surplus, while a decrease in such asset values increases surplus. This inverse relationship becomes clearer after further review of the basic accounting equation.

Since an insurer can include only admitted assets for the purposes of the statutory Balance Sheet, the basic accounting equation for insurers can be stated as:

$$\textit{Admitted Assets} = \text{Liabilities} + \text{Capital} + \text{Surplus}$$

An increase in the value of an insurer's nonadmitted assets generally occurs as a result of a decrease in an admitted asset account such as Cash. For example, assume that an insurer has purchased new office furniture (a nonadmitted asset), using cash (an admitted asset) to make the purchase. Since the admitted asset, cash, has been replaced with a nonadmitted asset of equal value, the effect of the furniture purchase is to reduce the left side of the insurer's Balance Sheet equation. Thus, the right side of the equation must be reduced by the same amount in order to keep the equation in balance. Regulatory authorities require that this reduction be made to surplus. In fact, this reduction could logically be made only to surplus, since no reduction in the company's liabilities or capital has occurred.

On the other hand, a decrease in the value of an insurer's nonadmitted assets results in an increase in the insurer's surplus. To illustrate, assume that an insurer recorded receipt of agents' balances due. Upon collection of this receivable, which was classified as a nonadmitted asset, the amount received is (1) subtracted from the total of nonadmitted assets and (2) simultaneously added to the amount of the insurer's admitted assets. Since the company's admitted assets are increased by this event, the value of the left side of the accounting equation is increased by the admitted asset amount. The value of the right side of the equation must then be increased to keep the equation in balance. The surplus total would be increased to compensate for the reduction in nonadmitted assets.

Change in liability for reinsurance in unauthorized companies

An insurer will occasionally reinsure some of its business with a company that is not licensed in the same state where the insurer is domiciled. Such a reinsurance company is considered to be an *unauthorized company*. The liability for reinsurance in unauthorized companies is the excess of the reserve taken on ceded business minus the amounts withheld from or deposits made by the reinsurer. The change in liability for reinsurance in unauthorized companies is the difference between the liability for such reinsurance on the previous-year Balance Sheet date and the liability for such reinsurance on the current-year Balance Sheet date. Determination of the liability for unauthorized reinsurance is accomplished on a company-by-company basis. Thus, the excess in the reinsurance liability for one company cannot offset a deficiency for another unauthorized reinsurer.

The reinsurance liability arises when (1) the amount due from an unauthorized reinsurer exceeds the balances owed to it or (2) amounts payable to a reinsurer are covered by letters of credit from the insurer. The purpose of this liability is to protect policyowners by ensuring that the direct company—the insurer with which the policyowner placed his or her policy—adequately covers its liabilities. Establishment of the unauthorized reinsurance liability is necessary because the direct company's domiciliary insurance department has no jurisdiction over the unauthorized reinsurer and, thus, has no means by which to make that reinsurer meet its obligations.

Similar to the change in nonadmitted assets, a change in the liability for reinsurance in unauthorized companies affects surplus in an opposite manner—that is, an increase in this liability decreases surplus, and a decrease in this liability increases surplus. This relationship can once again be demonstrated through the insurer's Balance Sheet equation. Since the total of the right side of the Balance Sheet equation is increased by an increase in a liability account, in order to keep the equation in balance, an insurer must either (1) increase the left side of the equation or (2) decrease the right side of the equation by an equal amount in order to offset the increased liability. Since no asset is affected by the increase in liability, the equation is kept in balance through an equal decrease in surplus.

Change in reserve on account of change in valuation basis

When a policy reserve amount changes, the amount of the change is typically treated as a net gain or loss resulting from the insurer's operations. However, when a policy reserve amount is altered because of a change in the valuation basis of that reserve, the amount of the change is not treated as a gain or loss, but instead is treated as a direct change in the insurer's surplus.

An insurer would generally change the valuation basis of a policy reserve if the valuation method on which the reserve was originally based no longer accurately reflected the company's mortality, morbidity, or financial experience. When reserves are increased as a result of such revaluation, the increase is known as *reserve strengthening*. On the other hand, an insurer might decrease the amount in reserve when interest assumptions have proved to be too low. In a case where the interest rates available are greater than those assumed when the reserve was established, an insurer can eventually realize the necessary projected payment with a decreased current reserve amount.

Since policy reserves constitute liabilities for an insurer, an increase in the policy reserve amount caused by a change in the valuation basis of the policy reserve results in a decrease in the insurer's surplus. As mentioned earlier, when reconciling the Capital and Surplus Account to compensate for an increased liability amount, surplus must be decreased to keep the Balance Sheet equation in balance. Similarly, when the amount of policy reserves is decreased as a result of a change in the valuation basis of those reserves, the amount of surplus is necessarily increased.

Change in Mandatory Securities Valuation Reserve

Similar to the change in liability for unauthorized reinsurance, the Mandatory Securities Valuation Reserve (MSVR) is also a liability whose change during the year does not affect net gains from operations and therefore must be included directly in the reconciliation of the Capital and Surplus Account. As with the liabilities discussed earlier, an increase in the MSVR causes a corresponding decrease in surplus, and a decrease in the MSVR results in an increase in the insurer's surplus.

Change in treasury stock

Treasury stock—stock that a company has issued and subsequently repurchased—is treated as a separate item in the Capital account (see Figure 10-5). The amount of treasury stock directly reduces the company's capital. Usually, a company will repurchase its own shares for cash. Since the payment reduces total admitted assets and since the liabilities and surplus are unchanged, the capital section must be reduced.

Changes in surplus in separate accounts Statements

The separate accounts Statement and the variable life insurance separate accounts Statement reported in the Capital and Surplus Account are similar and can be discussed simultaneously. The Balance Sheet of an insurance company includes the total assets and total liabilities of any separate accounts maintained by the insurer. Usually, the total assets and liabilities for an insurer's separate accounts are equal. However, when these totals are not equal, the difference between the totals must be reported in the Surplus account to keep the company's basic accounting equation in balance. If the assets of the separate accounts exceed the liability totals for those accounts, the amount of excess increases the insurer's surplus. On the other hand, if total liabilities exceed total assets for the separate accounts, the excess decreases the total of the Surplus account.

Miscellaneous Capital and Surplus Account adjustments

Several lines in the reconciliation of the Capital and Surplus Account reflect direct changes in the capital and surplus of a stock company. *Capital changes* shows any change in capital paid up resulting from the sale of stock, from the declaration of a stock dividend, and from the direct transfer of capital paid up to surplus. *Surplus adjustments* records the effects on surplus of the capital changes mentioned above. The surplus adjustments line also reflects any increase in paid in and contributed surplus that results from a decrease in the par value of an insurer's stock. *Dividends to stockholders* shows the amount of cash dividends that have been paid to the company's stockholders plus any change in declared but unpaid dividends. Payments of cash dividends are made directly from unassigned surplus and thus serve to decrease the total of the Capital and Surplus Account.

Write-in items in the reconciliation

Insurers can use write-in lines to make any necessary capital and surplus adjustments that are not explicitly listed among the other reconciliation items in the Capital and Surplus Account. Insurers can use these write-in lines to show, for example, corrections of previous years' information or special losses or expenses that should be charged directly to surplus, but which have not otherwise been reported. Among the write-in reconciliation items that can be found in an insurer's Capital and Surplus Account are

- prior year's federal income tax
- federal income tax refunds
- adjustments for employee stock ownership plans
- changes in loading resulting from changes in reserve valuation basis
- cancellation of real estate sale
- cost of officers' life insurance
- payment and return of seed money from separate accounts
- charitable contributions not reported elsewhere
- additional contributions to fund pension plans

Accounting for Changes in Surplus—Canada

Canadian insurers must report their annual change in surplus in the Reconciliation of Unappropriated Earned Surplus report on page 5 of the Canadian Annual Statement (see Figure 10-6). The method of reconciling surplus changes between reporting years is essentially the same method that U.S. insurers use for the Capital and Surplus Account. However, a number of significant differences for Canadian insurers should be noted:

(1) The Canadian Reconciliation of Surplus does not show items similar to "Change in Mandatory Securities Valuation Reserve," "Change in value of nonadmitted assets and related items," "Change in liability for reinsurance in unauthorized companies," or "Change in treasury stock."

(2) Unappropriated earned surplus, the item equivalent to *unassigned surplus* in the U.S. Statement, is divided among the following three totals: *surplus in shareholders' funds, surplus in insurance funds,* and *surplus in segregated funds.* Under the Canadian system, a specified amount must also be set aside for appropriated surplus. This surplus is used to cover the necessary asset reserves, cash value policy deficiency reserves, and the amounts necessary to cover potentially uncollectible amounts from unauthorized reinsurers. This appropriated surplus cannot be distributed.

Minimum Capital and Surplus Requirements

Each state in the United States requires that an insurance company must (1) have an initial amount of capital and paid in surplus to begin operations and

FIGURE 10-6
Reconciliation of Unappropriated Earned Surplus—Canadian Annual Statement.

IV. RECONCILIATION OF UNAPPROPRIATED EARNED SURPLUS ($'000)		LIFE 01	ACCIDENT AND SICKNESS 02	TOTAL 03
UNAPPROPRIATED EARNED SURPLUS, 31 DECEMBER 19 IN SHAREHOLDERS' FUNDS	15			
IN INSURANCE FUNDS	16			
IN SEGREGATED FUNDS	17		▓▓▓	
SUB-TOTAL (15 TO 17)	▶18			
	19			
	20			
NET INCOME FROM INCOME STATEMENT (+ OR -)	21			
DECREASE (INCREASE) IN RESERVES REQUIRED - BY THE DEPARTMENT	22			
- BY FOREIGN JURISDICTIONS	23			
DECREASE (INCREASE) IN ADDITIONAL RESERVES	24			
DIVIDENDS TO SHAREHOLDERS (-)	25			
NET INCREASE (DECREASE) IN UNAPPROPRIATED EARNED SURPLUS DURING THE YEAR (SUB-TOTAL 19 TO 25)	▶26			
UNAPPROPRIATED EARNED SURPLUS, 31 DECEMBER 19 IN SHAREHOLDERS' FUNDS	27			
IN INSURANCE FUNDS	28			
IN SEGREGATED FUNDS	29		▓▓▓	
TOTAL UNAPPROPRIATED EARNED SURPLUS, 31 DEC. 19 (27 TO 29)	▶30			

(2) maintain a minimum amount of capital and surplus in order to continue operations. The minimum requirements for these totals differ from state to state. Minimum capital and surplus requirements serve to protect a company's policyowners by guaranteeing that a certain amount of funds will exist for satisfaction of those policyowners' claims. Though each state bases its minimum capital and surplus requirements on different calculations, typical components of these calculations include:

For Stock Companies
Capital paid up
Gross paid in and
  contributed surplus
Subordinated debt
Special surplus
Unassigned surplus

For Mutual Companies
Guaranty fund surplus
Special surplus
Unassigned surplus

In Canada, federal and provincial insurance authorities each specify the minimum capital and surplus requirements.

If a company's surplus falls below the minimum requirements for the jurisdiction in which the company is domiciled, that company is considered to be **impaired.** If an impaired company is not able to increase one of the necessary capital or surplus components in order to meet minimum requirements, the insurance department of the company's home jurisdiction will often begin some form of supervisory action that could possibly lead to liquidation of the company's assets. As mentioned earlier, to help ensure that the company's surplus amount does not fall below the required minimum, mutual companies frequently designate the minimum required surplus amount to a special surplus fund.

Key Terms

stock company
capital paid up
gross paid in and contributed surplus
mutualization
issue strain
unassigned surplus
reserve strengthening

par value
capital stock paid
contributed surplus
treasury stock
liquidation
special surplus funds
unappropriated earned surplus
impaired company

Review Questions and Exercises

1. What is the difference between capital paid up and gross paid in and contributed surplus?
2. What journal entry would you make for retirement of 2,000 shares of $2 par value treasury stock, assuming that the stock's market value was $30 per share?
3. List and briefly describe the three surplus classifications that a U.S. insurer would use. Give the Canadian equivalents.
4. Define *reserve strengthening*.
5. Calculate the amount of an insurer's surplus given the following totals:

$$\text{Assets} = \$100,000,000$$
$$\text{Liabilities} = \$\ 35,000,000$$
$$\text{Capital} = \$\ \ 7,000,000$$

6. State three transactions that increase the total of an insurer's Capital and Surplus Account. State three transactions that decrease this total.

11
Summary of U.S. and Canadian Annual Statements

Learning Objectives

After reading this chapter, you should be able to:

- Understand the objectives of expense reporting in a life and health insurance company
- State the three different categories of expense liabilities
- Describe the Annual Statement presentation of a life and health insurance company's expenses
- Understand the purpose of Exhibits 12 and 14 in the U.S. Annual Statement
- Understand the basics of fund accounting in the Canadian Annual Statement
- List some of the items presented in the "Notes to the Financial Statements" portion of the U.S. Annual Statement

Introduction

This chapter includes discussions of some portions of the Annual Statement that have not yet been covered. In addition, certain parts of the Annual Statement that have previously been introduced are discussed in greater detail to show how the information from the Annual Statement is used to gauge an insurer's present financial performance in relation to both past performance and the performance of other life and health insurers. The Annual Statement schedules and exhibits reviewed in this chapter include the expense exhibit, the U.S. reconciliation of ledger assets and analysis of nonadmitted assets, and the Canadian reports relating to fund accounting.

Expense Reporting

In both the U.S. and Canadian Annual Statements, a major exhibit is devoted to reporting expenses, including both general operating expenses and expenses incurred in the investment of the company's cash assets. In both statements, this exhibit classifies expenses into three groupings according to whether the expenses were incurred in connection with the company's (1) investment activities, (2) life insurance operations, or (3) accident and health—in Canada, accident and sickness—operations. By monitoring and attributing expenses, companies can do a better job of controlling their expenses. Such control can often help achieve more successful and efficient operations. Before discussing Annual Statement treatment of expenses, however, we will cover the types of expenses incurred by an insurer as well as the ways in which the amounts of these expenses are determined for Annual Statement purposes.

Gains from operations in any industry result in large part from proper control of expenses. In the life and health insurance business, however, major expenses such as claims and commissions are essentially unavoidable. Management's efforts to control these expense categories are limited to ensuring adequate underwriting standards and avoiding overpayment. Operating expenses, then, are the only major costs over which management can have meaningful control.

Accounting for expenses in a life and health insurance company is centered around four primary objectives. First, the company must try to prevent excessive expenditures. A second objective is to maintain an audit trail from the approval of an expenditure to the presentation of the expense item in the Annual Statement. A third objective, relative to supplies and fixed assets, is to maintain adequate records for calculating depreciation expense and for determining the amount of liability at the end of the year in connection with orders placed. Adequate records must also be maintained for amortizable assets and for those assets that might involve nonadmitted amounts. Fourth, the company must ensure that each expenditure is properly authorized before it is made.

Many employees have the authority to approve expenses. Each person with such authority usually is restricted as to the types and amounts of expenses that he or she can approve. Wide dispersal of expense approval authority is considered desirable because the person most familiar with the need for an expense is generally in the best position to control it. To aid in ongoing control and analysis, management ordinarily requires reports that analyze expenses by (1) the persons responsible for incurring the expense, (2) the type of expense, and (3) each insurance function, line of business, or product to which expenses are attributable.

These reports, some of which are included in or based on reports in the Annual Statement, enable management to recognize and eliminate unnecessary expenses and to reward individuals or departments that conscientiously control expenses.

Types of Expense Liabilities

An insurer's expense liabilities can be classified into three general categories:

1. liabilities incurred on the date that merchandise is ordered, the date a service is performed, or the date a contract for purchase is signed;
2. liabilities incurred subsequent to the order date, such as when merchandise is received; and
3. continually accruing expenses on which some portion of the cost is incurred each day.

The characteristics of each of these categories is discussed below.

Liabilities incurred at time of performance or delivery

Liabilities incurred at the time of performance or delivery include printed brochures and supplies carrying the company's name. Such items typically have no value to any other person or company. Also included in this category are medical examination fees, inspection report fees, and any items purchased under a contract specifying that the company may not cancel the order once it is placed. As mentioned in Chapter 9, a considerable amount of judgment must be used in determining the amount of this type of liability.

Liabilities incurred subsequent to the order date

Liabilities incurred subsequent to the order date include amounts for products or services that have been received but for which money has not yet been paid. Invoices and bills for many types of items can be received after the reporting date, and incurred liability amounts must be established for each of these items. During examinations of life and health insurers, insurance departments typically examine the methods a company uses in establishing this type of liability.

Continually accruing expenses

Typically, the largest expense liability category for an insurer is for the following continually accruing expenses: (1) services received for which the company is liable and (2) taxes incurred for a period prior to December 31. Most expense items and many tax items are continually accruing. Salaries and wages are usually partially incurred at the time the statement is prepared, creating a liability for the portion incurred but unpaid. A liability may also exist for contributions to employee benefit plans, for professional services and fees, for utility services used, and for a number of investment expenses. Premium taxes and income taxes are continually accruing expenses. Most of these liabilities must be calculated separately.

Annual Statement Presentation of Expenses

The presentation of expenses in both the U.S. and Canadian Annual Statements is basically the same. In U.S. Statement Exhibit 5 (see Figure 11-1), the total for each expense category is allocated between insurance and investment operations. Within the insurance category, expenses are classified as either life insurance expenses or accident and health insurance expenses. Summary totals for each type of expense are then presented in the last column of Exhibit 5. In Canada, the total of each expense category is presented in column 1 of Exhibit 9 (see Figure 11-2). Each type of expense is then allocated among the company's life business, accident and sickness business, and segregated funds. In the United States, the total of general insurance expenses is reported in the Summary of Operations. Similarly, a Canadian insurer's general insurance expenses are reported on the statutory Income Statement. For each Annual Statement, investment amounts are segregated from insurance amounts to facilitate calculating the net investment income before allocating it to lines of business.

Annual Statement instructions for allocating expenses are quite comprehensive. Some expenses can be allocated directly to the appropriate line of business by maintaining separate general ledger accounts for each type of expense within each major line of business. Premium taxes can easily be charged directly to a line of business because premiums must be reported by line of business to each jurisdiction's insurance department. Many other expenses, such as cafeteria expense and payroll taxes, must be allocated periodically using a formula, such as a percentage of total employees or a percentage of total salaries. In some cases, expenses might be allocated first to different operational units and then reallocated to lines of business in accordance with the work volume involved in servicing and administering each line of business.

If a company is functionally organized—with centralized departments for marketing, underwriting, claims, and policyowner service—expense allocation to line of business must be based on special internal company reports. General expenses—such as the president's salary—and many other expenses can be allocated to lines of business using the same techniques used in allocating cost by function. (Functional cost allocation is discussed more fully in Chapter 16.) Salaries of supervisors and executives can be allocated to lines of business in proportion to the total salaries paid to subordinate employees in each line.

11 Summary of U.S. and Canadian Annual Statements

FIGURE 11-1
Exhibit 5—U.S. Annual Statement.

```
Form 1    ANNUAL STATEMENT FOR THE YEAR 1985 OF THE _____     9
                                                          Name
```

EXHIBIT 5 — GENERAL EXPENSES

	INSURANCE		(3) INVESTMENT	(4) TOTAL
	(1) LIFE	(2) ACCIDENT AND HEALTH		
1. Rent				
2. Salaries and wages				
3.11 *Contributions for benefit plans for employees				
3.12 *Contributions for benefit plans for agents				
3.21 Payments to employees under non-funded benefit programs				
3.22 Payments to agents under non-funded benefit programs				
3.31 Other employee welfare				
3.32 Other agent welfare				
3.4				
4.1 Legal fees and expenses				
4.2 Medical examination fees				
4.3 Inspection report fees				
4.4 Fees of public accountants and consulting actuaries				
4.5 Expense of investigation and settlement of policy claims				
4.6				
5.1 Traveling expenses				
5.2 Advertising				
5.3 Postage, express, telegraph and telephone				
5.4 Printing and stationery				
5.5 Cost or depreciation of furniture and equipment				
5.6 Rental of equipment				
5.7				
6.1 Books and periodicals				
6.2 Bureau and association dues				
6.3 Insurance, except on real estate				
6.4 Miscellaneous losses				
6.5 Collection and bank service charges				
6.6 Sundry general expenses				
6.7 Group service and administration fees				
6.8				
7.1 Agency expense allowance				
7.2 Agents' balances charged off (less $_____ recovered)				
7.3 Agency conferences other than local meetings				
8.1				
8.2				
9.1 Real estate expenses				
9.2 Investment expenses not included elsewhere				
9.3				
10. GENERAL EXPENSES INCURRED				
Reconciliation with Exhibit 12	(To Page 4, Item 22)		(To Exhibit 2, Line 2)	
11. General expenses unpaid December 31, previous year				
12. General expenses unpaid December 31, current year				
13. General expenses paid during year (10 + 11 − 12)	X X X	X X X	X X X	(To Exhibit 12, Line 27)

ORDINARY LIFE INSURANCE AND INDIVIDUAL ANNUITY BUSINESS ONLY
A. Compensation to agents on a plan other than commissions, included in Col. (1): First year $_____, Renewal $_____
B. Agency supervision, except home office, included in Col. (1): Line 2 $_____, Line 5.1 $_____, Line _____ $_____
C. Branch office expenses other than those in A and B included in Col. (1): Line 1 $_____, Line 2 $_____, All other lines $_____

*These items include $_____ on account of prior service.

Another method of allocating salaries is by the actual time spent by each employee in performing work for each line of business.

Rent is generally charged to a department on the basis of the amount of space occupied. This expense is then allocated to each line of business in the same proportion as the allocation of departmental salaries. Many expenses, such as telephone, postage, etc., can be charged to departments on the basis of actual usage and then allocated by line of business. Certain indices, such as premium volume, number of policies in force, or amount of insurance in force, are sometimes used as a basis for allocation.

FIGURE 11-2
Exhibit 9—Canadian Annual Statement.

	30		
NAME OF COMPANY ▶			YEAR OF STATEMENT 19

EXHIBIT 9 – GENERAL AND INVESTMENT EXPENSES ($'000)

		TOTAL INCURRED	TOTAL INCURRED CHARGED AS INVESTMENT EXPENSES	TOTAL DUE AND ACCRUED
		01	02	03
RENT:				
HEAD OFFICE RENTS	01			
BRANCH OFFICE RENTS	02			
	03			
TOTAL RENT ▶	04			
SALARIES, WAGES, AND ALLOWANCES:				
HEAD OFFICE EMPLOYEES' SALARIES AND WAGES	05			
BRANCH OFFICE EMPLOYEES' SALARIES AND WAGES	06			
MANAGERS' AND AGENTS' SALARIES	07			
DIRECTORS' FEES	08			
AGENTS' EXPENSE ALLOWANCES	09			
	10			
	11			
TOTAL SALARIES, WAGES AND ALLOWANCES ▶	12			
EMPLOYEES' AND AGENTS' WELFARE:				
CONTRIBUTION TO COMPANY PENSION AND INSURANCE PLANS FOR EMPLOYEES	13			
CONTRIBUTIONS TO COMPANY PENSION AND INSURANCE PLANS FOR AGENTS	14			
EMPLOYER'S CONTRIBUTION TO CANADA/ QUEBEC PENSION PLANS	15			
CONTRIBUTION TO MEDICAL AND HOSPITALIZATION PLANS	16			
UNEMPLOYMENT INSURANCE CONTRIBUTION	17			
CAFETERIA EXPENSES	18			
	19			
	20			
	21			
TOTAL EMPLOYEES' AND AGENTS' WELFARE ▶	22			
PROFESSIONAL AND SERVICE FEES AND EXPENSES:				
LEGAL FEES AND EXPENSES	23			
MEDICAL EXAMINATION FEES	24			
INSPECTION AND INVESTIGATION FEES	25			
AUDITORS' FEES	26			
	27			
	28			
TOTAL PROFESSIONAL AND SERVICE FEES AND EXPENSES ▶	29			

FIGURE 11-2 (cont.)

31

NAME OF COMPANY ▶
YEAR OF STATEMENT 19

EXHIBIT 9 - GENERAL AND INVESTMENT EXPENSES (CONCLUDED) ($'000)

		TOTAL INCURRED	INCURRED CHARGED AS INVESTMENT EXPENSES	TOTAL DUE AND ACCRUED
		01	02	03
MISCELLANEOUS EXPENSES:				
ADVERTISING	01			
AGENCY CONVENTIONS	02			
BOOKS AND PERIODICALS	03			
BUREAU AND ASSOCIATION DUES	04			
COLLECTION AND BANK CHARGES	05			
COMMISSIONS ON MORTGAGES	06			
CUSTODY OF SECURITIES	07			
INSURANCE, EXCEPT ON REAL ESTATE	08			
POSTAGE, TELEX, TELEPHONE, EXPRESS	09			
PRINTING, SUPPLIES AND STATIONERY	10			
DEPRECIATION EXPENSE RE MISCELLANEOUS ASSETS	11			
RENTAL OF EQUIPMENT	12			
TRAVELLING EXPENSES, HEAD OFFICE	13			
TRAVELLING EXPENSES, BRANCH OFFICE	14			
	15			
	16			
TOTAL MISCELLANEOUS EXPENSES	▶ 17			
REAL ESTATE EXPENSES, EXCLUDING TAXES:				
	18			
	19			
	20			
TOTAL REAL ESTATE EXPENSES, EXCLUDING TAXES	▶ 21			
GRAND TOTAL	▶ 22			

ALLOCATION OF TOTAL GENERAL AND INVESTMENT EXPENSES

		LIFE	SEGREGATED FUNDS	ACCIDENT & SICKNESS	TOTAL
		01	02	03	04
GENERAL EXPENSES	23				
INVESTMENT EXPENSES	24				
ADJUSTMENT EXPENSES	25				
TOTAL INCURRED	▶ 26				
DUE AND ACCRUED	27				

The direct cost of entering a new line of business is normally charged entirely to that line, even though expenses are incurred before any premium income is realized. U.S. Annual Statement instructions require insurers to use expense allocation methods that reasonably reflect the actual incidence of cost by line of business. The instructions also suggest methods that can be used to allocate each expense item. Expenses as shown in the Annual Statement expense exhibits can be divided into several broad categories: (1) rents; (2) salaries, wages, and allowances; (3) employees' and agents' benefits; (4) professional service fees and expenses; (5) investment expenses; and (6) miscellaneous expenses. For a complete list of expenses, refer to Figures 11-1 and 11-2, which show the expense exhibits of the U.S. and Canadian Annual Statements.

Reconciliation of Ledger Assets (Exhibit 12)—United States

The primary purpose of the Reconciliation of Ledger Assets exhibit is to serve an audit function for supervisory authorities. Other purposes of Exhibit 12 are (1) to provide an audit trail from figures in the trial balance to the figures used in the various exhibits and (2) to prove that all cash basis figures in the trial balance—except the Balance account (if applicable)—have been entered either as a receipt or as a disbursement in this exhibit, or as a ledger asset in the asset exhibit.

The formula used in the reconciliation of ledger assets can be expressed in the form of an equation:

$$\begin{aligned} & \text{Ledger assets at the beginning of the year} \\ + \ & \text{increases in ledger assets} \\ - \ & \text{decreases in ledger assets} \\ \hline = \ & \text{Ledger assets at the end of the year} \end{aligned}$$

Increases in ledger assets refers to (1) cash-basis income, including realized capital gains; (2) increases in the book values of assets; and (3) increases in cash-basis liabilities. *Decreases in ledger assets* includes (1) cash-basis costs, including realized capital losses; (2) decreases in the book values of assets; and (3) decreases in cash-basis liabilities. Note that increases in both cash-basis liabilities and the book value of ledger assets are generally treated as receipts, and decreases in both cash-basis liabilities and the book value of ledger assets are generally treated as disbursements. A sample entry should help to explain this treatment.

If an insurer receives $1,000 to be placed on deposit for the payment of future premiums, the entry is:

```
Cash ................................1,000
    Premium Deposits .........................1,000
```

The credit in this example is to a cash-basis liability account. This credit is equal to the increase in Cash, which is a ledger asset. Therefore, an increase in a cash-basis liability also reflects an increase in ledger assets—Cash, in this case—and must be included as a receipt item in the reconciliation equation. Similarly, a decrease in a cash-basis liability reflects a decrease in a ledger asset and must be included as a disbursement item in the reconciliation. Increases and decreases in cash-basis liabilities are usually summarized and entered in the reconciliation exhibit on a net-increase or a net-decrease basis. All cash-basis account balances from the trial balance are consolidated into broad classification totals before being entered into this exhibit. Most of these totals are obtained from other Annual Statement exhibits.

The last section of Exhibit 12 is entitled *reconciliation between years*. In this section, the difference between receipts and disbursements during the year is added to or subtracted from the total of ledger assets at the beginning of the current year to arrive at the total of ledger assets at the end of the current year.

Analysis of Nonadmitted Assets and Related Items (Exhibit 14)—United States

The Analysis of Nonadmitted Assets and Related Items (Exhibit 14—see Figure 11-3) shows increases and decreases in the book value of many nonadmitted assets. These assets are typically used in, or created through, insurance operations. No investment totals are included. As mentioned in Chapters 2 and 10, a net increase or decrease in the total of nonadmitted assets results in a direct change in Surplus, and any net increase or decrease is reflected in the Surplus account of the Annual Statement. Items shown in this analysis can be divided into two general categories: (1) prepaid expenses and (2) loans and amounts receivable.

Prepaid Expenses

The Prepaid Expenses category covers items that can either be treated as operating expenses in the next accounting period or that will be systematically charged to future periods through depreciation. Such items include inventories of supplies and commuted commissions of sales agents. For example, the item *supplies, stationery, and printed matter* is usually treated as an expense in the year of purchase. However, such expenditures may be capitalized if the purchase is related to a subsequent period, in which case the expenditures are reported in Exhibit 13—Assets. This treatment is consistent with the accounting principle of matching revenues and expenses. The amount of these assets must be nonadmitted, and the subsequent change in surplus from one year-end to the next is recorded in the nonadmitted asset exhibit.

FIGURE 11-3
Exhibit 14—U.S. Annual Statement.

EXHIBIT 14—ANALYSIS OF NON-ADMITTED ASSETS AND RELATED ITEMS
(Excluding Investment Adjustments Not Listed)

	(1) END OF PREVIOUS YEAR	(2) END OF CURRENT YEAR	(3) CHANGES FOR YEAR INCREASE (—) OR DECREASE (+)
1. Loans on company's stock			
2. Supplies, stationery, printed matter			
3. Furniture and equipment			
4. Commuted commissions			x x x
5. Agents' balances (net)			
6. Cash advanced to or in the hands of officers or agents			
7. Loans on personal security, endorsed or not			
8. Bills receivable			
9. Premium notes, etc., in excess of net value and other policy liabilities on individual policies			x x x
10. Accident and health premiums due and unpaid			
11. Other assets not admitted (itemize):			
11.1			
11.2			
11.3			
12. Agents' credit balances (Page 3, Item 19 inside)			
13. TOTAL CHANGE	x x x	x x x	*

*(Carry to Item 35, Page 4)

Commuted commissions can be defined as the present value of amounts paid to agents in lieu of renewal commissions that would otherwise be payable in future years. Agents who terminate their services with a company are sometimes willing to sell their unpaid renewal commissions to the company at a substantial discount. This commission cost can be recorded as an expense and then decreased annually to spread the expense over the years in which it would otherwise have been payable. The entry each year is a debit to a commission expense account and a credit to Commuted Commissions.

Loans and Amounts Receivable

Most miscellaneous assets of a life insurance company come under the general classification of Loans and Amounts Receivable. Some of the assets included in this category are discussed below:

- *Loans on company's stock* represents loans taken by the company against the value of company stock. Because the value of the stock is not acceptable as an admitted asset, the loan is unsecured for Balance Sheet purposes and must be nonadmitted.

- *Agents' balances (net)* describes the balance in the general ledger control account relating to individual accounts with agents. *Agents' credit balances* is also an item in Exhibit 14. The change in the control account balance and the change in the credit balances equal the change in agents' debit balances.
- *Cash advanced to or in the hands of officers or agents* represents amounts that the company has placed at the disposal of agents or officers for the purpose of carrying on necessary daily activities. An example of this type of nonadmitted asset is advances against travel expenses to be incurred by these persons. Such advances are not sufficiently secured to be considered admitted assets.
- *Loans on personal security, endorsed or not,* are loans made to individuals. These loans can either be collateral loans secured by assets of the borrower or notes receivable with no collateral backing. This Annual Statement item represents a minor amount since life insurance companies do not typically make loans on personal security. If such loans are made, they must be nonadmitted.
- *Bills receivable* represents small amounts due from outside sources. These amounts are unsecured and, thus, are nonadmitted.
- *Premium notes, etc., in excess of net value and other policy liabilities on individual policies* represents amounts receivable on notes given by a policyowner in payment of premiums. Some companies permit agents to accept notes in payment of premiums and may agree to buy these notes from the agent under certain conditions. When a note is taken in connection with a premium, the note is usually payment for a premium in the first policy year when the policy has no cash value to support a policy loan. If a premium note is secured by sufficient cash value in the policy, the note is acceptable as an admitted asset. However, most such notes are not secured and must, therefore, be nonadmitted.
- *Accident and health premiums due and unpaid* covers premiums that must be nonadmitted because of time limitations. For example, any premium that became due prior to October 1 of the reporting year must be nonadmitted.

Fund Accounting—Canada

In Canada, most life and health insurance companies, both stock and mutual, write participating and nonparticipating business. The interests of the participating policyowners are protected by a legal requirement that separate funds be maintained for participating business, nonparticipating business, and the shareholders' equity in the company (in the case of stock companies). The process used to account for and allocate revenue to the various funds in Canadian companies is referred to as **fund accounting.**

A **fund,** as the term is used in the Canadian Annual Statement, can be defined as all liabilities and surplus held for a particular purpose or for a particular group of persons. For example, the participating fund consists of all major liabilities for (1) participating policies and (2) surplus held for participating policyowners. Assets, on the other hand, are not segregated by funds. Fund accounting is comparable to an accounting arrangement for a group of companies, each with its own liabilities and surplus but joined together in a common investment program.

All interest-bearing liabilities—including policy reserves and amounts on deposit—and dividends payable in the following year are included in one of the funds. Capital stock outstanding is included in a separate fund, the shareholders' fund. Large common liabilities or reserves set aside, such as an investment reserve fund and various retirement funds, are each treated as separate funds. Miscellaneous liability items—primarily current liabilities on which interest is not required—are not included in a fund but are treated as general liabilities called *Amounts Owing by the Company,* or simply *Amounts Owing.* Included in this classification are all advance premiums, unearned investment income, and all incurred but unpaid costs, including unpaid claims.

To segregate the surplus belonging to each fund, insurers must account for all income, costs, and net income by fund. Net investment earnings and capital gains (or losses) from assets are allocated to each fund on an equitable basis. Expenses and other costs are allocated on an exact basis whenever possible. If direct allocation is impractical, expenses and costs are apportioned by methods that produce equitable results. Companies are required to describe their allocation methods in their Annual Statements.

Amounts can be transferred between funds under certain conditions, but Canadian law places restrictions on the amounts of surplus that may be transferred from insurance funds to the shareholders' fund in any one year. These special statutory requirements demand a considerable amount of fund accounting information. This need for information is served by the following financial reports that are included in the Canadian Annual Statement:

- The *Analysis of Income by Fund,* in which income, insurance costs, and expense items are analyzed by fund—the total of the life funds and the accident and sickness funds matches the total income reported in the Income Statement on Annual Statement page 4;
- The *Summary of Funds and Amounts Owing by the Company* (hereafter referred to as the *Summary of Funds),* in which the various liability, capital, and surplus amounts in the Balance Sheet at the end of the year are classified by fund or as *Amounts Owing*; and
- The *Reconciliation of Funds,* which shows the amount of change in fund liabilities and the sources of change in surplus of each fund during the year.

These reports are found on pages 14-16 of the Canadian Annual Statement and are shown at the end of this chapter.

Reports relating to fund accounting include sufficient detail so that an audit trail is clearly established from the source of change to the resulting surplus or liability amount in each fund. While we will not cover the detailed accounting steps required to produce these special reports, we will discuss the purpose of these reports as well as the items included in them. The Analysis of Income by Fund and the Reconciliation of Funds report on the following funds:

<u>Life Business</u>
participating fund—column 1
nonparticipating fund—column 2
shareholders' fund—column 3
other company funds—columns 4-6
segregated fund—column 7
total of life business funds—column 8

<u>Accident and Sickness Business</u>
insurance fund—column 9
shareholders' fund—column 10
total of accident and
sickness business funds—column 11

Before the analysis and reconciliation exhibits related to funds are examined, the method of classifying liabilities and surplus by funds should be understood.

Summary of Funds and Amounts Owing by the Company

The Summary of Funds and Amounts Owing by the Company attributes all of the liability, capital, and surplus items to a fund classification or to Amounts Owing by the Company. The purpose of the report is to show (1) that the total of a company's funds and amounts owing equals the company's total assets, (2) the specific amounts in each fund, and (3) the difference between the company's funds at the end of the current year and the funds at the end of the preceding year. The final total of funds and amounts owing is referred to as the *grand total all funds*. The amounts in this grand total column must agree with the totals shown on the Liabilities, Capital and Surplus page of the statutory Balance Sheet.

The first item in the Summary is entitled *insurance funds*. The liabilities listed under insurance funds are actuarial reserves, amounts on deposit with the company, and provisions for dividends and experience rating refunds. The first two of these items were discussed in earlier chapters. The third category covers the liability for (1) policy dividends that will become payable in the following year, including deferred dividends then payable, and (2) additional experience rating refunds set aside for payment in years other than the following year. Dividends currently payable to policyowners but not yet paid are not considered a fund liability but are instead treated as Amounts Owing by the Company.

Lines are provided in this Summary for special reserves established by the company. These reserves include portions of surplus set aside within each of the insurance funds to meet future mortality and other cost contingencies. A surplus item is also included in this Summary for each of the two insurance funds. The amounts shown are the surplus balances at the end of the year. These insurance surplus amounts are held in their respective insurance funds for the protection of policyowners. Surplus in insurance funds does not become shareholders' surplus until transferred by order of the board of directors.

Below the liabilities and surplus amounts related to insurance funds, three amounts make up the shareholders' fund. These totals are for capital, surplus, and reserves allocated within the shareholders' fund. Dividends to shareholders are paid only from this surplus. Surplus set aside each year for shareholders includes an allocation from investment earnings and from capital gains less capital losses during the year. The surplus in the Summary is shown after transfers between insurance funds.

Surplus and liabilities can be transferred between funds under certain conditions. Any surplus transferred or investment income allocated to a fund other than an insurance or shareholders' fund becomes a liability to the company as a whole. For example, if $1,000 is transferred from the company's surplus to the employees' pension fund, the $1,000 is thereafter a liability to the company in much the same manner as a declared dividend is a liability. Funds of this type do not have surplus as such and are shown as liabilities in this Summary.

Analysis of Income by Fund

The Analysis of Income by Fund allocates amounts resulting from investments and operations directly to the different established funds. Among the types of amounts allocated in this Analysis are

- premiums and annuity considerations
- investment income
- contributions to staff pension or insurance funds
- claims incurred
- payments of settlement annuities
- increases in reserve
- interest received on claims and amounts on deposit

Transfers between funds are also shown in the Analysis. In addition, net income before unusual or extraordinary items is calculated and allocated to each fund.

Reconciliation of Funds

The Reconciliation of Funds report shows the amount of surplus change in each liability and the source of change in surplus for each fund during the year. Items in this Reconciliation that relate to surplus changes include

- balances carried from the Analysis of Revenue account
- net nonamortizable gains (or losses) on investments
- transfers of surplus to shareholders' fund
- transfers of surplus from other funds
- transfers of surplus to other funds
- dividends to shareholders

The items related to transfer of surplus provide a clear audit trail between surplus balances in the participating, nonparticipating, and shareholders' funds.

Periodically, surplus may be transferred from the nonparticipating fund to the shareholders' fund. Under some conditions and limitations, surplus can also be transferred from the participating fund to the shareholders' fund. These transfers and any other surplus transfers permitted by statute are entered on the appropriate descriptive lines. The journal entry for such a transfer between funds can be demonstrated in the following example. Assume that a company transferred both $1,000 from the participating fund and $3,000 from the nonparticipating fund to surplus in the shareholders' fund. The journal would show a debit to each of the insurance surplus accounts, reflecting a decrease in these accounts, and a credit to shareholders' surplus to reflect an increase in this account. The entry is:

```
Surplus, Participating Fund ............... 1,000
Surplus, Nonparticipating Fund ............ 3,000
    Surplus, Shareholders' Fund ................. 4,000
```

Other Annual Statement Reports

In addition to the reports already covered in this text, U.S. and Canadian Annual Statements present a great deal of other information. This section briefly discusses some of these other Annual Statement reports.

An important portion of the U.S. Blank is the "Notes to the Financial Statements" that appears on page 17A of the Annual Statement. These Notes contain a great deal of additional information and explanatory remarks regarding other schedules and exhibits of the Annual Statement. The information in Notes to the Financial Statements includes

- the basis of valuation of invested assets and information regarding the company's investment income;
- the companies included, if applicable, in the insurer's consolidated federal tax returns;

- information concerning the insurer's parent company, subsidiaries, and affiliates;
- information on the company's deferred compensation and retirement plans;
- capital and surplus and stockholder dividend restrictions; and
- information regarding life insurance and annuity actuarial reserves.

Page 15 of the U.S. Annual Statement presents an Exhibit of Life Insurance that shows the changes during the reporting year in the number of policies issued by the company and the amount of insurance in force. The Exhibit analyzes these changes for each line of life insurance business—industrial, ordinary, credit, and group. The analysis takes into account issue of new policies, claims on existing policies, lapses, and policy surrenders. The Exhibit of Life Insurance also shows the amount of additional accidental death benefit coverage in force at year's end. Following the Life Insurance Exhibit is an Exhibit of Annuities and Supplementary Contracts with Life Contingencies that analyzes annuities and supplementary contracts by new issues and amounts currently payable or deferred. Canadian Annual Statement Exhibits A through G and I present information similar to that displayed in the U.S. Life Insurance and Annuity Exhibits.

Two other schedules in the U.S. Annual Statement present information that aids an analysis of the status of a company's life business. Schedule F—Policy Claims Resisted or Compromised—shows policyowner, policy, and claim information for each claim that was resisted or for which a compromise settlement was paid. Also presented in this exhibit are the settlement amounts paid during the reporting year, and the reasons for which each claim was compromised or resisted. Canadian insurers use Schedule L of the Canadian Blank to present this information. Schedule M of the U.S. Blank applies to policyowner dividends and lists the amount of dividends paid or to be paid per $1,000 of insurance in force. This exhibit is separated into two parts. Part 1 analyzes dividends paid per year on policies issued during the twenty years prior to the statement date. Part 2 of Schedule M presents the dividends that the company expects to pay for the next twenty years on policies issued during the reporting year. Canadian Exhibit 18 is the primary dividend exhibit.

Aside from strictly financial reports, the Annual Statement also presents other information regarding the company itself. The U.S. Annual Statement contains one report entitled "General Interrogatories" that presents information about the nature of the company's activities, its holding companies and subsidiaries (if any), and its ownership. Another schedule that presents non-financial information is Schedule L, which reports on the results of the last annual election of the insurer's board of directors. In Canada, Annual Statement page 11 presents information about the insurer's corporate history, while Schedule M lists the company's stockholders. Since the amount of information required by Schedule M can be quite extensive, this Schedule is often presented as a printout attached to the Annual Statement. Though much of the information described in this paragraph does not directly represent financial accounting activity or transactions, an insurer's accounting department is still responsible for accurate completion of these and all other portions of the Annual Statement. Since the Annual Statement also requires the signatures of a company's Controller, Chief Executive Officer, Chief Actuary, and other company officers, each of these individuals is also responsible for the information in the Annual Statement.

Use of Annual Statement Information

The information in the Annual Statement can be used by an insurance company as the basis for comparing itself to other companies or to the industry as a whole. These comparisons can take several different forms, generally referred to as *tests*. Such tests are performed not only by the insurers themselves, but also by such outside agents as governmental regulatory authorities or firms such as the A.M. Best Company, an insurance industry statistical service that administers **Best's Advance Rating Report Service (BARRS)**.

BARRS bases its ratings of a company's overall financial performance on a number of different types of tests. Two common categories of tests are profitability tests and liquidity tests. Most tests produce a ratio with ranges of outcome that can be from −100 percent to in excess of +100 percent. Because test results are generally expressed as ratios, cross-company comparisons are relatively easy to make. Industry standards are also easily derived over a period of years.

Best's uses eight tests to ascertain a company's *profitability*. The following list shows some of these tests, the usual percentage range resulting from each test, and the industry norm as determined by BARRS.[1] These industry norms fluctuate from time to time. The norms presented here were effective in 1985.

Test	Typical range	Industry norm
Yield on investments (Net investment income expressed as a percentage of the mean of cash and invested assets plus accrued investment income minus borrowed money)	7-12%	9.9%
Net operating gain as a percentage of net premiums written	any result greater than zero	4.6%

Test (cont.)	Typical range (cont.)	Industry norm (cont.)
Net operating gain as a percentage of total operating income	any result greater than zero	3.1%
Benefits paid as a percentage of net premiums written	less than 90%	59.9%
Commissions and expenses as a percentage of net premiums written	less than 85%	23.9%

Liquidity tests are concerned with the ease with which a company can meet any immediate claims upon its assets. Common liquidity tests and industry ranges and norms are as follows:

Test	Typical range	Industry norm
Common stocks and real estate as a percentage of capital and surplus	less than 95%	95.1%
Nonadmitted assets as a percentage of admitted assets	maximum value: 3%	.7%

(Note that the 1985 industry norm for the first liquidity test was outside the typical range for the industry.)

Key Terms

commuted commissions
Best's Advanced Rating Report Service (BARRS)
fund accounting

Review Questions and Exercises

1. What are the three categories of expense liabilities for a life insurer? Give an example of each.
2. What are the primary expense exhibits in the U.S. and Canadian Annual Statements?
3. Define *commuted commissions*.
4. What is the purpose of Canadian fund accounting?
5. Describe two of the tests used in BARRS to measure a company's profitability.

NOTES

1. *Best's Insurance Management Reports*, Release #8. ©A.M. Best Company—used with permission.

Chapter 11 Appendix
Fund Accounting Exhibits—Canadian Annual Statement.

14 (LS)

NAME OF COMPANY ▶

YEAR OF STATEMENT
19

XIII. ANALYSIS OF INCOME BY

		LIFE		
		PAR 01	NON-PAR 02	SHAREHOLDERS 03
PREMIUMS	01			
CONSIDERATIONS FOR SETTLEMENT ANNUITIES	02			
POLICY DIVIDENDS AND PROCEEDS OF CONTRACTS DEPOSITED IN SEGREGATED FUNDS	03			
NET INVESTMENT INCOME	04			
NET INVESTMENT GAIN (LOSS) ON SEGREGATED FUND ASSETS	05			
CONTRIBUTIONS TO STAFF PENSION AND INSURANCE FUNDS	06			
NET GAIN (LOSS) ON CURRENCY EXCHANGE TRANSACTIONS	07			
RESERVE ADJUSTMENT ON REINSURANCE CEDED	08			
	09			
	10			
NET TRANSFERS IN RESPECT OF MORTALITY, EXPENSES AND TAXES FROM (TO) SEG. FUNDS	11			
NET TRANSFER OF POLICY LIABILITIES (TO) FROM SEGREGATED FUNDS	12			
INTER FUND TRANSFERS TO MEET LIABILITIES TRANSFERRED	13			
SUBTOTAL (01 TO 13)	▶ 14			
CLAIMS INCURRED	15			
CLAIMS INCURRED PAID DIRECTLY FROM SEGREGATED FUNDS	16			
PAYMENTS UNDER SETTLEMENT ANNUITIES	17			
POLICY DIVIDENDS AND PROCEEDS OF CONTRACTS WITHDRAWN FROM SEGREGATED FUNDS	18			
NORMAL INCREASE IN ACTUARIAL RESERVES (TOTAL)	19			
NORMAL INCREASE IN SEGREGATED FUNDS	20			
INCREASE IN STAFF PENSION AND INSURANCE FUNDS	21			
INTEREST INCURRED ON CLAIMS	22			
TAXES, LICENCES AND FEES EXCLUDING INVESTMENT TAXES AND INCOME TAXES	23			
COMMISSIONS INCURRED (NET)	24			
GENERAL EXPENSES (EXCLUDING INVESTMENT EXPENSES)	25			
PAYMENTS FROM STAFF PENSION AND INSURANCE FUNDS	26			
DIVIDENDS AND INCREASE IN PROVISION FOR DIVIDENDS TO POLICYHOLDERS	27			
EXPERIENCE RATING REFUNDS PAID AND INCREASE IN PROVISION	28			
INTEREST INCURRED ON AMOUNTS ON DEPOSIT	29			
	30			
	31			
INCOME TAXES - CURRENT	32			
- DEFERRED	33			
SUBTOTAL (15 TO 33)	▶ 34			
INCOME BEFORE UNUSUAL OR EXTRAORDINARY ITEMS (14 - 34)	▶ 35			

Chapter 11 Appendix (cont.)

14 (RS)

NAME OF COMPANY ▶   YEAR OF STATEMENT 19___

FUND ($'000)

	LIFE					ACCIDENT & SICKNESS		
	04	05	06	SEG. FUND 07	TOTAL 08	INS. FUND 09	SHAREHOLD-ERS 10	TOTAL 11
01								
02								
03								
04								
05								
06								
07								
08								
09								
10								
11								
12								
13								
14								
15								
16								
17								
18								
19								
20								
21								
22								
23								
24								
25								
26								
27								
28								
29								
30								
31								
32								
33								
34								
35								

Chapter 11 Appendix (cont.)

15 (LS)

NAME OF COMPANY ▶   YEAR OF STATEMENT
                                                                           19

XIV.- RECONCILIATION

		LIFE		
		PAR FUND 01	NON-PAR FUND 02	SHARE-HOLDERS FUND 03
FUNDS, 31 DECEMBER 19	▶ 01			
INCOME BEFORE UNUSUAL OR EXTRAORDINARY ITEMS (FROM ANALYSIS OF INCOME)	02			
NORMAL INCREASE IN ACTUARIAL RESERVE (MANDATORY & ADDITIONAL)	03			
NORMAL INCREASE IN SEGREGATED FUNDS	04			
INCREASE IN STAFF PENSION AND INSURANCE FUNDS	05			
NET INCREASE IN AMOUNTS ON DEPOSIT	06			
INCREASE IN PROVISION FOR DIVIDENDS TO POLICYHOLDERS	07			
INCREASE IN PROVISION FOR EXPERIENCE RATING REFUNDS	08			
NET NON-AMORTIZABLE GAINS (LOSSES) IN RESPECT OF INVESTED ASSETS	09			
TRANSFERS OF SURPLUS FROM OTHER FUNDS	10			
TRANSFER OF "SEED MONEY" TO (FROM) SEGREGATED FUNDS	11			
	12			
	13			
INCREASE/DECREASE IN VALUE OF SECTION 64 AND 65 SUBSIDIARIES	14			
NET INCOME FROM ANCILLARY OPERATIONS	15			
EXTRAORDINARY ITEMS	16			
CURRENCY ADJUSTMENT OF FUNDS	17			
	18			
	19			
	20			
	21			
TOTAL (02 TO 21)	▶ 22			
TRANSFERS OF SURPLUS TO SHAREHOLDERS' FUND	23			
TRANSFERS OF SURPLUS TO OTHER FUNDS (GIVE DETAILS BELOW)	24			
DIVIDENDS TO SHAREHOLDERS	25			
INCOME TAXES ON UNUSUAL ITEMS: CURRENT	26			
DEFERRED	27			
	28			
	29			
TOTAL (23 TO 29)	▶ 30			
FUNDS, 31 DECEMBER 19 (1+22-30)	▶ 31			

Chapter 11 Appendix (cont.)

15 (RS)

NAME OF COMPANY ▶ YEAR OF STATEMENT 19

OF FUNDS ($'000)

	LIFE					ACCIDENT & SICKNESS		
				SEGREGATED FUND	TOTAL	INSURANCE FUND	SHARE-HOLDERS FUND	TOTAL
	04	05	06	07	08	09	10	11
▶01								
02								
03								
04								
05								
06								
07								
08								
09								
10								
11								
12								
13								
14								
15								
16								
17								
18								
19								
20								
21								
▶22								
23								
24								
25								
26								
27								
28								
29								
▶30								
▶31								

Chapter 11 Appendix (cont.)

```
                                    16 (LS)

NAME OF COMPANY ▶                                    YEAR OF STATEMENT
                                                              19
                                                 XV. SUMMARY OF FUNDS AND


INSURANCE FUNDS; 31 DECEMBER OF CURRENT YEAR

NET ACTUARIAL RESERVE                                              01

AMOUNTS ON DEPOSIT WITH THE COMPANY                                02

PROVISION FOR DIVIDENDS AND EXPERIENCE RATING REFUNDS              03

                                                                   04

                                                                   05

DEFERRED INCOME TAXES                                              06

RESERVES REQUIRED - BY THE DEPARTMENT                              07

                  - BY FOREIGN JURISDICTIONS                       08

ADDITIONAL RESERVES                                                09

UNAPPROPRIATED SURPLUS                                             10

            TOTAL INSURANCE FUNDS, 31 DECEMBER OF CURRENT YEAR  ▶ 11

SHAREHOLDERS' FUND:  CAPITAL                                       12

                  :  RESERVES ALLOCATED                            13

                  :  UNAPPROPRIATED SURPLUS                        14

STAFF PENSION AND INSURANCE FUNDS                                  15

                                                                   16

                                                                   17

SEGREGATED FUNDS (EXCLUSIVE OF AMOUNTS OWING)                      18

                                              TOTAL FUNDS       ▶ 19

AMOUNTS OWING BY THE COMPANY
ON SEGREGATED FUNDS        (PAGE 13, ITEMS 04, 06, 08 TO 16) INCLUDING $_____  20

                                    TOTAL FUNDS AND AMOUNTS OWING ▶ 21

                                                    TOTAL ASSETS ▶ 22

INSURANCE FUNDS, 31 DECEMBER OF PREVIOUS YEAR:
NET ACTUARIAL RESERVE                                              23

AMOUNTS ON DEPOSIT WITH THE COMPANY                                24

PROVISION FOR DIVIDENDS  AND EXPERIENCE RATING REFUNDS             25

                                                                   26

                                                                   27

DEFERRED INCOME TAXES                                              28

RESERVES REQUIRED - BY THE DEPARTMENT                              29

                  - BY FOREIGN JURISDICTIONS                       30

ADDITIONAL RESERVES                                                31

UNAPPROPRIATED SURPLUS                                             32

            TOTAL INSURANCE FUNDS, 31 DECEMBER OF PREVIOUS YEAR ▶ 33

SHAREHOLDERS' FUND, 31 DECEMBER OF PREVIOUS YEAR                ▶ 34
```

Chapter 11 Appendix (cont.)

```
                                    16 (RS)
NAME OF COMPANY ▶                                          YEAR OF STATEMENT
                                                                   19
AMOUNTS OWING BY THE COMPANY ($'000)
```

	LIFE			ACCIDENT & SICKNESS FUND	GRAND TOTAL ALL FUNDS
	PAR FUND 01	NON-PAR FUND 02	TOTAL FUNDS 03	04	05
01					
02					
03					
04					
05					
06					
07					
08					
09					
10					
▶11					
12					
13					
14					
15					
16					
17					
18					
▶19					
20					
▶21					
▶22					
23					
24					
25					
26					
27					
28					
29					
30					
31					
32					
▶33					
▶34					

12
Taxation of Life and Health Insurance Companies

Learning Objectives

After reading this chapter, you should be able to:

- Identify the types of taxes paid by U.S. and Canadian insurers
- Define and give an example of a retaliatory tax law
- Describe the difference between the tangible personal property tax and the intangible personal property tax
- Calculate the amount of a life insurer's small company deduction based on the insurer's tentative life insurance company taxable income (LICTI)
- Identify the basic income and deduction components of federal taxation in both the United States and Canada

Introduction

Taxes and other fees payable to governmental authorities represent a large operating expense for most insurance companies. In 1985, U.S. life insurance companies incurred state and local taxes, license fees, and other fees of approximately $2.8 billion and Social Security payroll taxes of $814 million. Federal income taxes paid by life insurers in 1985 totaled $4.1 billion in the United States. During the same year, Canadian life insurance companies paid federal, provincial, and local taxes, licenses, and fees on life and health business of approximately $315 million.

One of the accounting functions in an insurance company is calculating and recording the tax liability that the company has incurred during the reporting year. A primary aspect of this accounting function is ensuring that the company does not pay any more or any less taxes than required by law. Accurate calculation of taxes due is thus an essential part of the accounting process. This chapter discusses the different types of taxes paid by insurance companies in the United States and Canada. Among the types of taxes discussed in this chapter are premium taxes, real estate and property taxes, and income taxes. (Figure 12-1 shows some types of taxes paid by U.S. and Canadian insurers.) To record the payment of these taxes, an insurer generally debits a Tax expense account and credits the Cash account.

Premium Taxes

Premium taxes are generally imposed at the state, provincial, or local level. Each tax jurisdiction in the United States and Canada has different regulations defining taxable premiums, deductions, tax rates, offsets, and retaliatory provisions. (*Offsets* and *retaliatory tax laws* are defined later in this chapter.) Although the premium tax base differs in most jurisdictions, all jurisdictions share some basic considerations in defining the premium tax base. Some of these considerations and basic rules are as follows:

- Gross premiums collected on life and health business are taxed. Some jurisdictions, however, exempt premiums collected by domestic companies.
- Annuity considerations are exempt from taxation in Canada and in most jurisdictions of the United States. Among the jurisdictions that tax annuities, most tax them at a lower rate than insurance premiums.
- Some jurisdictions vary the tax rate between life and health business.
- Most jurisdictions require a breakdown of the insurer's tax liability into life, health, and annuity business (if annuities are taxable). The NAIC Annual Statement Blank requires further classification of tax liabilities into ordinary, industrial, and group categories.
- The premiums collected by Blue Cross and Blue Shield plans are taxed in some states, but not in others.
- Each Canadian province levies a tax on life and health premiums collected from residents in that province. The same method of calculating taxable premiums is used in all provinces except British Columbia. This province has a different method of premium taxation for insurance that has been ceded to a reinsurer, but the method does not have a significant bearing on the amount of tax collected.
- A few Canadian provinces collect premium taxes from fraternal societies.

FIGURE 12-1
Types of taxes paid by insurers.

>   Real Estate Tax
>   Premium Tax
>   Income Tax
>   Business Tax (Canada)
>   Tangible Personal Property Tax
>   Intangible Personal Property Tax
>   Sales Tax
>   Use Tax
>   Franchise Tax
>   Other Fees and Assessments

Jurisdictions typically allow some deductions and exemptions from premium income when calculating the premium tax base. Taxable premiums are reduced by certain allowable deductions, such as dividends paid to policyowners on participating business. Currently, approximately 80 percent of the jurisdictions in the United States allow this deduction. Some U.S. jurisdictions also allow a deduction for premiums on insurance and pension plans that qualify under the Internal Revenue Code. One jurisdiction taxes such qualified premiums at a reduced rate.

For certain items, about half of the jurisdictions in the United States allow a direct offset or a credit against premium taxes. An **offset** allows an insurer to use the amount paid for one type of tax to reduce another aspect of the company's tax liability. The items listed below are examples of some of these offsets and credits. The amount that an insurer pays in these types of taxes, fees, and assessments can often be used to reduce, or offset, the insurer's premium tax liability:

- state income taxes
- municipal taxes
- property taxes
- neighborhood assistance contributions
- valuation and examination fees
- registration fees
- guaranty association assessments

Guaranty associations are created to protect policyowners from losses suffered through the insolvency of an insurance company. In many states, solvent insurers are required to contribute money to these guaranty associations so that, if an insurer becomes insolvent, claims can still be paid or policy coverage can continue for persons who own policies issued by that insolvent insurer.

Premium tax rates vary considerably among jurisdictions. Most jurisdictions in the United States and Canada have a premium tax rate of two percent or less. Approximately twenty percent of the jurisdictions tax premiums at a rate between two and three percent, while some impose a premium tax of more than three percent. The state of New York has the lowest premium tax rate—one percent—but imposes a state income tax of nine percent on a net income basis. Certain states reduce an insurer's premium tax rate if the insurer invests a certain percentage of its assets in that state.

Retaliatory Tax Laws

The primary purpose of retaliatory tax laws is to protect domestic companies from unreasonable tax burdens being placed upon them by other states. **Retaliatory tax laws** impose taxes on a foreign insurer—an insurer from another state or province—at the rate the home state's domestic companies would be taxed by the foreign state, but only if that tax rate is higher. For example, assume that (1) State A has a premium tax rate of two percent, (2) State B taxes premiums at a rate of three percent, and (3) retaliatory tax laws are in effect in State A. An insurer domiciled in State B that also sells insurance in State A would pay premium taxes on its State A business at a rate of three percent, the tax rate of that insurer's home state. Almost all of the jurisdictions in the United States have retaliatory tax legislation in place. Some provinces in Canada have passed permissive legislation whereby retaliatory taxes can sometimes be assessed.

Taxes Based on Property Values

Real Estate Taxes

Real estate taxes are generally ad valorem taxes, i.e., "based upon the value" of the real estate that is being taxed. Real estate taxes may be imposed by the state, county, city, or other local taxing jurisdiction in which the real estate is located. This tax is the mainstay of most city and county governments, often constituting 50 to 70 percent of their total revenues.

Different jurisdictions have different ways of valuing real estate for taxation purposes. Generally, the taxable value represents the dollar amount at which the real estate would change hands between a willing buyer and a willing seller, with neither being under a compulsion to buy or sell. Determining the value of real estate is the responsibility of a jurisdiction's tax assessor. In most jurisdictions, the assessor normally considers—either collectively or individually—such factors as the original cost of the property, the cost of reproducing or replacing the property, recent sale prices of comparable properties, and income from the property capitalized at an appropriate rate. California's laws, on the other hand, limit the property tax basis to the property's value at the time of the most recent sale or addition to the property. In California, each year's increase is also limited to one percent per year.

An insurer may feel that the value established by the assessor is too high, either in an absolute sense or in comparison to valuations of similar properties. Since an assessor generally cannot appraise each of the properties within his or her jurisdiction each year, inequities can develop among the various properties under assessment. The insurer can, in such circumstances, appeal the assessor's valuation to a tax board or similar review board and present proof that the assessment should be reduced. Frequently, this process will require first challenging the basis or method of valuation and then presenting an alternative method of establishing value. If not satisfied at this level of appeal, the company can often proceed to the judicial system for resolution of the issue.

In Canada, the real estate tax is levied at the local government level. However, real estate taxation may occur at the provincial level in New Brunswick and Prince Edward Island, as well as in municipally unorganized areas in other provinces. The basis of assessment is becoming more uniform throughout the provinces as they assume a role in valuation and administration on behalf of municipalities. Real property forms the principal municipal tax base in every province.

In 1985, U.S. life and health insurance companies incurred real estate taxes totaling $537 million. Real estate taxes paid by Canadian insurers totaled $105 million during the same year. The real estate tax applies to both the home office and branch offices as well as to real estate properties owned as investments. In cases in which an insurer rents its home office or branch offices, the company may have to pay the real estate tax as part of the lease agreement. In some states, the real estate tax on the home office can be credited, at least in part, against the company's premium tax liability.

Controlling real estate taxes

An insurer's real estate tax burden can be controlled to some degree by an annual program in which the company uses the property tax rolls to determine whether the assessed values of its properties are comparable to those of similar properties in the same taxing jurisdiction. A company should consider using the appeal process when this annual review discloses adverse discrepancies in valuation.

In addition, company personnel should check any of the company's buildings that have been abandoned or destroyed so that the value of the property can be reassessed. Many property tax managers use the services of valuation consultants, private or staff attorneys, and staff investment personnel in order to monitor real estate taxes. In some cities, firms specialize in appealing real estate tax assessments for a contingent fee, such as half of the first year's savings.

The Tangible Personal Property Tax

In addition to the real estate tax, another ad valorem property tax paid by insurers is the *tangible personal property tax*. The personal property tax is imposed on such items as an insurer's office furniture and equipment either located within the office or on loan to an agent. This tax is also imposed upon the company's data processing equipment, vehicles used for transportation, and other types of personal property.

The collection of this tax differs from the collection of the real estate tax. In the case of real estate, an assessor independently determines the value of an insurer's real estate. With tangible personal property, though, insurers must annually render to the tax assessor a statement that lists the company's personal property subject to taxation. Each statement must also include an estimate of the property's value or an analysis of the property's cost, age, and condition. The assessor either accepts such valuation or returns a notice of his or her revised valuation along with information explaining the manner in which the taxpayer can appeal the revised assessment. In many jurisdictions, tangible personal property under lease is also subject to taxation, and the tax is generally imposed upon the lessee.

In some states, personal property taxes can be used to offset the premium tax owed to the state. Other jurisdictions provide, as a portion of their premium tax laws, that the premium tax is imposed in lieu of the personal property tax. This provision relieves the insurance company of paying the personal property tax. Some jurisdictions offer cash discounts if the personal property tax bill is paid early. Insurers often consult with dealers specializing in certain types of personal property, such as electronic data processing equipment and transportation vehicles, in order to determine the values to be rendered on personal property listings. Also, the company's tax records should exclude all items of personal property that have been sold, destroyed, abandoned, or made obsolete.

The Intangible Personal Property Tax

The purpose of the *intangible personal property tax* is to note intangible assets that otherwise would escape the personal property tax. Financial assets such as cash, promissory notes, bonds, and deferred or uncollected premiums are often subject to this tax. In some taxing jurisdictions, the intangible personal property tax is measured by the value of the assets subject to the tax. In other jurisdictions, the tax is measured by the yield derived from the assets. Fewer jurisdictions assess an intangible personal property tax than a tangible personal property tax.

The Business Tax in Canada

Canadian municipalities generally levy a business tax in addition to the real property tax. The tax is based upon the real property assessment base. In addition, the business tax usually includes, if applicable, a percentage or rate factor of the real property tax base. This rate factor accounts for the office area occupied as a percentage of the entire rentable area of the building. The occupant is liable for the payment of business tax whether he or she is the owner or tenant, except in British Columbia where the owner is solely liable. Some provinces have mandatory municipal business taxes, but in most provinces, the tax is an option of the municipality under general provincial legislation.

Non-federal Income Taxes in the United States and Canada

United States

Among the many tax jurisdictions in the United States, little uniformity exists in the methods of income taxation of insurance companies. Not all states have an income or excise tax for life and health insurance companies, and among the states that impose these taxes, some treat domestic and foreign insurance companies differently. (Federal income taxes are discussed later in this chapter.)

Most states that have an income tax allow offsetting between premium and income taxes so that no additional tax burden is imposed on the companies. However, a few states impose an income tax in addition to premium taxes. Although a state may allow offsetting, states generally require a company to file the income tax forms and pay the tax before granting the premium tax offset. In some jurisdictions, a combined or consolidated return is permitted for certain members of an affiliated group of companies. A **consolidated tax return** is a single tax return filed for an affiliated group of corporations. Consolidated tax returns represent the aggregate income, deductions, and resulting tax liability of the group. By filing a consolidated return, the operating losses of one member of the group can be offset against the operating gains of another group member in order to reduce the entire group's tax liability.

All states use a general formula to compute state taxable income. Most states begin with the amount of federal taxable income as a base and require certain increases and decreases as adjustments to that income. The following items are typical required *additions* to federal U.S. taxable income in order to arrive at state taxable income:

- the state income tax for that state that was deducted on the federal return,
- interest income from municipal obligations of states other than the taxing state that were excluded from the federal return,
- the state premium tax for that particular state if an offset is allowed,
- adjustments necessitated by the filing of a consolidated federal return, and
- undistributed net long-term capital gains of regulated investment companies and real estate investment trusts excluded from the federal return.

The following items are typical required *subtractions* from U.S. federal taxable income that are used for computing state taxable income:

- net income from outside the United States,
- interest on U.S. government obligations, and
- tax credit adjustments for new jobs if the credit was claimed on the federal return.

The state net taxable income that results from these types of adjustments is then apportioned to the particular state. Finally, the state tax rate is applied to the apportioned income to determine the income tax liability to that state.

Canada

Canadian insurance companies determine taxable income in accordance with the rules of the Federal Income Tax Act. Ontario and Quebec collect their own taxes using rules similar to those contained in the Federal Income Tax Act. The federal government collects income taxes on behalf of the other provinces. The federal tax levy is 46 percent of taxable income with a tax credit of 10 percent of the taxable income allocated to provinces. Each province and territory taxes the income of life and health insurers at a rate between 10 and 15 percent.

Other State, Provincial, and Local Taxes

Insurers in the United States and Canada are subject to various other types of state, provincial, and local taxes. Permit fees, certificates of authority to engage in an insurance business, agent's license fees, and other miscellaneous fees are required in many jurisdictions. Although the dollar amounts are usually small, the administrative complexity involved in these fee payments requires monitoring to see that all such fees are paid before they become delinquent. State insurance departments in some states base the fee for periodic examination of the company partially on the amount of the company's assets and partially on the number of person-days spent on the examination. Some states also charge a valuation fee for assessing the company's reserves and other liabilities. A few jurisdictions impose a franchise tax or annual license fee based on the net worth of the company, which includes both the company's capital stock and earned, paid-in surplus. In Canada, some provinces impose a corporation capital tax. In many cases, fees are subject to the same type of retaliatory provisions as premium taxes. Jurisdictions vary as to which fees are treated on a retaliatory basis.

Local taxes normally take the form of occupational or regulatory licensing by counties or municipalities. Counties and municipalities generally license both individual agents and the companies that the agents represent. These license fees can range from as little as $3 for agents' licenses to as much as $100,000 or more for a company's operating license. The majority of occupational license fees are based on premiums collected in each municipality. However, one exception is Florida's occupational license tax, which cannot be based on premiums, income, or the volume of the insurer's transactions. In Florida, the tax is based on the number of insurance companies and agents conducting business in that municipality.

Other local taxes include sales taxes on supplies, personal property purchases, and services rendered; usage taxes on transportation equipment; utility taxes on telephone service and utilities; and the municipal income taxes assessed in some states. Some municipal taxes are allowed as offsets against the state premium taxes.

Federal Income Taxation—United States

Since the inception of the federal income tax in 1909, Congress has recognized, at least in part, the unique nature of the life insurance industry. This unique nature stems primarily from two factors: the interest that the public has in the solvency of insurance companies and the long-term nature of the business that insurers conduct with their policyowners. Since a whole life insurance policy is a long-term contract—with premiums often paid over many years before any benefits are returned—much of the premium income in a policy's early years is set aside as a reserve for future benefit payments and thus is not regarded as taxable income. Therefore, insurance companies generally receive a deduction from their tax burden for annual increases in these policy reserves.

To try to accommodate the unique nature of the life insurance industry, Congress has used several different tax plans in the period from 1909 to the present. Currently, insurance companies are taxed primarily according to the provisions of the Deficit Reduction Act, or Tax Reform Act ("the 1984 Act"). The provisions of the 1984 Act affecting the taxation of life insurance companies represent the most comprehensive revision to the life insurance company sections of the U.S. Tax Code since the Life Insurance Company Tax Act of 1959. The 1984 Act was intended to be a permanent legislative revision of the temporary stop-gap provisions enacted in 1982 under the Tax Equity and Fiscal Responsibility Act (TEFRA). Generally, the 1984 Act applies to tax years beginning after December 31, 1983.

The 1984 Act introduced a new, single-phase tax structure that embodies the tax rules generally applicable to all other corporations with only a few special provisions unique to the life insurance industry. The special provisions unique to life insurance companies included

- a special deduction for small life insurance companies,
- a generally applicable special life insurance company deduction designed to reduce a life insurance company's taxable income, and
- a reduced deduction for dividend distributions by mutual life and health insurance companies.

In addition, the 1984 Act mandated, for the first time, a specific method for computing life insurance reserves.

Definition of a Life Insurance Company

In order to be taxed as a life insurance company, a firm must meet the legal definition of an insurance company. Before the 1984 Act, the Tax Code contained a definition of the term "life insurance company" but did not specifically define the term "insurance company." Under the 1984 Act, a firm is an *insurance company* if more than half of its business during the year is in issuing insurance or annuity contracts or reinsuring risks underwritten by insurance companies. Thus, the 1984 Act replaced the previous regulatory definition of an insurance company as a company whose "primary and predominant business activity" was insurance with the statutory "more than half of the company's business" requirement.

Relevant factors in determining whether the "more than half" requirement is satisfied include the number of employees involved in the various business activities, the space allocated to the activities, and the net income derived from the various business activities. If these factors indicate that more than half of the company's activities is devoted to insurance operations, then the company is considered, for taxation purposes, to be an insurance company.

For a company to be considered a *life* insurance company under the 1959 Act, more than 50 percent of the company's total reserves had to be represented by (1) life insurance reserves; (2) unearned premiums; or (3) unpaid losses on noncancellable life, accident, or health policies not included in life insurance reserves. The 1984 Act did not change the definition of the reserve test, nor the requirement that the test be satisfied. However, the 1984 Act did exclude from the computation of life insurance reserves and total reserves certain reserves on contracts that do not contain permanent guarantees as to life, accident, or health contingencies.

LICTI under the 1984 Act

Under the 1984 Act, a tax is imposed on the life insurance company taxable income (LICTI) of every life insurance company. **LICTI** is defined under the 1984 Act as the difference between life insurance gross income and life insurance deductions. As mentioned earlier, LICTI is taxed under the 1984 Act at standard corporate rates under a single-phase system. The 1984 Act is designed to adjust for the investment-related life insurance products.

The items that a life insurance company must include in its gross income under the 1984 Act parallel the items included in the 1959 Act. (Figure 12-2 lists the income and deduction elements of U.S. income taxation of life insurers.) Generally, life insurance gross income includes premiums, decreases in life insurance reserves, and other amounts generally included in gross income, such as investment income. The gross amount of premiums and other considerations includes advance premiums, deposits, fees, assessments, considerations arising from assumption of liabilities under contracts not issued by the company, and the amount of policyowner dividends reimbursable to the insurer by a reinsurer. The deductions permitted under the the 1984 Act can be categorized into two broad areas: (1) general deductions and (2) special deductions.

General deductions

Under the 1984 Act, a life insurance company is permitted to deduct the following amounts from the amount of its taxable income: (1) death benefits and all other benefits, (2) increases in certain reserves, (3) policyowner dividends, (4) a modified dividend received deduction, (5) an operations loss deduction, (6) considerations paid in connection with certain reinsurance agreements, (7) reimbursable dividends arising out of reinsurance agreements, and (8) all of the other deductions permitted in computing a corporation's taxable income.

Special deductions

In addition to the various general deductions allowed to other corporations and the particular deductions allowed to life insurance companies, the 1984 Act introduced two special deductions for life insurance companies: (1) a small life insurance company deduction and (2) a special life insurance company deduction. The special life insurance company deduction was repealed effective January 1, 1987.

FIGURE 12-2
Income and deduction elements of U.S. federal income taxation.

Income elements
   premiums (advance premiums, deposits, fees, assessments, etc.)
   decreases in life insurance reserves
   investment income

Deduction elements
   death benefits and all other benefits
   increases in certain reserves
   policyowner dividends
   losses from operations
   certain reinsurance considerations
   deductions allowed to non-insurance corporations
   small company deduction

For the *small life insurance company deduction*, a life company must satisfy a two-part test to determine whether and how much of a small company deduction can be taken. The two parts of this test relate to (1) the amount of the company's assets and (2) the company's tentative life insurance company taxable income (tentative LICTI). The assets test defines a *small company* as one having less than $500 million in assets. The assets test uses a fair market value basis for items such as real property and stock but an adjusted tax basis for other items. In addition, if an insurer belongs to a controlled group of companies, the assets of all group members, including those companies not involved in the life insurance business, are included in making the $500 million assets test. As a result of this provision, some life insurance companies may not be entitled to the small company deduction if other members of the controlled group cause the group's assets to exceed the $500 million limit.

The second test for the small life company deduction is based on a company's tentative LICTI. Tentative LICTI is calculated as the amount of life insurance company taxable income excluding the small company deduction, other deductions as allowed, and any items attributable to noninsurance business. Thus, if a life insurance company is also engaged in manufacturing activity, the income from such trade or business is not included in the company's tentative LICTI. However, if the activity is one that is normally conducted by a life insurance company for investment purposes, then income from the activity is included in the tentative LICTI. Under the 1984 Act, a small company is allowed to deduct 60 percent of its first $3 million of tentative LICTI. The deduction is phased out as tentative LICTI approaches $15 million. If the phase-out applies, the deduction is reduced by 15 percent of the excess of tentative LICTI over $3 million.

For example, assume that the Alpha Life Insurance Company has $400 million in assets on December 31, 1985, and has tentative LICTI of $5 million for calendar year 1985. Since Alpha has under $500 million in assets and tentative LICTI under $15 million, the insurer is entitled to the small company deduction. As mentioned, the small company deduction is calculated as 60 percent of the first $3 million of tentative LICTI minus 15 percent of the balance of tentative LICTI up to $15 million. For Alpha Life, then,

	60% of the first $3 million of tentative LICTI	$1,800,000
minus	15% of the balance of tentative LICTI	− $ 300,000*
equals	Alpha's small company deduction	= $1,500,000

(*In Alpha's case, 15 percent of $2,000,000 [$5,000,000 tentative LICTI minus the first $3,000,000] = $300,000.)

Federal Income Taxation—Canada

The Federal Business Income Tax

The most significant income tax on insurance companies in Canada is the *Part I Business Income Tax*. The Part I tax law is the basic income tax law applicable to all individuals and corporations. In other words, these sections of the Income Tax Act apply equally to insurance and non-insurance companies. Figure 12-3 shows the general calculation used to determine the Part I Business Income Tax that an insurance company must pay. However, as in the United States, to recognize the unique nature of long-term life insurance contracts, certain special taxation provisions are required.

A significant factor in the income taxation of both resident life insurance companies and all non-resident non-life insurance companies is that Canadian income is confined to the income that is generated from the company's insurance business *in Canada*. This tax treatment contrasts with that of other Canadian businesses, including resident non-life insurers, which pay Canadian income tax on their worldwide income and receive tax credits for any foreign income taxes paid.

The income element of business income taxation

As Figure 12-3 indicates, "income" is the first basic element entering the Part I tax calculation. For most corporations, "income" refers to the total of investment

FIGURE 12-3
Calculation of Part I—Business Income Tax.

```
           Life Income minus Deductions      = Business Income
  plus     Non-Life Income minus Deductions  = Business Income
                                   Subtotal  = Total Business Income
  minus    Other Deductions
  plus     Special Shareholders' Tax Liability = Part I Taxable Income

           Part I Taxable Income × Tax Rate = Part I Tax
```

income, net taxable capital gains, the sale of goods or services, etc. (Figure 12-4 lists the income and deduction elements of Canadian income taxation of life insurers.) For an insurance company, the five major items of income are:

1. **premium income**, which consists of insurance premiums and annuity considerations from business in Canada.
2. **gross investment revenue**, which includes interest, taxable investment dividends, rents, royalties, etc.
3. **miscellaneous income**, which includes all other items of taxable income not included elsewhere. One such item is employee and employer contributions to pension and insurance funds for staff and agents, if these funds are held as a separate liability and not as a part of policy reserves.
4. **net taxable capital gains**. One-half of net capital gains, known as "net taxable capital gains," is included in income and is taxed at the usual personal or corporation tax rates.

The question of what constitutes *capital gains* and what constitutes *ordinary income* is a difficult one and has been the subject of frequent consideration by the judicial system. The single most important determinant in distinguishing between capital gains and ordinary income is the taxpayer's intentions with respect to the asset, as evidenced by that taxpayer's course of conduct. These factors include the relationship between the assets sold and the taxpayer's regular occupation, the length of time the asset was owned, the nature of the property disposed of, and the reasons for and the circumstances surrounding the sale.

Capital gains and losses arise only on the disposition of capital property such as stocks, most bonds, real estate, home office properties, furniture, and equipment. The definition of a "disposition" for tax purposes is extremely broad and encompasses not only the sale or exchange of capital property but also other transactions including gifts or bequests.

5. **Canada securities—profit on sale and accrual of discount.** The Income Tax Act provides that the disposition of certain types of properties, called "Canada securities," that are used in the course of carrying on a life insurance business shall result in ordinary income gains or losses rather than capital gains or losses as would be the case for most other businesses. **Canada securities** are defined in the Canadian Income Tax Act as bonds, mortgages, or agreements of sale applicable to a company's life insurance business in Canada (other than segregated fund business). The profit is calculated as the excess of sale price over amortized cost. No equivalent definition of "Canada securities" exists

FIGURE 12-4
Income and deduction elements of Canadian federal income taxation.

Income elements
  premium income
  gross investment revenue
  miscellaneous income
  net taxable capital gains
  Canada securities—profit on sale and accrual of discount

Deduction elements
  benefit costs
  interest paid or credited
  expenses
  increase in policy reserves
  dividends and experience rating refunds
  increase in investment reserve
  Canada securities—loss on sale and amortization of premium
  capital cost allowances
  other deductions allowed to non-insurance corporations

for non-life (health) business, however. Therefore, realized gains and losses on similar assets used in the course of non-life business are subject to capital gains treatment.

In summary, the Canadian income tax provisions regarding gross income of a life insurance company are essentially the same as those applicable to any Canadian company, except for certain special provisions. One important difference is that a life insurance company's income is determined on a Canada-only basis rather than on a worldwide basis with foreign tax credits.

The deductions element of business income taxation

The next step in computing the Part I Business Income Tax is to make a series of deductions from the amount of the company's gross income. Generally, a life company's deductions are similar to those taken by any corporation. Such deductions include the cost of goods sold and the amount of overhead expenses. For an insurance company, the major deductions of this type are benefit costs and expenses. In addition, certain special deductions are allowed. The major deductions are:

1. **benefit costs.** Benefit costs consist of all claims incurred under insurance and annuity contracts in Canada. These costs include payments under settlement annuities arising from Canadian business as well as the increase or decrease in the provision for unreported death claims.
2. **interest paid or credited.** This item is comprised of interest credited to amounts on deposit, interest paid on claims, and interest paid on money borrowed in connection with investment operations.
3. **expenses.** The expense provisions of the Income Tax Act are basically the same for insurers and other types of businesses. Deductions are allowed for expenses if they are for the purpose of gaining or producing income and if they are considered reasonable for the circumstances. In general, the items of expense considered by an insurance company for tax purposes are the Canadian parts of those expenses reported in the Canadian Annual Statement (both investment expenses and general expenses), modified for certain types of expenses if the tax basis differs from the Statement basis. Commissions and premium taxes are also included here.
4. **increase in policy reserves.** The most important of the special deductions for insurance companies is the net increase in policy reserves for the year. If reserves decrease in the year, the net decrease is added back into income. In practice, the previous year-end total reserve is added to income and the current year-end reserve is taken as a deduction.
5. **dividends and experience rating refunds.** The deduction for policy dividends paid to insurance policyowners can be divided into two categories: (1) dividends allocated and paid to policyowners either during the year or payable to them at the end of the year, and (2) the increase

or decrease in the provision for dividends allocated to policyowners at year's end for dividends that will become payable in the following year.

6. **increase in investment reserve.** For non-life business, the Income Tax Act allows a mortgage-lending corporation to deduct a "special mortgage reserve" relative to conventional mortgages in Canada as a provision for doubtful debts. The actual deduction is the increase in reserves or a lesser amount calculated in accordance with the Tax Act. This provision is applicable to non-life insurance companies and to the other-than-life business of life companies. If the special mortgage reserve were to decrease, the amount of the decrease would be included in income.

   In lieu of the deduction for special mortgage reserves, a life insurance company is allowed to deduct an "investment reserve" with respect to its life insurance operations. This reserve is determined essentially by the same formula as the special mortgage reserve but is applicable to all Canada securities rather than just to conventional mortgages. Net losses on Canada securities, if any, must be deducted.

7. **Canada securities—loss on sale and amortization of premium.** Just as profit from the sale of Canada securities and accrual of discount on Canada securities are included in income, the losses on the sale of Canada securities and the amortization of premiums on Canada securities are allowed as deductions in computing income. The loss to be included is the excess of the amortized cost over the sale price at disposition.

8. **capital cost allowances.** *Capital cost allowance* (CCA) is the name given to the amount of depreciation expense that is deducted in computing income for Canadian tax purposes. CCA deductions are permitted on certain classes of property and equipment such as real estate (excluding the cost of land), buildings owned and occupied by the company, and other fixed assets such as electronic data processing equipment, furniture, and machinery.

When the eight deductions just described have been subtracted from income, the net result is "total business income." The next step in an insurer's tax calculation is to subtract four other deductions from total business income. The four deductions, similar to those allowed for any Canadian corporation, are (1) taxable dividends from stocks in taxable Canadian corporations, (2) charitable donations, (3) business losses from other years, and (4) net capital losses from other years. The resulting figure may be subject to one more adjustment— adding a special shareholders' tax liability that can arise. The figure obtained by subtracting "other deductions," and adding the special shareholders' tax liability if applicable, is called *taxable income*.

Annual Statement Aspects of Taxation

While information regarding the payment of an insurer's taxes is presented throughout the Annual Statement, such as on the liabilities page of the Balance Sheet and in the Summary of Operations, the primary summation of an insurer's tax liability is shown in Annual Statement Exhibit 6 for U.S. insurers and Exhibit 10 for Canadian insurers (see Figures 12-5 and 12-6). The U.S. exhibit does not include federal income taxes.

Many aspects of the tax and expense exhibits used in both countries are the same. Both exhibits present information about the taxes, license expenses, and fees that an insurer has incurred during the year. Both break the total dollar amounts of these taxes, expenses, and fees into two components for a company's life and health business. In addition, the two exhibits show tax and expense amounts relative to the company's investments. The major difference between the two exhibits is that federal income taxes are excluded from U.S. Exhibit 6, while a Canadian insurer's federal income tax liability must be shown in Exhibit 10 of the Canadian Annual Statement. A second difference between the two exhibits is that the U.S. data includes, where appropriate, totals for business transacted in Canada, while the Canadian exhibit does not require information about a company's U.S. business.

FIGURE 12-5
Exhibit 6—U.S. Annual Statement.

	INSURANCE		(3)	(4)
EXHIBIT 6 — TAXES, LICENSES AND FEES (EXCLUDING FEDERAL INCOME TAXES)	(1) LIFE	(2) ACCIDENT AND HEALTH	INVESTMENT	TOTAL
1. Real estate taxes				
2. State insurance department licenses and fees				
3. State taxes on premiums				
4. Other state taxes, incl. $_____ for employee benefits				
5. U.S. Social Security taxes				
6. All other taxes				
7. TAXES, LICENSES AND FEES INCURRED . . . Reconciliation with Exhibit 12	(To Page 4, Item 23)		(To Exhibit 2, Line 3)	
8. Taxes, licenses and fees unpaid December 31, previous year				
9. Taxes, licenses and fees unpaid December 31, current year				
10. Taxes, licenses and fees paid during year (7+8—9) . . .	X X X	X X X	X X X	(To Exhibit 12, Line 28.1)

NOTE: Canadian and other foreign taxes are included appropriately in Lines 1, 2, 3, 4 and 6.

FIGURE 12-6
Exhibit 10—Canadian Annual Statement.

```
                                    32
NAME OF COMPANY ▶                                        YEAR OF STATEMENT
                                                              19
              EXHIBIT 10 - TAXES, LICENCES AND FEES ($'000)
```

		LIFE			ACCIDENT & SICKNESS		
		TOTAL INCURRED	INCURRED CHARGED TO INVESTMENT	DUE AND ACCRUED	TOTAL INCURRED	INCURRED CHARGED TO INVESTMENT	DUE AND ACCRUED
		01	02	03	04	05	06
PREMIUM TAXES:							
PROVINCIAL	01						
OTHER	02						
TOTAL PREMIUM TAXES ▶	03						
INCOME TAXES - CURRENT							
CANADA: FEDERAL	04						
PROVINCIAL	05						
OTHER	06						
TOTAL INCOME TAXES - CURRENT ▶	07						
SUPERVISION AND EXAMINATION:							
CANADA: FEDERAL	08						
PROVINCIAL	09						
OTHER	10						
TOTAL SUPERVISION AND EXAMINATION ▶	11						
LICENCES AND FEES:							
PROVINCIAL	12						
OTHER	13						
TOTAL LICENCES AND FEES ▶	14						
REAL ESTATE TAXES	15						
OTHER TAXES EXCLUDING DEFERRED INCOME TAXES	16						
TOTAL TAXES ▶	17						
LESS TAXES PERTAINING TO SEGREGATED FUNDS INCLUDED IN LINE 17	18						
SUB-TOTAL (17-18) ▶	19						
LESS INCURRED CHARGED TO INVESTMENT	20						
TOTAL TAXES, LICENCES AND FEES (EXCLUDING INVESTMENT TAXES) ▶	21						
LESS INCOME TAXES PERTAINING TO GENERAL FUNDS	22						
TOTAL EXCLUDING INCOME TAXES (21-22) ▶	23						
INCOME TAXES - DEFERRED							
CANADA: FEDERAL	24						
PROVINCIAL	25						
OTHER	26						
TOTAL INCOME TAXES - DEFERRED	27						

Key Terms

offsets
retaliatory tax laws
tangible personal property tax
consolidated tax return
tentative LICTI
special deduction
capital cost allowances

guaranty associations
ad valorem tax
intangible personal property tax
LICTI
small company deduction
Part I Business Income Tax

Review Questions and Exercises

1. What items can be used to offset a U.S. insurer's premium tax liability?
2. For U.S. federal taxation purposes, what makes a company an insurance company? A life insurance company?
3. List (a) four income elements and (b) four deduction elements of Canadian income taxation of insurance companies.
4. What is the purpose of retaliatory tax laws?
5. What items are subject to intangible personal property taxes?
6. How does collection of tangible personal property taxes differ from collection of real estate taxes?
7. In what ways do the U.S. and Canadian Annual Statement presentation of a company's tax liability differ?

13
Internal Control and Auditing

Learning Objectives

After reading this chapter, you should be able to:

- Understand the objectives of internal accounting control
- Understand the differences between administrative controls and accounting controls
- List ways in which assets can be safeguarded
- Describe a number of different types of internal controls
- Differentiate between internal and external auditing
- Describe some of the activities undertaken in an internal audit

Introduction

One function that impacts directly on all areas of a life and health insurance company's operations is the control and auditing of the company's systems, procedures, methods, and accounts. Because of the information, personnel, and methods involved, auditing and control activities are distinctly accounting-related. Most often, however, this function is separated from the duties of the accounting department since auditing and control personnel must maintain a high degree of independence and objectivity regarding other departments—including the accounting department—in order to perform effectively and without bias. The purpose of this chapter is to introduce the quality control function known as internal control and auditing and to show the different forms that this activity can take.

Internal Control[1]

Internal control can be defined as the methods and operations used by a business in order to protect its assets, monitor the accuracy of its accounting records, and encourage both operational efficiency and adherence to managerial policies. While this definition is broad, it covers the operation not only of the accounting and financial departments but of every area of an insurance company. The basic goals of internal accounting control are to provide reasonable, though not absolute, assurance that (1) assets are safeguarded from unauthorized use or disposition and (2) financial records are reliable enough to permit the accurate preparation of financial statements.

When a company's management establishes internal controls, its main objective is to ensure that the company's methods and procedures support the financial and operating decisions made by management. For example, if a company has budgeted only a certain amount of money for advertising expenses, the purchase of advertising must be regulated so that the company's advertising budget is not exceeded without proper authorization. In such a case, controls on advertising expenses would be established. These controls would serve to ensure that the intentions of management are followed with regard to the amount spent on advertising, the types of advertising purchased, as well as which individuals in the company will have the authority to approve the expenditure of funds for such purposes. In other words, one important aspect of internal control is making sure that each financial transaction is approved or authorized either by management or by certain personnel designated by management.

Management typically uses two types of internal control to achieve its objectives. **Administrative control** can be defined as the system of procedures and records that leads, either directly or indirectly, to the authorization of transactions by managerial-level employees. **Accounting control** can be defined as the system of procedures and records concerned with maintaining and ensuring the accuracy of financial records as well as safeguarding company assets.

Accounting control is designed to provide reasonable assurance that the following objectives are met:

(1) Transactions should be executed in accordance with the general or specific authorization of management.
(2) Transactions should be recorded as needed in order
    (a) to permit preparation of financial statements that conform to generally accepted accounting principles, statutory accounting practices, or any other applicable criteria, and
    (b) to maintain accountability of assets.
(3) Access to assets should be permitted only in accordance with proper authorization of management.

(4) The company's record of its assets should be compared with existing assets at reasonable intervals, and appropriate action should be taken with respect to any discrepancies.

The goals and objectives of internal accounting control are independent of the methods used to process data. That is, internal accounting control has the same basic concepts and objectives whether the accounting function is performed by a manual data collection system, a highly sophisticated data processing system, or a combination of the two. The only impact these different systems would have on the control function would be on the accounting methods used to accomplish the control objectives.

Classification of a specific control as either an accounting control or an administrative control is difficult. The American Institute of Certified Public Accountants (AICPA) recognizes this difficulty and indicates in its Statement of Auditing Standards No. 1 that the two types of internal controls are not mutually exclusive. For example, personnel records provide wage and salary information that is necessary to accounting control as well as performance evaluation information that can be used as an administrative control in improving employee productivity.

The first part of this chapter focuses on the essential role of internal accounting control in the preparation of accurate and timely financial information, not only for distribution to outside parties such as regulatory authorities, stockholders, and banks, but perhaps more importantly for managerial decision-making purposes.

Basic Concepts of Internal Accounting Control

To better understand internal accounting control, we must first understand its basic concepts:

- Internal control is concerned with a certain type of risk
- Management should evaluate controls on a cost-benefit basis
- Internal control has inherent limitations
- Company personnel must be competent and motivated for successful internal control

Each of these concepts is discussed below.

Internal control is concerned with a certain type of risk

All businesses encounter risk in the course of their daily operations. In the Statement of Auditing Standards No. 30, the AICPA identifies two different types of risk: (1) the risk of loss arising from mistakes and irregularities in the processing of transactions and the handling of assets and (2) the risk of loss arising from a company's operational or strategic decisions, such as developing and trying to sell an unprofitable product. Internal accounting controls are concerned with safeguarding assets only from the first type of loss. Such controls have nothing to do with losses from normal business operations.

Management's responsibility is to determine the level of risk and the probability of loss associated with the possession of various assets and to develop safeguarding controls accordingly. For example, the risk in handling policy loans and other receivables is less than that involved in the handling of cash and marketable securities, both of which could easily be diverted for personal use. Because of the greater risk involved, access to cash and marketable securities is limited by strong internal controls, such as requiring two signatures on a check or requiring the presence of two officers to open the company's safe-deposit box. Internal controls also take into account the probability that a given type of loss will occur. For example, cash is more likely to be stolen than office furniture and is generally subject to stricter internal controls.

Management should evaluate controls on a cost-benefit basis

In addition to assessing the level of risk and the probability of loss associated with a specific area of concern, management must evaluate both the cost of implementing controls and the benefits derived from those controls. Evaluation and comparison of the projected costs and benefits of a certain action is known as a **cost-benefit analysis.** The assessment of cost-benefit relationships can include consideration of more than monetary effects. For example, some insurance companies place a high priority on maintaining agent satisfaction and may have extensive control procedures to ensure that no errors are made in agent billings. Management in these companies believes that such procedures, though expensive, are worthwhile because they contribute to agent satisfaction. For a company that does not place as high a priority on agent satisfaction, such control procedures might not be worth the cost.

Internal control has inherent limitations

Even a perfect system of internal controls has built-in limits to its effectiveness. Four such limitations are discussed below:

1. Internal control systems are only as effective as the people who operate them, and even the most competent employees make mistakes. The potential for error may be reduced by hiring competent personnel, but mistakes can still occur because of misunderstandings, carelessness, distraction, or fatigue.
2. No system of internal control is immune to employee collusion. **Collusion** can be defined as a secret agreement entered into for the purpose

of perpetrating fraud or some other illegal activity. The presence of collusion in an organization does not necessarily indicate that the entire system of internal control is deficient. Such action by employees usually means that one portion of the internal control system has been circumvented. Collusion can occur at any level in the organization.
3. Management usually has the power of overriding established control procedures, either temporarily or permanently. A member of management may conclude that a certain control is unnecessary or too time-consuming and thus either bypass the control or order subordinates to bypass it.
4. The circumstances under which a company operates are constantly changing. Changes in personnel, legislation, the economy, the products or services that a company offers, and many other factors can alter the effectiveness of a system of internal controls. Management should evaluate its system of internal controls in light of any changes in both the company's external and internal environments.

Personnel should be competent and motivated

Developing an effective system of internal control requires that the employees performing the tasks be both competent and motivated. Not only must an employee be able to comply with a control, but he or she should also understand both the control itself and why that control is in place. Accordingly, effective communication is essential. Management should provide effective channels of communication by providing up-to-date organization charts, accounting and procedural manuals, charts of accounts, and training for all employees. Whenever possible, employees should be allowed to use their own ideas and suggestions in developing internal controls. Allowing such input generally helps to encourage and monitor employees' compliance with established procedures.

Methods Used in Maintaining an Effective Internal Accounting Control System

Any internal accounting control system must rely on certain methods in order to be effective. Some methods used in developing an effective internal accounting control system can be stated as follows:

- Accounting duties must be segregated
- Transactions must be executed as authorized
- Transactions must be recorded as executed
- Assets must be safeguarded
- Physical comparison to recorded amounts must be made

We will discuss each of these methods in more detail.

Accounting duties must be segregated

Sound internal accounting control demands segregation of duties among employees, so that a different employee is responsible for each of the following duties:

- authorizing a transaction,
- recording that transaction, and
- having custody of the assets involved in the transaction.

In terms of internal accounting control, these duties are **incompatible functions,** i.e., job duties that place any person in a position to perpetrate and to conceal errors or irregularities in the normal course of his or her employment. Proper segregation of duties provides an environment in which errors and irregularities will more likely be detected.

The concept of segregation of duties also requires that procedures to detect errors and irregularities should be performed by persons other than those who are in a position to cause such errors or irregularities. For example, the person responsible for depositing the day's cash receipts in the bank should not be the same person who records the amount of the deposit in the general ledger. If one person performed both duties, that person could easily steal some of the cash and use fraudulent ledger entries to conceal the theft. However, if different people perform these duties, misappropriation requires more effort.

Transactions must be executed as authorized

In an insurance company, as in any other company, many different types of transactions take place each day. Transactions include purchasing and selling securities or other assets, issuing policies, paying benefits, paying operating expenses, and so on. Whatever the type of transaction, good internal control dictates that each transaction will in some way be authorized by management. Certain transactions may be authorized individually, while other transactions may be authorized by policies and operating procedures that have already been established by management. For example, a claim examiner may be required to obtain specific authorization by a senior officer to make any benefit payment of $50,000 or more, although the same claim examiner might be allowed to make payments of lesser amounts according to established operating procedures. Regardless, no transaction should occur without some form of authorization.

To provide effective authorization controls, management should attempt to set realistic authorization levels. Authorization levels should reflect the significance of the transaction and the experience and responsibility of the employee concerned. For example, a claim examiner with only two months experience may have to obtain management approval for all claims over $2,500, while an experienced examiner may be authorized to approve claims up to $50,000. Unless authorization levels are realistic, employees may attempt to circumvent the controls.

Transactions must be recorded as executed

A company's accounts and records should reflect transactions as they occur. This concept can be subdivided into six specific requirements:

1. *All recorded transactions should be valid.* For example, if a premium payment is due but has not been received, no transaction has occurred. If a premium receipt is recorded even though no money has been received from the policyowner as billed, then an invalid transaction has been recorded.
2. *All valid transactions should be recorded.* Accurate records should be kept of all valid transactions.
3. *All transactions should be recorded in their proper amounts.* Records of valid transactions must reflect the proper dollar amounts involved.
4. *All transactions should be recorded in the proper accounts.* For example, the purchase of a large computer should be recorded as a debit to an asset account rather than as a debit to an office supplies expense account. Similarly, a loan to a policyowner should be recorded as a policy loan rather than as a benefit expense.
5. *All transactions should be recorded in the proper period.* A transaction taking place in December of one year should be recorded in that year, rather than waiting until the following year. Failure to record transactions in the proper accounting period could result in either omission of the transaction altogether or incorrect adjustment for differences between the accounting records and detailed ledgers or inventory records.
6. *Transactions must be regularly summarized for inclusion in the company's financial statements.* The summation of all transactions during the reporting year should accurately reflect the result of the company's financial activities during that year.

Assets must be safeguarded

The responsibility of an insurance company to its policyowners makes the safeguarding of assets more crucial to an insurer than to many other types of companies. The problem of safeguarding assets requires sensitive handling. Certain assets must be sufficiently accessible so that business operations are not stifled. However, access to these assets must be restricted to authorized persons. Protection of assets may be accomplished by procedures such as limiting access to offices, documents, and records; storing negotiable documents in vaults to which no person has sole access; maintaining written disaster plans and off-premises storage of back-up files for all critical records; investigating the integrity of personnel hired to fill sensitive positions; and periodically reviewing the adequacy of the company's insurance coverage of its assets.

Physical comparison to recorded amounts must be made

As a further step in accounting for and safekeeping assets, the assets actually on hand should be inventoried and compared at reasonable intervals to the recorded amounts for those assets. A critical element of this method is that appropriate action should be taken with respect to any differences. In some companies, this procedure is performed either by the company's internal auditors, company personnel not involved in accounting for or maintaining custody of the assets, or independent auditors. In other companies, an inventory is performed by the employees responsible for maintaining the asset. The inventory is then tested or checked by an independent group.

Examples of Specific Types of Internal Controls

Up to this point, the discussion of internal controls has been general. Students should recognize that every company is different, and the specific controls actually in use vary widely from company to company. However, the types of controls used are universal. Identified below are examples of different types of controls that might be found in an insurance company.

1. *Approval, review, checking, or recalculation.* Examples of this type of control include additional approval of all claims over $20,000, random recalculation of premiums charged to policyowners, and completion of checklists that indicate that all required documents have been received prior to paying a claim or making a policy loan.
2. *Comparing information on independently generated documents.* Examples of this type of control are comparing information from a policy application to the new business worksheet and comparing the amount of a policy loan requested by a policyowner to the loan check generated before the check is mailed.
3. *Prenumbering.* Examples of controls that fall into this category include prenumbering checks, numbering applications when received, and numbering claims when received. Documents so numbered are then used or processed in numerical order and any numbers that are out of sequence or missing must be explained.
4. *Maintenance of control totals.* This type of control includes listing all policy loans separately and reconciling the total amount on the listing to the total amount of policy loans on the general ledger. Another example of the use of control totals is the use of batch totals on premium receipts. When premium checks are received, they are grouped together in a "batch" and the amounts are added together to obtain a "batch total." When the receipts are entered in the computer, the batch total is entered first. If the total of the checks entered does not equal the batch total, then the employee entering the figures must locate and correct the error.

5. *Comparison with third-party information.* The most obvious control fitting into this category is the reconciliation of bank statements. However, this type of control also includes (1) reconciliation of internally generated listings of securities held in safekeeping with listings provided by the holders of the securities, (2) reconciliation of notes payable with statements provided by owners of the notes, and (3) the follow-up and resolution of discrepancies and unreconciled differences.
6. *Soliciting third-party information.* This type of control could include periodically sending agents or policyowners statements that request (1) notification of errors in payment or policy records or (2) confirmation of amounts receivable from persons or companies owing the insurer. For example, some companies routinely send letters to policyowners asking them to confirm that the information concerning their policies is recorded correctly or that information regarding benefits paid under an accident and health policy is correct.
7. *Cancellation of documentation.* This method requires defacing documents in some way so that they cannot be sent through normal channels of processing. For example, a company should void all checks on which an error has been made. In addition, claim worksheets should include an indication of payment so that a check cannot be requested twice.
8. *Timeliness of operation.* All transactions should be processed promptly. Ways to ensure timeliness of operation may include requiring daily deposits of cash receipts, monthly reviews of the claim register and follow-ups on unresolved claims, and periodic reviews of the new business register with subsequent resolution of policies that have neither been issued nor denied.

The AICPA, in Appendix D of its *Audits of Stock Life Insurance Companies,* provides examples of questions that might be asked when evaluating the types of internal controls used by an insurer. (Such evaluations are part of the auditing function, which is discussed below.) Two examples of such questions, which apply to the areas of securities and policy liabilities, are shown in Figure 13-1. These lists are not intended to provide all of the questions that might be asked in the evaluation of controls in these areas, and more complete internal control questionnaires can generally be devised to suit a particular company or situation.

Auditing

When the terms "examination" and "auditing" are used, some people think of examinations performed by the Internal Revenue Service (IRS) for the purpose of determining whether or not the appropriate amount of federal income

FIGURE 13-1
Sample internal control questionnaires.[2]

Securities
1. Are security transactions authorized by:
   a. The board of directors?
   b. The investment committee?
   c. An officer?
   d. Other? _____
2. Does release of securities require the signatures of more than one officer where securities are under:
   a. Control of a safekeeping bank or independent custodian?
   b. Dual control of two officers other than those authorized to sign the release?
3. Are the securities periodically inspected or confirmed with independent custodians and balanced with security records?
   a. By internal auditors?
   b. By executives?
   c. By others? _____
4. Is the investment portfolio reviewed by an executive with the responsibility for determining that investments are in compliance with the State insurance code?

Policy Liabilities (policy valuation reserves)
1. Does the company maintain insurance in-force transaction registers and use such registers to reconcile insurance in-force to corresponding totals of number and amounts of policies shown in valuation summaries?
2. Does the company have provisions for reviewing the reasonableness of life reserves and the yearly changes by reference to plan, year, and age-at-issue valuation analyses?
3. Does the company match data contained in the valuation file with corresponding data in the following records:
   a. Application file?
   b. Premium record file?
   c. Premium billing file?
   d. Dividend file?
   e. Other files? _____
4. Were the following items included in the comparison?
   a. Policy number?
   b. Policy plan?
   c. Year of issue?
   d. Age at issue?
   e. Amount?
   f. Mode of payment?
   g. Paid-to date?
5. Does the company make other checks as to the completeness or accuracy of the in-force file?
6. Are the reserve factors and calculations checked?
7. Does the company utilize consulting actuaries to review or verify reserve valuations? Identify.
8. Do the consulting actuaries test the accuracy of the in-force listings and other summary items relied on in calculating policy reserves?
9. Does the company check the reasonableness of the "tabular cost" and "tabular net premiums" with respect to its ordinary life business?
10. Does the company establish active life reserves on non-cancellable or guaranteed renewable A&H contracts?

Copyright © 1985 by the American Institute of Certified Public Accountants, Inc. Reprinted by permission.

taxes has been paid. In the life and health insurance industry, many think of examinations performed by representatives of the regulatory authorities. Others think of independent examinations performed by certified public accountants (CPAs) for the purpose of expressing an opinion on the financial statements of an entity. Auditing encompasses much more, however. **Auditing** can be defined as the process of obtaining, examining, and evaluating data regarding a company's financial and operational actions and events. The process of auditing is undertaken in order (1) to determine the degree of correspondence between certain standards and the company's actual financial and operational actions and (2) to communicate the results to interested parties. This definition highlights several important points about audits or examinations, regardless of the type of examination or who is performing the examination. The following statements can also be made about auditing:

1. *Auditing is planned.* Before beginning an examination, an auditor generally develops a program of what procedures should be performed to achieve his or her objectives.
2. *Auditing has a purpose.* The purpose of an audit is to gather information that either supports or refutes an assertion. For example, governmental taxing authorities perform audits to determine if the amount of income tax that a person or company claims it owes is, in fact, the correct amount. IRS and Revenue, Canada, audits are based on criteria established by the Tax Codes for each country. In addition, independent audits of an insurer's financial statements are performed in the United States by CPAs, and by chartered accountants (CAs) in Canada, to determine if the amounts reported in those statements are in accordance with defined accounting principles. In the United States, this type of review is based on criteria established by the National Association of Insurance Commissioners (NAIC) and the Financial Accounting Standards Board (FASB). In Canada, the criteria are established by the Superintendent of Insurance, Canada, and the Canadian Institute of Chartered Accountants (CICA).
3. *The parties interested in the results of an audit are varied.* Interested parties may include the stockholders, creditors, and suppliers of a company, as well as various governmental agencies. In addition, the results of audits are reported to company management and the board of directors. In this way, management can determine if the company's products and services are being produced and sold as efficiently as possible and in accordance with either internally or externally established criteria.

External Auditing and Internal Auditing

The field of auditing is divided into two main categories: external auditing and internal auditing. **External auditing** is carried out primarily for the benefit of interested third parties, including the board of directors, investors, creditors, policyowners, and others that depend on the company's financial statements. People or entities generally performing external audits are tax auditors, public accountants, and government examiners, i.e., people who are not employed by the company being audited. **Internal auditing,** on the other hand, is performed by employees of the company being audited and is undertaken primarily for the benefit of that company's management. The primary purpose of internal auditing is to assist management in the effective discharge of its responsibilities. Since this text focuses on accounting within life and health insurance companies, the focus of this chapter is on the internal auditing function.

Internal auditing is one of the control tools used by insurers. The internal auditing function could be considered an independent means by which management evaluates and measures the effectiveness of other controls. The activities undertaken by internal auditing staff include

- reviewing and appraising the soundness and adequacy of accounting, financial, and other operating controls;
- investigating the extent to which company assets are accounted for and are safeguarded from all types of losses;
- ascertaining the reliability of statistical data and other managerial data that have been developed internally;
- appraising the quality of employee performance in carrying out assigned duties;
- reporting the results of audits objectively and making recommendations for corrections or improvements;
- coordinating, as necessary, internal auditing activities with those of external auditors; and
- investigating areas of suspected or proven fraud or irregularity.

Current accounting and auditing literature identifies two major types of auditing—(1) fiscal auditing and (2) performance or operational auditing—each of which is further subdivided into two subcategories (see Figure 13-2). Fiscal auditing can be subdivided into financial auditing and compliance auditing, while performance auditing can be subdivided into management auditing and program results auditing. Both fiscal and performance auditing can be conducted on an internal and external basis. A more detailed discussion of the various types of auditing follows.

FIGURE 13-2
Types of auditing.

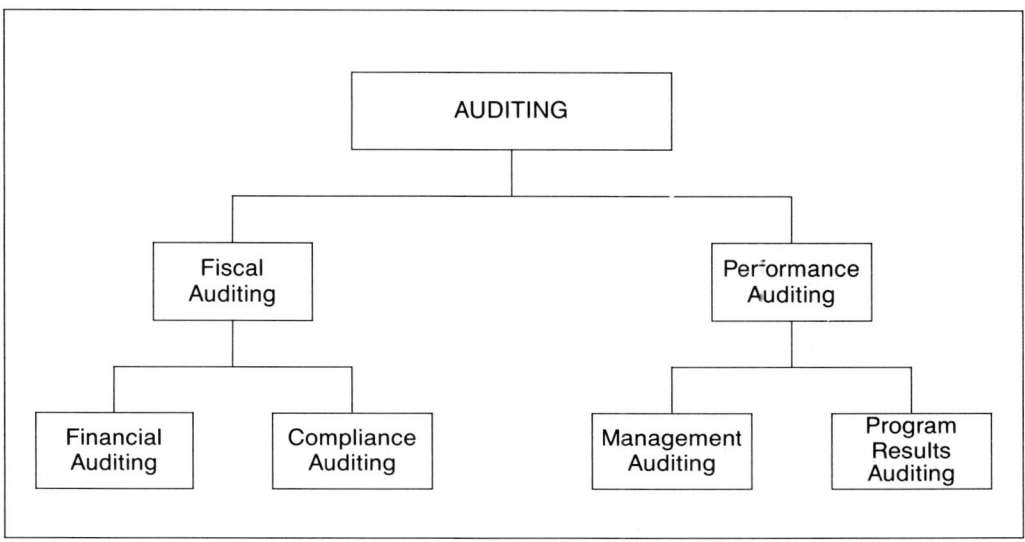

Fiscal Auditing

Financial auditing

Financial auditing is the traditional auditing of financial information and includes both the overall examination of a company's financial statements and the examination of individual accounts and accounting records. Financial audits are generally performed by several different persons or organizations including independent certified public accountants (CPAs) or chartered accountants (CAs), internal auditors, and auditors from various governmental agencies.

Examinations by independent CPAs or CAs are generally made to determine whether the financial statements of a company are presented fairly and in conformity with either generally accepted accounting principles (GAAP) or statutory accounting practices (SAP). The Securities and Exchange Commission (SEC) requires that all companies registered with the SEC—known as **public companies**—be audited annually to determine whether their financial statements conform to GAAP. On the other hand, companies that are not registered with the SEC may be audited to determine if their financial statements conform to statutory accounting practices. SAP serves as the basis for financial reporting to state insurance departments. Many states require non-public companies to be audited on a SAP basis. A CPA's opinion on a non-public company's internal controls must also be submitted.

Audits of public and non-public companies by state authorities are performed at least every three years. In the case of companies considered by regulatory authorities to be large and stable, these audits may be performed every five years. If the company is having financial difficulties, these examinations may take place annually. Taking into account internal audits, regulatory audits, and independent audits, life insurance companies are generally subject to at least two and often three financial audits annually. The different groups of auditors often rely on certain aspects of each others' work in order to minimize duplication of effort.

Students can gain a greater understanding of financial auditing through a short description of the ledger auditing process, which is described in Report #24 of LOMA's Financial Planning and Control Division. The purpose of the ledger audit is to determine if an account's balance is fairly stated. Such an audit can also be undertaken if fraud is suspected. The ledger audit starts with the balance in the general ledger and validates either all amounts or at least the major amounts in the account being audited. A typical ledger audit traces each ledger entry back to the respective source document such as an invoice, cash receipt listing, or deposit slip. In a large company, however, the volume of receipts and disbursements is such that only a random selection of entries, generated by statistical sampling techniques, would be used to test the validity of the ledger balance.[3] In any size company, discrepancies between ledger entries and source documents must be reconciled. Figure 13-3 shows other areas of a life and health insurance company's operations and financial records that are typically audited.

Compliance auditing

The distinction between financial auditing and compliance auditing is that the focus of financial auditing is to render an opinion as to the fairness of the presentation of financial statements, while the thrust of **compliance auditing** is to verify adherence to the laws, regulations, policies, and procedures prescribed by either internal or external authorities. Examinations of an insurance company by state regulatory authorities include compliance auditing since part of such examinations includes the determination of whether the company has complied with applicable laws and regulations. An IRS examination is another example of a compliance audit. Reports of both compliance and financial audits are reports of facts and transactions that have occurred and, thus, are reports of past events. However, past performance is not always the subject of the auditing function.

Performance or Operational Auditing

Management auditing

The focus of **management auditing,** also known as economy and efficiency auditing, is on improving the effectiveness and efficiency of a company's operations. Management audits are performed to identify areas in which costs can be reduced and improvements in operations can be made. Alternatively, such audits

FIGURE 13-3
Company audit program areas.[4]

(Note: The following list is not intended to be a complete listing of areas in a life insurance company that are subject to audits. The list is, however, shown as a representative example.)

Financial Division
Bank Reconciliations
Bonds and Stocks
Dividends Received on Stocks
Home Office Building and Real Estate
Interest Received on Bonds
Mandatory Security Valuation Reserve
Mortgage Loans
Petty Cash
Real Estate Purchased for Income
Security Vault Control
Separate Accounts

Group Division
Accident and Health Benefits
Accident and Health Claims
Claim Drafts Payable
Commissions Due and Unpaid
Commissions Paid
Contingency Reserve
Death Claims
Death Claims—Due and Unpaid
Dividends to Policyowners
Periodic Annuity Payments
Policy Reserves
Premiums
Service Fees
Unearned Premium Reserves—Accident and Health

Ordinary Division
Commissions Due and Unpaid
Commissions Paid
Death Claims
Death Claims—Due and Unpaid
Disability Claims
Dividend Accumulations

Ordinary Division (continued)
Dividends Paid to Policyowners
Periodic Annuity Payments
Policy Account
Policy Loans
Premiums
Surrender Benefits

Corporate
Advertising
Agency Expense Allowance
Agents' Financing Loans
Benefit Plans—Agents
Benefit Plans—Home Office
Budgets
Capital Stock
Data Processing
Furniture and Equipment
General Expenses
Inspection Report Fees
Medical Examination Fees
Payroll
Postage and Expenses
Rent Paid
Rental of Equipment
Restaurant
Surplus—Stockholders and Policyowners
Taxes
Telephone
Travel

Other
Agency Offices
Equity Investments
Mortgage Loan Correspondents
Subsidiaries

can be described as evaluations of management effectiveness and efficiency. Management auditing includes not only reviews of operational controls but also the formulation of possible improvements and cost reductions. Depending on the needs of the company, the scope of management audits can vary widely, addressing a single area or undertaking a review of all company operations. Internal auditors, external auditors, and regulatory agencies can perform management audits.

One example of a management audit is a departmental audit, which is also described in LOMA's Financial Planning and Control Report #24. The departmental audit evaluates and tests the performance of a department's personnel by first identifying the responsibility involved in each person's job and then determining if the responsibility is being met. To conduct this type of audit, the auditor must become familiar with the company's policies and procedures as well as all of the controls in the department's activities. Towards this end, the auditor reads all departmental reports for accuracy and usefulness. From this type of audit, the auditor can report to management if the department is functioning properly and efficiently and whether it is effectively meeting its responsibilities.[5]

Program results auditing

The purpose of **program results auditing,** or effectiveness auditing, is to determine whether the results or benefits desired from a particular program are actually being achieved. Additionally, such an audit would include an analysis of whether the desired results could be achieved at a lower cost. Inherent in this process is the determination of whether the program goals and objectives are realistic and well defined.

A fairly recent offshoot of program results auditing is known as **social auditing,** which tries to determine how a corporation's actions affect society. For example, areas evaluated under social auditing may include the impact of corporate actions on (1) the marketplace, (2) the external environment, or (3) the minority groups of a society's population.

Key Terms

internal control	administrative control
accounting control	cost-benefit analysis
segregation of duties	incompatible functions
external auditing	internal auditing
fiscal auditing	performance auditing
financial auditing	compliance auditing
management auditing	program results auditing
public company	ledger audit
departmental audit	social auditing

Review Questions and Exercises

1. List and describe three of the methods used in developing an effective internal accounting control system.
2. Define these two terms:
   (a) collusion
   (b) cost-benefit analysis
3. What are the two types of fiscal auditing?
4. Why is segregation of duties important to an effective accounting control system? If applicable, in what ways are duties segregated in your area of work?
5. Look at the definition of *administrative control* on p. 270. What types of administrative controls are in place in your company? In the area in which you work?

NOTES

1. Much of the information in the "Internal Control" section of this chapter is based on *Reporting on Internal Accounting Control*, Statement of Auditing Standards No. 30 (New York: American Institute of Certified Public Accountants, 1979) and *Adherence to Generally Accepted Accounting Principles*, Statement of Auditing Standards No. 1 (New York: AICPA, 1958).
2. From Appendix D of *Audits of Stock Life Insurance Companies*, American Institute of Certified Public Accountants (New York: AICPA, 1972), pp. 161, 163.
3. *Establishing an Internal Audit Function in a Life Insurance Company*, Financial Planning and Control Report #24 (Atlanta: Life Office Management Association, 1972), p. 9.
4. FP&C Report #24 (Life Office Management Association, 1972), p. 32.
5. FP&C Report #24 (Life Office Management Association, 1972), p. 9.

14
Generally Accepted Accounting Principles for Life and Health Insurance Companies

Learning Objectives

After reading this chapter, you should be able to:

- Understand the need for financial statements based on both statutory accounting practices (SAP) and generally accepted accounting principles (GAAP)
- Describe the primary purposes of SAP and GAAP as well as the different philosophies used to fulfill these purposes
- Describe the SAP and GAAP financial statement requirements for both stock and mutual insurers
- List and describe a number of ways in which SAP and GAAP reporting differ
- Explain the two primary components involved in the income determination process
- Understand the different methods of expense recognition
- Compare Canadian accounting practices with U.S. SAP and GAAP

Introduction

Life and health insurers have historically followed accounting procedures that concentrated on both demonstrating solvency and displaying the companies' interests in their policyowners. The economic and financial environment of the last two decades, however, has brought about recognition of the informational needs of another group: the suppliers of the insurer's capital. An insurance company's investors and lenders were, and still are, largely unfamiliar with statutory accounting practices and the Annual Statement described thus far in this text. Such investors and lenders are, in general, more familiar with financial reports based on the generally accepted accounting principles used by other types of businesses. This situation has led to the adoption of generally accepted accounting principles (GAAP) by stock life and health insurers in the United States. Since mutual life companies receive their capital from earnings retained from their policyowners, and thus are not open for outside investment, GAAP applies predominantly to stock life insurers. Many large mutual companies, however, are adopting GAAP for internal reporting purposes.

This chapter explores generally accepted accounting principles as they apply to life and health insurance companies. The chapter also compares GAAP with both U.S. statutory accounting practices and the accounting procedures followed by Canadian life and health insurers. Before beginning a discussion of generally accepted accounting principles, though, a look at the underlying philosophies of SAP and GAAP should be helpful.

SAP and GAAP Philosophies

In the United States, statutory accounting for life insurers consists of practices prescribed or permitted by the states in which insurers operate. Such practices must be followed in the preparation of the financial reports included in the NAIC Annual Statement that must be filed in all states in which a company is licensed to do business. The primary purpose of statutory accounting and reporting is to help state insurance departments supervise insurance companies. Regulators are concerned with protecting the interests of policyowners. Regulatory agencies thus strive to ensure a company's solvency, i.e., the ability to meet both debts to creditors and the future claims of policyowners and beneficiaries. Accordingly, SAP is oriented first towards a study of each company's financial position as shown by the insurer's Balance Sheet. A secondary concern of state regulators is the success of each insurer's operations as shown by the Annual Statement's Summary of Operations.

In order to enforce these regulatory stances most effectively, state insurance departments require that a company's statutory accounting practices employ the liquidation approach to accounting rather than the going-concern approach that is one of the underlying principles of GAAP. These two approaches were discussed in Chapter 1. Through use of the liquidation approach and other statutory accounting practices, the financial statements of life and health insurers reflect a more conservative financial position than would be the case if they followed the accounting practices generally accepted in other industries.

Conservatism in accounting can be defined as the choice of a financial reporting alternative that results in the projection of lower values for a company's assets, higher values for its liabilities, and a reduced level of income than would be the case if a non-conservative approach had been used. Thus, the usual outcome of taking a conservative reporting position is the inclusion of extra safety margins in Balance Sheet items and a lower net income in any given year. Since GAAP reporting is oriented towards potential investors, however, it places greater emphasis on reporting realistic net income on the Income Statement than on reporting a liquidation value for the company's net worth. Though GAAP reporting is generally conservative, it employs a less conservative accounting approach than statutory accounting.

As we noted in Chapter 1, the going-concern concept that is essential to GAAP reporting assumes that, in the absence of evidence to the contrary, a firm will continue in business indefinitely. Therefore, the presentation of GAAP financial statements is designed to provide information that is useful in making financial decisions. One application of the going-concern concept is the matching of major expenses with the future accounting periods in which the benefits from those expenses will be realized. As a result, under GAAP, fewer expenses are deducted from current income, and net income is greater than it would be if those expenses were deducted in full when incurred.

Development of GAAP for the Life Insurance Industry

In the 1960s, investors began to be attracted to stock life insurance companies because of their market performance, their stable and relatively high earnings, and the nature and extent of these companies' assets. Life company wealth, in general, is in the form of secure financial assets—marketable securities, real estate, and loans—as opposed to the other businesses' tangible goods that can lose value as a result of perishability, obsolescence, consumer attitudes, wear and tear, and other reasons. Unfortunately, from an investor's point of view, evaluation and interpretation of insurance company financial statements were difficult if not impossible. Differences between statutory accounting and the generally accepted accounting practices of other industries were unfamiliar to potential investors and were not typically explained in insurers' financial statements. Furthermore, statutory statements included many terms and account titles—reinsurance ceded, deferred premiums, policy reserves, the Mandatory Securities Valuation Reserve (MSVR), nonledger assets, and nonadmitted assets, for example—that were not present in the reports of other business concerns.

At the same time, stock life insurance companies were seeking ways to reach the private-investor market as a source of capital. Since education of countless investors about life insurance accounting practices was not practical, insurers developed financial statements based on GAAP in order to facilitate tapping this source of capital. At first, various rules were developed so that certain items in insurers' statutory financial statements could be modified to reflect GAAP reporting standards. Then, insurers began completing a set of financial statements distinct from those filed with regulatory authorities. These statements conformed to the generally accepted accounting principles followed by noninsurance companies, and thus, insurers' GAAP financial statements were comparable to the financial reports of companies in other industries. As a result, many insurers now issue two types of financial statements:

(1) one financial statement that contains the kind of information investors use in the investment risk evaluation process for noninsurance companies, and
(2) one financial statement that contains the information and presentation necessary to satisfy regulatory requirements.

Over a period of years, the evolutionary process for the first type of financial statement resulted in generally accepted accounting principles that were specifically applicable to stock life insurance companies, though *not* to mutual, fraternal, or government insurance organizations. Generally, these latter organizations are not involved in the search for outside capital, nor are they open for investment by outside sources.

Another factor contributing to and accelerating the trend toward adapting life insurance accounting to general accounting practices was the growth in the number of holding companies since the 1960s. A **holding company** can be defined as a company that controls one or more other companies, or **subsidiaries,** through ownership of a sufficient amount of the subsidiaries' common stock. Holding companies typically monitor and control their subsidiaries' operations, rather than being involved in the subsidiaries solely for investment purposes. Because the SEC requires publicly held holding companies to follow generally accepted accounting principles, many life insurance companies that either owned other companies or were owned by other companies had to prepare financial statements on a GAAP basis in addition to their SAP financial statements.

A third factor in the development of GAAP for life companies also related to holding company operations. When a holding company is borrowing money in order to acquire a subsidiary—such as a finance company or another insurer—lenders generally require that the borrower's financial statements be based on accounting practices comparable to those found in other types of enterprises. This requirement is understandable because such lenders, similar to potential investors, are usually unfamiliar with insurers' statutory accounting.

A fourth factor encouraging the application of GAAP to life companies arose when the AICPA began to require independent auditors to indicate in their reports to clients whether the audited firm's financial statements were prepared in accordance with GAAP. This requirement meant that an auditor's report on an insurance company for which GAAP statements had not been prepared must state that the company's financial statements were in accordance with statutory accounting practices, but were not presented on a GAAP basis. To avoid the presence of such disclaimers on audit reports, more and more insurers began preparing financial statements on a GAAP basis in addition to their Annual Statements filed with regulatory authorities.

The Audit Guide

As a result of changes in the financial environment and in insurers' accounting procedures, the AICPA and the life insurance industry developed a guide entitled *Audits of Stock Life Insurance Companies* (known as the *Audit Guide*) and required in 1973 that the principles prescribed in that Guide be implemented in the preparation of life insurers' GAAP financial statements. Remember that this Guide prescribes GAAP only for stock life insurers, and not for mutuals, fraternals, or government insurance organizations. Statutory accounting practices, however, are considered to be generally accepted accounting practices for mutuals.

After the AICPA Audit Guide was issued, the SEC required GAAP financial statements from all life insurance companies—both stock and mutual, whether or not associated with a holding company—that file reports with the SEC. Since SAP is considered GAAP for mutuals, the SEC accepts statutory accounting financial statements from mutual insurers. However, a stock company under the jurisdiction of the SEC is required to prepare two sets of financial statements—one that meets state insurance regulations and another that meets generally accepted accounting principles. Only when a company files a financial statement that fulfills GAAP requirements for that type of company can an auditor file an *unqualified* report stating that the company's financial statements have been prepared according to generally accepted accounting principles. In certain situations in which GAAP figures are prepared but do not meet explicitly prescribed guidelines, the auditor must issue a *qualified* opinion.

Some states historically have required companies that prepare separate statements based on SAP and GAAP to include a reconciliation of SAP and GAAP figures for two items: net income and stockholders' equity. In recent years, states have also begun requiring companies to file SAP and GAAP reconciliations for assets, liabilities, and the Statement of Changes in Financial Position. In addition, some states require reconciliation on a company by company basis if consolidated GAAP statements are prepared. A few states, on the other hand, prohibit the distribution of GAAP statements. Thus, in these states, if a company prepares GAAP-basis financial statements for managerial, investor, or regulatory purposes, the company cannot use those figures in its annual report or in other publications distributed to or available to the public.

SAP-GAAP Comparisons

Because of the basic differences in statutory accounting practices and generally accepted accounting principles, the appearance and content of certain aspects of an insurer's financial statements will differ depending on the accounting "language" being used. That is, a financial report prepared under the guidelines of statutory accounting practices will differ in a number of respects from a financial report prepared using generally accepted accounting principles. Among the ways in which the reports will differ include

- the manner of determining income for a certain period,
- the valuation of assets,
- the valuation of policy reserves,
- the accounting for dividends paid to stockholders and policyowners, and
- the treatment of federal income taxes.

Explanations of these differences are presented below.

Income Determination

The process of determining the amount of a company's net income for financial reporting purposes entails both revenue recognition and expense recognition. We will describe these two components separately.

Revenue recognition

Not all of a company's income before expenses is actually earned in the accounting period in which the income is received. Thus, certain procedures are required in order to match a company's income with its proper accounting period, i.e., the period in which the income is considered to be earned. These procedures are mandated by the generally accepted accounting principle known as the **realization principle,** which holds that income should be recognized, or *realized,* when it is earned rather than when it is received. Thus, if a publisher that is selling magazines by subscription receives income of $100 in December 1986 on sale of a three-year subscription running through November 1989, under the realization principle, the publisher's income statement for 1986 would not show $100 of income for this subscription. Instead, under GAAP, the $100 would be apportioned as follows:

1986 statement	Income for December 1986 only, or 1/36 of $100	$ 2.78
1987 statement	Income for 1987 only, or 12/36 of $100	33.33
1988 statement	Income for 1988 only, or 12/36 of $100	33.33
1989 statement	Income for January–November 1989 only, or 11/36 of $100	30.56
		$100.00

Note that when financial statements are prepared using GAAP, the present value of money is generally ignored.

In insurance, revenue recognition applies primarily to the receipt of premiums. In both SAP and GAAP, incoming insurance premiums are recognized as they are earned over the course of the *premium-paying* period of the policy. In GAAP, however, single-premium contracts provide an exception to this practice. Under GAAP, premiums for single-premium contracts are recognized as earned revenues over the *coverage* period of the policy, though this revenue recognition method for single-premium contracts has been the subject of recent debate.

Expense recognition

Expense recognition under statutory accounting practices is relatively simple. In many companies, expenditures are generally recognized as expenses when money is disbursed. In other companies, accounting is done on an accrual basis, and expenses are recognized as they are incurred. Accounting for expenses under GAAP, however, is more complicated. Expense recognition under GAAP involves three principles: (1) associating cause and effect (known as the *matching concept*), (2) systematic and rational allocation, and (3) immediate recognition. Actual application of the principles varies with the circumstances of the situation.

Associating cause and effect. Accountants recognize some costs as having a direct association with specific revenues. This direct relationship is described in accounting literature as *associating cause and effect,* or as *matching revenue and expense.* Under this principle, costs that can be recognized as having a direct relationship to certain future earnings or specific elements of revenue are charged to earnings of future accounting periods instead of to the current accounting period. An example of expenses falling into this category is commissions paid to sales agents.

Under GAAP for life and health insurance companies, one particular adjustment that is made to establish a cause-and-effect matching of revenues and expenses involves amounts that are grouped together under the category of policy acquisition costs. **Policy acquisition costs** are those amounts that are directly attributable to the production of new business. Sales commissions are the largest single item incurred to acquire business, but other components are physicians' fees, paramedical fees, inspection report fees, policy issue costs, and salaries of those directly involved in the production of new business. In order to defer until future accounting periods the recognition of policy acquisition costs as expenses, most of a company's acquisition costs are capitalized. **Capitalization** is a term used to describe the process of deferring costs, treating them as assets, and then amortizing the value of those assets over the period of time in which the benefits resulting from the expenses occur. The benefits resulting from acquisition costs are realized in those future periods in the form of premium revenue. Such amortization or capitalization of expenses is not made in statutory accounting. In SAP, expenses are instead attributed to the period in which they are incurred. Thus, no matching is made of the initial acquisition costs to future years' premium income derived from the reporting year's sales.

To illustrate the principle of associating cause and effect, assume that a company spent $1,000,000 one year for policy acquisition purposes. Experience for this company indicates that most of the business put on the books will continue in force for years into the future. If the company followed SAP, the entire $1,000,000 would be considered an expense for that year. However, if the company employed GAAP, then instead of charging off the entire $1,000,000 in policy acquisition costs as an expense this year, the company's accountants would charge off only a small part of the $1,000,000 and attribute the remainder to a deferred asset account. The balance in the deferred asset account would be amortized over future accounting periods as the related premium revenues were earned. The amount charged off as an expense each year would be calculated based on the relationship of current year's premiums to total future years' premium income.

The authorities that mandated GAAP have issued certain guidelines describing which acquisition costs may be deferred. Only those policy acquisition costs that are primarily related to the production of new business and that vary with the volume of business are eligible for deferral. Items that are *not* typically eligible for deferral include executive salaries, fees for accounting and legal services, and claims settlement expenses.

Similar to policy acquisition costs are **developmental costs,** which are incurred in efforts to acquire new business, or, in some cases, to support business that has already been acquired. Examples of developmental costs include amounts incurred in developing and printing a new rate book or revising an existing rate book, developing and implementing a training program to introduce a new policy, and developing or revising a data processing system for policy issue. Developmental costs are given immediate expense recognition under SAP, but under GAAP, certain guidelines determine which costs are eligible to be deferred. For example, costs arising from unusually large and extended training programs are eligible, but only if such programs serve to expand the marketing force. Advertising campaigns designed to sell specific products, rather than to promote the company or the industry, are also eligible.

Systematic and rational allocation. Sometimes, a direct association of cause and effect is not clearly recognizable or measurable. In such cases, another method must be used to achieve the desired matching of costs and benefits. This method, known as **systematic and rational allocation,** spreads the cost of an asset over its estimated useful life without regard to the revenues realized from use of the asset. One example of such systematic allocation is depreciation. As with the method of associating cause and effect, expenses are capitalized under systematic and rational allocation methods.

Systematic and rational allocation can be illustrated by the following example. Assume that a company spent $1,000,000 one year on the purchase and installation of a new computer system. Management cannot predict how long the system will provide financial benefits or what its financial benefits will be. In the absence of a recognizable and measurable relationship between cause and effect, the expense recognition approach used is to capitalize the million-dollar expense in the present accounting period and to begin systematic and rational depreciation. Assuming that the estimated useful life of the system is eight years and that the straight-line method of depreciation is used, $125,000 would be recorded as a full year's expense during each year of the system's estimated eight-year life. After eight years, the full $1,000,000 will have been allocated.

Immediate recognition. Under SAP, an expense is absorbed by either earnings or surplus in the accounting period in which the expense is incurred. This approach to expense recognition is justified under GAAP requirements in two sets of circumstances:

(1) The costs incurred provide no recognizable future benefits, and thus neither associating cause and effect nor systematic and rational allocation is applicable. Examples of expenditures in this category are the company's legal expenses and fees paid to consultants.
(2) Systematic and rational allocation has ceased to be applicable, e.g., if expense items that had been capitalized and have been in the process of being amortized no longer provide benefits to the company. In such a case, the unamortized amounts of deferred charges should be written off in a lump sum. Two examples of expenses in this category are prepaid rent and unamortized amounts of capitalized improvements on leased property. Either or both expenses may be recognized immediately if a company moves from leased premises before the end of its lease.

Asset Valuation

Statutory accounting requires that certain assets be designated as nonadmitted assets, which means that they are not shown on the Balance Sheet even though they are reported elsewhere in the Annual Statement. Examples of nonadmitted assets include furniture and equipment, automobiles, inventories of supplies such as paper and policy forms, amounts of money owed by employees and agents, and prepaid expenses. Such assets are considered nonadmitted assets for an insurance company because, in the event of the company's liquidation, they could not be easily converted into cash for use in the repayment of debts to creditors or payment of benefits and claims to policyowners and their beneficiaries.

Under GAAP, the possible liquidation of a company's assets is generally not considered. Thus, on GAAP Balance Sheets, all assets are shown, and no nonadmitted asset classification exists. All fixed assets are reported at their net book value, i.e., cost minus any accumulated depreciation. Other assets, such as inventories and prepaid expenses, are usually shown at the lower of cost or market value. Amounts owed by employees and agents are reported minus an estimated allowance for uncollectible accounts.

Marketable securities

The value at which marketable securities must be carried in SAP statements is dictated by state insurance regulations and practices. In general, bond and stock values are determined by use of rules and specific values set forth in the NAIC *Valuations of Securities* manual. Bonds and preferred stocks in good standing according to NAIC rules are valued at book value—i.e., cost or amortized cost, as applicable. Bonds and preferred stocks not in good standing are carried at a value prescribed by the NAIC. Common stocks are carried at their market value.

Securities that no longer have a book value are completely written off against the Mandatory Securities Valuation Reserve (MSVR) and are sometimes reported as unlisted assets in Annual Statement Schedule X. An **unlisted asset** has doubtful value and does not appear on the Balance Sheet. An unlisted asset differs from a nonadmitted asset in that the latter has a book value, but only its admitted book value is reflected on the Balance Sheet. Examples of unlisted assets include

- common stock or other securities that have become worthless because of the bankruptcy of the issuing company or, in the case of government bonds, because of the fall of the issuing government; and
- retained mineral interests. This situation occurs when an insurer has sold property yet has retained mineral rights to the property. If the insurer subsequently determines that the mineral rights have no value, then they are listed as unlisted assets in Schedule X.

GAAP reporting of marketable securities is often different from reporting under SAP. Under GAAP, preferred stocks and bonds with mandatory redemption features are carried at amortized cost. A **mandatory redemption feature** allows the security's issuer to redeem preferred stock that had been issued for a limited period of time or to pay back a bond's principal at a certain call date. Other preferred stocks and all common stocks are carried at market value. Realized gains (or losses) arising from the sale of securities are shown in the Income Statement rather than being credited to the MSVR as in SAP. Unrealized gains or losses, that is, changes in the value of securities that are retained and continue to be carried in financial statements at market value, are also credited or debited, respectively, to a separate account in the stockholders' equity section of the Balance Sheet.

GAAP mandates that securities that have become permanently impaired should be written down to their realizable value and the write-down should be recorded as a realized loss through income statement accounts. SAP mandates similar treatment for preferred stock that has become permanently impaired. **Permanently impaired securities** are ones in which investments will likely not be recovered because the securities' issuer has experienced financial difficulty or outright bankruptcy. To write down a permanently impaired security to a **realizable value** means to assign to that security a dollar value that represents the insurer's best estimate of the amount, if any, that the insurer will recover upon the security's sale or maturity. Once written down, securities cannot be written back up.

The Mandatory Securities Valuation Reserve

As mentioned earlier in this text, statutory accounting in most states requires life insurers to establish a liability account called the Mandatory Securities Valuation Reserve (MSVR). Amounts debited or credited each year to this account are calculated according to rules and formulas adopted by the NAIC. This account serves to negate the effect of both realized and unrealized capital gains and losses on the company's current-year surplus. Without the use of the MSVR as an intermediary account to offset changes in year-end account balances caused by realized and unrealized capital gains and losses, the amount of each year's surplus would fluctuate in proportion to changes in the market values of securities owned by the company.

In GAAP, the MSVR account is not treated as a liability. Instead, the MSVR is classified and treated as an appropriation of the company's accumulated earnings, or *retained earnings*. As a subdivision of retained earnings, the MSVR may, at the company's option, be reported as a separate item in the equity section of the Balance Sheet or be included in Retained Earnings.

Real estate

Home office property and investment real estate are carried in SAP at their cost less (1) accumulated depreciation and (2) any mortgages payable. Some states give approval for a company to carry home office property at an appraised value that exceeds cost. This option, justified when property values have increased significantly beyond book values, offers a means of increasing reported surplus and is used in situations where a company needs to increase that account. Foreclosures, or properties acquired in satisfaction of debt, are carried at the lesser of the unpaid balance of the foreclosed loan or the fair market value of the property. Under any statutory valuation, actual market values are sometimes in excess of book value and, thus, assets may be undervalued on the books.

Real estate valuations under GAAP are basically the same as valuations under SAP with some exceptions. One exception is that appraised values in excess of depreciated cost are not permitted under GAAP. This prohibition provides an example of where GAAP accounting is more conservative than SAP.

Policy Reserve Valuation

Policy reserves, sometimes known as policy benefit reserves, are collectively the largest liability of a life insurance company. To understand policy reserves from an accounting point of view, some basic information regarding premiums must be understood.

Under SAP, the total premium paid by the policyowner, known as the **gross premium,** is divided into the **net premium,** which is the portion that funds the benefit reserve, and the **loading,** which represents the amount needed for expenses, commissions, and profit for the insurer. Under GAAP, the gross premium is divided into the net benefit premium, the net expense premium, and profit, if any. The **net benefit premium** funds the benefit reserve, and the **net expense premium** pays the expenses of maintaining and acquiring the policy. The remainder of the gross premium represents the company's profit. No item known as "loading" exists in GAAP. (Figure 14-1 shows the different premium classifications under SAP and GAAP.)

In simple terms, policy reserves under both SAP and GAAP represent the present value of future benefits minus the present value of future net premiums. The policy reserve accumulates through the periodic addition of the net premiums, plus the constant addition of interest earned, less any benefits paid. Under both SAP and GAAP, increases to policy reserves in any given period are charged against expenses during that period. Decreases to policy reserves are treated as reductions to expenses. Thus, changes in policy reserves are recorded in both Balance Sheet and Income Statement accounts in the same time period in which the changes occur.

FIGURE 14-1
Premium terminology under SAP and GAAP.

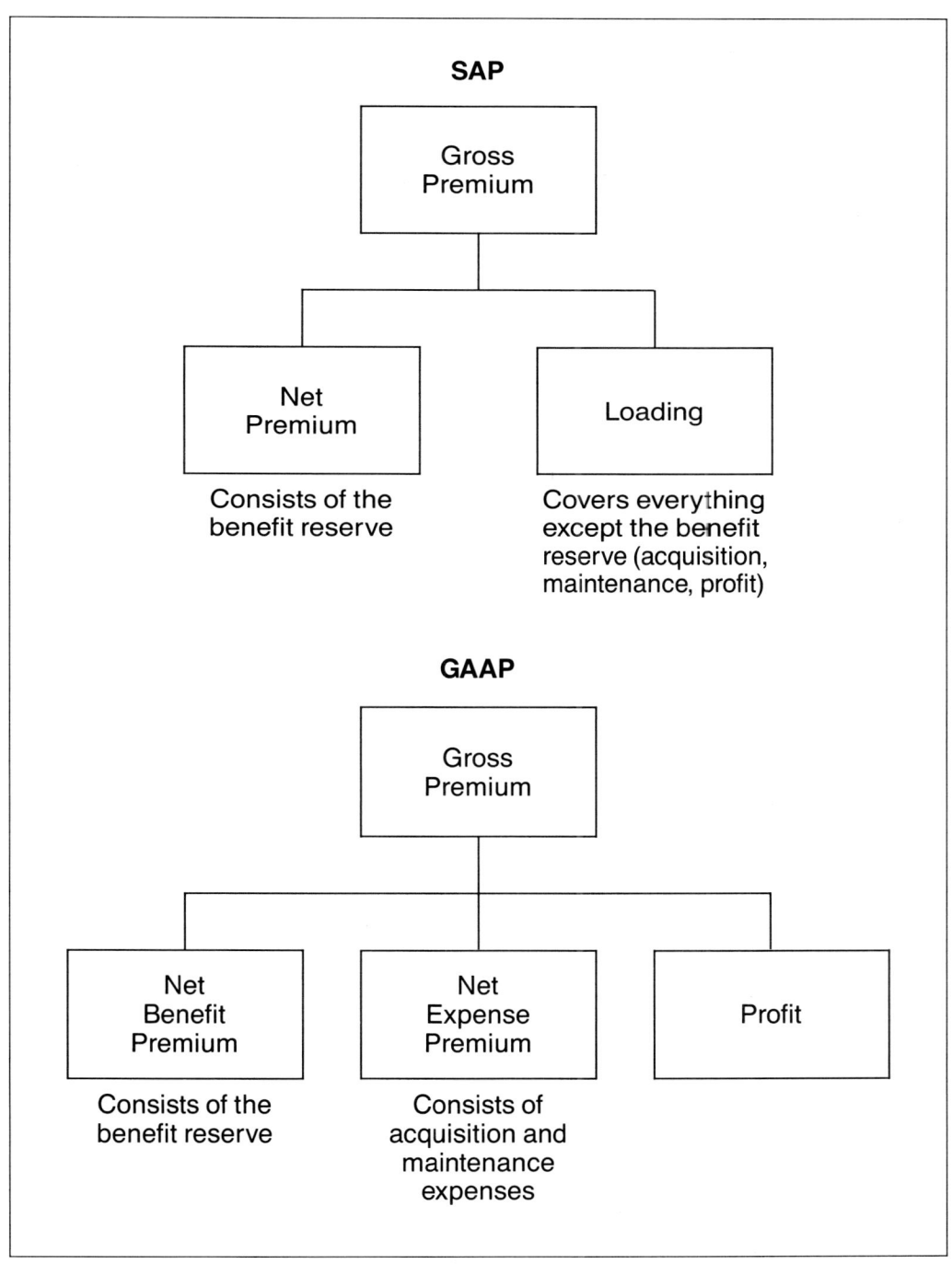

For a description of policy reserves, two other terms requiring comment are *net level reserves* and *modified reserves*. **Net level reserves** are reserves accumulated from policies for which the amount of premium set aside to fund the reserve remains level over the life of the policy. **Modified reserves** are reserves accumulated from policies for which the amount of premium set aside for reserves is lower in early policy years than in later premium-paying years.

SAP policy reserves

In general, policy reserves under SAP are actuarially computed using conservative interest and mortality assumptions that are prescribed by regulatory authorities. Reserves are calculated without consideration of possible withdrawals resulting from lapses and surrenders. By not considering withdrawals, a company assumes that all policies will stay in force until death of the insured and, accordingly, the reserve amount is higher than it would be if terminations not caused by death were considered.

Statutory policy reserves can be maintained, at the company's discretion, on either a modified or net-level reserve basis. Modified reserves are used in SAP financial statements to offset the high first-year expenses incurred in selling new business. By setting aside lower amounts of reserve in the first year, the company improves its surplus position on the Balance Sheet. Modified reserves are not used in GAAP.

GAAP policy reserves

GAAP policy reserves are actuarially computed using interest, mortality, and lapse assumptions that the company deemed to be reasonable and realistic at the time a given policy was issued, not at the time the policy was priced nor at the time reserve computations are being made for year-end statements. Such realistic assumptions are based, to the greatest extent possible, on the company's own experience rather than on multi-company studies, standard actuarial tables, or population statistics. In GAAP, during any given accounting period, these reserves are calculated on a net-level basis in order to match reserve increases to their related premium revenue.

Another difference between reporting of GAAP and SAP reserves is the time period reflected in the amount of reserves reported. SAP reserves are reported for an entire policy year, no matter when that year begins or ends. Thus, on December 31, reserves reported under SAP will include amounts for policy years extending into the next calendar year. To ensure the matching of assets, liabilities, revenues, and expenses, deferred and uncollected premiums are also recorded for the next year. GAAP reserves, on the other hand, are reported for the company's fiscal year, not the policy year. As a result, GAAP statements do not reflect deferred premiums.

Once a set of assumptions regarding a particular type or group of policies is adopted for a particular year or years of issue, these assumptions are to continue prospectively, i.e., they must be used for reserve calculations in future years. This feature of reserve calculation under GAAP is often referred to as the **lock-in concept.** When actual experience differs from expectations, results are reflected directly in company operations and various accounts. The particular account for policy reserves is not changed to show current conditions as future years' financial statements are prepared. SAP does not use the lock-in concept. Under statutory accounting practices, reserve assumptions can be changed when calculating the reserve liability.

Dividends to Policyowners

The amount shown on the statutory Annual Statement Balance Sheet for dividends to policyowners represents a company's anticipated liability for policy dividends to be paid out during the next calendar year. Most types of participating policies do not provide a policy dividend in the first policy year because of the high first-year costs associated with most insurance policies. The estimation of subsequent policy dividends is done annually and is based on projections made when those particular policies were issued.

Under GAAP, accounting for dividends paid on participating business is more complex than estimating the next calendar year's policy dividends. In general, companies estimate future dividend payout over the life of the policies, basing such estimates on the dividend scales that were contemplated when the policy was issued. The total projected dividend amount represents the present value of dividends expected to be paid over the life of the policy. This liability is often included with the amount reported for policy reserve liability, but may be reported as a separate item in GAAP financial statements.

State regulation is one factor that indirectly affects the amount of policy dividend liability shown on the GAAP-basis Balance Sheet. For example, states may restrict the amount of earnings on participating business that can be set aside for the benefit of stockholders or policyowners. Any restriction on how much a company is allowed to pay stockholders automatically affects what the company can pay policyowners and subsequently the anticipated liability for policy dividends. When a company is limited in the payout of earnings from participating business, the mandatory share owed to policyowners is excluded from calculations of the amount reported on the Balance Sheet for stockholders' equity. This exclusion is accomplished by debiting an income account and crediting a liability account. If and when dividends actually paid on such business exceed the anticipated liability amount, the difference should be debited to the liability account in an adjusting entry.

Dividends to Stockholders

In SAP, cash dividends to a company's stockholders are generally paid from unassigned surplus, and the company is subject to statutory limitations on the amount that can be paid. For example, the total amount of payment cannot be in excess of the company's unassigned surplus. If the insurance company is owned by a holding company, additional regulatory restrictions on the payment of dividends usually exist. These restrictions are typically based on prior years' earnings. Under GAAP, cash dividends are paid from retained earnings, which are equivalent to unassigned surplus under SAP. Both terms represent a company's accumulated earnings that have not been paid out as dividends to policyowners.

When dividends to stockholders are paid in the form of additional stock, the monetary value used for recording the transaction is either the par value of the stock or, in the case of stock that was issued without a par value, an amount determined by the board of directors. Under GAAP, rules for determining the stock's monetary value differ based on the size of the stock dividend. The dollar value used when recording the payment of dividends in the form of stock should be the total resulting from multiplying the number of shares involved by the stock's market value at the time of distribution.

A company's ability to pay dividends is governed by one primary factor: the amount available in unassigned surplus or retained earnings. The amount of cash available—that is, the amount of unassigned surplus that is in the form of cash—also enters into any decision regarding a distribution of dividends. However, if unassigned surplus is not available, neither cash nor stock dividends can be paid. Under GAAP, the amount available for dividends is disclosed in notes contained in the financial statements. The amount available is calculated on a SAP basis, even if financial statements are otherwise based on GAAP, because states place limits on the payment of stockholder dividends. The limitations are based on statutory earnings and surplus.

Changes in Surplus

As discussed in Chapter 10, various items affect surplus. Changes that occur among such items between the end of one year and the end of the next year result in changes in the balance of surplus on hand. A partial list of items that affect surplus in statutory accounting includes the following:

1. net income or loss for the accounting period;
2. change in liability for unauthorized reinsurance;
3. change in surplus because of appropriations of surplus—i.e., amounts of surplus set aside for some special purpose, such as a contingency fund; and
4. change in the MSVR.

GAAP follows what is known as the **clean surplus theory**, which holds that only certain prescribed items can be debited or credited directly to Retained Earnings. Limiting the activity in the Retained Earnings account keeps that account "clean," and analysis of results of the company's operations becomes easier. Adjustments to Retained Earnings are limited to recording items such as (1) the result of the current accounting period's operations as shown by net income, including realized gains or losses, and (2) dividends to stockholders.

Thus, in GAAP, no adjustments to Retained Earnings result from changes in nonadmitted assets, changes in liability for unauthorized reinsurance, or appropriations of surplus that are mandatory in SAP, because these items are not applicable to GAAP. However, the following items would appear in separate lines in the equity section of a GAAP Balance Sheet:

1. net unrealized gains or losses for the accounting period;
2. appropriations of retained earnings, if any; and
3. the MSVR. As previously discussed, this item can either be treated as an appropriation of retained earnings or can be included in the Retained Earnings account balance.

Federal Income Taxes

The federal income tax liability shown in statutory financial statements represents only the current year's tax as determined in accordance with the Internal Revenue Code. On the other hand, the federal income tax liability shown in GAAP statements represents the current year's liability plus the company's estimate of deferred taxes, i.e., taxes that, because of timing differences, will be paid in future years rather than in the current year. A **timing difference** refers to a situation in which a figure reported in financial statements differs from the figure shown on the tax return for the same item because the item is recognized in different accounting periods for GAAP and taxation purposes. Timing differences can also apply to situations other than taxation.

Canadian Accounting Compared with U.S. SAP and GAAP

As indicated earlier, Canadian life insurers currently have one accounting language: statutory accounting practices as promulgated by the federal Canadian and British Insurance Companies Act (hereafter referred to as *the Act*) and its related regulations and forms. The Act's objective is the same as that of statutory accounting practices in the United States: to help ensure the solvency of insurance companies and thus protect policyowner interests. Changes to the Act adopted in 1977 and 1978, however, brought about a basis of accounting that bears similarities to GAAP in the United States but that leaves the primary purpose of the Act unchanged. Although official GAAP for Canadian life insurance companies has, as of this writing, not yet been finalized, the Canadian Institute of Chartered Accountants, life insurance company executives, and actuaries are working together toward that goal. So far, only GAAP for the Canadian property and casualty insurance industry has actually been developed and adopted. The following section of this chapter discusses the accounting practices of Canadian life insurers and how those practices compare to both SAP and GAAP in the United States.

Policy Acquisition Costs

In both Canadian accounting and U.S. GAAP, most policy acquisition costs are deferred to future time periods extending over the expected premium-paying period of the relevant policies. This practice is in contrast to U.S. SAP, which requires that such costs be entirely charged to expense in the year the expense is incurred. A difference exists between U.S. GAAP and Canadian practices, however, in the way in which the deferral is handled. Under Canadian practice, acquisition costs are deducted from the policy reserve, and the amount deferred cannot exceed 150 percent of the net-level valuation premium. The **net-level valuation premium** is the portion of the gross premium used to fund the policy benefit reserve on a net-level basis. Under U.S. GAAP, acquisition costs are set up as an asset, and the only restriction on the amount that may be deferred is that such amounts must be recoverable from future premium revenues.

Nonadmitted Assets

Like U.S. GAAP, Canadian law permits the presence of certain assets in the Balance Sheet that are considered nonadmitted assets under U.S. SAP and thus do not appear on the SAP Balance Sheet. However, one difference from U.S. GAAP is that, under Canadian practices, the sum of the nonadmitted assets is treated as an appropriation of retained earnings and appears as a separate component of stockholders' equity in the financial statements.

Marketable Securities

Bonds

In Canadian practice, as in SAP in the United States, bonds are carried at amortized cost. However, one significant difference between Canadian practices and those in the United States concerns an adjustment that is made in Canada when a gain or loss results from the sale of bonds. Canadian insurers do not recognize the entire amount of any gain or loss as a lump sum in the accounting period during which the bond was sold. Instead, the gain or loss is amortized on a straight-line basis from the date of sale to the date the bond was scheduled to mature, subject to one limitation: the amortization period cannot exceed twenty years.

The rationale behind amortizing the gain or loss on the sale of a bond after it has been sold is that any such gain or loss incurred is part of an overall financial plan. For example, a company might deliberately sell an 8 percent bond at considerably less than its face value in order to invest the proceeds at a much higher rate of return that will continue to be earned for as long as the bond would have been held had the sale not occurred. In such circumstances, the company would realize a net gain in the long run, justifying amortization of the loss suffered at the time of the sale. Thus, part of the balance in a Canadian insurer's Bonds Owned account might derive from bonds no longer owned by the company.

Equities

In Canada, equity securities—principally preferred and common stocks—are reported in financial statements at an adjusted cost value. An equity's original cost is modified by two adjustments. One adjustment projects realized gains or losses over a period of time in a manner similar to the adjustment of bonds discussed above. A second adjustment achieves a leveling effect on the asset values reported for equity securities. This effect is similar to that achieved in the United States by use of the MSVR. This leveling adjustment is based on the difference between the book values and market values of the affected securities at the end of each year. In Canada, the amount of the adjustment is not the whole amount of the difference, as in the United States, but instead is 15 percent of the difference in values. The adjustment is added to or deducted from asset values and the current year's income. The effect of the two adjustments is to eliminate substantially the immediate, or current-year, impact of (1) realized gains or losses on stock investments and (2) market value changes.

Permanent impairments. In Canada, a permanent impairment in the value of equity securities requires an immediate write-down for the loss in value of a permanently impaired marketable security. This treatment is similar to U.S. GAAP.

Mortgage Loans

Canadian accounting practice is to carry mortgage loans at their unpaid principal balance adjusted for amortization of any premiums or discounts, as is the case in the United States under GAAP and SAP. However, unlike U.S. practice, when mortgage loans are sold, realized gains or losses are amortized on a straight-line basis for a period of time running from the date of sale to the date of maturity, but not to exceed twenty years. This amortizing of income or loss across a time span covering future Income Statements and Balance Sheets is the same treatment as that described above for realized gains or losses on marketable securities.

Real Estate

Canadian accounting methods for real estate are similar to those prescribed for U.S. SAP: (1) property is usually valued at cost less accumulated depreciation and (2) real estate mortgages payable are reported as a reduction of the asset value rather than as a liability. Unlike U.S. SAP, however, upward adjustments to the real estate's carrying value, based on appraised value, are allowable. However, upward adjustments require regulatory approval. These practices are in contrast to U.S. GAAP, which (1) requires that mortgages be shown as liabilities and (2) does not permit the use of appraised values that are higher than book values. For 1986 and subsequent years, though, the Superintendent of Insurance, Canada, has indicated that real estate may be revalued during periodic appraisals.

Policy Reserves

Amendments to the Act provide for policy reserves to be computed on a net-level basis. That is, the amount of an incoming premium used to fund the reserve is assumed to be level over a period of years. Such reserves must be computed by using interest and mortality assumptions deemed by the company to be realistic and up-to-date. The company cannot use the assumptions of the mortality table in use at the time the policy was written if that table no longer reflects current mortality assumptions. This accounting policy is similar to U.S. SAP and is in sharp contrast to U.S. GAAP. Under U.S. GAAP, once a company makes certain interest, mortality, and lapse assumptions for a block of policies, in most cases, the company must continue to use those assumptions, even if they are no longer accurate. Canadian companies need not adhere to their original reserve assumptions.

Additional reserves

Canadian accounting practices permit additional policy reserves, as do U.S. SAP and GAAP. That is, in all three systems, a company can hold reserves in excess of the amount actuarially required, thus providing the company with an extra measure of safety. When such contingency reserves are not needed, they can be used to pay policy dividends. If and when additional policy reserves are set up, the extra amounts must be disclosed in financial statements. In both Canadian practice and U.S. GAAP, additional reserves are treated as appropriations of retained earnings and therefore do not affect current-year income.

Solvency Reserves

Canadian accounting practices prescribe that certain solvency reserves, or required reserves, be appropriated from surplus and reported in the stockholders' equity section of the Balance Sheet. The most common solvency reserves provide for protection in the following areas:

- *fluctuations in investment valuations.* The value of an asset at the time financial statements are prepared is likely to be different from the value at the time the asset was acquired. Valuations also change from the end of one year to the end of the next year.
- *foreign currency.* Assets purchased with foreign currency and carried on the company's books at cost will likely have a different value at the end of each year and at the time the asset is sold because of fluctuations in the values of foreign currency.
- *reinsurance.* A solvency reserve account is protection against any potential loss from reinsurance that has been ceded to companies not registered in Canada.
- *miscellaneous assets.* Losses could develop in other asset accounts because of various circumstances. One reserve account can be established to cover all such miscellaneous assets.

Comparison of Canadian solvency reserve practices with accounting for reserves in U.S. GAAP and SAP is difficult because reserves are held for various purposes. Solvency reserves are similar to some reserves found in U.S. SAP. However, under U.S. SAP, such reserves are shown as liabilities whereas in U.S. GAAP and Canadian reserve accounting, solvency reserves are included in the equity section of the Balance Sheet and are not included in accounts of the Income Statement.

U.S. GAAP permits but does not require solvency reserves. If solvency reserves are established, U.S. GAAP requires that they be classified as "Appropriations of Retained Earnings."

Deferred Federal Income Taxes

The Act and related regulations do not address the issue of deferring federal income taxes. Thus, a variety of practices have evolved in Canadian insurance companies. A majority of life insurance companies do not defer taxes on their financial statements. Of the companies that do defer taxes, approximately half do so on a basis comparable to U.S. GAAP, while the other companies report the deferred liability at its present value. In Canada, the practice of discounting the tax liability to its present value is followed by some life and health insurers in the absence of a defined GAAP, but not by other insurance companies. In the United States, such practice is not acceptable under GAAP for insurers.

Key Terms

GAAP (generally accepted accounting principles)
liquidation
conservatism
holding company
policy acquisition costs
developmental costs
unlisted assets
permanently impaired securities
gross premium
loading
net expense premium
modified reserves
clean surplus theory
net-level valuation premium

SAP (statutory accounting practices)
liquidation approach
going-concern concept
realization principle
capitalization
systematic and rational allocation
mandatory redemption feature
realizable value
net premium
net benefit premium
net-level reserves
lock-in concept
timing differences

Review Questions and Exercises

1. Compare the liquidation approach to accounting with the going-concern approach. Which approach results in a more conservative picture of a company's finances?
2. What is the lock-in concept?
3. List some ways in which GAAP financial statements and SAP financial statements differ.

4. Obtain copies of your company's SAP and GAAP financial statements (if applicable). Look at the Balance Sheets of these statements and see what differences you can find in the totals of similarly listed assets and liabilities.
5. Do Canadian accounting practices more closely resemble U.S. GAAP or U.S. SAP? In which ways do they resemble U.S. SAP?

15
Planning and Budgeting

Learning Objectives

After reading this chapter, you should be able to:

- Distinguish between operations planning and strategic planning
- List different functions and topics that are the subjects of strategic planning and operations planning
- Describe different types of budgeting methods
- Discuss the respective advantages and disadvantages of top-down budgeting and bottom-up budgeting

Introduction

Much of this text has been devoted to the methods and procedures for recording accounting transactions that have already taken place. However, accounting information is also used to prepare for future events. This chapter discusses how a company prepares for the future through the activities known as planning and budgeting and how accounting information is essential to the planning and budgeting processes.

Planning

Constant changes in the insurance and financial services environment have made life and health insurance companies aware of the importance of comprehensive planning in achieving and maintaining growth, financial soundness, and profitability. More than ever, the survival of a life insurance company depends on its ability to adapt to a changing environment and to plan for the future. The activity known as **planning** consists of (1) setting goals, (2) determining company policy in accordance with managerial philosophy, (3) anticipating future events that may affect corporate performance, and (4) devising the strategies, methods, and procedures necessary to achieve desired results. Often, however, the unique and long-term nature of life insurance products makes planning difficult. Nonetheless, because the environment in which insurers operate has become increasingly complex, comprehensive planning is more important than ever.

Accounting data has an important place in comprehensive planning. Accurate compilation of accounting data is necessary to ensure the accuracy and relevance of an insurer's plans. Reported dollar totals must be accurate at the outset of the planning process so that managerial assumptions are based on correct and realistic amounts. In addition, proper and accurate accounting procedures are required throughout the planning process so that management can determine whether the company's financial plans are, in fact, being met. The management of insurance companies and other business concerns uses accounting data in various planning techniques for most, if not all, areas of operations. In general, a company's planning activities can be divided into two major segments: *operations planning* and *strategic planning*.

Operations Planning and Strategic Planning

Operations planning is primarily concerned with the short-term. Because of the complex and unpredictable financial environment, however, the definition of "the short-term" has become less universal in recent years. Some insurers consider any span of time up to five years to be the short-term, while other companies may restrict the scope of their operations planning to one or two years. Although its time frame varies from company to company, operations planning in most companies focuses primarily on day-to-day activities.

Each area of an insurance company has specific uses for operations planning. Figure 15-1 lists the topics that are typically covered in operations planning for the major insurance company functions.

In contrast to operations planning, **strategic planning** is concerned with the long-term. The time period past which a company's plans can be defined as *strategic* plans depends on the company's managerial philosophy. One company's strategic plans may focus on the period beginning two years from when the plans are made, while another company's strategic plans may focus only on activities five years or more into the future. As with operations planning, certain types of activities and goals are the primary topics of strategic planning. Figure 15-2 shows the topics of strategic planning for the same functional areas that are listed

FIGURE 15-1
Topics of operations planning.

Marketing	Advertising Plans and Promotions
	Agents' Compensation Plans
	Sales Forecasts
Risk Selection	Underwriting Targets and Guidelines
	Reinsurance Policies
Policyowner Service	Policy Issue Procedures
	Service Standards
Financial Planning	Cash Flow Planning
	Product Profitability Goals
Investments	Performance Planning
	Tax Planning
	Liquidity Planning
	Legal Restrictions
Human Resources	Recruiting Plans
	Wage and Salary Plans
	Job Design and Analysis
Electronic Data Processing	Software Needs
	Short-Term Capacity Requirements

FIGURE 15-2
Topics of strategic planning.

Marketing	Marketing Identification and Penetration
	Agency Development Strategy
	Customer/Product Suitability
Risk Selection	Underwriting Strategy
	Underwriting Standards Analysis
Policyowner Service	Desired Service Levels
	Policy Processing Alternatives
Financial Planning	Economic Research and Forecasting
	Capital Adequacy
	Allocation of Capital
Investments	Investment Strategy
	Risk Analysis
	Legal Restrictions
Human Resources	Long-Term Personnel Requirements
	Personnel Policies
Electronic Data Processing	Hardware and Software Needs
	Long-Term Capacity Requirements

in Figure 15-1. Note that overlap can exist between the topics covered by the two types of planning. For example, the legal restrictions placed on a company's investments are subjects of both operations and strategic planning.

Both strategic planning and operations planning call for the preparation of **budgets,** which are detailed financial plans for a company's operations over a given period of time. Approaches to planning and budgeting activities are numerous and diverse. When developing plans and budgets, however, companies must balance growth, risk, and profit. While even the simplest planning and budgeting techniques can produce valuable results, optimum results are achieved when the two activities are combined. In addition, the best results for a company are often achieved when all functional areas of a company have input into the planning and budgeting processes. Planning will not be effective if the accounting department is the only participant in the process. This chapter presents an overview of planning and budgeting activities and explains some planning and budgeting terminology commonly in use.

Factors in strategic and operations planning

Formalized planning focuses attention on common goals and helps to coordinate the efforts of managers in many different areas—e.g., marketing, underwriting, claims, accounting, and investments. If long-term planning decisions are usually made only after a specific need has arisen, the result is generally intuitive decisions, spur-of-the-moment decisions, and decisions made during a period of crisis. This type of decision making is generally unsatisfactory because it makes inefficient use of a company's resources and often allows insufficient time to develop and implement plans to meet newly discovered needs. A formalized planning process helps to avoid these problems.

An important step in both strategic and operations planning is the development of specific corporate goals and objectives. If goals are not specific enough, management may not be able to determine whether the goals have been met, even if accurate accounting data is available. For example, a particular company's objective might be to grow at a rate of 20 percent per year for the next five years. However, an objective of 20 percent annual growth is not specific enough to allow an accountant, executive, or potential investor to measure accurately the overall results of the company's operations. If the company succeeds in increasing assets and premium income by 20 percent but at the same time incurs substantial financial losses, is the company accomplishing its objective? Without specifically defining both "growth" and the standards used to measure it, one could not determine whether such losses were anticipated or whether the expected growth rate had been achieved. If premium income increases by 20 percent at the expense of heavier-than-anticipated underwriting losses, the marketing department may claim that the desired growth rate has been achieved, but the underwriting department could disagree.

While management often recognizes the need to establish specific plans for the future, the degree of flexibility used in formulating plans varies widely among companies. Defining objectives and setting specific and realistic quantitative goals is a complex process. Management must realize that any plan extending several years into the future is subject to many unforeseen forces that can affect any business. To be able to counter the effects of unexpected events, a company must create plans that are flexible enough to be changed as circumstances change.

When formulating a life and health insurance company's strategic and operational plans, management considers many past and prospective factors that can influence decisions. Some specific items of information provided by or used by accountants and analysts in developing a company's plans are the company's

1. performance as compared with similar companies in the life insurance industry;
2. geographic market area and the forecast for economic activity in the area;
3. amount of insurance in force;
4. product mix, which may be analyzed by line of business, type of policy, and other categories;
5. reinsurance requirements;
6. sales force and other human resources;
7. investment portfolio mix;
8. capital and surplus;
9. gains from operations;
10. dividends paid to stockholders; and
11. premium and income taxes to be paid to various governmental authorities.

Identifying potential problem areas is another important step in the planning process. One common way of anticipating problem areas is to analyze past operations and identify past goals and whether they have been achieved. This analysis should consider not only financial statistics from the company's past performance, but also economic projections applicable to the insurance industry, the business community, and the national economy. If the planning process does not allow for inflation, changing interest rates, and industry trends, management projections may leave the company unprepared to function effectively in certain environments. For example, the rapid increase in interest rates during the late 1970s led many policyowners to take advantage of the 5-8 percent interest rates available on policy loans. Some of these policyowners borrowed the cash values of their whole life policies and invested the proceeds in financial instruments that yielded higher returns than were available by leaving the funds on deposit with their insurers. As a result, many insurers experienced severe cash flow problems and reduced investment income. Now that they are aware of the possibility and potential consequences of such interest rate fluctuations, insurers can plan for such occurrences.

Potential problems resulting from a company's planning activities can also arise if management sets conflicting goals. For example, one company objective may be to increase insurance in force by 50 percent over a five-year period. Such a goal may be incompatible with another goal, such as increasing profits and surplus. These goals could be incompatible since the high production costs for new business may make a simultaneous increase in profits and sales volume unlikely.

Different ways of reaching goals and objectives are often available to insurers, and often more than one solution to any given problem is possible. For example, in planning for new-product development, the marketing and actuarial departments should first narrow down the new product possibilities to those having the best prospects of meeting projected revenue and expense goals. Similarly, the marketing department should plan to achieve its sales targets at a cost that falls within managerially prescribed limitations on expenditures. In addition, the alternative plans developed by each department should give the company the capability to adapt to changing economic conditions. A company planning to market tax-deferred annuities, for example, should have at least one alternative marketing strategy in case the federal government diminishes or removes that product's favorable tax status.

As part of the planning process, management generally develops a model that is capable of producing a variety of financial statement projections. These projections would show the expected results of planned operations after many different events and combinations of events occurred. A **model** can be defined as a mathematical representation that shows the relationships among the variables in a particular problem or situation. In terms of strategic planning or operations planning for an insurer, a model would show the financial effects of different economic and other situations on each decision that the planners could make. By constructing models, planners can determine the best course or courses of action to take within the context of many different situations.

The human relations factor in planning and budgeting. As with most employment-related activities, human relations are important in accounting, planning, and budgeting. Final responsibility for all company functions and operations rests with managerial staff. As a result, top levels of management generally review and analyze the assumptions underlying budget projections and long-term plans to be sure they are both reasonable and appropriate. Overly optimistic or pessimistic planning projections by management can have a disastrous effect on a company. Expectations that are excessively optimistic may result in production objectives that are difficult to attain. Such objectives can strain the capacities of personnel and thus cause dissatisfaction. Pessimistic expectations, on the other hand, tend to result in easily obtainable objectives. Objectives that fail to challenge employees do not make full use of a company's human resources. For any type of planning to be most effective, employees must believe that the company's objectives are attainable, but not without those employees' best efforts. In addition, managerial staff should be aware of the best ways to motivate different employees and groups of employees so that these objectives can be attained.

Communication is also essential to an effective planning process. The results as well as the objectives of the planning process must be communicated well in order for the plan to be implemented properly throughout the company. Lower management as well as rank-and-file employees must be aware of specific company and departmental goals. The recordkeeping requirements needed to measure progress toward or fulfillment of these goals must also be clear. One way in which progress is monitored is through the comparison of a company's operational performance to the projected budget amounts for the same time period. The next section of this chapter introduces the different budgeting techniques that are available to insurers and other businesses for use in their planning process.

Budgeting

As we noted earlier, *budgets* are financial plans that show a company's anticipated income or expenditures over a specified period of time. Budgets for different spans of time can generally be classified into three categories: short-term budgets, long-term budgets, and rolling or continuous budgets. **Short-term budgets** generally address a one-year period and relate mainly to a company's operations during that period of time. **Long-term budgets,** on the other hand, address periods of two, three, five, or ten years. Budgets that project into future years should generally allow for income and expenditures that correspond to the company's strategic planning objectives. For example, long-term budgets are often used to plan for the large capital expenditures that will be necessary to the future operations of the company. Also, budgets for longer periods try to project the company's future potential sources of capital.

Many companies also prepare rolling budgets. A **rolling budget,** also known as a **continuous budget,** allows a company to maintain projections for a certain time period into the future. A company with a rolling budget for a time period of one year would thus create a one-year budget and then update it at certain intervals throughout the year so that the projections always apply to the coming twelve-month period. For example, assume that the Practical Life Insurance Company creates a budget for the period January 1, 1990, to December 31, 1990. If Practical Life uses a rolling budget that is updated quarterly, then a new budget would be prepared on April 1, 1990, to reflect the period from that date until March 31, 1991. The procedure would be repeated for July 1, 1990, to June 30, 1991; October 1, 1990, to September 30, 1991; and so on. Each new budget would reflect revised amounts projected for the coming one-year period, even though the period itself changed during the year.

Budgets are used in a wide variety of circumstances and for various purposes. At one company, a budget may give formal authorization to spend money, while at another company, a budget may be used as no more than a planning guideline or target goal. Budgets can be used as management tools for the following purposes:

- to control and reduce expenses through monitoring of performance as well as evaluation of personnel and financial operations,
- to communicate information among various levels of the company,
- to motivate personnel, and
- to help in financial planning.

The sophistication and complexity of budgets differ from company to company. Budgets also vary greatly in scope, ranging from those that include only some expenses to those that include all items of income and expense.

Types of Budgets

When a company is creating budgets for its different planning needs, various budgeting methods can be used. Budgets can be classified in a number of ways, such as by subject matter, by degree of variability, and by type of approach.

Classified by subject matter

When budgets are classified by subject matter, three types of budgets are common: capital expenditure budgets, operational budgets, and financial budgets. **Capital expenditure budgets** show a company's plans for management of the company's fixed assets. (See Figure 15-3 for an example of a capital expenditure budget.) Capital budgeting refers to the process of evaluating, selecting, and acquiring long-term assets, such as furniture, computer equipment, and buildings. Because of the long-term nature of capital expenditure budgets, they are used extensively in strategic planning.

A budget covering part or all of a company's operations is referred to as an **operational budget** (see Figure 15-4). Operational budgets set forth the income or expenses that a company expects over a definite period of time. These plans may cover only a small subdivision of a company's operations, such as a single department's expenses, or may represent the plans for an entire line function,

FIGURE 15-3
A capital expenditure budget.

**Design and Construction Summary Budget
for a Proposed New Facility
Expected Completion Date: July 19X7**

Demolition	$ 30,000
General construction ($25.66 per square foot)	8,536,851
Mechanical	1,979,511
Electrical	1,367,360
Vertical transportation	605,498
Construction manager fee	375,941
Sitework (including landscaping and surface parking)	1,400,000
Parking deck	754,784
Renovation of existing building	1,067,209
Architect/Engineers	967,029
Construction contingency reserve	427,105
Estimated total	$17,511,288

FIGURE 15-4
An operational budget.

The format and content of all budgets vary widely among companies. This exhibit illustrates just one of many possibilities for presenting budgetary data. In this particular case, the company has facilitated decision making by providing comparative data and combining an operational budget with a financial report showing current-year and prior-year actual dollars.

ABC INSURANCE COMPANY
OPERATING BUDGET AND REPORT
for the period ending December 31, 19X7

INCOME/EXPENSE ELEMENT $000 omitted ( ) = negative amount	PRIOR YEAR Actual Dollars	CURRENT YEAR Actual Dollars	CURRENT YEAR Budget Dollars	VARIANCES Dollars	PERCENT OF PREMIUM Actual	PERCENT OF PREMIUM Budget
Net premiums	11,030	13,523	12,686	837	100.0	100.0
Policyholder benefits	7,797	10,177	7,813	(2,364)	75.3	61.6
Increase in reserves	1,664	2,643	1,681	(962)	19.6	13.3
Commissions & fees	1,613	1,815	1,822	7	13.4	14.4
Operating taxes and services	355	431	418	(13)	3.2	3.3
Operating expense	1,470	1,545	1,537	(8)	11.4	12.1
Provision for uncollected premium	(21)	19	5	(14)	.1	—
Policyholder dividends	192	255	157	(98)	1.9	1.2
Total underwriting expenses	103	270	218	(52)	2.0	1.8
	13,173	17,155	13,651	(3,504)	126.9	107.7
Underwriting income (loss) before tax	(2,143)	(3,632)	(965)	(2,667)	(26.9)	(7.7)
Federal income tax (refund)	(1,006)	(1,800)	(655)	1,145	(13.3)	(5.2)
Net Underwriting Income (Loss)	(1,137)	(1,832)	(310)	(1,522)	(13.6)	(2.5)
Gross investment income	1,906	1,863	1,961	(98)	N/A	N/A
Less: Investment expense	16	15	15	—		
Internal investment expense	53	40	63	23		
Investment income before tax	1,837	1,808	1,883	(75)		
Federal income tax	415	319	434	115		
Net Investment Income	1,422	1,489	1,449	40		
Earnings Before Capital Gains (Losses)	285	(343)	1,139	(1,482)		
Gross realized gains (losses)	(422)	141	—	149		
Federal income tax	(67)	56	—	(56)		
Net Realized Gains (Losses)	(253)	93	—	93		
Foreign Exchange Income (Expense)	(6)	(2)	—	(2)		
Net Income (Loss)	26	(252)	1,139	(1,391)		

such as underwriting or marketing. The same operational budget can be used for two or three purposes. For example, a cash flow statement, one type of operational budget, can be used in financial statement analysis as well as in management of the company's operations. **Financial budgets** include a company's plans regarding its asset, liability, and capital accounts.

Classified by degree of variability

When budgets are classified by the degree of variability inherent in them, they are often referred to as fixed-amount or flexible-amount budgets. In a **fixed-amount budget,** the dollar amounts are generally not subject to change unless the changes have been approved by management. As a result, fixed-amount budgets are of limited managerial usefulness if projected amounts of income and expenses are uncertain. Fixed-amount budgets provide no alternative guidelines or financial predictions when actual experience differs from the assumptions underlying the fixed budget figures. Fixed-amount budgets are normally used when the budget's objective is to reduce or limit expenditures. For example, if $10,000,000 is allocated to a certain division within a company for the coming fiscal year, the division generally cannot spend more than this fixed amount, nor would the division receive more than this amount. In certain cases, overspending may be allowed, but a good explanation to management of the reasons for the overspending would typically be expected. The division can, of course, spend less than the budgeted amount.

A **flexible-amount budget,** on the other hand, provides one or more alternative sets of figures that can be used under the different circumstances that may arise during the course of a budgeting period. For example, assume that a company is expecting $25,000,000 in new business and is trying to budget for the coming year's commission expenses. Since the exact amount of sales often cannot be predicted, the company might prepare budgets for several sales figures that approximate the projected dollar amount. A flexible-amount budget prepared for both higher and lower sales experience might show three columns of possible commission expenses based on $22,000,000, $25,000,000, and $28,000,000 of new business. In each case, the amount budgeted for commissions and other direct sales expenses would be different.

Classified by type of approach

Three basic approaches to preparing a budget are top-down budgeting, bottom-up budgeting, and zero-base budgeting (ZBB). In practice, various combinations of the three approaches are generally used.

Top-down budgeting. In the **top-down budgeting** approach, upper levels of management establish the company's budget with little or no participation from lower ranks of employees. Often, the amounts budgeted are based on a combination of (1) experience reflecting prior years' decisions and (2) management's desires and objectives for the company's future. The primary advantages of top-down budgeting are that it requires less preparation time than other budget creation methods and reflects management's intentions more accurately. One disadvantage of top-down budgeting is that staff cooperation in budget implementation is apt to be minimal. Lower-management personnel, if they provide little or no input to the development of the budget, might exhibit a lack of commitment to meet goals. Another disadvantage is that budget figures developed exclusively by executives may be inaccurate or less realistic than those that could be developed by lower-level employees with hands-on experience in areas where the budget will be implemented.

Bottom-up budgeting. The converse of top-down budgeting is **bottom-up budgeting,** in which employees in lower organizational ranks play a key role in determining their own budgets. Final budgetary approval remains the responsibility of top management, however. The two major advantages of bottom-up budgeting are (1) high-quality informational input and (2) employee support and cooperation. The monetary projections obtained in bottom-up budgeting are generally more accurate and realistic than those obtained in top-down budgeting. The people in lower echelons of the organization are in a better position to determine which costs can be cut and which proposed budgetary measures will be effective. Also, lower-level employee participation in the budgetary process increases the likelihood that the company will achieve its budgeting goals.

One disadvantage of bottom-up budgeting is the amount of time consumed in preparation. With the bottom-up approach, all levels of management must spend more time in the budgeting process than would generally be required with the top-down approach. Lower-level managers must devote time to budgeting, and top management must also devote additional time (1) to make effective use of lower management's input and (2) to properly evaluate managerial recommendations. If top management does not spend enough time in the bottom-up budgetary process, the end result will often fail to meet top management's objectives. As a result, lower-management recommendations may be too easily met and budget goals may offer little or no challenge to lower-level employees.

The top-down and bottom-up approaches to budgeting can each result in negative motivation for employees. For example, if management claims to adhere to the bottom-up approach and then (1) disregards or overrules the recommendations of advisors and lower-level managers or (2) switches methods from bottom-up to top-down in the middle of the budgeting process, adverse results in morale and attitude are likely to occur. Such practices can cause lower-level employees to lose the motivation to put forth their best efforts.

Zero-base budgeting. Unlike the budgeting approaches discussed previously, which can be applied to both income and expense budgets, zero-base budgeting (ZBB) generally applies only to expense budgets. In **zero-base budgeting,** a manager begins with the premise that no resources will be allocated for the following year unless and until each dollar to be spent is justified and is in accord with departmental plans as well as the company's overall plans. Zero-base budgeting operates on the premise that each organizational unit, function, and activity should cost-justify its existence each year. ZBB differs from conventional approaches to budgeting which assume that current levels of spending are justified and therefore can be taken as reasonable starting points for developing the next year's budget. No such assumption is made with ZBB.

Many results of ZBB come from the financial analysis and planning requirements that are imposed on all levels of management in order to carry out the zero-based budgetary process. In this process, every operation must be evaluated in terms of efficiency and need. Alternative courses of action must be created to prepare for the different needs that may arise during the coming year. Other advantages of ZBB are (1) the high quality of information contained in the budgets because of extensive employee participation and (2) the training and education that occurs as a result of employees' contributions to the budget-building process. Although such training and educational benefits are indirect, they can be quite valuable to the company.

The main disadvantage of ZBB is its high cost in terms of the time consumed in performing the extra work that is not part of the conventional budgeting process. A great deal of extra work is involved in collecting and analyzing data in order to (1) cost-justify every item in a budget and (2) prepare additional budgets that represent alternative courses of action. Another disadvantage of ZBB is that the executives who are best qualified to review and evaluate alternative courses of action are also generally least able to devote much time to the review and evaluation process. In the context of budgetary review, "best qualified" refers to having both varied experience and a company-wide perspective of operations. Since qualified executives and managers can rarely find enough time to perform all of the steps required by "pure" zero-base budgeting, most companies practice modified ZBB. With a modified zero-base budget, either the budgetary process is only partially zero-based or the zero-based process is performed on a less-than-annual basis.

Budget Preparation

Because use of zero-base budgeting is not widespread, the starting point of budget development in most companies is usually the prior year's allocated amounts. The budgeted amounts of the previous year are generally modified to reflect desired or anticipated changes for the coming year. Often, a budget system will consist of a master budget, supported by numerous detailed supporting budgets. A **master budget** can generally be described as a comprehensive plan that encompasses the financial projections for an entire organization. **Supporting budgets** are used to define and articulate the projections and objectives that are generally stated in a company's master budget plan. Examples of supporting budgets for a life insurance company include the following:

(1) a *sales* budget to project first-year and renewal premium income, as well as selling costs related to that income;
(2) an *operating expense* budget to project general expenses;
(3) a *cash-flow* budget to estimate the amount of cash that will become available from insurance operations for the purpose of investment;
(4) an *investment* budget to project the types of investments to be made, as well as the amounts of expected investment-related income and expenses; and
(5) a *capital expenditures* budget to outline or detail any plans for major expenditures of capital.

As indicated earlier, expenses related to marketing, investments, and capital expenditures may be set forth in separate specialized expense budgets, or they may be combined into one overall operating expense budget. In larger companies, with relatively autonomous departmental or functional structures, specialized budgets are often more appropriate. While many smaller companies also use specialized budgets, some smaller companies find the most desirable and efficient method of budgetary preparation to be the creation of a single expense budget for the entire organization.

Regardless of whether a company prepares a single budget or a master budget with supporting budgets, the objective of the budget is the quantitative projection and allocation to each department of all anticipated income and expense items. Each department is theoretically accountable for its share of income and expenses. However, in practice, the degree of responsibility varies significantly depending on the department, the budget item, and the company's operational philosophy. Even though a specific department is generally responsible for its budget, in some circumstances, the department has little actual budgetary control.

For example, the marketing department of a company might be responsible for increasing sales and for the development of new products, such as the investment-oriented products designed and introduced in the early 1980s. However, if the government were to pass tax legislation that was unfavorable to annuities or a company's universal life products, then the marketing department's control over its efforts to increase sales would be greatly diminished. Such a lack of effective control does not render the budget process useless, but the degree of control that a department has over its budget is an important managerial consideration in evaluating how well or how poorly a department has stayed within its budget.

Budget Analysis and Evaluation

Preliminary budget work, such as statistical analysis of a company's operations, provides a great deal of useful information. However, much of a traditional budget's usefulness stems from the analyses of variances from the budget as well as the follow-up actions taken after the budget has been put into operation. Prompt and frequent comparison of actual results with budget expectations is necessary to the validity of a budget. Rarely does the budget follow-up show actual results that coincide exactly with budgeted amounts. Variances must be identified and then classified by type and department in order to determine who bears responsibility for the variances. Many companies make comparisons on a monthly basis, while others do so more frequently. Large variances between budgeted and actual figures, whether from controllable factors, uncontrollable factors, or incorrect assumptions, often result in the creation, as soon as possible, of a revised or updated budget. Rolling budgets make use of this process.

When analyzing budget variances, management has a natural tendency to pay attention only to negative or unfavorable variances from projected figures. However, seemingly favorable variances should also receive close scrutiny to determine whether they are indeed favorable to the company. For example, a department may have been budgeted $38,000 for a given activity but spent only $29,000. On the surface, this expenditure appears to be a favorable variance. Upon reviewing such figures, however, management should attempt to determine the reason for the seemingly superior performance. The favorable variance may have resulted from overly pessimistic projections, indicating that what at first appeared to be a performance that exceeded budget expectations was actually an indication of poor judgment in making budget estimates.

Favorable variances can also be misleading in another manner. Assume, for example, that an investment budget based on a certain prime interest rate projects a 14 percent rate of return on new investments, and that actual experience results in a 15 percent rate of return. The 15 percent rate of return is apparently better than the 14 percent rate that was expected. If the actual prime rate happened to rise by 4 percent during this same period, however, then a 1 percent greater rate of return might actually reflect unsatisfactory investment performance.

Favorable variances can also occur as a result of overzealous or shortsighted actions such as lowering quality standards, delaying training, or changing operating procedures in an attempt to reduce expenses. For example, a dramatic increase in new business that might appear to be a favorable budgetary variance could actually be the result of increasingly lax underwriting standards which may result in extensive losses at a later date.

Committed costs and discretionary costs

In budgetary analysis, company expenditures are often classified as committed costs and discretionary costs. **Committed costs** are expenses that result from decisions or commitments made at an earlier time. Ownership of computer equipment provides one example of committed costs. The depreciation expenses related to computer ownership are a result of a previous decision to acquire the equipment. Another example of a committed cost arises from a mortgagor's promise to maintain property insurance in order to protect the mortgagee-lender. The property insurance premiums paid to protect the mortgaged real estate fall within the committed costs classification. The amount actually spent on committed costs generally does not vary greatly from the amount projected for these costs in a company's budget. On the other hand, for any given *discretionary* cost, no "correct" amount is generally spent. **Discretionary costs** are partially or wholly under the control of current management and are flexible components of an insurer's budget. Advertising, research and development, public relations, and charitable donations are examples of discretionary costs.

The concepts of committed costs and discretionary costs are important to planning and budgeting. A company's future committed costs typically appear in the company's present long-term budgets and strategic plans. The committed costs that appear in a company's present budget can also be controlled, to some degree, by current management. Management can decide to sell a company-owned building, for example. Discretionary costs typically are most predominant in a company's short-term budget and operations planning. In a company's rolling budget, the amount of discretionary costs would be constantly changing.

Key Terms

planning	operations planning
strategic planning	model
budgeting	short-term budget
long-term budget	rolling budget
capital expenditure budget	operational budget
financial budget	fixed-amount budget
flexible-amount budget	top-down budgeting
bottom-up budgeting	zero-base budgeting
master budget	supporting budget
committed costs	discretionary costs

Review Questions and Exercises

1. Can the same topic be the subject of strategic planning and operations planning? Give three examples.
2. Why is the development of specific corporate goals and objectives important to the planning process?
3. What type of information is used in developing a company's plans?
4. How can budgets be used as management tools?
5. Does your department use top-down budgeting methods or bottom-up budgeting methods? Is zero-base budgeting used in your company?
6. In what circumstances could an expenditure under budgeted amounts indicate an unfavorable situation for a company?
7. What is the difference between a short-term budget and a rolling budget?
8. Distinguish between discretionary costs and committed costs.

16
Cost Accounting

Learning Objectives

After reading this chapter, you should be able to:

- Enumerate the primary uses of cost accounting in life and health insurance companies
- State ways in which the information gathered by a cost accounting system can be used in the decision-making process
- Describe the difference between an operating cost center and a service cost center
- Describe three basic methods of time analysis
- State typical base units used in determining functional unit costs

Introduction

Companies can determine their financial effectiveness through analysis of various aspects of their operations. By using accounting data to perform this type of analysis, a company's management is involved in the practice of *managerial accounting*. One branch of managerial accounting that provides valuable information is cost accounting. **Cost accounting** accumulates data on current-period actual costs in order to give management unit-cost information. A **unit cost** can be defined as the incurred expense that can be attributed to a single measured unit of work. Knowing the unit cost of products sold or services performed can guide management in (1) predicting future costs; (2) evaluating personnel, operations, and equipment; (3) setting premium and dividend scales; and (4) performing various other managerial activities.

Cost accounting is generally associated with manufacturing and commercial companies, but it has also been used in life and health insurance accounting, although traditionally to a lesser extent. Because of increased competitive pressures in the current financial environment, however, cost accounting has become more important to the life and health insurance industry. This chapter discusses cost accounting in the life insurance industry as well as some of the cost accounting procedures that are commonly used to produce meaningful managerial accounting information.

Before discussing the specifics of cost accounting, students should understand the role of computerization and of automated accounting systems—as described in Chapter 3—in cost accounting. Before extensive computerization of the accounting function, costs had to be recorded, accumulated, and allocated through numerous manual operations. With the advent of advanced accounting information systems, however, expense transactions can easily be identified as applying to a certain product, function, or line of business as they are made. When a company's managerial or financial accounting reports are prepared at the end of an accounting period, the cost accounting system can be programmed to allocate expenses to each area for which the company needs cost information. The cost accounting system can also be designed to provide the information in any number of formats. Costs can be accumulated for GAAP and statutory reporting purposes for presentation in both the company's expense reports and the Analysis of Operations.

The Uses and Purposes of Cost Accounting

Insurers generally use cost accounting for seven primary purposes:

(1) To determine the costs of creating and marketing a company's products so the products can be priced appropriately;
(2) To match the costs incurred during a given accounting period to the income earned in or attributed to that same period;
(3) To determine the costs incurred during a given accounting period for different products, lines of business, or subsidiary companies that the insurer might control;
(4) To give management information that can be used to save money in less productive areas of the company;
(5) To budget the company's resources, either for purposes of holding the company's market share or for expanding, contracting, or changing the focus of the company's operations;
(6) To determine premium and dividend scales for the company's products; and
(7) To maintain and exercise control over operations by evaluating the efficiency of company procedures and personnel. Such control can be

accomplished through comparison of forecasted and actual costs and through the internal control procedures mentioned in Chapter 13.

For financial reporting reasons, the matching of income and costs to specific accounting periods, different products, and different lines of business (#2 and #3 above) has become important to the insurance industry. For GAAP financial statements of stock companies, the American Institute of Certified Public Accountants (AICPA) requires that policy acquisition costs—commissions, underwriting expenses, and other expenses—be deferred and recognized as expenses in future accounting periods when the income associated with these acquisition costs is received. Cost accounting data is used to match income and expenses. On the other hand, statutory accounting requires that a company match its expenses to the products for which the expenses were incurred. Cost accounting facilitates that process, also.

Cost accounting provides information that serves as a valuable management tool for planning and control. Management uses cost information—e.g., total costs for each product being marketed and the costs of performing various functions in company operations—to set target costs for each product or function. Through use of cost accounting information, management can be reasonably assured that these target cost goals are fair and achievable. By accurately projecting costs for a particular product, management can have a better idea of the profits that should be realized upon marketing the product. Future operations often depend on such projections. For example, an insurer's actuarial department relies on the accuracy of output from the company's cost accounting system when setting premium rates on new products. Since newly introduced products generally have smaller profit margins than established products, accurate projections are extremely important when pricing these products.

Basics of an Effective Cost Accounting System

One essential element of an effective cost accounting system is accurate and complete accounting data. Before a company can develop a cost accounting system that will provide management with useful and important information, a general accounting system that produces reliable financial data must already be in place. The information provided by cost accounting is only as reliable as the historical and current data on which the cost accounting system is based.

Another necessary element of an effective cost accounting system is the identification of costs by product lines as well as organizational lines or functions. Many insurance accounting systems provide at least some itemization in cost gathering, usually by department. As cost identification by department becomes more specific, the effectiveness of a company's cost accounting system increases.

Top management participation in the development and implementation of a system is generally considered mandatory to successful cost accounting. Executive participation is typically an effective way of communicating top management's desires and interests to lower levels of management. Such participation also tends to motivate employees to make the cost accounting system work and to make it as useful as possible.

Management must be able to measure long-term plans and budgets against actual performance, even when changes in organizational structure and cost accounting systems have occurred in the interval between financial reports. Therefore, a cost accounting system must be carefully designed to assure that the cost information can meaningfully be compared to previous and future accounting periods.

Cost accounting systems can be developed to analyze and plan for many different aspects of a company's performance. Among the possible types of cost accounting analyses are determinations of marginal costs and functional costs. The remainder of this chapter discusses both the methods of determining these different costs and the uses for this cost information.

Marginal Costs

A **marginal cost** is the additional expense incurred as a result of producing one additional unit of a product or service. Marginal cost information is often useful in determining the monetary effect of a specific action and, in certain cases, whether an action should or should not be taken. Once a certain volume of production or sales has been reached, the decision whether to produce or sell more units involves different cost considerations than the earlier decision to produce or sell the initial amount. Some of the costs involved in producing the initial amount may not apply to the additional production. Alternatively, the additional production may incur additional costs not required for the initial amount of production. Thus, the marginal cost of each additional unit is different from the unit cost of the initial amount produced. The decision whether to increase production must take into account the marginal unit cost.

If an agent produces 50 new applications per year at a total expense of X dollars, the cost of producing the 51st application would be the subject of a marginal cost study. The cost of producing the 52nd application and then the 53rd application would also be subjects for marginal cost analyses. Production of the 51st application would probably not cost as much as one-fiftieth of X dollars. Most of the agent's total expenses—advertising, use of office supplies and other equipment, and required office space—are not affected when only a single additional application is produced. Perhaps additional transportation or telephone expenses would be incurred, but they would probably be minimal in comparison to the total production costs.

A simple example should help explain the concept of marginal cost analysis in an insurance company. The following table (Figure 16-1) refers to the costs incurred in the Policy Issue Department of the Principle Life Insurance Company, a hypothetical life company. This example assumes that no salary increases occurred during these years. Note that as the number of policies issued increases each year, total expenses do not rise in proportion to the rise in costs already incurred. That is, the marginal cost of producing an extra 1,000 applications does not significantly affect the unit cost of the first 50,000 applications.

As you can see in Figure 16-1, in the first year, 40 employees issued 50,000 policies. These 40 employees had total salaries and other employee-related expenses (such as fringe benefits; office space; and furniture, equipment, and telephone expenses) of $600,000—the equivalent of $15,000 per employee. Printed-form expenses of $75,000 also related directly to the policies issued during Year 1. The sum, $675,000, represents an overall unit cost for Year 1 of $13.50 per policy issued ($675,000 ÷ 50,000).

When the number of policies issued in the second year increased by 1,000 to 51,000, the department manager determined that the present work force could handle the additional work load without a significant change in productivity. While this decision did not affect the amount of salaries and other employee-related expenses, the decision did result in a $1,500 increase in printed-form

FIGURE 16-1
Costs incurred in Principle Life's Policy Issue Department.

	(1) Number of policies issued	(2) Number of employees	(3) Employee-related expenses	(4) Printed Forms	(5) Total Expenses (3) + (4)	(6) Unit Cost (5) ÷ (1)
Year 1	50,000	40	$600,000	$75,000	$675,000	$13.50*
	+1,000			+1,500	+1,500**	$ 1.50***
Year 2	51,000	40	$600,000	$76,500	$676,500	$13.26*
	+1,000	+1	+15,000	+1,500	+16,500**	$16.50***
Year 3	52,000	41	$615,000	$78,000	$693,000	$13.33*

  * Unit cost for each policy
 ** Marginal cost for additional 1,000 policies
*** Marginal unit cost for each additional policy

expenses. Because this $1,500 amount is the only additional expense incurred in issuing the additional 1,000 policies, the marginal unit cost of each additional policy is $1.50. With the addition of 1,000 policies for this amount of expense, the overall unit cost per policy issued in Year 2 declined to $13.26.

In Year 3, an additional 1,000 policies were issued so that the total number of policies processed by the department increased to 52,000. The manager determined that, to handle this additional work load effectively, an additional employee must be hired. As a result of adding an employee, salaries and other employee-related expenses increased by $15,000. As with the earlier addition of 1,000 issued policies to the department's work load, policy-form printing expenses increased again by $1,500. These increased expenses resulted in a total increase of $16,500, representing a marginal unit cost of $16.50 per additional policy. The end result of adding one person to the department and issuing another 1,000 policies was thus an increase of the total departmental expenses to $693,000, representing an overall unit cost of $13.33 per issued policy.

Note that when the manager faced the situation of processing an additional 1,000 policies in the third year, the marginal unit cost per additional policy jumped from $1.50 to $16.50 per policy because of the hiring of an additional employee. Statistics of this type are useful to managers in determining the optimal production that can result from resources available and currently in use. These statistics generally cannot be considered on their own, however, when deciding whether to use additional resources, such as the new employee hired in the example. The statistics often must be compared to the marginal unit costs and other costs that might be incurred if other, alternative actions were taken.

For example, if an additional employee was *not* hired in the third year, the manager might have to pay current employees overtime pay that would still raise the marginal unit cost of issuing additional policies. The necessary overtime might even exceed the cost of a new employee. In addition, reduced accuracy in performing job duties might result, thus increasing the costs of policy issuance because of the mistakes that would have to be corrected. If no additional employee were hired *and* no employees worked overtime, more time would probably be required to issue the policies and more policy lapses could result, thus causing a reduction in the amount of business written by the company.

Functional Costs

Another subdivision of cost accounting that is applicable to the business of life and health insurance is *functional cost accounting*. A functional cost accounting system combines all component costs of a particular series of operations into one total, without regard to traditional departmental lines or account classifications. For example, the cost of collecting renewal premiums is determined by collecting cost data from all departments involved in the collection process, not just from the cashiers' section that receives and records premiums. Other costs incurred in receiving premiums include printing and postage expenses, machine costs for preparing and mailing premium notices, and the indirect costs of other departments involved in premium collection. The costs of all of these operations would be included in a functional cost analysis of the renewal premium collection process.

The greatest advantage that management derives from using a functional cost accounting system is generally the ability to determine costs without concentrating on organizational structures. A functional cost accounting system allows management to ascertain the cost of (1) relatively small functions, such as file maintenance or policy issuance; (2) products, such as term insurance or variable life insurance; and (3) larger areas of operations, such as entire lines of insurance. Having functional cost data and product-line cost data, in addition to the traditional departmental accumulation of data, also helps management control current operations as well as develop plans for future operations.

With a functional cost system, management can identify trends that are not recognizable with conventional analyses and can obtain more relevant statistics than when concentrating simply on departmental costs. Thus, statistical information and estimates of projected budget changes are apt to be more accurate. For example, under conventional budgeting methods, management would normally approve tentative budget increases without requiring cost justification. On the other hand, evaluations based on functional cost accounting provide management with an alternative to conventional "across the board" budget changes when cost-cutting is desired. Instead of flat percentage cuts applicable to all departments, management can pinpoint inefficient or unnecessary areas of operations and cut costs in those areas without harming more efficient departments or operations.

A functional cost system is also a valuable managerial tool for controlling operations. With functional cost data, a company can evaluate the performance of managers, determine the costs and effectiveness of procedures, and ascertain the accuracy of product pricing and budget estimates. A functional cost system can also be useful and meaningful for many analysis and planning activities. LOMA performs functional cost analysis for selected life and health insurance products and annuities through the Intercompany Cost Analysis Program (ICAP). ICAP calculates—on an annual basis—functional costs by product line for a number of life and health insurers. Participating companies can then use this information (1) to compare functional cost data with that of other insurers and (2) to analyze internal cost accounting procedures.

Development of a Functional Cost Accounting System

Developing an effective functional cost system with an appropriate and necessary level of detail requires identifying and defining each business function within the company—marketing, claims processing, data processing, underwriting, etc.—as well as each line of business or product offered. These functions, lines, or products may or may not coincide with the departmental units of the company. For example, mail handling is a function that is likely to be the responsibility of one department in the company's organizational structure, but the policy change function could be administered by a single subdivision of one department or could be spaced over two or more departments.

Companies that have cost accounting systems establish cost centers in order to compile the company's cost information. A **cost center** can be defined as an operation or department to which costs can be charged. Examples of cost centers are a sales office, an executive's office, or a section within a department. In most instances, a certain amount of research in each operating and service department is necessary to identify which cost centers would be the most effective. Training is also necessary to make certain that the operating personnel and the personnel assigned to gather cost information understand the cost accounting duties that they are expected to perform. To be most effective, cost centers should break down the total costs associated with each job function or department into components such as product, distribution system, or line of business.

The two primary types of cost centers are operating cost centers and service cost centers. In **operating cost centers,** products or services are actually produced, while in **service cost centers,** work indirectly related to production is performed. In an insurance company, examples of operating cost centers would be the underwriting, policy issue, and claim processing departments. Service cost centers would be the mailroom, the personnel department, the legal department, and often the data processing department. Either type of cost center can involve one or more functions.

The number and size of cost centers within a company depend on the company's size, organizational and operating procedures, degree of functional breakdown desired, and the availability of personnel and equipment to accumulate costs. The number of cost centers in a company and the number of employees in each cost center vary from one company to another. Each company must do its own research in order to establish cost centers that will facilitate the accurate and complete compilation of functional cost data.

When developing a functional cost accounting system, system designers must be careful to include all activities—and only those activities—that are relevant to the specific function under study. Two other important considerations when establishing a functional cost accounting system are expansion and special needs. The entire functional cost accounting system must be designed to be expandable as the company grows or diversifies. The system must also be able to provide for exceptions and peculiarities within any function or line of business.

A functional cost accounting system should usually be designed with detailed functional subdivisions at the outset rather than with consolidated information classifications. For example, expenses of the claim processing function should be subdivided, perhaps into areas such as "Claim—Administration," "Claim—Adjusting," and "Claim—Contested," rather than merely being grouped together into one account for claim processing. With a subdivided system, management has the option of consolidating functions at some later time to produce a single cost figure for the entire function. Once the system is in operation, however, conversion of a consolidated system into a subdivided system is difficult.

Besides allocating costs by functions, companies also allocate costs by line of business. Such allocations enable management to know more about the cost of the company's products or product lines. In addition, this kind of allocation is required by insurance regulatory agencies and is reported in the Analysis of Operations and expense exhibits of the company's Annual Statement. The allocation of expense by line of business is influenced by volume and by a particular product's innate administrative complexity. For example, a policy change action for an ordinary life policy may involve much more administrative detail than such a change in an industrial policy. Therefore, even if 40 percent of the policies processed by a policy change unit are for industrial policies, the industrial insurance line may be charged for less than 40 percent of the policy change unit's operating costs.

Cost Accumulation and Allocation

A functional cost accounting system must include procedures for accumulating costs. In an effort to ensure that functional cost totals are complete and that no information has been omitted accidentally, cost totals should be compared with the historical costs of the organizational units under study. **Historical costs** are the expense amounts recorded in the general ledger. A fully developed functional cost system should cover all investment and operating expenses as well as tax and license expenses. When the complete amount of costs has been tabulated, functional costs can be allocated among those products or lines of business responsible for incurring them.

The following factors are important considerations when evaluating an allocation method: (1) the length of time necessary to produce useful results, (2) the required accuracy of the results, (3) the cost of producing the results, and (4) the availability of data. When choosing from among available methods, however, the company should select the allocation method that is most reasonable with respect to speed, accuracy, and cost. In addition, the results of allocation must be easily understandable by management. Different allocation methods are generally appropriate for different types of costs. The types of costs for which allocation methods are discussed in this chapter are salary costs, expenses other than salaries, and service department costs.

Salary costs

Allocation of each type of salary cost should be as precise and practical as possible for the following reasons: (1) salary costs usually constitute an insurance company's largest operating expense and (2) many other expenses are allocated in proportion to salary costs. The most common basis for allocating salary expense is time analysis. The three basic methods of time analysis are *estimated, actual,* and *standard* time analysis.

Estimated time analysis. In **estimated time analysis,** estimates are made of how much time is spent on various jobs and functions. These estimates become the basis for allocating both salaries and certain other cost center expenses that must be allocated in relation to salary costs. The estimated time method is inexpensive and easy to implement, and it generally gives quick results. However, estimated time analysis is also more likely to give incomplete or inaccurate results than actual or standard time analysis. Estimates are usually based on guesswork and intuitive judgments that may actually be wrong. Cost analysts should make particular effort to find the sources of significant changes in the estimated times for performing various functions. Estimated times could change as a result of changes in both the products that a company offers and the production methods used in the company. For example, a company can expect cost variances when new electronic data processing programs or systems are implemented. Changes may also take place when significant economic or financial events outside the company occur.

Actual time analysis. In **actual time analysis,** the times used in cost allocation calculations come from employees' records of their own work. These time records are usually samplings that cover a limited and specific period of time (e.g., two weeks to one month) that is representative of normal conditions. When a company is initiating a functional cost system, the actual time approach is recommended because it is more accurate than using estimated times and (1) less expensive, (2) less difficult to implement, and (3) faster than using the standard time method.

Standard time analysis. Traditionally, **standard time analyses** have been derived from time-and-motion studies made by job analysts rather than projections made by accountants or employees. **Time-and-motion studies** determine the amount of time necessary to perform certain job-related activities. The process of developing standards from time-and-motion studies is both complex and technical. Generally, managers and analysts work together to establish work standards based on these studies.

Once time standards have been established, functional cost distribution of the amount of expense applicable to certain job functions can be made more readily and accurately than with the actual-time or estimated-time methods. The standard time method is the least used method of time analysis, however, for a number of reasons. First, time-and-motion studies are very expensive. Also, employee dissatisfaction often results when standard job performance times are set by systems analysts and managerial personnel who do not actually perform the job activity. Finally, job duties and activities change frequently so that a time-and-motion study for a particular activity may quickly become obsolete. Also, cost allocations may be inaccurate when employees' performance differs from the standards established by the time-and-motion study.

Expenses other than salaries

Expenses other than salaries include office supplies, utilities (including telephone), and postage. A decision whether to distribute nonsalary expenses among cost centers should depend on a company's size, the company's entire cost control program, and the level of information that management requires. The difficulties involved in compiling and allocating many indirect expenses are sometimes disproportionate to the dollar amounts of the expenses being allocated, especially if the company does not have a highly automated cost accounting system.

Many methods of allocating expenses other than salaries are somewhat arbitrary and differ from company to company. The most common allocation method is to apportion certain costs in the same proportion as the directly chargeable payroll costs for that department or function. Thus, when a number of cost centers are involved in a function, overhead expenses—often referred to as *indirect costs*—are allocated based on each cost center's share of the total payroll. If cost accountants are trying to allocate the office supply expenses of a number of cost centers and no direct method of allocation is available, the office supply expense can be allocated in the same proportion as the salary expense.

For example, assume that Cost Centers A, B, C, and D draw the following percentages of salaries for personnel involved in a particular function:

Cost Center A	60 percent of salaries
Cost Center B	20 percent of salaries
Cost Center C	15 percent of salaries
Cost Center D	5 percent of salaries

In this case, the indirect office supply expenses would be allocated in the same percentages as the salary expenses for those cost centers. Thus, 60 percent of the office supply expense would be allocated to Cost Center A, 20 percent to Cost Center B, 15 percent to Cost Center C, and 5 percent to Cost Center D.

Service department costs

Costs incurred by service departments include (1) salaries and other costs related to the president's office, (2) board of directors' compensation, (3) certain association dues, and (4) expenses related directly to the particular service department. Allocation of service department costs can be based on ratios such as salaries to total company costs or the general expense of each function to total company costs.

Since no single allocation method is entirely suitable for all service departments, the company's objective should be to find the method that is most suitable for the company's particular circumstances. For example, the methods of allocation in the personnel department and the legal department might be quite different. In the personnel department, the allocation may be based on either the (1) number of employees in each operating cost center or function or (2) salaries in each operating cost center or function. The most appropriate method for a particular company is the one that most closely approximates the value of services rendered by the personnel department to each cost center or function. The legal department's functional allocation, on the other hand, may depend on the functions or cost centers serviced by the company's legal staff and should be based on either periodic or continuing cost studies. Occasionally, certain legal expenses may apply indivisibly to several functions. In such instances, basing the expenses on a percentage of the total charges allocated to each function or line of business would be a valid approach. Quite often, substantial expenses of the legal department are allocated directly to the corporate overhead function.

Effective Utilization of Functional Cost Information

Once the best possible unit of measurement has been selected and the functional cost system has been designed and installed, accountants must present the cost information in a format that is comprehensible to management and that can be used in decisior making. Providing functional cost information that can assist managerial decision making requires the presentation of a narrative report that accompanies basic statistical information. The narrative should comment on such factors as volume fluctuations, industry or product trends, deviations from planned performance, and forecasts of future costs.

Presentations of output from a cost accounting system vary according to factors such as (1) the types of decisions to be made, (2) the management level at which decisions will occur, (3) the timing of the presentation, and (4) the personalities of the individuals involved. To help management evaluate organizational cost control and measure productivity, operational unit costs are often presented for separate organizational units or cost centers.

Determination of unit costs

As defined earlier, a unit cost is the incurred expense that can be attributed to a single measured unit of work. *Functional* unit costs are calculated by dividing the total cost of a function by a basic, predetermined unit of measurement. A functional unit cost can only be calculated when the total cost of a function, from start to finish, has been determined. For accurate determination of a functional unit cost, appropriate weight must be given to each element or phase of work that contributes to the total cost of the function. The functional unit cost of the premium collection function, for instance, would cover the cost of

(1) preparing and mailing a premium notice,
(2) issuing a premium receipt if requested,
(3) receiving and depositing each premium,
(4) recordkeeping in both home and field offices, and
(5) other activities related to the premium collection function.

These activities consume differing amounts of time and, therefore, must be given different weights in the process of cost accumulation.

FIGURE 16-2
Typical base units used in determining functional unit costs.

Function	Typical Base Units
Selling or acquisition	Per thousand paid for (adjusted for term, juvenile, single premium, other special plans, and reinsurance) Per policy issued
Policy issue	Per policy issued Per policy paid for
Premium collection	Per item Per $100 of premiums reported Per $100 of premiums collected
Underwriting	Per policy paid for Per application Per $1,000 of insurance
Policy changes	Per item Per $1,000 of insurance in force Per policy in force
Commission payment	Per item Per $100 of commissions Per $100 of premiums
Investments	Per $1,000 of mean admitted assets Per $1,000 of investment revenue Per classification (policy loans, mortgage loans, etc.)

The unit of measure used in determining functional unit costs is known as the **base unit.** Typical base units in life and health insurance accounting are the number of claims processed, the number of premiums collected, and the number of policy changes made. However, for certain functions, functional unit costs can also be expressed in terms such as "per $1,000 of admitted assets" or "per $1,000 of premiums collected." In order to offer different cost perspectives on a certain function, though, use of more than one unit of measurement in the cost system is often advisable. For example, policy issue unit costs may be expressed in several ways, such as by number of policies issued, number of applications submitted, and face amount of insurance paid for (in thousands of dollars). Typical base units for different insurance company functions are presented in Figure 16-2.

Key Terms

cost accounting
marginal cost
cost center
service cost center
indirect costs
actual time analysis
base unit

unit cost
functional cost accounting
operating cost center
historical costs
estimated time analysis
standard time analysis

Review Questions and Exercises

1. State four reasons that insurers use cost accounting.
2. What are two prerequisites to an effective cost accounting system?
3. How do marginal costs and functional costs differ?
4. What is the main advantage of using a functional cost accounting system?
5. Define *cost center.*
6. At the outset of the functional cost accounting process, is it preferable to have cost information consolidated or subdivided within each function? Explain your answer.
7. Why is standard time analysis of salary costs the least used of the three time analysis methods?

Glossary

accounting control. The system of procedures and records concerned with maintaining and ensuring the accuracy of financial records as well as safeguarding company assets.

accrued income. Income that has been earned but that is not receivable until a specified date in the next reporting period.

actual time analysis. A method of time analysis in which the times used in cost allocation calculations come from employees' records of their own work. These time records are usually samplings that cover a limited and specific period of time that is representative of normal conditions.

ad valorem taxes. Taxes that are based upon the value of the real estate or personal property that is being taxed.

administrative control. The system of procedures and records that leads, either directly or indirectly, to the authorization of transactions by managerial-level employees.

administrative system. An accounting information system that maintains records and processes daily transactions that involve insurance contracts.

admitted assets. Assets shown on a life insurance company's Annual Statement Balance Sheet as required by law or by insurance department ruling.

advance premium. A premium that is received before the statement date but that is not due until after that date.

agents' subsystem. An accounting subsystem that calculates both commissions for agents and compensation for field office managers.

alpha system. A system used in an insurance company to organize information on (1) each person insured by the company, (2) recent applications that have been received and whether those applications have been accepted or declined, and (3) other records that the company has collected in doing business; short for *alphabetical index system.*

amortization. The process by which the book value of an investment is periodically and systematically adjusted so that, on the maturity date, the investment's book value equals its par value.

application program. Software that instructs a computer in how to perform one particular task or function.

appropriated surplus. *See* **special surplus funds.**

asset duplication. A situation that arises when assets are recorded twice on a company's financial statements.

assigned surplus. *See* **special surplus funds.**

assuming company. In a reinsurance transaction, the reinsuring company.

auditing. The process of obtaining, examining, and evaluating data regarding a company's financial and operational actions and events.

automated system. A system that uses computers to perform one or more of the four basic tasks—input, processing, output, or control—that together form a system.

automatic transaction. A type of computer transaction that is internally generated by the client and policy data base.

balance account. A composite of all of a company's nonledger accounts and nonadmitted asset accounts, usually used for keeping the trial balance and ledger in balance at all times. Also called the *general fund*, *ledger surplus*, and *net ledger assets*.

base unit. The unit of measure used in determining functional unit costs.

bond discount. The difference between the price paid for a bond and the bond's par value, if the price paid for the bond is lower than par.

bond premium. The difference between the price paid for a bond and the bond's par value, if the price paid for the bond is higher than par.

bonds. Certificates of indebtedness that are issued by corporations, governmental units, and other legal entities and that are typically secured by the assets or the general credit of the issuing party.

bottom-up budgeting. A budgeting approach in which employees in lower organizational ranks play a key role in determining their own budgets.

budget. A detailed financial plan for a company's operations over a given period of time.

Canada securities. Bonds, mortgages, or agreements of sale applicable to a company's life insurance business in Canada.

capital. The amount of money invested in a company by its owners or stockholders.

capital cost allowance (CCA). The amount of depreciation expense that is deducted in computing income for Canadian tax purposes.

capital expenditure budget. A budget that shows a company's plans for managing its fixed assets.

capital paid up. The number of outstanding shares of an insurer's stock multiplied by the stock's par value. In Canada, *capital paid up* is referred to as *capital stock issued and paid* or *capital stock paid*.

capital stock. The par value of all shares of outstanding stock.

capital stock issued and paid. *See* **capital paid up.**

capital stock paid. *See* **capital paid up.**

capitalization. The process of deferring costs, treating them as assets, and then amortizing the value of those assets over the period of time in which the benefits resulting from the expenses occur.

cash-basis accounting. An accounting system in which journal entries are not made until cash transactions take place.

cash flow statement. A statement showing the sources and uses of a company's cash during a specified period of time.

ceding company. In a reinsurance transaction, the original insurer.

chart of accounts. A detailed listing of all of the accounts maintained in a company's accounting systems.

claim reserves. Health insurance claim liabilities, including the present value of amounts not yet due on claims and the reserve for future contingent benefits, that are treated as health insurance reserves.

claims. Requests for payments under the terms and conditions of life and health insurance policies.

claims in the course of settlement. Claims that have been reported to a company and are being investigated.

clean surplus theory. Under generally accepted accounting principles, a theory which holds that only certain prescribed items can be debited or credited directly to Retained Earnings.

client and policy master file. The data base that provides much of the data on individuals and individual policies for an insurer's accounting information system.

client/policy accounting system. An accounting information system that handles all the activities that can occur, either automatically or by request, for a given client or policy.

collateral trust bonds. Bonds that are secured by negotiable securities owned by the bond issuer.

collected income. The amount of income actually received in cash during a reporting period, including certain adjustments for amortization as well as interest paid on home office purchase and occupancy.

collected premiums. The amount of premium income received by an insurance company during an accounting period.

committed costs. Expenses that result from decisions or commitments made at an earlier time.

commuted commissions. The present value of amounts paid to agents in lieu of renewal commissions that would otherwise be payable in future years.

compliance auditing. A type of auditing that verifies adherence to the laws, regulations, policies, and procedures prescribed by either internal or external authorities.

conservatism. In accounting, the choice of a financial reporting alternative that results in the projection of lower values for a company's assets, higher values for its liabilities, and a reduced level of income than would be the case if a non-conservative approach were used.

consolidated tax return. A single tax return filed for an affiliated group of corporations.

contingency reserves. *See* **special surplus funds.**

continuous budget. *See* **rolling budget.**

contract payments. Payments on annuities and supplementary contracts.

contributed surplus. On a Canadian company's Balance Sheet, the amount in excess of par value paid in by stockholders minus the amount of stock dividends paid.

conventional mortgage loans. Mortgage loans that are not insured or guaranteed by a government agency.

cost accounting. A branch of managerial accounting that involves the accumulation of data on current-period actual costs in order to give management unit-cost information.

cost-benefit analysis. An evaluation and comparison of the projected costs and benefits of a certain action.

cost center. An operation or department to which costs can be charged.

coupon rate. The rate of interest specified on a bond certificate. Also called the *nominal rate* or *stated rate*.

data. Any representation of facts or figures.

data base. All of the information and data retained by a company. In the current generation of computers, a data base can be defined as a nonredundant collection of data that has been organized for easy access, update, and retrieval.

deferred premiums. Premiums that are due after the statement date but before the next policy anniversary.

departmental audit. A type of management audit that is designed to evaluate and test the performance of a department's personnel by first identifying the responsibility involved in each person's job and then determining if the responsibility is being met.

developmental costs. Costs incurred in efforts to acquire new business, or, in some cases, to support business that has already been acquired.

disability income insurance. A form of health insurance that provides a monthly income benefit should the insured become disabled as defined in the policy.

disabled life reserves. A claim reserve liability that is the present value of all amounts that are predicted to become payable while an insured is disabled.

discretionary costs. Costs that are partially or wholly under the control of current management and are flexible components of an insurer's budget.

dividend accumulations. Amounts that result from a policyowner's decision to leave the dividends owed to him or her on deposit with the company.

dollar control. A process for continuously maintaining a total of separate amounts in a particular file while amounts are being added to and deleted from the file.

draft. A means of paying a claim against an insurance company. A draft is similar in appearance to a check but is not automatically charged by the bank against the insurer's bank account.

due and unpaid claims. Claims that have been approved by a company but that have not been paid.

due income. Income that was scheduled for payment prior to the financial reporting date but that has not been received by the insurer as of the reporting date.

earmarked surplus. *See* **special surplus funds.**

earned income. The amount of income actually earned during an accounting period, as opposed to the amount that has been received during that period.

effective rate. The actual rate of return on the amount paid for a bond. Also called *yield*.

estimated time analysis. A method of time analysis in which estimates are made of how much time is spent on various jobs and functions.

ex-date. *See* **ex-dividend date.**

ex-dividend date. The date that determines whether a stockholder is eligible to receive a declared dividend. Also called the *ex-date*.

external auditing. Auditing that is carried out primarily for the benefit of interested third parties, including the board of directors, investors, creditors, policyowners, and others that depend on the company's financial statements.

face value. *See* **principal.**

financial accounting. The area of accounting that is oriented primarily towards reporting financial information about a company to interested parties outside the company.

financial auditing. The traditional auditing of financial information, including both the overall examination of a company's financial statements and the examination of individual accounts and accounting records.

financial budget. A budget that covers a company's plans regarding its asset, liability, and capital accounts.

financial information system. An accounting information system that provides data on both the flow of money through the company and the ways in which the money is being used to achieve the company's objectives.

fiscal auditing. A type of auditing that encompasses both financial auditing and compliance auditing.

fixed-amount budget. A budget in which the dollar amounts are generally not subject to change unless the changes have been approved by management.

flexible-amount budget. A budget that provides one or more alternative sets of figures that can be used under the different circumstances that may arise during the course of a budgeting period.

foreclosure. A legal procedure by which a lender recovers an unpaid loan balance by gaining title to the real estate offered as collateral.

functional cost accounting. A subdivision of cost accounting that combines all component costs of a particular series of operations into one total, without regard to traditional departmental lines or account classifications.

fund accounting. The process used to account for and allocate revenue to various funds in Canadian insurance companies.

general accounting system. An accounting information system that records and classifies the company's financial transactions from the client/policy accounting system, the investment accounting system, and all areas of the company's operations.

general fund. *See* **balance account.**

general obligation bonds. Bonds that are secured by the general taxing power of the issuing governmental unit.

generally accepted accounting principles (GAAP). The set of accounting principles used by most firms outside the life insurance industry and sometimes used by life and health insurance companies. GAAP is based on the going-concern concept of asset valuation.

going-concern concept. An asset valuation concept that assumes, for financial reporting purposes, that the reporting company will continue to do business in the future.

gross paid in and contributed surplus. The excess of the price paid for a stock over its par value, multiplied by the number of outstanding shares.

gross premium. The total premium paid by a policyowner.

guaranty association. An organization whose purpose is to protect policyowners from losses suffered through the insolvency of an insurance company.

hardware. A computer system's physical component: the computer itself, input/output devices, and secondary storage devices.

historical costs. Expense amounts previously recorded in the general ledger.

holding company. A company that controls one or more other companies, or subsidiaries, through ownership of a sufficient amount of the subsidiaries' common stock.

income recognition process. The process by which income is allocated to the period in which it was earned.

incompatible functions. Job duties that place any person in a position to perpetrate or to conceal errors or irregularities in the normal course of his or her employment.

incurred but unreported claims. Claims that were incurred in an accounting reporting period but that had not been reported to the company as of the Annual Statement date.

indirect costs. Overhead expenses.

information. Data that has been processed and manipulated in various ways to make it meaningful and useful.

intangible personal property tax. A tax on financial assets such as cash, promissory notes, bonds, and deferred or uncollected premiums.

integrated software. Computer programs that perform several different applications.

internal auditing. Auditing that is performed by employees of the company being audited and that is undertaken primarily for the benefit of that company's management.

internal control. The methods and operations used by a business in order to protect its assets, monitor the accuracy of its accounting records, and encourage both operational efficiency and adherence to managerial policies.

invested assets. Assets that produce income in the form of interest, rent, dividends, and capital gains.

investment accounting system. An accounting information system that provides inventories and valuations of all stocks, bonds, mortgage loans, real estate, and other invested assets.

ledger accounts. In a cash-basis accounting system, accounts that are included in a company's cash-basis ledger.

ledger asset. An asset that is recorded on the insurer's books.

ledger audit. A type of audit that determines if an account's balance is fairly stated.

ledger liability. A liability that is recorded on the insurer's books.

ledger surplus. *See* **balance account.**

LICTI. *See* **life insurance company taxable income.**

life insurance company taxable income (LICTI). The difference between a life insurance company's gross income and deductions.

line of business. A segment of the insurance market that has a cost pattern distinctively different from that of other segments.

liquidation. The process of selling a company's assets and terminating the company's operations.

liquidation concept. An asset valuation concept that assumes, for financial reporting purposes, that the reporting company will have to terminate its operations immediately and liquidate all of its assets in order to satisfy the claims of creditors.

loading. Under statutory accounting, the portion of an insurance premium that is applied toward expenses, commissions, and profit for the insurer.

lock-in concept. Under generally accepted accounting principles, a feature of reserve calculation which holds that once a set of reserve assumptions regarding a particular type or group of policies is adopted for a particular year or years of issue, these assumptions are to continue prospectively, i.e., they must be used for reserve calculations in future years.

long-term budget. A budget that generally addresses periods of two, three, five, or ten years.

management auditing. A type of auditing that focuses on improving the effectiveness and efficiency of a company's operations.

managerial accounting. The area of accounting responsible for providing a company's management with financial information about the company.

mandatory redemption feature. A feature of bonds and preferred stocks that allows the security's issuer to redeem preferred stock that had been issued for a limited period of time or to pay back a bond's principal at a certain call date.

Mandatory Securities Valuation Reserve (MSVR). In the United States, a liability account that is designed to absorb, within certain specified limits, realized and unrealized capital gains and losses resulting from the company's investments.

marginal cost. The additional expense incurred as a result of producing one additional unit of a product or service.

market value. The price that an asset would command if it were offered for sale instead of being retained in the insurer's portfolio.

master budget. A comprehensive plan that encompasses the financial projections for an entire organization.

maturity date. The date on which the principal amount of a bond is to be repaid or the last principal payment is to be made.

maturity value. *See* **principal.**

mean reserve. The average of a policy's reserve at the beginning and end of one policy year.

medical expense insurance. A form of health insurance that pays for the cost of hospital room and board, miscellaneous hospital expenses, surgical expenses, and medical care as set forth in the policy.

model. A mathematical representation that shows the relationships among the variables in a particular problem or situation.

modified reserves. Reserves accumulated from policies for which the amount of premium set aside for reserves is lower in early policy years than in later premium-paying years.

mortgage bonds. Bonds that are secured by land and buildings owned by the bond issuer.

mortgage correspondents. Real estate firms or mortgage brokers that service mortgage loans for a fee.

mutualization. The process of converting a stock company into a mutual company.

net benefit premium. Under generally accepted accounting principles, the portion of the premium that funds the benefit reserve.

net capital gain. The amount of realized and unrealized capital gains in excess of the amount of realized and unrealized capital losses.

net capital loss. The amount of realized and unrealized capital losses in excess of the amount of realized and unrealized capital gains.

net cash value. An amount equal to the cash surrender value of both a policy and any paid-up additions minus any existing indebtedness, including accrued interest.

net expense premium. Under generally accepted accounting principles, the portion of the premium that covers the expenses of maintaining and acquiring the policy.

net gain. The total of an insurer's income minus the total of its expenses, benefit payments, federal income taxes, and policyholder dividends, if the difference is positive.

net investment income. The total of gross investment income minus any expenses, taxes, and depreciation recorded or incurred during the reporting year.

net ledger assets. *See* **balance account.**

net level reserves. Reserves accumulated from policies for which the amount of premium set aside to fund the reserve remains level over the life of the policy.

net loss. The total of an insurer's income minus the total of its expenses, benefit payments, federal income taxes, and policyholder dividends, if the difference is negative.

net premium. Under statutory accounting, the portion of the premium that funds the benefit reserve. The net premium equals a policy's gross premium minus the policy's expense loading.

nominal rate. *See* **coupon rate.**

nonadmitted assets. Assets not shown on a life insurance company's Annual Statement Balance Sheet as required by law or by insurance department ruling.

nonforfeiture options. The choices available to a policyowner concerning the methods under which he or she can apply the policy's cash surrender value when the policy expires.

nonledger accounts. Accounts that are separate from the company's cash-basis ledger and that are generally incorporated into the Balance Sheet, Summary of Operations, and other Annual Statement reports through the use of working papers.

offset. A tax law provision that allows an insurer to use the amount paid for one type of tax to reduce another aspect of the company's tax liability.

operating cost center. A cost center in which products or services are actually produced.

operational budget. A budget that covers part or all of a company's operations, setting forth the income or expenses the company expects over a definite period of time.

operations planning. Planning that is primarily concerned with the short-term.

outstanding premiums. In Canada, premiums that are due on or before the statement date but that have not been received by that date.

paid-to date. The date to which a policyowner has paid his or her premium.

par value. The designated legal value assigned to each outstanding share of stock. Also, the amount borrowed by the issuer of a bond. *See* **principal**.

Part I Business Income Tax. In Canada, the basic income tax applicable to all individuals and corporations.

performance auditing. A type of auditing that encompasses both management auditing and program results auditing.

permanently impaired securities. Investments the value of which is not likely to be recovered because the securities' issuer has experienced financial difficulty or outright bankruptcy.

planning. The activity that consists of setting goals, determining company policy in accordance with managerial philosophy, anticipating future events that may affect corporate performance, and devising the strategies, methods, and procedures necessary to achieve desired results.

policy acquisition costs. Costs that are directly attributable to the production of new business.

policy loan. A loan that is made to a policyowner by an insurer and secured by a policy's cash surrender value.

premium assets. *See* **deferred premiums** and **uncollected premiums**.

premium deposits. Amounts that are left on deposit with the insurer for the payment of future premiums.

premium suspense. A premium income classification used to record amounts that are intended as premiums but that cannot be accepted as income until a particular event occurs.

present value of amounts not yet due on claims. An amount set aside as a reserve for future payments on claims currently being paid in installments, as in the case of disability income coverages and waiver-of-premium benefits.

principal. The amount borrowed by the issuer of a bond. Also called *face value*, *maturity value*, and *par value*.

private placements. Bonds offered by the bond issuer directly to specific financial institutions.

program results auditing. A type of auditing that determines whether the results or benefits desired from a particular program are actually being achieved and whether the desired results could be achieved at a lower cost.

public companies. All companies registered with the Securities and Exchange Commission.

public offerings. Bonds offered for sale to the general public.

purchase money mortgage. A mortgage in which the seller of a property grants credit to a purchaser and the purchaser uses the real estate being purchased as collateral for the loan.

real estate mortgage loan. A loan under which a person, business, or other entity borrows money from a lender and offers some specific piece of real estate, such as a house, farm, or office building, to the lender as collateral.

realizable value. A dollar value that represents an insurer's best estimate of the amount, if any, that will be recovered upon the sale or maturity of a permanently impaired security.

realization principle. A generally accepted accounting principle which holds that income should be recognized when it is earned rather than when it is received.

realized capital gain (or loss). The difference between an asset's sale price and its book value or amortized cost.

redundant data. Data that appears in more than one place in a data processing system.

reinsurance. A type of insurance transaction between insurers in which companies buy, sell, or exchange risks on certain policies in order to reduce potential losses on certain insurance risks.

requested transaction. A type of computer transaction that is externally generated by action on the part of a policyowner, assignee, or beneficiary.

required reserves. In Canada, reserves required by the insurance department of the province in which an insurer operates as well as reserves required by foreign jurisdictions.

reserve destrengthening. The reduction of policy reserves in order to increase surplus.

reserve for future contingent benefits. An amount established as a reserve for deferred maternity benefits and for any other claims that may have already been incurred but that may be contingent upon a future event or circumstances beyond the company's control.

reserve released. A policy reserve, established in connection with an in-force policy, that is no longer required.

reserve strengthening. The process of setting up additional policy reserves.

resisted claims. Claims that a company has refused to pay but that may be paid in the future.

retained earnings. In GAAP accounting, the net change in owners' equity resulting from gains or losses in the company's operations as well as any dividends paid to the stockholders.

retaliatory tax laws. Tax laws that impose taxes on a foreign insurer at the rate at which the home state's domestic companies would be taxed by the foreign state, if the home state's tax rate is higher.

revenue bonds. *See* **special obligation bonds.**

rolling budget. A budget that allows a company to maintain projections for a certain time period into the future. Also called a *continuous budget*.

segregated fund. In Canada, an asset account that stands apart from a company's general account.

segregation of duties. A concept of internal accounting control that requires that different employees be responsible for the following duties: authorizing a transaction, recording that transaction, and having custody of the assets involved in the transaction.

separate accounts. In the United States, accounts maintained apart from the company's general accounts for the purpose of managing the funds used for nonguaranteed insurance products.

service cost center. A cost center in which work indirectly related to production is performed.

short-term budget. A budget that generally covers a one-year period and relates mainly to a company's operations during that period of time.

small life insurance company deduction. A tax deduction that is permitted to certain life insurance companies if they meet criteria relating to the amount of the company's assets and tentative life insurance company taxable income (tentative LICTI).

social auditing. A type of auditing that is designed to determine how a corporation's actions affect society.

software. The programming instructions given to a computer in order to make it perform a specific data processing task, produce information, or solve a particular problem.

solvency. A company's ability to meet its current and future obligations.

special obligation bonds. Bonds that are secured by revenue from a restricted source, such as a toll bridge or water system, or by a special tax source such as gasoline taxes or special property taxes. Also called *revenue bonds*.

special surplus funds. Surplus that a life company's board of directors has segregated for the purpose of meeting unforeseen contingencies or paying for certain extraordinary expenses that may arise. Also called *appropriated surplus*, *assigned surplus*, *contingency reserves*, and *earmarked surplus*.

standard time analysis. A method of time analysis that has been derived from time-and-motion studies made by job analysts rather than from projections made by accountants or employees.

stated rate. *See* **coupon rate.**

statutory accounting practices (SAP). The accounting methods and principles that apply to the completion of the statutory Annual Statement which life insurance companies are required to submit to regulatory authorities.

stock company. An insurance company that sells stock in the company to obtain funds for starting and continuing its operations.

strategic planning. Planning that is primarily concerned with the long-term.

subsystem. A system contained within a larger system.

supplementary contract with life contingencies (WLC). A supplementary contract or annuity in which the duration of the payment period depends on the lifetime of the beneficiary.

supplementary contract without life contingencies (WOLC). A type of annuity contract or supplementary contract in which the proceeds are held at interest or paid in installments over a specified period.

supporting budgets. Budgets that are used to define and articulate the projections and objectives that are generally stated in a company's master budget.

surplus. The amount of a life insurance company's assets in excess of the amount of its liabilities and capital. *See* **contributed surplus, gross paid in and contributed surplus, special surplus funds,** and **unassigned surplus.**

system. A group of integrated elements—generally composed of four basic tasks: input, processing, output, and control—that interact to achieve a desired end.

systematic and rational allocation. A method of expense recognition in which the cost of an asset is spread over its estimated useful life without regard to the revenues realized from the use of the asset.

10-K report. A report that contains certified financial statements and that publicly held insurance companies are required to file with the Securities and Exchange Commission (SEC) on an annual basis.

10-Q report. An unaudited financial statement that publicly held insurance companies are required to file with the Securities and Exchange Commission (SEC) on a quarterly basis.

tangible personal property tax. A type of ad valorem tax in which a tax is imposed on such items as an insurer's office furniture and equipment, data processing equipment, vehicles used for transportation, and other types of personal property.

tentative LICTI. The amount of life insurance company taxable income excluding the small company deduction, other deductions as allowed, and any items attributable to non-insurance business.

terminal policy dividend. A substantial extra dividend or pro-rata dividend covering the period between the last policy anniversary date and the termination date of the policy.

time-and-motion studies. Management studies that determine the amount of time necessary to perform certain job-related activities.

timing difference. A situation in which a figure reported for a certain item in financial statements differs from the figure shown on the tax return for that item because the item is recognized in one accounting period for GAAP and in another period for taxation purposes.

top-down budgeting. A budgeting approach in which upper levels of management establish the company's budget with little or no participation from lower ranks of employees.

treasury stock. Stock repurchased by the issuing company.

unappropriated earned surplus. In Canada, the amount of an insurer's surplus remaining after determination of an insurer's reserve, capital, and other surplus amounts.

unassigned surplus. The amount of surplus remaining after the creation of any special surplus funds.

uncollected premiums. Life insurance premiums and annuity considerations that are due on or before the statement date but that have not been received by that date.

unearned income. Income that was collected by the insurer during the reporting period but that is applicable to a later period.

unearned premium. A premium or portion of a premium that is due or received before the Annual Statement date but that is applicable to the following reporting year.

unit cost. The incurred expense that can be attributed to a single measured unit of work.

unlisted asset. An asset that has doubtful value and that does not appear on the statutory Balance Sheet.

unrealized capital gain (or loss). The difference between an asset's book value and its market value.

waiver-of-premium benefit. A form of disability insurance that specifies that the insurer will not require premium payments as long as the insured is disabled.

work sheets. *See* **working papers.**

working papers. An informal tool that accountants use to adjust journal and general ledger information to the formats or valuations necessary for the preparation of formal financial statements. Also called *work sheets*.

yield. *See* **effective rate.**

zero-base budgeting. A budgeting approach in which a manager begins with the premise that no resources will be allocated for the following year unless and until each dollar to be spent is justified and is in accord with departmental plans as well as the company's overall plans.

Index

Accounting, life insurance, 2-3. *See also* Annual Statement, Generally accepted accounting principles, Statutory accounting practices
  and commissions, 80-82
  information systems in, 53-68
  organization of, 15
  and premiums, 71-80
Accounting control, internal, 270-277
Accounting information systems, 53-68
  evolution of, 54
  financial and managerial, 57-68
Accrual-basis accounting, 8, 9, 19, 96-99
Accrued bond interest income, 104-105
Accrued income, 97-98
Actual time analysis, 338
Actuarial reserves, 23
Administrative control, 270
Administrative system, 64-65
Admitted assets, 6-8, 188-192
Advance premiums, 27, 79-80
Agents' subsystem, 66-67
AICPA. *See* American Institute of Certified Public Accountants
Alpha system, 64
American Institute of Certified Public Accountants (AICPA), 12-13, 271, 277, 291
Amortization, 19
  bond, 107-110
  mortgage loan, 126

Analysis of Income by Fund, 234, 235, 236
Analysis of Income by Line of Business, 29-30
Analysis of Increase in Reserves during the Year, 42
Analysis of Nonadmitted Assets and Related Items, 231-233
Analysis of Operations, 29-36
Annual reports, 49-50
Annual Statement (Canada), 4, 6-8, 9, 18
  Analysis of Income by Fund, 234, 235, 236
  Analysis of Income by Line of Business, 29-30
  Balance Sheet, 18-28, 92, 93
  capital and surplus, 206
  Changes in Financial Position, Statement of, 38-42
  Changes in Reserves, 42
  claims, 181-186
  dividend liabilities, 156-158, 238
  electronic data processing equipment, 188
  expenses, 48, 226-230
  five-year schedule of data, 42
  fund accounting, 233-237
  Income Statement, 28, 226
  investment income information, 43, 99, 116-119
  policy reserves, 48
  premiums and commissions, 48, 88-93
  Reconciliation of Funds, 234-235, 237
  Reconciliation of Surplus, 36-38, 220
  segregated accounts, 196
  Summary of Funds, 234, 235-236

surplus on Balance Sheet, allocation of, 213
taxes, 266
Annual Statement (U.S.), 3-4, 6-8, 9, 13, 18, 60
   Analysis of Increase in Reserves during the Year, 42
   Analysis of Nonadmitted Assets and Related Items, 231-233
   Analysis of Operations, 29-36
   assets, 188-192
   Balance Sheet, 18-28, 88, 153-155
   Capital and Surplus Account, 36-38, 205-206, 214-220
   Cash Flow statement, 38
   claims, 48, 179-181
   commissions paid, 86
   dividend liabilities, 153-155
   electronic data processing equipment, 188
   Exhibit of Life Insurance, 238
   expenses, 48, 226-230
   Five-Year Historical Data, 42
   foreign exchange rates, 191-192
   General Interrogatories, 238
   investment income information, 43, 96-99, 105, 113-116
   liabilities, 192-196
   Notes to the Financial Statements, 237-238
   Policy Claims Resisted or Compromised, 238
   policy reserves, 48
   premium income, 48, 83-88
   Reconciliation of Ledger Assets, 230-231
   reinsurance ceded, 188-190
   reserve analysis, 42
   separate accounts, 196-202, 219
   Summary of Operations, 28-29, 226
   surplus changes, 36-38, 167-168, 214-220, 231, 302-303
   taxes, 266
Annuities, 171-173
Appropriated surplus, 212
Asset classifications, 19-23
   admitted, 6-8, 188-192
   ledger, 9, 230-231
   nonadmitted, 6-8, 37, 216-217, 231-233, 296, 304
   nonledger, 10-11
   premium, 22, 80
   unlisted, 296
Asset valuation, 5-6
   under GAAP, 296-298
Assigned surplus, 212
Auditing, 269, 277-284
   external, 280

fiscal, 281-282
and use of GAAP in life companies, 290-291
internal, 280
management, 282-284
program results, 284
social, 284
Audits of Stock Life Insurance Companies, 12-13, 277, 291
Automatic premium loan (APL), 132
Automatic transactions, 66
Automation, uses of in insurance company accounting, 54, 57-68
   client/policy accounting system, 61-67
   general accounting system, 60-61
   investment accounting system, 67
   transaction processing, 58

Balance account, 5, 11-12
Balance Sheet, 18-28
   allocation of surplus, 213
   asset classifications and valuations, 19-23, 188-192
   Canadian, 18-28, 92, 93
   capital stock, 28, 206-208
   liability classifications, 23-27, 192-196
   purpose of, 18
   surplus, 28, 210-211
   U.S., 18-28, 88, 153-155
BARRS. *See* Best's Advance Rating Report Service
Base unit, 342
Best's Advance Rating Report Service (BARRS), 239-240
Bonds, 99-110
   accounting for purchase and sale of, 102-105
   and Canadian accounting practices, 304-305
   as reported on Canadian Annual Statement, 43, 116
   as reported on U.S. Annual Statement, 43, 113-116
   coupon rate, 101
   discounts and premiums, 105-110
   effective rate, 105-106
   nominal rate, 101
   par value, 99
Bonus additions, 145
Bottom-up budgeting, 322
Budgets, 51, 314, 317-326
   analysis and evaluation, 325-326
   bottom-up budgeting, 322
   fixed-amount, 321
   flexible-amount, 321

long-term, 317
preparation of, 323-325
rolling, 317-318
short-term, 317
top-down budgeting, 321-322
types of, 318-323
zero-base budgeting, 323
Business tax (Canada), 255

Canada securities, 263-264, 265
Canadian accounting practices, 303-308
    See also Annual Statement (Canada)
  federal income taxes, deferred, 308
  marketable securities, 304-305
  mortgage loans, 305-306
  policy acquisition costs, 304
  policy reserves, 306-307
  real estate, 306
  solvency reserves, 307
Canadian and British Insurance Companies Act, 303-304
Capital, 18
  minimum requirements for insurance companies, 220-221
  in mutual companies, 210
  in stock companies, 205-210
Capital and Surplus Account, 36-38, 205-206, 214-220
Capital cost allowances (CCA), 265
Capital expenditure budgets, 318
Capitalization, 130, 294
Capital paid up, 206-210
Capital stock, 28
Capital stock issued and paid, 206-210
Cash-basis accounting, 4-5, 8-12
Cash dividends, 28, 112-113, 302
Cash Flow statement (Annual Statement), 38
Cash flow statement (internal), 50-51
Cash surrender, 150-152
Changes in Financial Position, Statement of, 38-42
Chart of accounts, 60
Claim liabilities, 26, 176-178
Claim reserves, 177
Claims, 161-171
  accounting for, 162-164
  as reported on Canadian Annual Statement, 181-186
  as reported on U.S. Annual Statement, 48, 179-181
  drafts, 175-176
  due and unpaid, 177
  health insurance, 168-171
  incurred but unreported, 178
  in the course of settlement, 177
  liabilities, 26, 176-178
  life insurance, 164-168
  present value of amounts not yet due on, 178
  records and controls, 174-176
  resisted, 178
Clean surplus theory, 303
Client and policy master file, 63-65
Client/policy accounting system, 61-67
Collateral trust bonds, 101
Collected income, 96-97
Commission accounting, 80-82, 86
Committed costs, 326
Common stock, 110
Commuted commissions, 232
Compliance auditing, 282
Conservatism in accounting, 4, 5, 6, 289
Consolidated tax return, 255
Contingency reserves, 212
Continuous budget, 317
Contract payments, 161-162
Contributed surplus, 28, 208, 213
Conventional mortgage loan, 122
Conventional policy loan, 132
Cost accounting, 329-342
  basics of, 331-332
  functional, 334-342
  marginal costs, 332-334
  purposes of, 330-331
Cost-benefit analysis, 272
Cost centers, 336

Death benefit, adjustments to, 164-166
Developmental costs, 294-295
Disability income insurance, 168, 169-170, 186
Disabled life reserves, 171
Discount
  bonds, 105-110
  mortgage loans, 126
Discretionary costs, 326
Dividend accumulations, 145, 147, 153
Dividend liabilities, 26-27, 144-145, 153-155, 156-158, 238, 301
Dividends, policy. *See* Policy dividends
Dividends due and unpaid, 144, 153
Dividends payable in the following year, 144, 153-155
Dollar control, 153
Drafts, 175-176
Due income, 97

Earmarked surplus, 212
Earned income, 98-99
Effective rate (bonds), 105-106
Electronic data processing equipment
  valuation of, 188
Estimated time analysis, 338
Ex-dividend date, 113
Expense recognition, 293-295
Expense reporting, 224-230
  on Annual Statements, 48, 226-230
  liabilities, 225-226
Extended term insurance, 152-153
External auditing, 280

Federal Income Tax Act (Canada), 256
Financial accounting, 14
Financial auditing, 75, 281
  and premium reporting, 75
Financial budgets, 321
Financial information system, 58
Fiscal auditing, 281-282
Five-Year Historical Data, 42
Fixed-amount budgets, 321
Flexible-amount budgets, 321
Foreclosure, 122, 126-127, 130-131
Foreign exchange rates, adjustments
  due to, 191-192
Functional cost accounting systems, 334-342
  cost accumulation and allocation, 337-340
  development of, 335-337
  effective use of information from, 340-342
Fund accounting, 233-237

GAAP. See Generally accepted accounting
  principles
General accounting system, 60-61
General fund, 11
General ledger subsystem, 61
Generally accepted accounting principles
  (GAAP), 2, 5, 12-14, 49, 206, 288
  and Canadian accounting practices, 303-308
  as compared with SAP, 13-14, 292-303
  development of for life companies, 289-291
  in mutual companies, 13-14
  philosophy behind, 288-289
General obligation bonds, 102
Going-concern concept, 5, 13, 289
Gross premiums, 86, 298
Guaranty associations, 252

Health insurance claims, 168-171
  as reported on U.S. Annual Statement, 179-181
  disability, 169-170
  medical expense, 170-171
Health insurance premiums, 88
Historical costs, 337
Holding companies, 290

Immediate recognition, 295
Impaired company, 221-222
Income classifications, 96-98
Income recognition process, 75, 292-293
Income Statement, 28-29, 226
Income taxes, federal (Canada), 256, 261-265
  deferred, 308
Income taxes, federal (U.S.), 257-261, 303
Income taxes, non-federal, 255-256
Incompatible functions, 274
Insurance company, as defined for tax
  purposes, 258-259
Intangible personal property tax, 254-255
Internal auditing, 280
Internal control, 269, 270-277
  basic concepts of, 271-273
  examples of, 276-277
  methods used in, 273-276
  and policy benefit accounting, 142
Investment accounting system, 67
Investment income
  accounting for, 96-99
  and Canadian Annual Statement, 43, 99,
    116-119, 139
  and U.S. Annual Statement, 43, 96-99,
    113-116, 135-139
  bonds, 99-110
  mortgage loans, 122-127
  policy loans, 131-134
  real estate, 127-131
  role of in life and health insurance companies,
    95-96
  stocks, 110-113

Ledger accounts, 10-11
Ledger assets, 9, 230-231
Ledger audit, 282
Ledger surplus, 11
Liability classifications, 23-27, 192-196
LICTI. See Life insurance company taxable
  income
Life insurance company taxable income
  (LICTI), 259-261
Liquidation, 210
Liquidation concept, 5-6, 13, 288

Loading, 298
Lock-in concept, 301
Long-term budgets, 317

Management auditing, 282-284
Managerial accounting, 14. *See also* Auditing, Budgeting, Cost accounting, Planning
Mandatory redemption feature, 297
Mandatory Securities Valuation Reserve (MSVR), 37, 195-196, 218, 296, 297
Marginal costs, 332-334
Master budget, 324
Master dividend record, 143-144, 148
Matured endowments, 167, 168, 179
Mean reserve, 23
Medical expense insurance, 168, 170-171
Modified reserves, 300
Mortgage bonds, 101
Mortgage correspondents, 125
Mortgage loans, 122-127
  accounting for, 123-127
  and Canadian accounting practices, 305-306
  as reported in Canadian Annual Statement, 43, 139
  as reported in U.S. Annual Statement, 43, 135
  conventional, 122
  first, 122
  foreclosure, 122, 126-127, 130-131
  government-backed, 122
  purchase money, 135
  purchase of, 125-126
  second, 122
  subsidiary ledger account information, 123, 124
MSVR. *See* Mandatory Securities Valuation Reserve
Mutualization, 209-210

Net ledger assets, 11
Net-level valuation premium, 304
Nonadmitted assets, 6-8, 37, 216-217, 231-233, 296, 304
  and changes in Surplus, 37
Nonadmitted investment income, 98
Nonforfeiture options, 150-153
  cash surrender, 150-152
  extended term insurance, 152-153
  reduced paid-up insurance, 152-153
Nonledger accounts, 10-11

Offset, 251
Operating cost centers, 336
Operational budgets, 318-321
Operations planning, 312-317

Paid-to date, 72, 75
Paid-up additions, 148, 155
Part I Business Income Tax (Canada), 261-265
Par value (of a bond), 99
Par value (of a stock), 110, 206-209
Permanently impaired securities, 297, 305
Planning, 311-317
  operations, 312-317
  strategic, 312-317
Policy acquisition costs, 294, 304
Policy benefits, 141-158
  dividends, 142-150
  nonforfeiture options, 150-153
  objectives of accounting for, 142
Policy dividends, 142-150
  accounting for, 145-150, 301
  as reported on Canadian Annual Statement, 156-158
  as reported on U.S. Annual Statement, 153-155
  disbursements of, 148-150
  liabilities, 144-145, 153-155
  payment options, 145
  records, 143-144
  terminal, 146
Policy loans, 131-134, 139
  accounting for, 132-134
  automatic premium loans, 132, 133
  as reported in Canadian Annual Statement, 139
  as reported in U.S. Annual Statement, 139
  conventional, 132
  interest on, 133-134
Policy reserves, 23-26
  as reported on U.S. and Canadian Annual Statements, 48
  and Canadian accounting practices, 306-307
  and change in valuation basis, 218
  net level, 300
  under SAP versus GAAP, 298-301
  valuation of, 10
Preferred stock, 110
Premium
  paid for bonds, 105-110
  paid for mortgage loans, 126
Premium accounting system
  objectives of, 72-75
Premium assets, 22, 80
Premium billing and collection, 65

accounting systems for, 71-72
control process, 72
Premium deposits, 78-79
Premium Income account, 48, 75-77, 83-88, 146, 147
Premium Suspense account, 77-78
Premium taxes, 75, 250-252
   offsets, 251, 254, 255
   and paid-up additions, 148
Premiums
   advance, 27, 79-80
   Annual Statement treatment of, 48, 83-93
   gross, 86, 298
   health insurance, 88
   net benefit, 298
   net expense, 298
   and returned checks, treatment of, 76-77
   uncollected, 80
   unearned, 79
Prepaid expenses, 231-232
Principal (bond), 99
Private placements, 99-101
Program results auditing, 284
Property taxes, 129-131
Public companies, 281
Public offerings, 99

Real estate, 127-131
   accounting for, 128-131
   and Canadian accounting practices, 306
   as reported in Canadian Annual Statement, 43, 139
   as reported in U.S. Annual Statement, 43, 135-139
   property taxes, 129-131, 252-254
   rental income and expense, 131
   sale of, 128-129
   valuation under GAAP versus SAP, 298
Real estate mortgage loans. *See* Mortgage loans
Realizable value, 297
Realization principle, 292-293
Realized capital gain or loss, 102, 103-104, 111, 112, 128-129
   bonds, 102, 103-104
   real estate, 128-129
   stocks, 111, 112
Reconciliation of Funds, 234-235, 237
Reconciliation of Ledger Assets, 230-231
Reconciliation of Surplus, 36-38, 220
Reduced paid-up insurance, 152-153
Reinsurance
   as admitted asset, 188-190
   and Annual Statement valuations, 36, 188-190
   change in liability for, 217-218
   as nonledger liability, 195
   retention limits, 189
Reinsurance benefits
   accounting for, 173
Requested transactions, 66
Reserve for future contingent benefits, 178
Reserve released, 150-151
Reserves. *See* Claim reserves, Policy reserves, Solvency reserves
Reserve strengthening, 38, 218
Retained earnings, 206, 297, 303, 307
   and cash dividends under GAAP, 302
   and clean surplus theory, 303
Retaliatory tax laws, 252
Retention limits, 189
Revenue bonds, 102
Revenue recognition, 292-293
Rolling budgets, 317-318

SAP. *See* Statutory accounting practices
Segregated accounts, 196-202
Segregated fund, 158
Separate accounts, 196-202, 219
Service cost centers, 336
Short-term budgets, 317
Solvency reserves, 307
Special obligation bonds, 102
Special surplus funds, 28, 211-212
Standard time analysis, 338-339
Stated rate, 101
Statement of Changes in Financial Position, 38-42
Statutory accounting practices (SAP), 3-12, 13-14, 49, 288
   and Canadian accounting practices, 303-308
   as compared with GAAP, 13-14, 292-303
   philosophy behind, 288-289
   and solvency, 3
Statutory Annual Statement. *See* Annual Statement
Stock companies, 206-210, 289-291
   and GAAP, 289-291
Stock dividends, 110, 111-112, 302
Stocks, 110-113
   accounting for the purchase and sale of, 111-113
   as reported on Canadian Annual Statement, 43, 119
   as reported on U.S. Annual Statement, 43, 113-116

par value, 110, 206-209
Strategic planning, 312-317
Summary of Operations, 28-29, 155, 226
Supplementary contracts, 172-173
Supporting budgets, 324
Surplus, 28, 205-206
   calculation of, 210-211
   changes in, 36-38, 167-168, 214-220, 231, 302-303
   classifications of, 28, 211-213
   contributed, 208, 213
   gross paid in and contributed, 208
   minimum requirements for, 220-222
   unassigned, 209, 212-213
Suspense accounts, 77-78, 194
Systematic and rational allocation, 295

Tangible personal property tax, 254
Tax accounting, 14, 50, 249-250
Taxation of insurance companies, 249-265
   and agents' commissions, 82
   Annual Statement aspects of, 266
   business tax (Canada), 255
   Federal Income Tax Act (Canada), 256, 261-265, 308
   income taxes, federal (Canada), 261-265
   income taxes, federal (U.S.), 257-261, 303
   income taxes, non-federal, 255-256
   intangible personal property tax, 254-255
   local taxes, 256-257
   premium taxes, 250-252
   real estate taxes, 252-254
   retaliatory tax laws, 252
   tangible personal property tax, 254
   Tax Reform Act (1984), 258-261
   tax returns, 50
10-K reports, 49-50
10-Q reports, 49-50
Tentative LICTI, 260-261
Time-and-motion studies, 338-339
Timing difference, 303
Top-down budgeting, 321-322
Treasury stock, 208, 209, 219

Unassigned surplus, 28, 209, 212-213
Uncollected premiums, 80
Unearned income, 27, 97
Unearned premiums, 79
Unit cost, 329, 341-342
Unlisted assets, 296
Unrealized capital gain or loss, 102

Valuation of Securities manual, 114, 296

Waiver-of-premium benefit, 168, 169-170
Working papers, 8
Work sheets, 8

Yield (bond), 105-106

Zero-base budgeting, 323